30

The Family Handyman

Home Improvement

2008

The Family Handyman

Home Improvement

2008

by The Editors of *The Family Handyman* magazine

THE FAMILY HANDYMAN HOME IMPROVEMENT 2008
(See page 288 for complete staff listing.)
Editor in Chief: Ken Collier
Managing Editor: Mary Flanagan
Contributing Designers: Teresa Marrone, Bruce Bohnenstingl
Contributing Copy Editors: Donna Bierbach, Peggy Parker
Indexing: Stephanie Reymann
Vice President Book Marketing: Robert Botta

Publisher: Rick Straface
Vice President, Consumer Marketing: Cara Schlanger
Vice President, Retail Sales: David Algire

Reader's Digest Association, Inc.
President and Chief Executive Officer: Mary Berner
President, Home & Garden and Health & Wellness: Alyce C. Alston
President, North American Consumer Marketing: Dawn Zier

Warning: *All do-it-yourself activities involve a degree of risk. Skills, materials, tools, and site conditions vary widely. Although the editors have made every effort to ensure accuracy, the reader remains responsible for the selection and use of tools, materials, and methods. Always obey local codes and laws, follow manufacturer's operating instructions, and observe safety precautions.*

ISBN 978-0-7621-0939-5

Address any comments about *The Family Handyman Home Improvement 2008* to:
Editor, Home Improvement 2008
2915 Commers Drive, Suite 700
Eagan, MN 55121

To order additional copies of *The Family Handyman Home Improvement 2008,* call 1-800-344-2560.

For more Reader's Digest products and information, visit our Web site at rd.com.
For more about *The Family Handyman* magazine, visit thefamilyhandyman.com.

Printed in the United States of America.
1 3 5 7 9 10 8 6 4 2

INTRODUCTION

Why DIY? The top three reasons: To save money, take pride in a job well done, and sometimes even save time! Here at *The Family Handyman*, we celebrate the can-do spirit we share with all of our readers.

Senior editor Gary Wentz says, "Hiring pros isn't just expensive—it can be a real hassle. The hassle factor is huge even with small jobs: searching for a pro, making calls, waiting for some knuckle-dragger to show up (while using up a half-day of your vacation time). If you add up the time you spend hiring out a small or mid-size job, you often find that you saved very little time, if any. Friends and neighbors tell me, 'I'd like to do it myself, but I just don't have the time.' Personally, I'd like to hire it out, but I just don't have the time!"

Senior editor Travis Larson credits his father with passing on the DIY attitude. "I got my 'chops' from my dad, a career Marine who refused to pay anyone to do anything he could do himself. That included pouring concrete, ripping apart appliances, installing retaining walls, tiling and anything else that needed work around the house. Somehow I inherited that same cheapskate mind-set. And it's still true, even though now I could afford to hire people to do the stuff I hate doing (drywall taping, painting, etc.). But that just doesn't seem right somehow. I can't stand the thought of looking at anything in my house that someone else had a hand in—and of course, cost me money to boot!"

So whatever got you started as a DIYer, and whatever keeps you going, we hope this book helps you successfully carry out your projects, and saves you some time and money in the process.

—The staff of *The Family Handyman* magazine

Contents

Safety First 8

1   INTERIOR PROJECTS, REPAIRS & REMODELING

Home Care & Repair 10
10 Tips for a Perfect Paint Job 16
Handy Hints 20
One-day Floor Revival 25
Tile a Shower with Panache! 30
Great Goofs 36
Regrout a Shower 38
Sharpen Your Skills: Tough
   Tile Cuts with a Grinder 42
Five Ways to Seal
   Attic Air Leaks 45
New Products 50
DIY Granite Countertop 52
Ask TFH .56
Laundry Room Makeover 60
Home Care & Repair 65
Heated Floors 68
10 Tips for Smoother Drywall 73

2   ELECTRICAL & HIGH-TECH

Home Care & Repair 78
Top 10 Electrical Mistakes 82
Ask TFH 87
Everything You Need to Know
   About CFLs 89
New Products 94

3   PLUMBING, HEATING & APPLIANCES

Ask TFH 96
Install a New Shower Faucet 98
Stop Sink Leaks 102
Handy Hints 107
Plumbing with PEX 108
Flip a Switch, Save $200 112
Great Goofs 115
Do's & Don'ts: Soldering Copper . .116
10 Pitfalls of Sink Replacement . .118

4   WOODWORKING & FURNITURE

Workshop Tips 122
Classic Arch-Top Bookcases 126
Summer Lounge Chair 132
Charging Station 136
Wordless Workshop: Bathroom
   Reading Rack 138

EXTERIOR MAINTENANCE & REPAIRS

Handy Hints 140
Sprinkler System Fixes 142
Ask TFH .148
Deck Rescue 151
Add an Outdoor Faucet 156
Home Care & Repair 159
Roof Tear-off 162
New Products 167
Installing an Outdoor Handrail . . .168

OUTDOOR STRUCTURES & LANDSCAPING

Garden Archway 172
Ask TFH .176
Slay the Crabgrass Monster 178
Cast a Concrete Fountain 182
Storage Bench 187
Build a Vinyl Fence 192
Handy Hints 199
8 Tips for an Easy-Care Yard 200
Arched Planter 203
New Products 208
Pour Your First Big Slab 211
Rain Garden 217
Home Care & Repair 221
Gallery of Ideas 222

AUTO & GARAGE

Ultimate Garage Wall System . . .226
Car & Garage 232
Garage Bump-out 240
Handy Hints 247
Car & Garage 248
Car Caddy 256
Home Care & Repair 261
New Products 263

SPECIAL BONUS SECTION

Storage & Organizing 265
Dirty, Dusty Great Goofs 274
Our Best Cleaning Tips 278
Sturdy, Simple Sawhorses 282

Index 284
Acknowledgments 288

SAFETY FIRST–ALWAYS!

Tackling home improvement projects and repairs can be endlessly rewarding. But, as most of us know, with the rewards come risks. DIYers use chain saws, climb ladders and tear into walls that can contain big and hazardous surprises.

The good news is, armed with the right knowledge, tools and procedures, homeowners can minimize risk. As you go about your home improvement projects and repairs, stay alert for these hazards:

Aluminum wiring

Aluminum wiring, installed in about 7 million homes between 1965 and 1973, requires special techniques and materials to make safe connections. This wiring is dull gray, not the dull orange characteristic of copper. Hire a licensed electrician certified to work with it. For more information visit inspect-ny.com/aluminum.htm.

Asbestos

Texture sprayed on ceilings before 1978, adhesives and tiles for vinyl and asphalt floors before 1980, and vermiculite insulation (with gray granules) all may contain asbestos. Other building materials, made between 1940 and 1980, could also contain asbestos. If you suspect that materials you're removing or working around contain asbestos, contact your health department or visit epa.gov/asbestos for information.

Backdrafting

As you make your home more energy-efficient and airtight, existing ducts and chimneys can't always successfully vent combustion gases, including potentially deadly carbon monoxide (CO). Install a UL-listed CO detector.

Buried utilities

A few days before you dig in your yard, have your underground water, gas and electrical lines marked. Just dial 811 or go to call811.com.

Five-gallon buckets

From 1984–2003, more than 200 children drowned in 5-gallon buckets. Store empty buckets upside down and store those containing liquids with the cover securely snapped.

Lead paint

If your home was built before 1979, it may contain lead paint, which is a serious health hazard, especially for children six and under. Take precautions when you scrape or remove it. Contact your public health department for detailed safety information or call (800) 424-LEAD to receive an information pamphlet.

Spontaneous combustion

Rags saturated with oil finishes like Danish oil and linseed oil, and oil-based paints and stains can spontaneously combust if left bunched up. Always dry them outdoors, spread out loosely. When the oil has thoroughly dried, you can safely throw them in the trash.

Mini-blind and other cords for window coverings

From 1991–2003, more than 160 children died of strangulation from window covering cords. Most accidents occur when infants in cribs near windows become entangled in looped cords or when toddlers looking out windows or climbing furniture lose their footing and becoming wrapped up in cords. Recalls, regulations, new products and new designs have lessened the dangers, but older existing window covering cords still pose a threat, and some experts maintain that no corded window treatment—old or new—is completely safe. In addition, some older vinyl blinds present a lead poisoning threat. For more information visit windowblindskillchildren.org or the Consumer Product Safety Commission at cpsc.gov or (800) 638-2772.

1 Interior Projects, Repairs & Remodeling

IN THIS CHAPTER

Home Care & Repair 10
  *Keyless lock, dry lubricants, fix a sliding
  door, renew a wood finish and more*

10 Tips for a Perfect Paint Job 16

Handy Hints 20
  *Remove grout haze, restore dented
  carpet, lint-free paint roller and more*

One-day Floor Revival 25

Tile a Shower with Panache! 30

Great Goofs 36

Regrout a Shower 38

Sharpen Your Skills 42
  Tough tile cuts with a grinder

Five Ways to Seal Attic Air Leaks 45

New Products 50
  *Six new products to make painting
  less messy; plus magnetic paint!*

DIY Granite Countertop 52

Ask TFH 56
  *Heat-reducing window film, drilling in
  a floor joist, tiling countertop and more*

Laundry Room Makeover 60

Home Care & Repair 65
  Insulate rim joists and more

Heated Floors 68

10 Tips for Smoother Drywall 73

GIVE YOUR FRONT DOOR A KEYLESS LOCK

What with friends, contractors, pet sitters and others, it's easy to lose track of extra house keys. For better control of who can get in and out—and a permanent solution to the lost-key problem with kids—replace one of your dead bolt locks with an electronic keypad entry ($100 to $200 at home centers). Instead of using a key, you just punch in a four-digit number, so you don't have to worry about being locked out. You can pick your own number and change it anytime. You can also program in additional four-digit codes for visitors, then delete them later.

Start by removing the old dead bolt (and the handle if you're replacing it). Set the new dead bolt to match the existing 2-3/8-in. or 2-3/4-in. "backset" (measured from the door edge to the center of the dead bolt hole), then install it in the deadbolt hole. Make sure that "TOP" is facing up and that the bolt is fully retracted.

Install the outside keypad first (**Photo 1**), then secure it in place with the inside mounting plate (**Photo 2**). Connect the wires to the battery and tuck them out of the way before attaching the inside cover plate (**Photo 3**). (Note: We used a Schlage lock; other manufacturers may have different installation procedures.)

With the door open, check to make sure the dead bolt extends and retracts smoothly. If it doesn't, disassemble the lock and make sure the parts were installed correctly. To unlock the dead bolt, just punch in the code and turn the latch.

The lock we installed comes preprogrammed with two unique user codes. To change them or add more, follow the lock's programming instructions.

SCHLAGE

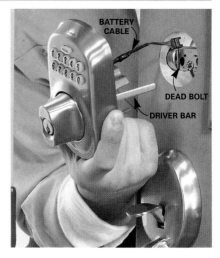

BATTERY CABLE

DEAD BOLT

DRIVER BAR

1 HOLD the keypad upright and slide the battery cable over the top of the dead bolt and the driver bar through the center slot of the dead bolt.

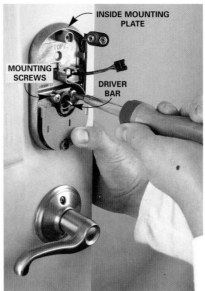

INSIDE MOUNTING PLATE

MOUNTING SCREWS

DRIVER BAR

2 PULL the battery cable through, then hold the keypad and the inside mounting plate together while you tighten the screws.

DEAD BOLT RETRACTED

INSIDE COVER PLATE

3 HOOK UP the battery and snap it into place, make sure the keypad and inside plate are level, then screw on the cover plate.

The lock will send a signal when the battery needs replacing. A key is also included in case the lock ever malfunctions or loses battery power and needs to be opened manually. One big caution: Don't lose the programming guide. It contains the user codes, programming codes and instructions for changing codes.

STRIPPED-OUT
SCREW HOLE

SOLID SOLUTION FOR
STRIPPED HINGE SCREWS

One day the door closes smoothly; the next day it's sticking. And the sticking grows worse as the weeks pass. It's a common old-house problem, but it can happen anywhere kids hang from doorknobs.

The screws holding the top hinges carry most of the weight of the door and are almost always the first to pull out, especially after they've been repeatedly tightened over the years (inset photo). The best way to beef them up is to replace the standard 3/4-in. hinge screws with at least two 3-in. screws that go through the jambs and solidly anchor into the framing. If the door has a large hinge with four screw holes, just drive 3-in. screws straight through the two holes toward the center of the door. However, if the hinge has only three holes, add a 3-in. screw through the middle hole and redrill the top screw hole at a slight

angle so the screw hits solid wood (photo right).

Start the drill bit at a sharp angle so the bit doesn't follow the old screw hole. As soon as you feel a fresh hole starting, tip the drill bit back to an angle that will hit the stud— the angle shown here should work for most doors. If the bit or screw feels like it's sliding off to the side between the drywall and wood, redrill at a sharper angle.

Screw the hinge back in with yellow dichromate (zinc-plated) screws—the color and head size of these rust-resistant drywall screws are a good match for standard brass hinge screws. If the door doesn't shut properly after all the screws are driven in, they may have been driven in too far, pulling the door frame out of plumb. Just back the screws out a few turns.

1/2"
DRYWALL

1/4" TO 1/2"
SHIM SPACE

TOP
HINGE

Replace short hinge screws with long screws when the screw holes no longer hold. Angle the long screws toward the studs to make sure they catch.

FOR LESS MESS AND BETTER RESULTS, USE DRY LUBRICANTS

Penetrating spray lubricant is not always the best lubricant for everything around the house. Drawers, cabinets, locks and latches, windows, sliding and bifold doors, and other metal, wood and plastic surfaces inside the house all need lubricants that stay dry and clean.

Use graphite to lubricate locks; unlike oil or penetrating sprays, it won't collect dust, which will clog the mechanism.

Rub a solid lubricant made from wax on wood drawers, wood windows and other porous surfaces.

Use silicone spray on drawer rollers, window tracks and other plastic, rubber and metal surfaces. It dries almost instantly.

HomeCare&Repair

FIX A STICKING SLIDING DOOR

Years of dirt, exposure to the elements and hard use can turn sliding doors into sticking doors, but the problem is usually easy to fix.

Start with a good cleaning. Scrub caked dirt and grime out of the track with a stiff brush and soapy water. If the door still doesn't slide smoothly, the rollers under the door either need adjusting or are shot.

Locate the two adjusting screws at the bottom of the door (on the face or edge of the door) and pry off the trim caps that cover the screws. If one side looks lower, raise it until the door looks even on the track (**Photo 1**). If the door still sticks, turn both screws a quarter turn to raise the whole door. Then slide the door just short of the jamb and be sure the gap is even.

ROLLERS

If the door still doesn't glide smoothly, you'll have to remove the door and examine the rollers. Get help for this—the door is heavy! Unscrew the stop molding on the inside of the jamb (**Photo 2**). Be sure to hold the door in place once the stop is removed—if you forget and walk away for a moment, the door will fall in, requiring a much bigger repair! Tilt the door back (**Photo 3**) and set it on sawhorses. Inspect the rollers for problems. If they're full of dirt and debris, give them a good cleaning and a few drops of lubricant and see if they spin freely. However, if the rollers are worn, cracked or bent, remove them (**Photo 4**) and replace them with a new pair ($8 to $16 a pair). You can order rollers and other door parts through lumberyards and home centers or online (alcosupply.com or blainewindow.com). Look for the door manufacturer's name on the edge of the door or the hardware manufacturer's name on the roller.

HIDDEN ADJUSTING SCREW

TRIM CAP

1 LIFT OR LOWER the door on the track with a screwdriver or Allen wrench. Raise it just enough to clear the track and roll smoothly.

STOP MOLDING

2 REMOVE the screws that hold the stop molding. Cut the paint or varnish line on the room side of the stop molding so the molding will pull off cleanly.

…

COOK HARDWARE TO REMOVE PAINT

If you want to strip paint from metal without the nasty fumes and mess of chemical strippers, just fill a slow cooker with water and set the dial to high. The heat and moisture will soften the paint, and often it will fall off as a single piece.

This works on oil, latex and spray paints, but it may not remove some clear finishes like lacquer. Cooking the hardware may stain or contaminate the pot, so use an old one or buy a new one for less than $20. This method won't harm hardware made of non-rusting metals like copper, brass or aluminum. You'll end up with a little rust on steel—not enough to ruin hidden parts like hinge pins or screws, but possibly enough to roughen shiny surfaces. If the steel has a plating like chrome or brass and the plating is already flaking off, this method will cause more flaking.

Some paints will loosen within a couple of hours, but for best results, plan to cook the hardware overnight. If the paint doesn't fall off by itself, scrub lightly with a stiff plastic brush. The paint will harden as it cools, so scrub the hardware as soon as you pull it

out of the water. The paint may contain lead, so catch all the sludge and throw it in the garbage. To clean the metal and restore its shine, use a metal polish like Brasso or Noxon.

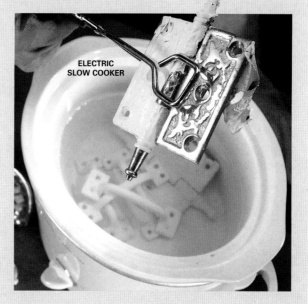

ELECTRIC SLOW COOKER

3 GRIP the door by the edges and tip it about a foot into the room. Lift it up and out of the track one edge at a time.

ADJUSTING SCREW

NEW ROLLER

4 UNSCREW and pry out the screws that hold the roller in, then carefully lever it out with a screwdriver. Clean or replace the rollers.

HomeCare&Repair

RENEW A WOOD FINISH IN 30 MINUTES

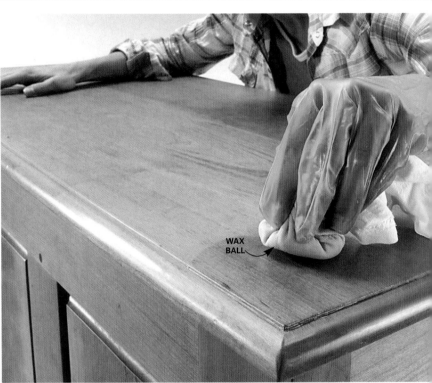

WAX BALL

1 CLEAN the wood using a soft cloth dampened with mineral spirits. Open windows for ventilation.

2 WRAP a ball of wax in a cloth and apply a thin, even coat of wax. Rub on the wax in a circular pattern.

If you have wood furniture that's looking dull, revive the shine with paste wax. Wax is a more durable coating than liquid furniture polish and it won't attract dust as many polishes do. Wax will fill and hide very fine scratches, but it won't hide dents or deeper scratches.

Wax is available in several colors. Most home centers and hardware stores carry only light-colored wax ($8), which is fine for most finishes. But don't use light wax on dark finishes that have recesses in the grain. Yellowish wax that fills the tiny crevices in the surface will look bad. (This won't happen on glossy, solid dark finishes.) For wax in a variety of colors, go to briwax-online.com (800-527-4929; $13, plus shipping). You can also use dark wax to deepen the color of a finish.

Clean the wood with mineral spirits to remove grime as well as residue left by furniture polishes (**Photo 1**). When the mineral spirits dries, buff off any residue with a dry cloth. Then cut a rag from an old cotton T-shirt and wrap it around a walnut-sized ball of wax. As you rub with the ball, wax will ooze through the rag (**Photo 2**). Apply only

enough wax to form a thin gloss—a heavy coat just leaves you with more wax to buff off later. If you haven't used wax before and you're working on a large piece of furniture, wax and then buff small areas no more than 3 x 3 ft.

Don't wait for the wax to dry completely and form a haze the way you would with car wax. Fully dried furniture wax is very hard to buff smooth. Wait only until the wax partially dries and begins to look dull (typically 15 to 30 minutes). Then rub the surface with a cotton cloth to remove the excess wax. The rag should glide smoothly over the wax with only a little elbow grease. If you've waited too long and can't rub out the swirls of wax, simply apply more wax, then wait and wipe again (solvent in the second coat of wax will soften the first coat).

Tip Touch up scratches with a fine-tip marker before you wax. Visit an art supply store to find a wide array of browns.

14

3 WIPE OFF the excess wax with a soft cloth. Turn and refold the cloth frequently to expose clean cloth.

A wax finish doesn't require any special care; simply dust with a dry or damp cloth. A wax coating will last months or even years depending on how heavily the furniture is used. When the finish again looks worn, scuffed or dirty, just clean and rewax. Don't worry about wax buildup. Each new wax job dissolves and removes much of the previous coat.

LIGHT WAX

DARK WAX

WAX BALL

TEST PAINT COLORS ON A VIRTUAL HOUSE

Picking paint colors from little paint chips is very difficult, and if you make a mistake you're usually stuck with it—paint stores don't take custom colors back.

You can improve the odds of picking a good color by visiting paint company Web sites. Benjamin Moore, Sherwin-Williams and Glidden all have sample interiors and exteriors where you can experiment with different colors. Just pick a room, click on a paint sample or a paint combination and the whole room is instantly painted. Save the rooms you like and compare them all when you're done. Benjamin Moore even sells a downloadable program from its Web site ($10, for PCs or Macs) that allows you to color digital photos of your own house.

Colors on a computer screen won't be an exact match, but at least you can get a good preview before you buy $100 worth of paint.

The Web sites also calculate the amount of paint you need, list recommended primers and supplies, and offer how-to and problem-solving sections.

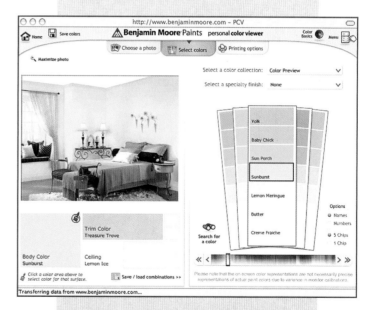

- benjaminmoore.com (free Personal Color Viewer or $10 Personal Color Viewer 2.0)
- glidden.com (Color Visualizer)
- sherwin-williams.com/do_it_yourself/ (Color Visualizer)

10 TIPS FOR A
PERFECT PAINT JOB

Professional painters share secrets for great-looking interiors

by **Brett Martin**

COTTON
DROP CLOTH

1 Roll paint along the edges for consistent texture

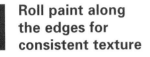

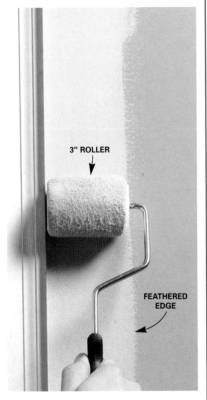

3" ROLLER

FEATHERED
EDGE

Corners and areas next to trim that are painted only with a brush have a noticeably different texture than the surrounding paint. To ensure the finished texture will be consistent in these areas, brush on the paint, then immediately roll it out before the paint dries.

Use a 3-in. roller with a nap that's the same thickness that was used for the rest of the wall. Roll as close as you can without bumping the opposite wall or slopping paint onto the trim. Finish brushing on the paint and rolling it out in one area before moving on to the next section.

2 Feather out the paint where you can't keep a wet edge

You can't cover large areas like ceilings, extra-tall walls or stairwells in single, continuous strokes, so the best way to minimize lap marks on these areas is to feather out the paint along the edges that you can't keep wet. The thinner, feathered coat of paint will avoid the buildup that causes the lap mark.

To paint a large section without leaving lap marks, roll the nearly dry roller in different directions along the dry edge, feathering out the paint as you go. After completing the entire length of the wall or ceiling, move to the next section and paint over the feathered edges. For the second coat, apply the paint in the opposite direction. This crisscrossing paint application sharply reduces (if not eliminates) lap marks.

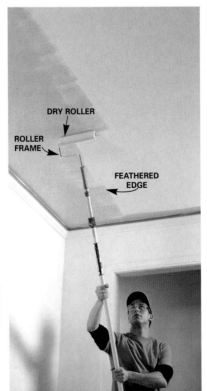

DRY ROLLER

ROLLER
FRAME

FEATHERED
EDGE

3 Use cotton drop cloths rather than plastic

Spills and spatters happen, regardless of how careful you are. It's a lot easier to prepare for them than to wipe them out of your carpeting or off your wood floor later. All it takes is canvas drop cloths in your work area (a 4-ft. x 15-ft. cloth costs $15). The thick canvas stays in place, so you don't need to tape it, and you can use it to cover any surface. Plastic drop cloths are slippery to walk on or set a ladder on and don't stay in place. Even worse, paint spills on plastic stay wet, and they can end up on your shoes and get tracked through the house. Canvas is slippery on hard floors, so rosin paper ($10 for 400 sq. ft. at home centers) is better over vinyl, tile and hardwood. Tape the sheets together and to the floor to provide a nonslip surface.

But even with canvas or rosin-paper drop cloths, large spills still need to get wiped up right away or they'll seep through. Clean spills with paper towels or cloth rags. Likewise, if you splatter paint on any other surface, wipe it up immediately.

4 Prime and texture wall patches to avoid a blotchy finish

Freshly painted walls often look blotchy. The color is uniform, but the sheen isn't consistent. This usually occurs over the holes and cracks you patched with a filler or drywall compound. The porous fillers absorb the paint, dulling the surface (a problem called "flashing"). When light hits these dull spots, they stick out like a sore thumb. The smooth patch also stands out in contrast to the slightly bumpy texture of the rest of the wall. A quick coat of primer is all it takes to eliminate flashing and texture differences.

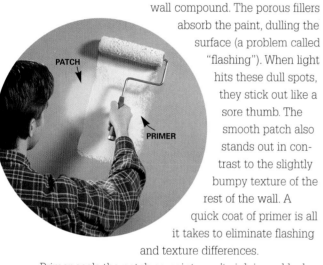

PATCH

PRIMER

Primer seals the patch so paint won't sink in and look dull. To match texture, prime with a roller, feathering out the edges. Choose a nap thickness to match the surrounding wall texture (a 3/8-in. nap roller for smooth walls; 1/2-in. for textured).

5 To avoid lap marks, roll the full height of the wall and keep a wet edge

Lap marks are those ugly stripes caused by uneven layers of paint buildup. They occur when you roll over paint that's already partly dry. (In warm, dry conditions, latex paint can begin to stiffen in less than a minute!) The key to avoiding lap marks is to maintain a "wet edge," so each stroke of your roller overlaps the previous stroke before the paint can begin to dry.

To maintain a wet edge, paint an entire wall all at once. Start at one end, running the roller up and down the full height of the wall, moving over slightly with each stroke. Move backward where necessary to even out thick spots or runs. Don't let the roller become nearly dry; reload it often so that it's always at least half loaded. Keep the open side of the roller frame facing the area that's already painted. That puts less pressure on the open side of the roller, so you're less likely to leave paint ridges.

"If you paint in sections, you double the amount of work and double the chances of lap marks. I always roll on the paint the full height of the wall, and I haven't had lap marks for 25 years."

Brad Karja, president of Brad Karja Decorating

6 Paint the trim first, then the ceiling and walls

Pros usually follow a certain order when painting a room. They paint the trim first, then the ceiling, then the walls. That's because it's easier (and faster) to tape off the trim than to tape off the walls. And you certainly don't want to tape them both off!

When painting the trim, you don't have to be neat. Just concentrate on getting a smooth finish on the wood. Don't worry if the trim paint gets slopped onto the walls. You'll cover it later when painting the walls. Once the trim is completely painted and dry (at least 24 hours), tape it off (using an "easy release" painter's tape), then paint the ceiling, then the walls.

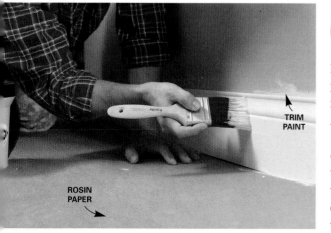

TRIM PAINT

ROSIN PAPER

SANDING
SPONGE

FIRST COAT
OF NEW
PAINT

"Painters are really just glorified sanders. Prep and sand the wood, and the final coat is so smooth it looks like it's been sprayed on."

7 Sand trim between coats for an ultra-smooth finish.

One coat of paint usually won't hide the underlying color and sheen on trim. And if you don't sand the surface smooth between coats, the finish may have a grainy texture. For a smooth finish, sand the trim before applying each coat of paint.

Sand the trim with a fine-grit sanding sponge. Sponges get into crevices where sandpaper can't go and apply even pressure. Then apply the first coat of paint, let it dry at least 24 hours, lightly sand it again for a completely smooth surface, and apply the second coat. After each sanding, vacuum the trim, then wipe it down with a tack cloth to remove the dust.

8 Mix several cans of paint in a large bucket for a consistent color throughout the room.

Paint color may vary slightly from one can to the next. If you have to open a new can in the middle of a wall, the difference may be noticeable. Mixing the paints together eliminates the problem. It's best to estimate the amount of paint you'll need and mix it in a 5-gallon bucket (a process called "boxing"). When coverage is difficult to estimate, add more rather than less. You can always pour the leftover back into cans.

For large jobs, use the bucket and a roller screen rather than a roller tray. It's much faster to load your roller with the screen than to use a roller pan. Simply dunk it into the paint bucket, then roll it along the screen until it stops dripping.

5-GALLON
BUCKET

ROLLER
SCREEN

9 Clean dirty surfaces so the paint can form a strong bond

DEGLOSSER

PREPAINT CLEANER

Paint dirty, oily surfaces and the paint will easily chip or peel off. So before painting, clean grimy areas with a deglosser or heavy-duty cleaner intended for prepaint cleaning. They work well to clean painted, varnished or enameled surfaces to improve the adhesion of the new paint. They're ideal for cleaning greasy or oily areas like kitchen and bathroom walls and removing hand marks around light switches and doorknobs.

Wipe on the cleaner in a circular motion using a lint-free cloth or abrasive pad. Start at the bottom and work up. After the surface is clean, fill in any nicks and holes, then sand them smooth before painting. The cleaners are available at paint stores and home centers. Be sure to wear rubber gloves and eye protection.

"Painting over grease, grime or hair spray is like painting over rust on your car—you've got to get rid of it or the paint won't hold."

Butch Zang, president (retired) of Premier Papering and Painting

10 Let the paint dry, then cut the tape loose for a perfect edge

Once paint is dry, you can't just pull the tape off the trim. Paint forms a film between the wall and the tape, and removing the tape tears pieces of dried paint off the wall. So before pulling off the tape, cut it loose.

Wait for the paint to completely dry, at least 24 hours, then use a sharp utility knife or box cutter knife to slice through the film. Start in an inconspicuous area to make sure the paint is hard enough to slice cleanly. If you cut the paint while it's still gummy, you'll make a mess. As you cut the paint, pull up the tape at a 45-degree angle.

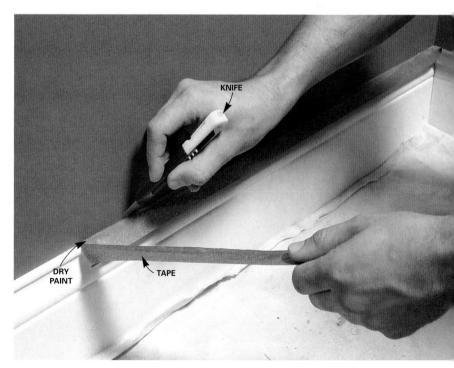

KNIFE

DRY PAINT

TAPE

HandyHints®

GROUT HAZE REMOVER

The Mr. Clean Magic Eraser product ($4 at discount stores) is designed to remove wall scuffs, but it also works great for removing dry grout haze from tile. Just wet the sponge-like pad and wipe off the grout residue.

GROUT HAZE

iTCH REMOVER

A sticky lint roller pulls those nasty insulation fibers off your skin and clothes—and reduces itching later.

KITCHEN CHALK-UP

Before you buy the appliances and cabinetry for your kitchen, "try them on" with a mock-up. Use tape, chalk and paper to make a scale drawing on the walls. Also tape the floor to indicate the depths of appliances and cabinets to ensure a good fit.

RAMON MORENO

SCUFF MARK ERASER

Clean off shoe scuff marks from vinyl flooring with a clean, dry tennis ball. A light rub and heel marks are "erased."

RESTORE DENTED CARPET

Old furniture depressions in carpets can be really ugly. Lay a wet, wrung-out towel over the carpet "dent" and iron with a hot clothes iron for about a minute. The steam will release crushed fibers and make them pliable. Lift the towel, hand-fluff and no more mark!

DRILL BIT GUIDE

Drill bits can wander when you're starting a hole on a hard, glossy surface like tile. Choose a washer slightly larger than the head of your drill bit and align the washer opening over your starting point. Tape the entire washer to the tile and you'll have a steady guide.

WASHER

MASONRY BIT

DUST-PROOF EYEWEAR

For dusty jobs that require both a mask and eye protection, swim goggles may be just the thing. They fit tight around your eyes, so they keep out airborne dust and fiberglass particles. And because of that tight seal, your breath won't fog them up—as often happens with safety glasses.

SWIM GOGGLES

HandyHints®

NUTTY STAIN MIXER

Pigment in stain settles to the bottom of the can and forms a hard sludge that requires a lot of stirring before it dissolves. For faster mixing, just drop in two or three nuts, press the cover back on and shake. But don't use this trick with polyurethane or varnish, since it creates air bubbles.

PEEL-AND-STICK TILE

DAMAGED CABINET BOTTOM

UNDER-CABINET CLEANUP

When the floor of your sink cabinet needs a spruce-up, lay down squares of self-adhesive vinyl tile. They're about a buck a square at home centers and provide an easy-to-wipe-clean surface.

HANDY DRY LUBRICANT

You can buy powdered graphite lubricant at hardware stores, but you already have it in a handy stick form in your pencil. Pencil "lead" is actually graphite and it's less messy than powder.

CITRUS PEELER CAULK REMOVER

The flexible head and cutting edges of a citrus peeler make for a great tool to remove old caulk from around the bathtub or windows. Wedge the tip under the caulking and with some luck, you'll be able to pull the whole bead out without scratching countertops and fixtures.

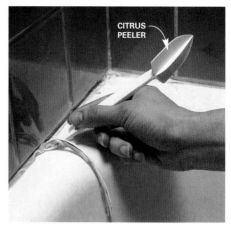

CITRUS PEELER

LINT-FREE PAINT ROLLER

The cheapest paint rollers shed all over the paint as you roll it on, but I like them because I can treat them as if they're disposable—no cleanup! Before I use one, I swipe it with a self-adhesive lint roller to remove all the loose fuzz—no more picking it off my wet wall.

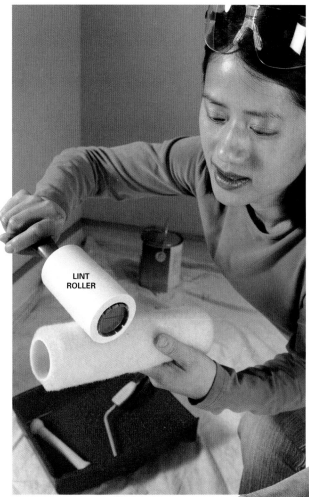

LINT ROLLER

CONTAINS DRIPS

PAINT BUCKET CADDY

Whether you're painting a whole room or just touching up, set your paint can in a bucket. The bucket prevents spills, catches drips and gives you a place to tuck your rag.

EASY TOOL CLEANUP

Wrap your putty knife or trowel with duct tape when you're mixing grout, thin-set or anything else that hardens. It makes cleanup a breeze. Tear off the tape before the compound gets crusty. A little WD-40 will clean away any adhesive residue.

ANYTHING THAT HARDENS

DUCT TAPE

HandyHints®

PAINTER'S REMINDER

When you're finishing a painting project, write on a piece of masking tape the date and how many gallons of paint were needed for the job. Stick the tape to the back of the light switch plate. To get the exact shade next time, also include the color formula sticker peeled off the paint can. When the room's due for a fresh coat, you'll be ready to go.

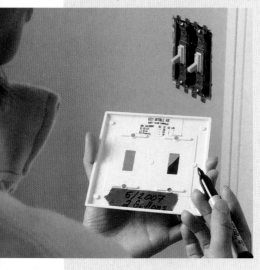

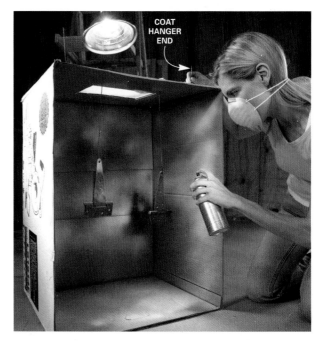

CARDBOARD SPRAY BOOTH

Prevent paint "overspray" with this clever spray booth made from a cardboard box. Cut a hole in the top of the box. Cover the opening with plastic wrap and position a shop light above to illuminate your project.

You can use coat hangers, poked through the cardboard, to hold and rotate the objects as you're painting them. Not only will your shop be neater, but your paint projects will now be thumbprint free.

SPRAY CAN SIX-PACK

A cardboard six-pack corrals loose spray cans for a neater shop.

COUNTERTOP GAP FILLER

If crumbs, papers or even flatware falls into the gap between your countertop and refrigerator, fill the void with nearly invisible plastic tubing. Clear tubing is available at home centers in several widths starting at 1/8 in.

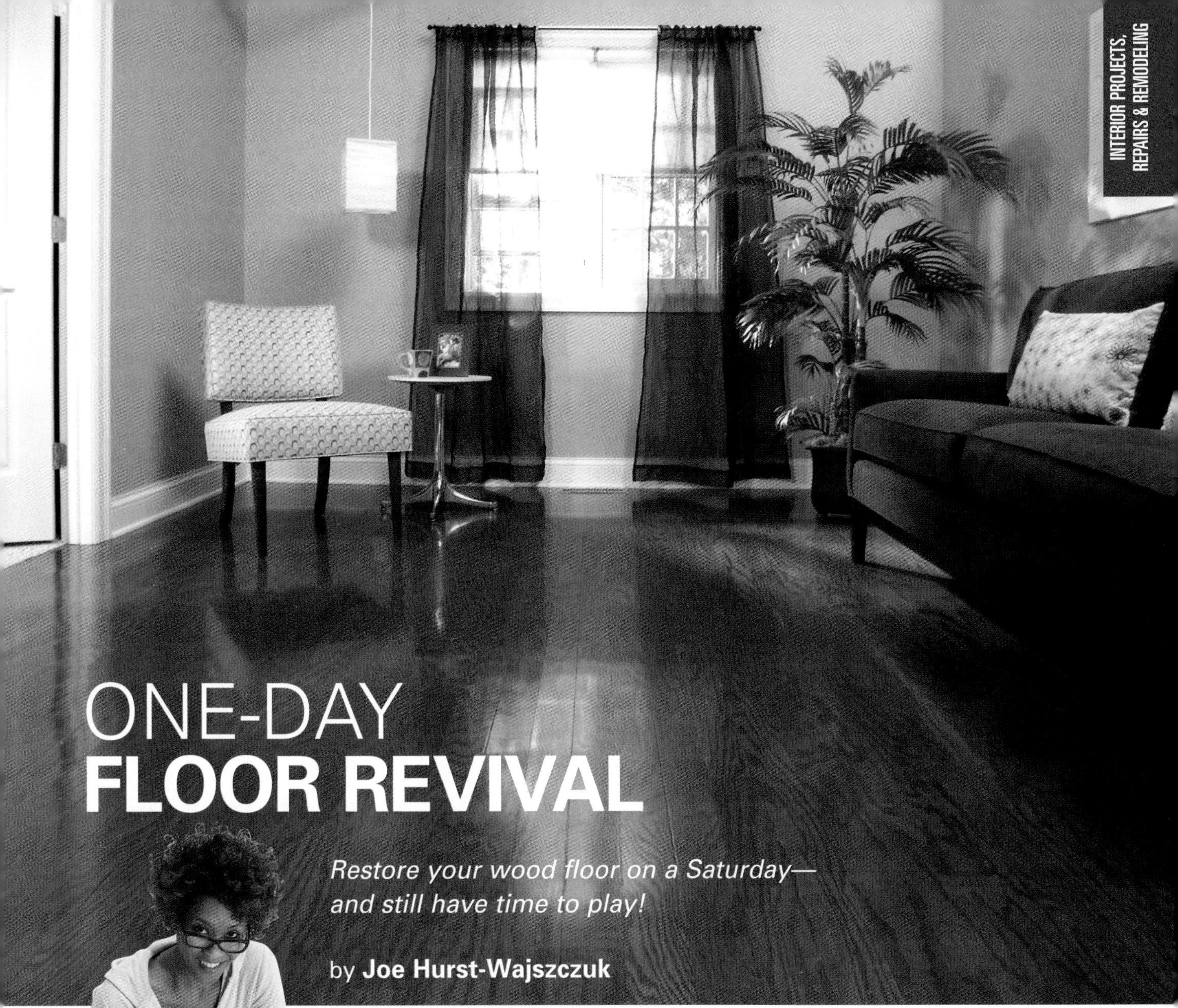

ONE-DAY FLOOR REVIVAL

Restore your wood floor on a Saturday—and still have time to play!

by **Joe Hurst-Wajszczuk**

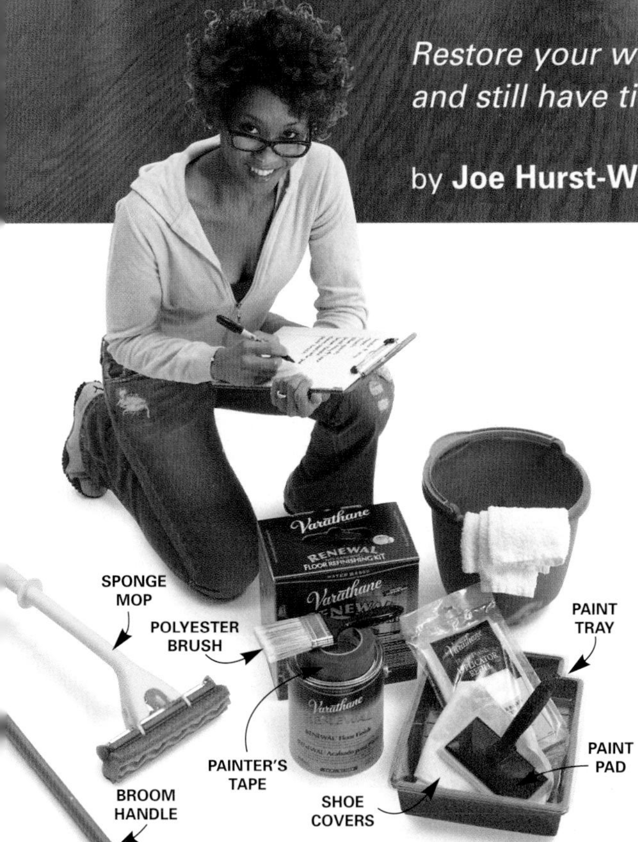
SPONGE MOP
POLYESTER BRUSH
PAINTER'S TAPE
BROOM HANDLE
SHOE COVERS
PAINT TRAY
PAINT PAD
Varathane
RENEWAL
FLOOR REFINISHING KIT

Restore your floor with a recoating kit and the other items shown above. The total bill for this project is about $100.

If the finish on your wood floor is worn and lightly scratched, you can make it look like new without the labor, mess and expense of sanding off the finish. This story will show you how to add a new coat of finish directly over the old by first applying a liquid that roughens the old finish so the new finish can bond to it. Unlike waxes or other products that provide a short-term shine, this added coat will last for years and extend the life of your floor. You can use this method on wood floors that you would otherwise sand or on flooring that's difficult or impossible to sand, such as prefinished or laminated wood. You can even use it on plastic laminate flooring such as Pergo.

Professional floor refinishers have used this "chemical etching" process for years, and now there's a system designed for the floor-finishing novice. The Varathane Renewal Floor Refinishing Kit ($68) includes enough liquid etcher and urethane finish to cover about 225 sq. ft. of flooring, plus an applicator block and pads. The finish dries slower than most water-based floor finishes, making it easier to use. The kit is available at Lowe's and some other home centers. If you need help finding it, call (800) 323-3584.

1 CLEAR the floor of furniture and clean the room thoroughly to minimize dust. Vacuum the floor and wipe it with a damp cloth.

2 PLUG heating ducts with old towels, close windows and turn off fans to limit dust. Protect baseboards with painter's tape.

Clear the floor and clean the whole room

To get started, remove all the furniture from the room. Then clean the room to make it as dust-free as possible. Dust in the air can mar a smooth finish by landing in the wet finish and creating "whiskers" as the finish hardens. To limit air movement, close windows, turn off the ceiling fan or window air conditioner, and block any ducts in the room (**Photo 2**). Next, give the room a top-to-bottom cleaning. Vacuum curtains and wipe down baseboards, windowsills and any other horizontal surfaces with a damp rag. Vacuum the floor, then clean it with a damp rag. Scrub off any stubborn gunk using a gentle abrasive pad such as a Scotch-Brite sponge. Finally, close curtains at any windows that allow direct sunlight to shine on the floor—that can create hot spots on the floor and cause the finish to dry too quickly.

"Sand" the floor with liquid

Once you're done cleaning, the floor is ready for liquid etcher, which roughens the surface (**Photo 3**). The etcher has very little odor, but if you want ventilation, open a window or turn on an exhaust fan in another room. Attach the abrasive pad from the kit to the wood applicator block and screw a broom handle into the block. Slip a shallow cardboard box into a plastic bag, set a paint tray in the box and pour in the etcher (the box catches drips and spills from the tray). Dip the pad in etcher and then press the pad against the tray to squeeze out the excess. Don't just mop the etcher onto the floor; scrub firmly with the grain,

Is this system right for your floor?

This process will make some floors look absolutely perfect. Others will look much better, though not quite perfect. Still others are not good candidates for this process at all and require sanding instead. The category your floor falls into depends on the amount and type of damage it has.

■ Normal wear and shallow scratches in the finish only (not the wood) are no problem; they'll disappear under the new coat of finish.

■ Deeper scratches that go through the finish and into the wood won't disappear completely, even if you touch them up with stain (**Photo 8**). A shiny new coat of finish may even accentuate deep scratches and dents. There's no harm in applying new finish over these spots. But if your floor has a lot of deep damage, sanding is your best option.

■ If you have heavy traffic paths where the finish is completely worn away or areas where the finish is flaking off (often caused by water damage), don't use this process. The etching chemical can discolor bare wood and won't remove water stains.

■ If your floor has been waxed or has a wax finish, the new finish won't stick. To check for wax, find a low-traffic spot behind a door or near an inside corner. Place a few drops of mineral spirits on the floor; let it stand for two to three minutes, and then wipe it off with a clean white rag. If the rag shows any brown or shiny residue, you've got wax. In that case, sanding is your best option. Alternatively, you can buff on a fresh coat of wax for a fresh, although temporary, shine.

BROOM HANDLE

APPLICATOR BLOCK

ABRASIVE PAD

3 SCRUB a small section of floor with the abrasive pad and the liquid etcher. Scrub with the grain, applying firm pressure.

4 WIPE UP the excess liquid etcher as soon as you're done scrubbing each section. Then move on to the next section.

5 WALK THE DOG for 30 minutes while you're waiting for the etching liquid to dry.

making sure you pass over each area several times. That way, the abrasive pad lightly scratches the finish, creating a rougher surface than the etcher alone would provide.

Left on the floor too long, the etcher can seep into cracks between flooring strips and damage the core of laminated flooring. To prevent this, work on small sections that you can complete in about five minutes (start with a 4 x 4-ft. area to get the hang of it). Wipe up the etcher with an old towel as soon as you're done scrubbing (**Photo 4**). You don't have to wipe the floor absolutely dry; just wipe up the excess etcher, leaving a light film of liquid on the floor. When the whole floor is done, remove the abrasive pad and rinse the applicator block and the paint tray. Let the floor dry for 30 minutes before the next step.

Damp-mop and touch up

When the etcher is dry, mix 2 tbsp. of dishwashing liquid in a gallon of warm water. Slip on the shoe covers and damp-mop the floor (**Photo 6**). This final cleaning removes any remaining residue and neutralizes the etcher. Water can damage flooring, so work in sections and wipe up puddles immediately just as you did with the etcher.

Let the floor dry and then give it one last inspection before you apply the finish. Now's the time to fix scratches (**Photo 8**). Dab on matching stain using an artist's brush, then blot the excess stain with a rag. Blow-dry the stain for about

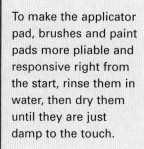

Tip To make the applicator pad, brushes and paint pads more pliable and responsive right from the start, rinse them in water, then dry them until they are just damp to the touch.

one minute with a hair dryer. Then seal the stain with floor finish from the kit. Apply a very thin coat of finish with an artist's brush and "feather out" the edges to avoid visible ridges around the patch. This repair might not be perfect, but if it's done reasonably well, you'll be the only one who knows it's there.

Apply the new finish—fast

The "waterborne urethane" finish included with the Renewal kit dries fast, though not as fast as most other water-based finishes. After spreading it on the floor, you have five to 10 minutes (depending on the heat and humidity) before it becomes gummy and impossible to smooth out. So line up a helper and make sure all your equipment is ready before you

6 DAMP-MOP the floor with water and dishwashing liquid to neutralize the liquid etcher. Wear shoe covers to keep the floor clean.

7 TAKE a 30-minute coffee break, allowing the damp floor to dry completely.

8 TOUCH UP any scratches that have cut through the finish into the wood. Apply stain and dry it with a hair dryer. Then brush on a light coat of finish and dry it.

begin. Attach the applicator pad to the block and prepare your paint tray just as you did before. Also have a paint pad and a 3-in.-wide polyester paint-brush handy for your helper.

Give your helper a short head start applying finish along the baseboards with the paint pad. Then follow close behind with the applicator pad. Dip the applicator into the paint tray, but don't squish out excess finish as you did with the etcher—that creates bubbles. Apply and spread the finish using as few strokes as possible. With beveled-edge flooring, you may need to make multiple passes, but one steady pull is usually all it takes. The trick is to keep the pad wet. Ideally, as you apply the finish, you want a little excess to puddle on the "unfinished side" of the floor. On your next pass, switch the angle of your attack so that the applicator snowplows the wet finish across the room. Have your helper

Tip

Keep tweezers handy while you apply the finish. That way, you can pull a piece of lint or hair off the wet finish without making a mess.

smooth out drips and puddles with a brush so you can keep moving (**Photo 11**). Don't worry about the milky, uneven color of the finish. It will become clear as it dries.

Resist the urge to fix imperfections after the finish becomes sticky. This almost always does more harm than good. If you notice a drip after it's too late to fix, just let it dry completely, then carefully slice off the bump with a razor blade.

If the original finish had only light wear and fine scratches, one coat of finish may be enough to restore the floor's brand-new look. But in most cases, a second coat is a good idea; it will hide deeper scratches that show through the first coat and will protect the underlying wood better. The kit contains enough finish for two coats over 225 sq. ft., but check the can to make sure it's at least half full. If not, buy another gallon of Varathane Diamond Water-Based Finish for Floors ($43). Apply the second coat following the same steps you took with the first coat.

Your final finish will be hard enough for "sock traffic" after eight hours, and ready for you to move furniture back after 24 hours. Give your floor two weeks to completely cure before putting down an area rug. 🏠

9 PLAN your strategy so you don't paint yourself into a corner. Have your helper work along walls with a paint pad while you follow close behind with the applicator pad.

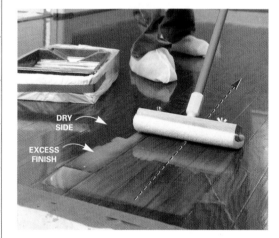

10 GENTLY PLOW the finish with the grain of the wood. Pull the applicator at an angle so the excess finish puddles on the dry side of the floor.

DRY SIDE

EXCESS FINISH

DETAIL MAN

LIGHT TOUCH

11 SMOOTH OUT drips or puddles with a polyester brush. Stick close to the "pad person" to fix drips before they begin to dry.

12 WATCH a long movie, allowing the finish to dry for at least three hours before you apply an optional second coat.

> **" If the original finish had only light wear and fine scratches, one coat of finish may be enough to restore the floor's brand-new look. "**

bench

TILE A SHOWER
WITH PANACHE!

Build an alcove, bench & shelf into your shower with these advanced tiling techniques

by **Travis Larson**

Showers used to be simple boxes for fear that any special architectural features could lead to a leak—and expensive repairs. But modern tiling materials, especially spreadable waterproof membranes, can put these fears to rest. Now you can build in a bench or other structure with confidence and make showering more convenient and pleasant.

In this article, we'll show you how to build in three features: a bench, a shelf and an alcove. We'll include the key planning steps and the waterproofing and special tiling techniques. This project isn't for a tiling rookie. You should have some hands-on tiling experience before tackling a complex project like this one. But if you

shelf

have rudimentary framing skills, and have successfully tiled floors, backsplashes or simple shower surrounds, the advanced techniques we show here will enable you to move on to a project like this.

Framing, sheathing and tiling a shower like we show here will take you about four full days. The tiling alone will take two days. Tile and tiling supplies will cost about $600 if you choose standard tile. If you want fancy glass tile accents like the ones we show, brace yourself. Glass tile starts at $30 per sq. ft. and can cost upward of $100 per sq. ft., so it's wise to think of it as an accent only. It pays to rent or buy a "score and snap" tile cutter if you're using 4 x 4-in. tiles like we show. But if you're using natural stone or larger tiles and your tile layout requires lots of cuts, especially notching, rent a tile saw for a day. You can score and snap glass tile (small mosaic tiles only), but you'll break about every 10th tile—not a big deal if you plan the tile layout well and only have to cut a few.

alcove

Plan the layout

First make sure you have enough space in your shower to add a bench. You'll need to leave at least 3 ft. of shower area so you can still move around. This bathroom originally had a 5-ft. tub, which we tore out and replaced with a 4-ft. shower base. (See "How to Plumb a New Shower Base," Oct. '06, p. 74.) This left a 1-ft. space for the bench and the overhead shelf at the end of the shower.

The key to an exceptional tile job is to plan the shower with the actual tile you intend to use. Use the tile to decide on exact dimensions and positions of benches, alcoves and even wall thicknesses so you can use whole tiles as much as possible and minimize cutting.

A foolproof method is to draw a full-scale template of each wall on rosin paper (**Figure A** and **Photo 1**). Be sure to draw the walls including the thickness of backer board and any plywood that's needed, like on the bench seat. Then mark existing studs that outline alcove positions. Next, lay the tile on the template to decide on the heights, widths and depths of shower features like benches, alcoves and shelves.

Try to wind up with full tiles outlining or covering those features whenever possible. Notice that our alcove is surrounded by full tiles. Those tiles determined the final position and size of the alcove. (It's easier to deal with cutting the tiles that cover the back of the alcove than the ones that border it.) Notice also that the exact height of the bench allowed for full tiles around it—no cutting needed.

Also adjust the thicknesses of walls and ledges for full tiles. We furred out the 2x4 wall with strips of 1/2-in.

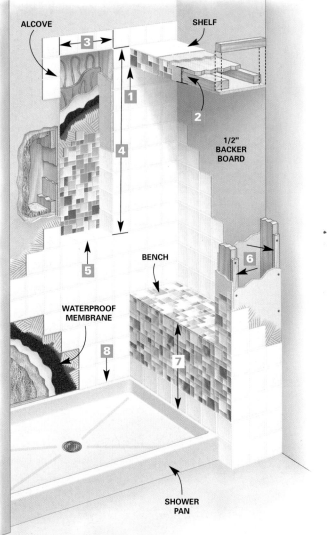

Figure A: Layout objectives

1 Shelf rests on full tile
2 Thickness matches face tile
3 Adjust alcove width for full field tiles
4 Plan height for full field tiles
5 Start alcove at top of tile row
6 Fur out as needed to avoid cutting
7 Full tiles define bench height
8 Start with full tiles at base

plywood so the glass tile would cap the end without any cutting. We chose framing and sheathing thicknesses to achieve the same aim with the shelf edge. If possible, plan the tile for the large wall expanses so that you'll have columns of similar-width tiles at both ends of each wall. Study **Figure A** to make all of this clear. You won't be able to avoid all tile cutting, of course. The goal is to simplify the tile work as much as possible. The more effort you put into planning the project, the easier it will be to install the tile. And you'll be rewarded with a first-class tile job.

1 PLAN the framing and tile layout for each wall on rosin paper cut to match the size of each wall.

Frame the shower

If you have a space between the shower base and the wall, as we show, start by framing a continuous wall, floor to ceiling, between the base and the wall (**Photo 2**). If there's no framing behind the ceiling for anchoring the wall, just screw it to the drywall and then add a bead of construction adhesive around the ceiling plate. Next, frame in the alcove. Use your template to establish the height of the top and bottom and then add blocking there. Fur out the side(s) if needed to accommodate tile sizes within and/or surrounding the opening. If your alcove is on an outside wall, glue 1-in.-thick foam insulation against the outside sheathing using special foam adhesive.

Frame the bench with a 1/4-in. slope so water won't pool. Cap the bench with 3/4-in. plywood, screwing it with 1-5/8-in. screws. Lastly, add 2x6 blocking to anchor shelves and missing blocking at inside corners.

Cement board tile backer is commonly used for shower walls, but we used a drywall-type tile backer called DensShield. It's slightly more expensive than cement board but much easier to work with. You score it, snap it and cut it just like drywall.

Whatever material you use, anchor it with 1-1/4-in. cement board screws spaced every 4 in. at seams and every 6 in. everywhere else. If you have a premade shower base, keep the bottom row of backer board just above the lip. The tile will hang down over the lip to direct water into the base.

Next lay a strip of fiberglass mesh tape over all seams and corners. It has adhesive on one side, but many brands don't stick very well or for very long. If you have trouble, use staples to hold it in place. Mix up about a quart of thin-set mortar to the consistency of creamy peanut butter and trowel it over all the seams with a 6-in. putty knife. Try to avoid big buildups, which keep the tile from lying flat.

BLOCKING
SHELF BLOCKING
ALCOVE
1" FOAM
SHOWER BENCH
INSIDE-CORNER BLOCKING
1' WALL

2 ADD blocking to the top and bottom of the alcove, shimming the sides as needed, and fill in the back with foam board. Frame the end wall and then the bench.

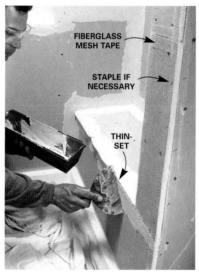

FIBERGLASS MESH TAPE
STAPLE IF NECESSARY
THIN-SET

3 COVER all seams and corners with fiberglass mesh tape. Embed the tape with a thin layer of thin-set.

FIRST COAT OF WATERPROOFING MEMBRANE

4 COAT water-prone areas with two coats of waterproofing membrane.

Apply waterproofing membrane

Any area that will be exposed to lots of water should be coated with two coats of a brush-on waterproofing membrane ($50 per gallon; available at some home centers and all tile stores). Use disposable brushes and let the first coat dry thoroughly before recoating. The RedGard product we show goes on pink and dries to red when it's ready for a second coat (Photos 4 and 5). Focus on areas that will get the lion's share of showerhead water, especially corners and horizontal bench surfaces and recessed alcoves. For extra protection, also coat all of the screw heads in areas that'll get deluged. As with the thin-set, try to avoid big buildups.

WATERPROOFING MEMBRANE

Tile the alcove wall

Use your template as a guide to snap exact tile layout lines. First establish lines

for the rows of tiles surrounding the alcove. Then dry-stack and measure tiles to get an exact measurement from the bottom of the alcove to the top of the first row of tile. Draw a level line and screw a 1x2 ledger to the wall (**Photo 7**). The ledger will ensure a perfectly straight bottom course of tiles and keep them from sliding down the wall before the adhesive sets. (You'll remove the ledger and add the bottom row of tiles later, cutting them to height if needed.)

Mix up about a quart of thin-set at a time (follow the directions on the bag). Comb the thin-set onto the back of the alcove with a 1/4-in. notched trowel (**Photo 5**). Then press the mosaic tile sections into the thin-set. Lightly tap the tiles with a grout float to embed each small tile evenly with its neighbors (**Photo 11**). Look carefully for grout that works its way out between the tiles and wipe it off with a damp rag; it's tough to scrape off after it sets.

Begin setting the field (wall) tile following your layout lines. After you set each tile, give it a little rap with your fist to better embed it. Dip tiles in water before sticking them to the wall so they form a better bond with the thin-set (**Photo 8**). Continually check the rows of tile for straightness. When the thin-set is still fresh, you can even out rows just by pushing a level against several tiles at once (**Photo 12**). Finish tiling the wall, cutting the top row to fit as needed. Leave out the row of tiles where the shelf will rest (**Photo 8**).

Tile the alcove sill and then the sides and top. Slightly slope the sill tiles toward the shower for drainage by piling on a little extra thin-set on the back side. Match the slope on the bottom tiles at the side by taping the bottom tile even with the row above it and scribing the angle with a full tile (**Photo 9**).

5 SPREAD thin-set on the back of the alcove with a 1/4-in. notched trowel and then embed the mosaic tile into the adhesive.

6 SUPPORT sagging mosaic tiles with shims and/or nails until the adhesive sets. Tamp all the tiles level as we show in Photo 11.

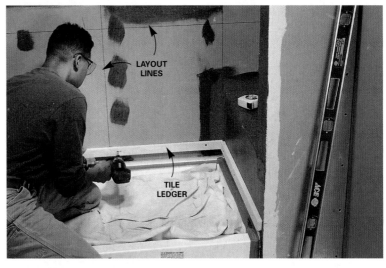

LAYOUT LINES

TILE LEDGER

7 LAY OUT the critical tile lines with a chalk line. Screw a 1x2 to the studs to support the second row of tiles.

FIELD TILE

DAMPEN TILE

8 SPREAD thin-set up to the horizontal layout line and around one corner of the alcove. Set those tiles and then continue tiling the wall, leaving out the row of tiles directly behind the shelf.

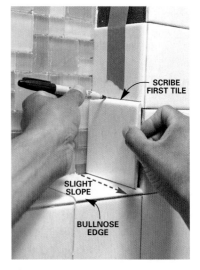

SCRIBE FIRST TILE

SLIGHT SLOPE

BULLNOSE EDGE

9 TILE the alcove bottom shelf first, sloping it slightly toward the shower. Scribe the bottom side tiles to get the proper angle, and then finish tiling the sides and top.

GROUT
FLOAT

TILE
LEDGER

TILE FRONT FIRST

10 TILE the front of the bench first. Cut the mosaic tiles into strips if you need to adjust the spacing to get a better fit with less cutting.

11 TILE the bench and the end of the short wall. Force mosaic tiles evenly into the thin-set with a grout float.

12 ADD the rest of the field tile, stopping at the underside of the shelf. Align tile edges at outside corners with a straightedge.

3/4"
PLYWOOD

BLOCKING
BEHIND

BACKER BOARD

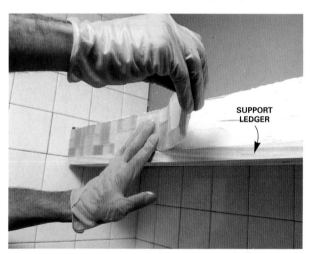

SUPPORT
LEDGER

13 FRAME the shelf. Sheathe the bottom with backer board, rest it on the tile and screw the sides into the blocking. Add the 3/4-in. plywood and cover the exposed wood with backer board.

14 SCREW a support ledger to the shelf underside to support the lip tile. Then tile the underside, top and the rest of the wall tile. The following day, grout the whole works and caulk all inside corners.

Tile the bench

Starting at one end, set the tile on the face of the bench. If you're left with a gap at the other end, cut the mosaic into

strips and slightly expand the grout lines between rows (Photo 10). Small variations in the width of the lines won't be noticeable. Lay tile on the seat to gauge the final grout line width between the seat and the face tile. Then add the seat tile, working from front to back and aligning the grout lines with the face tile. Make sure the seat tile edges align perfectly with the face tile surface—they shouldn't be backset or overhanging. Finish tiling the rest of the field tile above the bench, stopping at the shelf (Photo 13).

Mount and tile the shelf

Build the shelf 1/8 in. narrower than the opening so you can tip it into place. Leave off the plywood top but add backer board to the underside. Rest the shelf on the field tile and screw it to the blocking behind the backer board with two 3-in. screws at each side. Then screw the 3/4-in. plywood top to the framing with 1-5/8-in. screws (Photo 13) and add the backer board to the top and the front edge.

Tile the edge first, support-ing it with a ledger screwed to the shelf underside (Photo 14). Remove the ledger after an hour or so, and then finish tiling the underside and top and the field tile above it. Lastly,

remove the 1x2 ledgers and add the bottom row of tiles. ⟰

GreatGoofs®

In the bag

After removing an old toilet, I did the old handyman trick of stuffing a bunch of plastic bags into the sewer opening. This kept the stench from seeping into the bathroom while I installed the new toilet over the weekend.

After setting and hooking up the new commode, I did a test flush. It was very satisfying to watch the water swirl down and the bowl fill up—and up and up! The toilet gushed water all over the floor.

Turns out the other half of that trick is removing the bags from the sewer opening.

All spun up

My washing machine quit just before the spin cycle. After I opened up the washer, it was clear the belt needed to be changed. It's a bear of a job with a lot of disassembly and working in tight spots, but I wanted to save the 80-buck service call.

I drained the water from the washer and got to work. After a couple of hours (and some foul language), I was hovering over my machine with the lid open, watching my socks dance in the wash and praying for spin. The washer worked its way up to the cycle and then…nothing. I emptied it by hand again, took it all apart and reseated the belt.

Hours later I was once more peering at the agitating clothes and holding my breath, but just as the machine was supposed to spin—it shut down. "I give up!" I said to no one and called the repair service.

The repair person set down his tools, approached the washer and closed the lid. As the cover clicked into place and disengaged the safety mechanism, the washer transitioned perfectly to the spin cycle. My belt repair had been flawless, but I was still writing out an $80 check.

A blot on the day

My nephew, his wife and I had just finished paneling a new playroom. We were feeling pretty good about our achievement until we noticed a small dark mark on the wall.

First we tried cleaning it off with a damp cloth, then moved on to an abrasive cleaner and finally used straight mineral spirits. Nothing seemed to work on this stubborn stain. Just as I was considering sanding it out, I noticed the light fixture hanging from the ceiling. I tapped its pull chain and our "stain" swayed back and forth. I'm afraid our nemesis was just a shadow.

Decorator flooring

My husband and I put a smooth, flawless coat of epoxy on our garage floor. Then we lowered the overhead door, leaving it high enough that it wouldn't touch the wet floor but low enough that the cat couldn't squeeze in under it.

The next morning I peeked into the garage and my eyes grew to the size of silver dollars! We didn't keep the cat out of the garage; we kept her in—all night! (She must have been hiding on top of the rafters.)

It's a goof we're unlikely to forget; hundreds of little paw prints across the floor's mirror finish remind us every day.

It's NOT in the bag

I had just demolished a couple of nasty moldy shower walls for a client and decided the mess needed to be cleaned up straight away. I had forgotten my own shop vacuum that day, so I borrowed the homeowner's machine to knock out the task.

After sucking up all the insulation and drywall debris, I turned around to put the shop vacuum away but could scarcely see. The adjacent room was thick with haze and everything was covered with dust! The filter bag was missing and the vacuum had spewed every particle I had sucked up right back out the exhaust port and into the air behind me.

I put things right with several hours of cleaning and have not borrowed a tool since.

While you were out

All I wanted was a little more storage in our bathroom. But the shelf and hardware I had bought had been gathering dust for over a year while the men in my house procrastinated. So when my husband and sons announced that they were taking off on another hunting trip, I told them I was going to do the job myself.

Their grins and snickers as they headed out the door made me determined to do just that. But as I was driving one of the wall anchors, I bore down too hard on my drill and popped the whole end of the screw gun through the drywall. Remembering those giggles, I ran to the hardware store to buy patching materials and matching paint.

Late into the night I worked on camouflaging that large hole, only to realize in the morning light that the paint wasn't the right color at all! It stood out like a bull's-eye. I spent the whole next day repainting the entire bathroom so everything would match.

A few minutes before the guys were set to roll in, I finally hung the little shelf that had started the marathon bathroom makeover. I told the guys it took about 15 minutes.

REGROUT
A SHOWER

Replace that eroded, crumbling grout for just $50

by **Joe Hurst-Wajszczuk**

By itself, the tile in a shower enclosure is almost maintenance free. With an occasional wipe-down, it can look good for years. Grout, however, is a different story—eventually it's going to break down. Large cracks and crumbly chunks are alarming, but smaller fractures can be trouble too. Fractures, and stains that won't wash out, may indicate spots where water is wicking in and working its way behind the tiles. Sooner or later, that water will weaken the adhesive that's holding the tile or cause rot in the walls. When that happens, the only solution is to tear out the tile and start from scratch.

The good news is that if you catch it in time, you can quickly and easily give tiled surfaces a new lease on life—and a fresh look—by applying a new layer of grout. In this article, we'll walk you through the regrouting process from start to finish, and offer some tools and tips to prevent mid-job mishaps. You don't need previous tile experience; regrouting is mostly grunt work.

The materials needed for an average-size shower cost about $50. In some cases, you can finish the job in a few hours, but to be safe, give yourself a weekend. If you start on Saturday morning, you should be able to take a shower on Monday.

Choosing the right tools and grout

Before you begin digging into that old grout, make sure you have all the tools and materials you'll need to finish the job. To help make sense of what you'll need, think of this project in three parts: scraping and cleaning, regrouting and cleanup.

When you're choosing grout-removal tools, stick with steel to be safe. Many special grout scrapers equipped with carbide tips work well and stay sharp for a long time, but if you slip, the carbide can damage your tile or tub. Steel utility knife blades, on the other hand, may dull quickly, but they're less likely to scratch the tile. Buy a knife with easy-to-change blades, and also buy plenty of spare blades (a 100-blade pack only costs about $10). They're ideal for cleaning out narrow joints. A grout saw ($8; Photo 2) with a notched steel blade is also handy for snagging chunks of grout.

Tip

When you're shopping for grout, stick with brands that offer color-matching caulks. Factory-matched caulk/grout combinations blend almost perfectly.

38

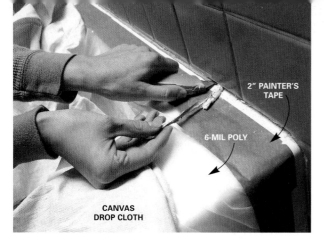

2" PAINTER'S TAPE

6-MIL POLY

CANVAS DROP CLOTH

1 SLICE along each edge of the caulk/wall joint with a sharp utility knife. Pull out the old caulk.

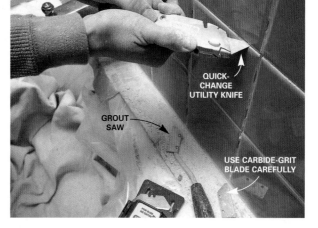

QUICK-CHANGE UTILITY KNIFE

GROUT SAW

USE CARBIDE-GRIT BLADE CAREFULLY

2 SCRATCH out at least 1/8 in. of grout from all the horizontal and vertical lines with a utility knife or grout saw. Change blades often.

STIFF BRUSH

3 CLEAN OUT all of the dust and loose debris from the grout joints using a stiff brush and vacuum.

As for grout, buy a 10-lb. bag—having some left over is better than running out. Grout comes in two forms: unsanded and sanded. For joints up to 1/8 in., choose the unsanded variety. For wider joints, choose sanded to avoid cracking. Whatever type you need, look for a "polymer-modified" mix. The extra ingredients help prevent future cracking and staining. It's almost impossible to match new grout to old, but don't worry. By scratching out the top-most layer from all the grout lines and adding new, you'll get a fresh, consistent color.

To apply the grout, buy a rubber-soled grout float ($9) and a grout sponge ($3). In case the grout starts hardening too quickly, you'll also want to buy a plastic scouring pad (see Editor's Note, p. 41). Last, buy a tube of tub-and-tile caulk ($3 to $6) that matches the grout color.

Slice out caulk and scratch out grout

Before you begin your attack, take a minute to protect your tub against scratches and debris that can clog your drain (**Photo 1**). Tape a layer of plastic sheeting to your tub's top edge. Next, lay a drop cloth on top of the plastic to protect the tub and cushion your knees. Then remove the faucet hardware or protect it with masking tape.

When the going gets tough

The basic arsenal of simple scratch-out tools works for most projects, but there are times when you might need a little extra help. This pair of not-so-secret weapons can make short work of super-stubborn grout and caulk.

The first is a **Grout Grabber** (**$17**). Attached to your reciprocating saw, this carbide-tipped clean-out tool works like a steroid-fueled electric toothbrush. Controlling the blade so it doesn't scratch the tile takes some getting used to, so start with light pressure. Once the blade digs in, it's not too difficult to keep it on the path.

GROUT GRABBER

CAULK REMOVER

The second weapon is 3M's Caulk Remover (**$7**). You'll find it indispensable if the previous installers used silicone caulk to seal cracks around tubs and showers. Silicone's stickiness can make removing it a real headache. The chemical requires a few hours to soften stubborn caulk, but waiting is better than the tedious chore of scratching off the silicone remnants with your knife and possibly damaging your tile or tub.

Getting rid of the old caulk and grout requires plenty of elbow grease, but it's not difficult work, especially if you take your time. Begin by cutting out the old caulk (**Photo 1**) and then move on to the grout (**Photo 2**). When you're using a utility knife, switch blades as soon as the edge stops digging and starts skating on the grout (**Photo 2**). At times, you may have more success with the grout saw. Whatever tool you choose, the goal remains the same: to remove about 1/8 in. from the top (or more, if the grout comes out easily).

When you're done, remove dust and debris, which can weaken the bond between the tile and the new grout (**Photo 3**).

4 MIX the grout with water in a tall bucket using a paint-mixing paddle. Mix slowly until the grout becomes a thick paste.

5 SPREAD grout at an angle to the grout lines with a rubber float. Press hard on the float to pack the joints full of grout.

6 SCRAPE OFF excess grout by tipping the float on edge and pushing it diagonally across the tile. Work quickly.

Mix the grout and pack the joints

Once the grout is mixed, the clock starts ticking toward the moment when it will harden on the wall…or in the bucket. Pro tilers can mix and use a 10-lb. bag of grout before it hardens, but to play it safe, mix up a few cups at a time and work in sections. A smaller batch will allow you plenty of time to apply it and clean the excess from one wall at a time. When you run out, rinse the container before mixing a new batch.

Before you make a batch from a bag, shake the bag to redistribute any pigment and Portland cement that might have settled out in shipment. After it's been dry mixed, scoop out a few cups (one cup equals about a half pound) into a bucket. The instructions on the bag indicate how much water to add per pound of mix. To ensure a strong mix, start with about three-quarters of the specified amount of water and gradually pour in just enough to make the grout spreadable. Aim for a fairly stiff consistency, somewhere between cake icing and peanut butter (Photo 4, inset). Don't worry if the grout looks a little lumpy. After it's mixed, allow it to sit, or slake, for 10 minutes. During this time, the remaining dry specks will absorb moisture. Give the grout one last stir (restirring also keeps the mix from hardening in your bucket) and it's ready for application.

Focus on one wall at a time. Scoop out a dollop and press it out across the tiles at a 45-degree angle (Photo 5). It's OK to be messy. The goal is to pack as much grout into the joints as you can. Press hard and work the float in several directions.

Immediately after you fill the joints, rake off the excess grout. Hold the float on edge, like a snowplow, and cut off most of the excess (Photo 6). Move the float across the joints diagonally to prevent the edge from dipping into the

7 WIPE OFF the excess grout with a damp sponge as soon as the grout lines are firm. To keep the rinse water clean, dip the sponge in the "dirty" bucket and wring it out. Then dip it in the "clean" bucket and wring it over the dirty bucket.

joints and pulling out too much grout. Work quickly before the grout starts to harden.

The time between scraping and sponging varies from job to job. Depending on your mix, the humidity or the temperature, the grout may take anywhere from five to 20

8 SCRAPE grout out of the inside corners and tub/tile joint so that you can seal these joints with caulk later on.

9 BUFF the haze off the tile after the grout dries (several hours). Use an old terry cloth towel.

10 APPLY painter's tape to control your caulk lines. Apply the caulk, smooth the joint with your finger and immediately remove the tape.

minutes to firm up. Begin sponging as soon as the grout feels firm and no longer sticks to your finger.

Using a well-wrung tile sponge, wipe away the bulk of the unwanted grout with short, gentle, circular strokes (Photo 7). Turn the sponge so that you're using a clean edge with each pass. Rinse and wring it out in the "dirty" bucket, then dip the sponge in a "clean" bucket, and finally wring it out again in the "dirty" bucket. This two-bucket technique helps keep your sponge and rinse water clean so that you can remove grout more effectively. Wring out as much water as possible. Too much water can pull cement and pigment from your fresh grout lines.

In addition to wiping away the excess, the sponge works for fine-tuning the shape of your grout lines. To shave down any high spots and make the lines slightly convex, run the sponge across the joint until the grout lines appear uniform. (If you find a low spot, use your finger to rub in a little extra grout.)

Finally, scrape out any globs of grout that may have gotten into the joints you intend to caulk (Photo 8). This includes all corners and the tub/tile joint. You could do this chore later, but it's a lot easier now, before the grout is rock hard.

The sponge-wiped walls may look clean at first, but as the surface moisture evaporates, the remaining grout particles will create a light haze. Give the grout an hour or two to dry, then buff off any residual haze with a soft towel (Photo 9).

Finish up with neat caulk joints

Let the grout dry overnight before applying the caulk along the tub/tile joint and inside corners. For clean, precise caulk lines, run painter's tape along the inside corner and at the tub/tile joint (Photo 10). Just remember to

remove the tape as soon as you finish smoothing. If you wait too long, the caulk will skin over or stick to the tape and you'll pull out the caulk when you try to remove the tape. Depending on the caulk, your bath should be ready for an inaugural shower in 24 hours.

To reduce mold growth, seal grout lines for extra stain and water resistance. Give the grout a week or two to cure completely before sealing. Remember that sealers wear off in time, so you'll need to reapply it every year or so. If you don't want to apply a sealer, wiping your walls down with a squeegee after each use works almost as well. 🏠

Editor's Note

The biggest mistake you're likely to make is waiting too long before sponging the excess grout off the tile. I've discovered that it only takes a few minutes before a shower stall can start looking like a sidewalk.

A plastic scrub pad ($3) is a cheap insurance policy. The coarse pad quickly and easily scours off hardened grout that would shrug off a sponge, but it won't scratch the tile. (In addition to emergencies, I like using it to tweak the shape of my grout lines.)

Of course, buying one may guarantee that you won't need it. On the other hand, should you need one, you won't be able to drive to the hardware store fast enough. *Joe*

SharpenYourSkills

TOUGH **TILE CUTS** WITH A **GRINDER**

S tone, porcelain and glass tiles offer beautiful options for bath and kitchen tiling projects. But cutting these hard materials presents a unique challenge. Straight cuts are easy to make with a diamond wet saw. But cutting curves and holes requires special techniques.

In this article, we'll show you how to use an inexpensive angle grinder with a diamond blade to cut perfect circles and squares in even the toughest tile. You can buy a 4-in. or 4-1/2-in. grinder for as little as $50 and a dry-cut diamond blade to fit it starting at $15. In general, more expensive blades will last longer. When you're choosing a diamond blade, look for one with a continuous, rather than segmented rim for the smoothest cut.

Be aware, though, that cutting with a dry-cut diamond blade creates a lot of dust and noise. So make sure you cut in a well-ventilated area (or better yet, outside!) and wear hearing protection, a good-quality two-strap dust mask and safety glasses.

BOSCH
Diamond Blade
Hoja de diamante
Lame de diamante

4½"
115mm

GENERAL PURPOSE
Uso general
Usage general

PREMIUM
DB4542C 2 610 027 850
MAX RPM 13,200
DRY/En seco/A sec

CONCRETE • BLOCK • BRICK • STONE
Concreto • Bloque • Ladrillo • La piedra
Ciment • Blocs • Briques • Pierre

SMOOTH
CONTINUOUS RIM

Tilt the blade for circles

Many tile jobs require you to cut one or more large round holes for floor drains or shower valves. Photos 1 – 3 show how to cut a hole for a shower valve. We're showing how to cut a hole that's entirely within a single tile, one of the most difficult cuts. In the next section we'll show you an easier method to use for cutting curves in the edge of a tile.

Even with this method, try to avoid a tile layout that places the edge of the circular cutout less than 1/2 in. from the edge of a tile. It's better to shift the entire layout instead. Otherwise, chances are good that you'll break the tile at the narrow point while cutting.

The method shown for cutting a circle with a grinder and diamond blade requires you to cut around the circle a number of times, making a deeper cut with each revolution. The key is to maintain the same angle and shave off progressive layers, moving the cut closer to the center of the circle (Photo 2).

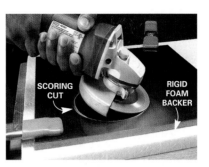

1 SCORE the front of the tile along the circle guideline with the diamond blade. Tilt the grinder about 30 degrees and cut about 1/16 in. deep.

2 MOVE the blade 1/8 in. to the inside of the line and make a deeper cut. Continue moving the blade away from the line and cutting deeper until you cut completely through.

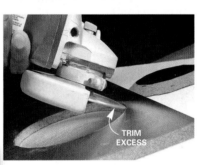

3 GRIND off rough edges and trim back to the line for a perfect curve.

Plunge-cut from the back to make square or rectangular cutouts

Cutting rectangular or square holes for electrical outlets is simple with this method. The key is to avoid cutting beyond the corners of the square where the cut might be visible. Plunge-cut slowly from the back and check often to avoid going too far.

1 MARK the cutout on the front and back of the tile precisely. Then score the front of the tile about 1/16 in. deep along the line.

2 FLIP the tile over and plunge the cut from the back. Stop and check often. Stop when the cut lines up with the corners of the marked square on the front. Plunge-cut the remaining three sides.

Rough out semicircular cuts before trimming to the line

The process for cutting semicircles from the edge of tiles is similar to the technique shown on p. 43 for full circles. You start by marking the cut and scoring the face of the tile on the line. Then, rather than deepen the scoring cut, simply remove the excess tile with straight cuts (**Photo 1**).

Before you remove the excess tile (**Photo 1**), be sure to make short cuts on both sides of the semicircle (1 and 2). Then connect the cuts as shown (3). Rather than make this connecting cut in one pass, make a series of progressively deeper shallow cuts until you're through the tile.

Now complete the semicircle with a series of radial cuts—like the spokes of a wheel (**Photo 2**). Finish by cleaning up the rough edges with the diamond blade. Or remove the "tabs" with a tile nipper (a pliers-like biting tool). Then grind the edges smooth.

Make a dish-shaped cutout for small, rough holes

Most plumbing pipe holes are covered by a decorative escutcheon or hidden by a fixture base. When a precise round hole isn't necessary, use the technique shown here.

Start by marking the circular cutout on the back of the tile. Then plunge the diamond blade down through the tile, keeping it centered on the hole so that the slot made by the blade extends equally on both sides of the circle marks (**Photo 1**). Check often to see when the slot through the front of the tile reaches the edges of the desired cutout. Then use the length of that plunge cut to gauge the diameter of a second, larger circle. Draw that larger circle on the back of the tile (**Photo 2**). Use this circle as a guide for making the rest of the plunge cuts. Rotate the grinder about a blade's width and make another plunge cut, stopping at the outer circle. Continue this process until you finish the hole.

1 SCORE the profile with the saw, then cut in from the edge of the tile to remove as much waste as possible.

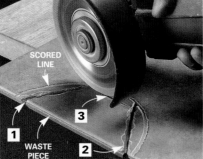

1 CENTER the cut on the hole and plunge slowly from the back. Stop when the slot through the face of the tile lines up with the edges of the desired cutout.

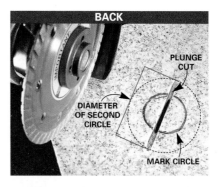

2 MAKE a series of closely spaced cuts up to the scored line. Break off the waste. Then grind the edges smooth.

2 DRAW another larger circle to guide the depth of the remaining cuts. Make repeated plunge cuts until the circle is complete.

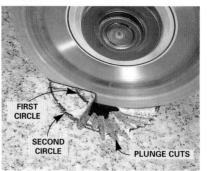

FIVE WAYS TO SEAL
ATTIC AIR LEAKS

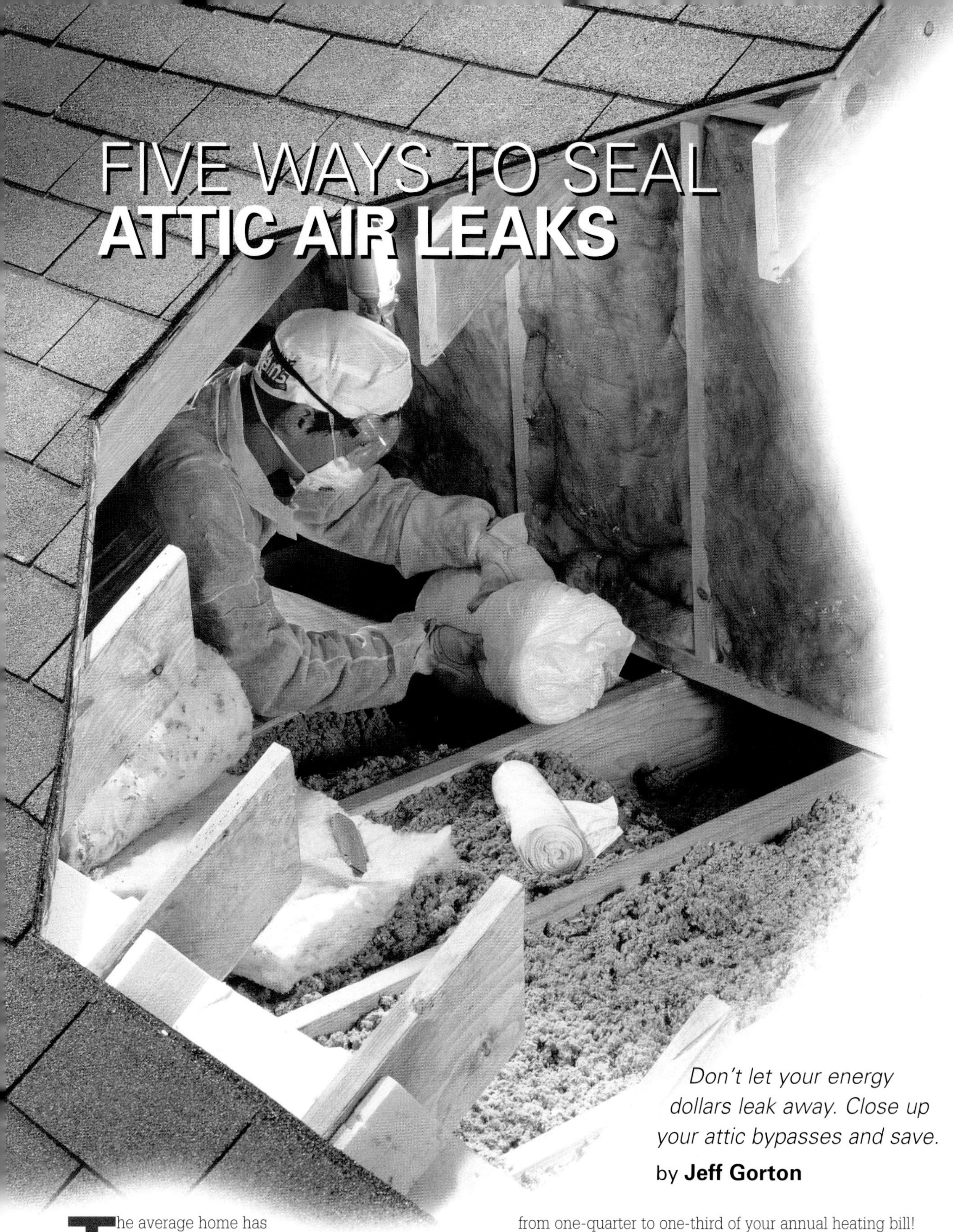

*Don't let your energy
dollars leak away. Close up
your attic bypasses and save.*
by **Jeff Gorton**

The average home has the equivalent of a 2-ft.-square hole in the ceiling that allows warm air to leak out through the attic. That hole is actually in the form of many smaller cracks and gaps around lights, plumbing pipe, chimneys, walls and other ceiling penetrations. In dollars and cents, this leakage accounts for anywhere from one-quarter to one-third of your annual heating bill! No small change.

Yet for less than $100 in caulk, foam and other materials available at a hardware store or home center, plus a day's labor, you can plug most of those holes and reduce your heating bill. In this article, we'll tell you how to find those attic "bypasses" and how to seal them.

How to find the gaps

Before you crawl into your attic, make a rough sketch of the floor plan and the ceiling below the attic. Sketch in the walls, the chimney, the main plumbing stack, ceiling electrical fixtures and lower sections of ceiling (soffits; Figure A). They all have high leak potential, and your sketch will help you find them when you're in the attic.

To help generate actual leakage, place a box fan in a window so it blows air into the house. Then close all other windows and doors. Tape cardboard around the fan to eliminate large gaps. When you turn the fan on high, you'll slightly pressurize the house, just like an inflated balloon. Then when you're in the attic (with the hatch closed), you can confirm a leaky area by feeling the air coming through. You may even spot the insulation blowing in the breeze.

Another helpful sign is dirty insulation (photo, right). Insulation fibers filter the household air as it passes, leaving a dirt stain that marks the leaky area.

Now gather up the gap-sealing materials we show on the next few pages and suit up. Attics are miserable places to work in. Be sure to read the tips on p. 47 before you start.

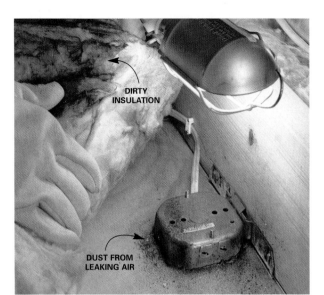

DIRTY INSULATION

DUST FROM LEAKING AIR

**Figure A
Common attic
air leak zones**

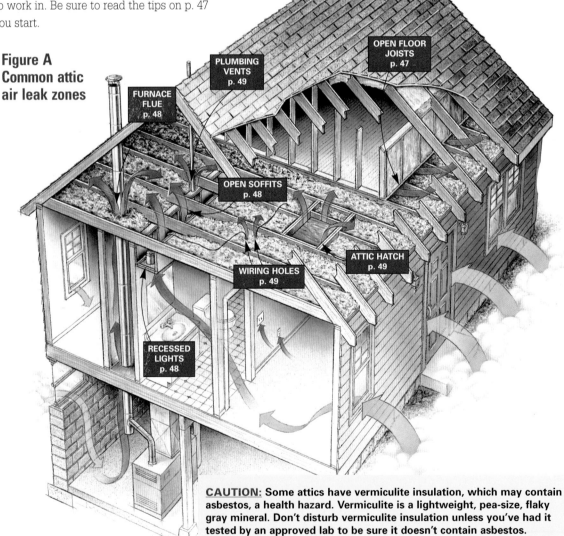

PLUMBING VENTS
p. 49

OPEN FLOOR JOISTS
p. 47

FURNACE FLUE
p. 48

OPEN SOFFITS
p. 48

ATTIC HATCH
p. 49

WIRING HOLES
p. 49

RECESSED LIGHTS
p. 48

CAUTION: Some attics have vermiculite insulation, which may contain asbestos, a health hazard. Vermiculite is a lightweight, pea-size, flaky gray mineral. Don't disturb vermiculite insulation unless you've had it tested by an approved lab to be sure it doesn't contain asbestos. Contact your local health department for the name of an approved lab.

Labels on image: GOGGLES, DUST MASK, 13-GALLON GARBAGE BAG, 16"-LONG FIBERGLASS BATT, OPEN STUD CAVITY, PAINTER'S COVERALL, DROPPED SOFFIT, RECESSED CAN LIGHT

1 CUT a 16-in. length from a batt of unfaced fiberglass insulation and fold it into the bottom of a 13-gallon plastic garbage bag.

1 Plug open stud and joist cavities

It's tempting to grab a can of expanding foam and squirt it into all the little holes you can find. But your biggest savings will come from plugging the big holes. Look for them first. Open stud cavities are the worst (**Photo 1**). Look for them around lowered areas of ceilings (soffits) and where the ceiling height shifts, especially in split-level homes. Pull back insulation to examine these areas, because the insulation itself doesn't stop the leaks. Plug them with a plastic bag partially filled with insulation. The plastic bag stops the airflow (**Photo 2**). The insulation makes the bag expand tightly to close off gaps.

Use the same method for open joist spaces under floors (**Photo 3**). You can't get to the potentially leaky areas under floors, but you can plug the cavity where it leads into the attic.

Labels on image: OPEN STUD CAVITY, PLUGGED STUD CAVITY, RECESSED CAN LIGHT

2 FOLD the bag over once and stuff it into the open stud cavity. Make sure there's enough insulation in the bag to achieve a tight fit in the cavity.

Labels on image: 24" BATT ROLLED INSIDE GARBAGE BAG, KNEE WALL, OPEN JOIST CAVITY, FIBER-GLASS BATT

3 PLUG open joist spaces under side walls. Cut a 24-in. length from a fiberglass batt and roll it into a garbage bag. Fold the bag over and stuff it into the joist cavity.

Editor's Note: Working in the attic

I've made almost every mistake you can make working in the attic. I've sweated in 110-degree F conditions when the roof sheathing felt like a hot radiator, endured itchy skin after working in short sleeves, bumped my head many times and inadvertently stepped through a ceiling. To avoid these goofs, do the following:

- Work when it's cool outdoors: early morning or on cloudy days in the summer.
- Wear an old long-sleeve shirt, work pants and a hat to protect your skin from insulation irritation. Wash the clothing or toss it when you're done.
- Wear a double-strap face mask or particulate respirator.
- Use a couple of short 2x6s or 3/4-in. plywood to kneel on and hold your supplies.
- Pull a clamp-on light around with you and carry a flashlight as well.
- Collect all your materials and tools and place them in the attic before you climb up. Ask a helper to remain within shouting range in case you forget something.

2 Cover open soffits

Builders often put a soffit where they want to put cabinets or recessed light fixtures, and sometimes they use soffits to contain heating ducts. Soffits have a high potential for leakage, especially if they contain recessed lights. Refer to your sketch and dig around in the insulation if necessary to find them. Reflective foil insulation, sometimes called "bubble-pack" insulation, works well as an air barrier for soffits. It's flexible and only about 1/4 in. thick, making it easy to cut with scissors. The photo at right shows how to install it. You have to clear insulation from the surrounding wood to get the caulk to stick. Then cover the foil with insulation when you're finished. However, don't put insulation within 3 in. of recessed lights unless the fixture is IC rated (for "insulation contact"). The rating will be listed on a label inside the recessed can.

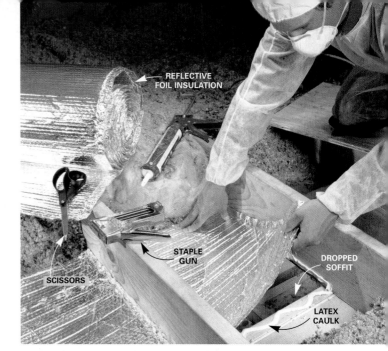

With scissors, cut a length of foil insulation about 6 in. longer than the opening to be covered. Apply a bead of latex caulk around the opening. Embed the foil in the caulk and staple it into place.

3 Seal around flues and chimneys

The opening around a furnace or water heater flue is a major source of warm air leakage into the attic. Because the pipe gets hot, building codes require at least a 1-in. clearance from combustible materials, including insulation. For masonry chimneys, the minimum clearance is 2 in. The trick then is to block airflow with aluminum flashing and high-temperature caulk ($5 to $10). Photos 1 – 3 show you how. Before you push insulation back into place, build a metal dam to maintain the required minimum clearance.

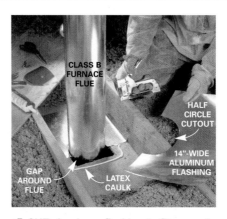

1 CUT aluminum flashing to fit around the flue. For round flues, cut half circles out of two pieces so they overlap about 3 in. Press the flashing metal into a bead of latex caulk and staple it to wood or drywall.

2 SEAL the gap between the flue and metal flashing with special high-temperature silicone caulk. Don't use spray foam here.

WARNING Insulation must be 1 in. from Class B flues.

3 FORM a 16-in.-high dam to keep insulation from contacting the flue. Cut enough aluminum to wrap around the flue plus 6 in. Cut 1-in.-deep slots spaced every 2 in. along the top and bend the tabs in. Cut slots about 2 in. deep along the bottom and bend the tabs out. Wrap the dam around the flue and secure the bottom by stapling through the tabs.

Recessed lights: No easy solution

Recessed lighting is a great lighting technique, but the cans are notorious energy-wasters when put into a ceiling with an attic above. They usually leak, and when hot, create a strong heat draft into the attic. If you find recessed lights protruding into your attic, take these steps:

- Replace incandescent bulbs with cooler-operating compact fluorescent bulbs.
- Replace the old cans with newer airtight models. They're available at home centers and lighting stores for $20 to $30 each.

4 Use foam or caulk for small gaps

Now concentrate on the small stuff. Actually it's best to keep your can or expanding foam and caulk gun handy and plug the obvious electrical cable holes and fixture boxes as you move around working on the bigger air leaks. Make sure you get to the plumbing vent, because the gap around it is usually large (Photo 1). Use your sketch to help find this and other features. Also look for the 2x4 top plates (framing) of interior walls and follow them, keeping a sharp eye out for electrical cable holes and dirty insulation, which would indicate a gap or long crack between drywall and a wood

1 STUFF fiberglass batt insulation into the space around the plumbing vent pipe as a backer for the expanding foam. Then follow the directions on the can to fill the space around the pipe.

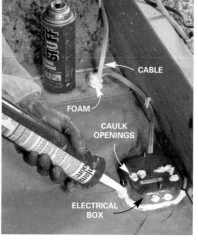

2 FILL wiring and plumbing holes with expanding foam. Caulk around electrical junction boxes and plug holes in the box with caulk.

plate. Seal these with caulk.

Work carefully with expanding foam because it's super sticky and

almost impossible to get off your clothes and skin. Wear disposable gloves when working with it.

5 Weatherstrip hatches and doors

When you're done sealing the attic bypasses, push the insulation back into place with an old broom handle or a stick as you back out of the attic. Then finish up by sealing the access hatch with self-sticking foam weatherstrip (Photo 1). You may have to add new wood stops to provide a better surface for the weatherstrip and enough room for hook-and-eye fasteners (Photo 2). Position the screw eyes so that you slightly compress the weatherstrip when you latch the hatch. Use a similar procedure if you have a hinged door that leads to the attic. 🏠

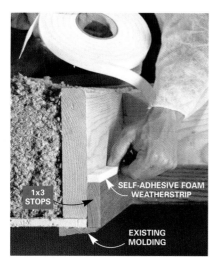

1 WEATHERSTRIP the attic access hatch or door. Cut 1x3 stops and nail them on with 6d finish nails. Apply self-adhesive foam weatherstrip to the top edge of the stop.

2 ATTACH hook-and-eye fasteners to the door and stops. Position the eyes so that the weatherstrip is compressed when you latch the hooks.

Check for backdrafting

If you do a good job, you'll quickly notice the results. Your home will feel less drafty and more snug. Your heating system will run less too. But whenever you tighten your home, there's less air turnover and a greater risk of carbon monoxide poisoning from a poorly adjusted furnace, gas water heater or other combustion appliances. Test your CO alarm to make sure it's working or install one if you don't have one already. And ask a furnace pro to check your furnace and water heater for backdrafting at the next regular service interval. (See "Prevent Carbon Monoxide Poisoning," Oct. '01, p. 64. To order a copy, visit thefamilyhandyman.com.)

NewProducts

BEST PAINT PRODUCTS UNDER $3

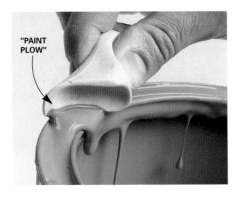

"PAINT PLOW"

Clean paint can rims

It's not often that we're impressed with a $1 gadget, but this simple little Paint Plow turned out to be one of our favorite products. It quickly cleans the lid grooves on paint cans, pushing the paint back into the container so you can put the lid back on without making a mess. No more pounding the lid down and watching the paint fly. Plus, a clean rim leads to a better seal, so stored paint will last longer. Buy it at some Ace Hardware stores and other select hardware and paint stores. **Foam Painting Tools, (949) 252-0112. foampromfg.com**

Hassle-free baseboard painting

Holding back strands of carpet while you paint baseboard can be a pain, and it doesn't always work. The carpet shield makes painting next to carpet easy. The 3-ft.-long, reusable "shield" slides under the baseboard, pushing down the carpet to keep it out of your way. You'll still want to put a drop cloth under the shield.

The shield also works great for protecting hard flooring while you apply a baseboard finish. Just butt it against the baseboard while you work. Home Depot sells the paint shield for $2 for a six-pack. **Trimaco, (888) 415-9888. trimaco.com**

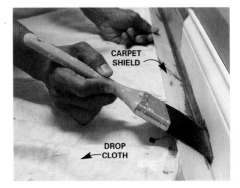

CARPET SHIELD

DROP CLOTH

MAGNETIC PAINT FOR KIDS' ROOMS

My kids like to hang things in their bedrooms—which usually means thumbtack holes and tape all over the walls. Magic Wall Magnetic Paint (it's actually a primer, so a conventional primer coat isn't needed) makes displaying things on the walls with magnets easy, thanks to iron particles in the paint. Roll on a couple of coats, apply the finish paint, and magnets stick to the walls. It's like having a sheet of steel behind the paint. You and your kids can hang awards, art projects and other lightweight objects without damaging the drywall—no more repairs!

At $25 a pint, it's not cheap, but you don't need to paint an entire wall. Just paint the display area you want magnetized. Find Magic Wall Magnetic Paint at Sherwin-Williams stores and Michaels arts and crafts stores. **Kling Magnetics, (518) 392-4000. kling.com**

MAGNETS

MAGNETIC PAINT

FINISH PAINT

ADORABLE KID

POP-OFF ROLLER COVER

Roller covers are often a pain to remove. You have to bang the roller frame on the edge of the sink or a trash can to get the cover off (sending paint everywhere) or grab the paint-filled roller with your bare hand (yuck!). Wagner has

RELEASE BUTTON

ROLLER COVER

made the task push-button simple and neat. Just press a button on the handle of the Mess Free Release Roller and the roller cover ejects. It doesn't get any easier than this.

At $13, it's more expensive than other 9-in. roller frames (starting at about $5). Find it at home centers.

Wagner, (800) 328-8251. wagnerspraytech.com

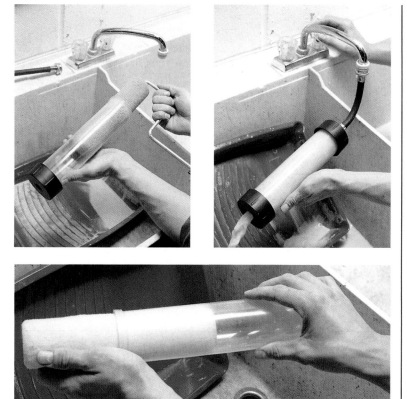

BEST WAY TO CLEAN ROLLER COVERS

If you do a lot of roll-on painting and use premium roller covers that you don't want to throw away, get a Roller Washer ($25). You'll be glad you did.

We've been using one of these roller cover cleaners for 20 years. They're easy to use and they do get the rollers incredibly clean—a task that takes a long time by hand, and even then you rarely get a truly clean nap. Just hook up the hose to a faucet, slide the roller cover into the tube, and watch the water flush out the paint in minutes. Get it at Sherwin-Williams stores or buy it directly from the company.

Paint Cleaners, (585) 335-9099. rollerwasher.com

A NO-HASSLE WAY TO STORE PAINT AND ROLLERS OVERNIGHT

If you can't finish your paint project in one day, you can clean all the tools and start over the next morning or wrap your paint tray in a bag overnight to keep the paint and roller fresh. You can also try a third option: Get Prazi USA's Seal Pro Paint tray. The attachable lid seals the tray, protecting the paint and roller from drying out while you snooze. That way, you don't have to hassle with cleanup until the job's done.

The rigid tray doesn't tip easily and holds up to a gallon of paint. A magnet on the side of the tray holds brushes upright so they're grabbable and keeps the handle out of the paint. Buy the tray at hardware stores and online for $20.

Prazi USA, (800) 262-0211. praziusa.com

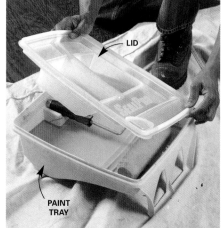

LID

PAINT TRAY

DIY **GRANITE COUNTERTOP**

Get the beauty and durability of granite for half the cost

by **Joe Hurst-Wajszczuk**

Gorgeous and tough, granite makes a great countertop material. Unfortunately, greatness has its price: Granite slab countertops start at about $100 per sq. ft. But you can have granite countertops for half that cost (or even less) by using granite tile instead of professionally installed granite slabs. Budget-conscious builders and homeowners have done this for decades—and now there are granite tiles designed especially for countertops.

This article will show you how to install these special tiles. Since a countertop sits just a couple of feet below eye level, minor mistakes are easy to see. So we'll show you how to set your tiles flat, even and perfectly aligned.

Money, time and tools

The materials bill for our countertop and backsplash was less than $50 per sq. ft., including everything from screws and backer board to the tiles themselves. The number of inside and outside corners has a big impact on the total cost: Corners cost us about $40 each. Standard bullnose tiles cost $20 and field tiles just $10 each.

This is a two-weekend project for a typical kitchen. You'll spend about half that time tearing out your old countertop and creating a solid base for the tile. A countertop requires a bit more skill and precision than a wall or floor, so we don't recommend this as a first-time tile project. In addition to standard tile tools, you'll need to rent a tile saw for a day (about $50). You can't cut the tiles with a manual cutter. Aside from the tile, all the tools and materials you'll need are at home centers.

Order the tile

A few weeks before you tear off your old countertops, pull out a pencil and pad and calculate the number and types of tiles needed. Measure, then sketch your countertop on graph paper, including the sink. Label the tiles (bullnose, field, corners) to assess what's needed where. To see some sample layouts, go to benissimosystems.com and click on "counter examples."

When you arrive at a final count, you're almost ready to place your order. Because the tiles are color-matched before shipping, order a few extra to allow for cutting mistakes. Three extra field tiles and two extra bullnose tiles is a safe allowance for a simple job, but for a complex project, you might want extra insurance.

Build a solid base

According to the manufacturer of our tiles, they can be installed directly onto an existing laminate countertop *if the laminate is attached to a 3/4-in.-thick plywood substrate.* Since the vast majority of countertops have a particleboard core, chances are you'll have to tear out your countertop and start from scratch. For step-by-step instructions on

Tip **More help online.** For help building a base for tile over your cabinets, plus more on granite tile installation, search for "granite tile countertop." For tips on cutting tile, search for "tile saw" at thefamilyhandyman.com

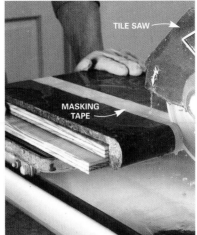

1 PROTECT the tile base against water damage with a coat of waterproofing membrane.

2 SET bullnose tiles on scraps of plywood to cut them. Granite is difficult to mark clearly, so stick on some masking tape and mark the tape.

3 RUB CUT edges with a honing stone to bevel the edge slightly. Rub in a circular motion to avoid wearing a groove in the stone.

how to remove your old countertop and build a base for the tile, go to our Web site (see Tip, p. 52). For construction details, see **Figure A**. Seal the backer board with a waterproofing membrane (**Photo 1**) for extra insurance. This coating prevents moisture from passing through the backer board and causing the plywood to swell or delaminate.

Make a dry run first

Once the base is in place, you're set to start laying tile. But first do a dry run. Dry-fitting gives you time to experiment with the arrangement of the tiles so that the natural color and grain variations flow from one tile to the next. A dry run also lets you cut the tiles all at once and minimizes the total rental fee for the tile saw.

The manufacturer recommends setting tiles tightly together and filling the shallow V-shaped bevels between them with grout. But we left 1/8-in. gaps between tiles using tile spacers. That gave us a little room for error in cutting and placing tiles and allowed the tiles to conform to our L-shaped countertop, which wasn't perfectly square.

Start the dry run from an inside corner and work outward so that the two mitered inside corner tiles fit together perfectly. Continue working out from the corner, laying a few bullnose tiles and filling in the back with field tiles.

Cutting bullnose tiles with a wet saw isn't any more difficult than cutting regular tiles, except that you'll need to stack a few plywood scraps under the tile so that you can cut the bullnose edge first (**Photo 2**). To avoid chipping or cracking the tile, guide it slowly and steadily past the blade. It's OK if a wall-facing cut is a little rough, but for visible cuts, smooth the sawn edge and create a slight bevel along the top edge with a honing stone (**Photo 3**).

After laying out all the tiles, label them and make a simple layout map (**Photo 4**) so you can set each tile right where it belongs later. Finally, remove the middle tiles and use the remaining end and corner pieces to draw guidelines (**Photo 5**).

Figure A: Granite tile countertop

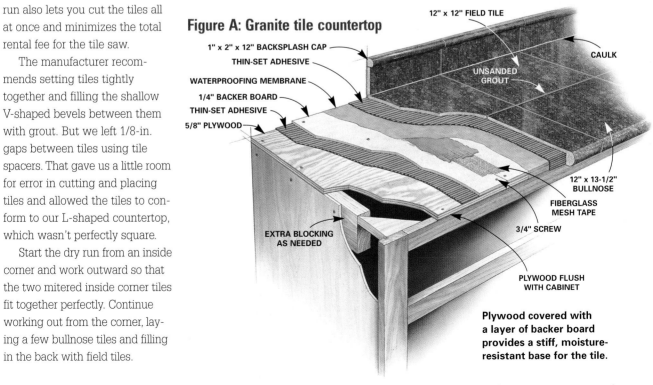

12" x 12" FIELD TILE

1" x 2" x 12" BACKSPLASH CAP

CAULK

THIN-SET ADHESIVE

UNSANDED GROUT

WATERPROOFING MEMBRANE

1/4" BACKER BOARD

THIN-SET ADHESIVE

5/8" PLYWOOD

12" x 13-1/2" BULLNOSE

FIBERGLASS MESH TAPE

3/4" SCREW

EXTRA BLOCKING AS NEEDED

PLYWOOD FLUSH WITH CABINET

Plywood covered with a layer of backer board provides a stiff, moisture-resistant base for the tile.

Granite tile made just for countertops

The tile we used has a thick, rounded "bullnose." That gives the front edge of the countertop a more elegant look than standard tile can and eliminates the slow, fussy task of cutting and installing thin strips of tile to cover the edge. There are outside corners, premitered inside corners and standard bullnose tiles. Special backsplash pieces are available too. The field tiles are just like standard granite floor tiles.

BULLNOSE

FIELD TILE

INSIDE CORNERS

OUTSIDE CORNER

LAYOUT MAP

4 NUMBER the tiles and sketch a layout map after the dry run. Remove the tiles and use the map to put each tile back in the correct order later.

5 DRAW a baseline from the inside corner tiles to the end tiles. Use this line as a guide as you set the front row of tiles.

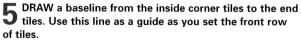

TESTER

SPACER

6 WORK in small sections, spreading just enough thin-set to set eight tiles. That gives you plenty of time to set and adjust tiles before the thin-set becomes too stiff.

7 LAY tiles perfectly flat using a straightedge. Set a "tester" tile on a spacer to account for the thickness of the thin-set. Run the straightedge from the tester to the tile you're setting to check for flatness.

8 PLOW OUT thin-set that oozes up between tiles before it hardens. An old credit card fits into the narrow gaps and won't scratch the tile.

9 SHIM the narrow tiles in front of the sink to keep them from tipping forward. Align the tops and fronts of these tiles using a straightedge.

10 "BACK BUTTER" the backsplash and cap pieces to minimize the mess on the wall. Support backsplash tiles with spacers to leave a 1/8-in. gap for caulk.

11 SEAL the tiles with a penetrating stone sealer after the grout has dried. A foam paint roller applies the sealer quickly and evenly.

Set the tiles

It's time to mix the thin-set. To prevent the tiles from sinking, aim for a peanut-butter-thick mix. When combed out with a 3/8-in. notched trowel, the thin-set should hold sharp ridges without slumping.

Lay the tiles from the inside corner out (Photo 6), just as you did during the dry run. Instead of fussing over each tile, lay two or three tiles at once, then treat them as a unit. Once you've positioned the tiles, use a straightedge to make sure they're set flat (Photo 7). At the beginning, you'll need to place a dry-laid tester tile on top of a 1/8-in.-thick spacer (such as a layer or two of cardboard). As you proceed, rest the level on the first tiles you've laid to help gauge the rest. After checking the height, nudge the straightedge against the bullnose edges to be sure the front edge stays straight and lines up with your guideline.

Be careful when adjusting tiles. Granite is tough stuff, but it's surprisingly easy to crack. To slide freshly set tiles, use your utility knife. Stab the point of the blade into the backer board, then lever the side of the blade against the bottom edge of the tile. If a tile sinks lower than its neighbors, lift it straight up, scrape off the old thin-set, trowel on a fresh layer, then reset. Trying to tap down a high tile almost always causes a crack. Instead, try gently pressing and wiggling so the excess thin-set can squeeze out an open end. If that doesn't work, lift the tile and scrape away the excess thin-set. Clean out any thin-set that oozes out between the tiles as you go, before it has a

chance to harden (Photo 8).

Thin-set sets quickly, but to be safe, give the counter a few hours (preferably overnight) to harden before starting the backsplash (Photo 10). Make sure your new backsplash isn't higher than your outlets before mixing any mortar. To prevent tiles from sliding, give your freshly tiled backsplash a day to cure before removing the spacers and packing the grout.

Grout, seal and caulk

Once the granite's in place, this job is like any other tiling project. Use a float to pack grout into most of the lines, but you'll probably need to use your finger to work grout into the curves, such as the bullnose front edge and the backsplash cap. Sponge off the excess when the grout begins to harden. Wait until the grout is fully dry before buffing off the remaining haze with a clean cotton towel. You can now reinstall the sink, stove and other appliances.

Some foods and cleaners can stain or even etch granite and grout, so apply a stone sealer (Photo 11). Finally, lay a thin bead of caulk along the joint where the counter meets the backsplash. 🏠

Buyer's Guide

We chose "Giardini Quartz" tile for our countertop. To find a dealer, go to benissimosystems.com. To find other manufacturers, search the Web for "modular granite tile countertop" or call a local tile dealer.

The Family Handyman

HEAT-REDUCING WINDOW FILM

My son's west-facing bedroom gets very hot in the spring and summer. Will a window film help, and if so, can I install it myself?

A heat control window film will help keep your son's room cooler, and yes, you can install it yourself. These films reflect the sun's heat and ultraviolet rays, and reduce glare without obscuring the view (**see photo**). The more direct sunlight coming through the window, the more the film will help (and it may lower your air-conditioning bills!).

Applying the film takes approximately 30 minutes per window (**inset photo**). It should last about 10 years. Prices vary with film size. A 3-ft. x 15-ft. film (which can cover two to three windows) costs $30. The film is sold at home centers and hardware stores. Gila is one company that makes heat control film (800-528-4481, gilafilms.com).

Different types of film are available, so get the one designed for heat control. The film can be applied to any window, including double-pane low-e windows, although they already reduce radiant heat loss and gain.

One drawback is that the film may void the manufacturer's warranty for the seal on double-pane windows, although the film representatives we talked to said the film shouldn't affect the seal. If the window warranty has already expired or reducing excessive heat is more important to you than possibly jeopardizing a warranty, then

Window film can be installed in about 30 minutes. The hazy appearance will disappear after 10 days.

FILM   NO FILM

apply the film. Otherwise, consider other options, such as installing shades, awnings or shutters over the windows or even planting a tree on the west side to block the sun.

Heat control film is composed of treated micro-thin layers of film that block ultraviolet rays and reduce the summer heat that comes through the window.

BETTER-PERFORMING WATERPROOFERS

I want to use my basement as a kids' playroom, but we have seasonal dampness. What's the best way to solve the water problem without shelling out big bucks?

Start with the easiest, least expensive fixes first, like grading the soil away from the house and adding extensions to the downspouts to channel water away from the basement. Then apply a waterproofing paint to the walls. The walls need to be clean, bare, dry and free of efflorescence. If they're already painted, you'll need to strip off the old paint before applying the waterproofing paint.

To prep the bare walls, start by scraping off dirt, dust and loose mortar with a wire brush. If efflorescence (a white, powdery substance) is present, wash it off with an etching solution or muriatic acid (**Photo 1**). If the muriatic acid isn't already diluted, dilute it in the ratio of two parts water to one part muriatic acid.

Then fill in any holes and cracks in the walls, and any gaps between the wall and the floor, with a cement-patching product (**Photo 2**).

Next, apply the first coat of the waterproofing paint in temperatures above 50 degrees F, using a paintbrush (**Photo 3**). The paint is designed to go on thick, not spread thin like house paint (so don't use a roller on the first coat). Once the first coat dries, apply a second coat with a 3/8- to 1/2-in.-nap roller. Two of these topcoats are needed to effectively block water.

Two companies that make waterproofing paints are United Gilsonite Laboratories (570-344-1202, ugl.com) and Zinsser (732-469-8100, zinsser.com).

CEMENT PATCH — WATERPROOFING PAINT — CRACK FILLER — ETCHER

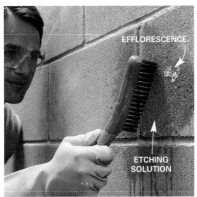

1 REMOVE dirt, loose mortar and efflorescence from the walls so the waterproofing paint can form a solid bond.

EFFLORESCENCE — ETCHING SOLUTION

2 WET the area around holes and cracks with water, then apply a patch with a trowel.

HOLE — CEMENT PATCHING MATERIAL

3 USE a 4-in. general-purpose paintbrush to apply the waterproofing paint fast.

WATERPROOFING PAINT

GROUT HAZE ON STONE

We noticed grout residue embedded in our new slate, giving the tile a gray, lifeless appearance. On a test basis, I've tried sanding, scraping and applying muriatic acid. Nothing seems to clean it off. Any suggestions?

Normally, a Scotch-Brite pad, water and a little rubbing will remove grout residue and the hazy appearance it causes. Since nothing you tried removed the grout haze, I'd guess that the slate probably wasn't properly sealed before the grout was applied. Porous tiles, especially a stone such as slate, need up to two or three applications of a special grout release. Tile and stone sealers will work sometimes, but not always.

Try using a grout haze remover, which is available at tile stores. It's not always effective on slate, however. If it doesn't work, chances are the grout haze isn't removable. Call in a professional tile setter for a final assessment. By the way, muriatic acid usually makes this situation worse.

SLATE NOT SEALED WITH GROUT RELEASE — SLATE SEALED WITH GROUT RELEASE

Ask TFH™

The Family Handyman

STRAIGHT SCOOP ON TRIPLE GLAZING

I'd like to replace the drafty single-pane windows in my house. Is upgrading to triple-pane windows a good idea in areas like mine where it's often below zero in the winter?

In cold regions, triple-glazed windows can save 2 to 3 percent of your heating bill, compared with double-glazed windows. From a cost standpoint, it'll take a few decades to recoup the 10 to 15 percent upcharge to go from low-e double-glazed windows to triple-glazed. For example, if you pay $1,000 per year in energy bills, have 20 windows in your house, and 22 percent of your energy is lost through your windows (which is average), then each window is losing $11 worth of energy per year. A triple-glazed window will reduce that loss by about $1, so it'll take 35 years to cover a $35 upcharge for triple-glazing. Of course, if your energy bills and energy loss are greater, you'll recoup the cost sooner.

However, the investment may be worth the cost in terms of comfort. Triple glazing will reduce condensation, which will allow you to maintain a higher indoor relative humidity in cold weather. These windows also reduce cold drafts. If you don't want to pay for triple-pane windows throughout the house, get them for the north- and east-facing rooms, where you'll get the biggest payoff.

Most of the major window manufacturers in the United States don't offer triple glazing. But here are two that do: Marvin (888-537-7828. marvin.com) and Weather Shield (800-222-2995. weathershield.com). Many Canadian window manufacturers offer triple glazing.

MARVIN

Marvin's triple-glazed window consists of three panes of glass, two of which have a low-e coating. The space between the panes is filled with krypton gas.

DRILLING IN A FLOOR JOIST

Where is the best place to drill a joist for running cable? Do you recommend at the bottom, the top or in the middle?

It depends on what type of floor framing you have. Keep the hole at least 2 in. from the top and the bottom if it's a dimensional lumber joist. The hole cannot be larger than one-third the depth of the joist, so the maximum hole size for a 2x12 joist (actual size 1-1/2 x 11-1/4 in.) is 3-3/4 in. diameter—plenty big enough for running cable! You can drill the holes anywhere along the length of the joist (**photo A, below**).

If you have manufactured I-joists, you can drill holes up to 1-1/2 in. diameter almost anywhere in the web area (the area between the flanges). Just stay 6 in. away from any end or load-bearing wall (**photo B, below**). Holes up to 4 in. can be drilled in the middle of the I-joist, away from the ends and load-bearing wall. Keep the distance between adjacent holes at least twice the diameter of the largest hole. For holes larger than 4 in., consult the lumber supplier.

NO-HOLES ZONE 2"

MAXIMUM DIAMETER IS 1/3 JOIST DEPTH

NO-HOLES ZONE 2"

A: Dimensional lumber
Drill holes with a diameter of no more than one-third the depth of the joist, staying 2 in. away from the top and bottom.

B: Engineered lumber
Drill 1-1/2-in. holes anywhere in the web area of engineered I-joists, except within 6 in. of walls and rim joists.

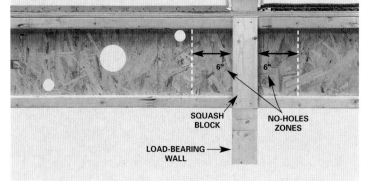

6"   6"

SQUASH BLOCK

NO-HOLES ZONES

LOAD-BEARING WALL

TILING COUNTERTOPS

I'd like to tile my kitchen backsplash and countertop. I have a plastic laminate top over plywood. Can I install tile over the laminate?

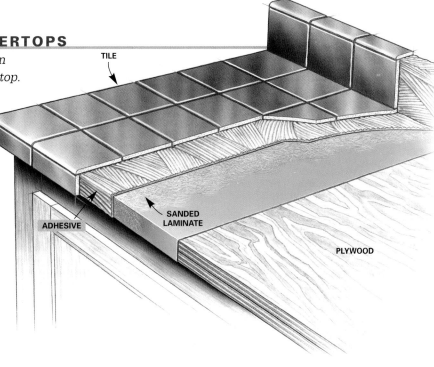

TILE

ADHESIVE

SANDED LAMINATE

PLYWOOD

Yes, but think carefully before you attempt it. If your counter has curved edges, as most do, you'll have to grind off the raised bead at the lip with a belt sander and you won't be able to tile the back-splash without cutting off the curved top edge. Some tile stores carry special tiles that will wrap around the front edge, but the selection will be limited. If you choose to go ahead, first rough up the laminate with 100-grit sandpaper and adhere the tile with an adhesive that's formulated to bond to plastic laminate (look for the adhesive at tile stores).

Frankly, this a dicey proposition and we don't recommend it. Some tiles can still come loose, and the grout may crack, especially at the front edge. The best course is to tear off the old top and install a solid 3/4-in. plywood underlayment and a layer of tile backer board before tiling. It's less work than it sounds and will ensure a long-lasting tile countertop.

UNDER IS BETTER

We're going to install ceramic tile in our entryway and the adjoining coat closet. Should we cut the tile to fit against the door trim or cut the trim shorter and slip the tile beneath it?

You'll end up with a better-looking floor if you slide the tiles under the casings like the pros do. If you butt the tiles against the casings (**photo below**), you'll usually end up with uneven gaps that you have to fill with grout. The gaps won't look good, and chances are the grout will crack from the vibration caused by the closing door.

Cutting the casings is fairly easy and only takes a few minutes if you have a sharp handsaw or special "jamb" saw. Simply place a tile next to each casing, add 1/8 in. for the adhesive thickness (use 1/8-in.-thick cardboard as a guide), mark the casings and saw at the mark. Sliding the tiles under the casings eliminates the need for grout and hides the cut edges (**photo below**).

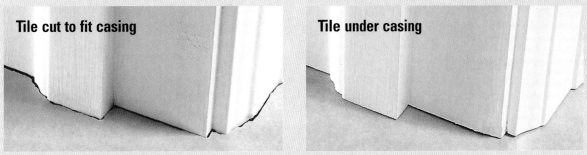

Tile cut to fit casing

Tile under casing

Installing tile under the casings eliminates gaps, giving the floor a cleaner, professional appearance.

LAUNDRY ROOM
MAKEOVER

Create a fresh, clean work space. We walk you through the toughest part — reworking the plumbing and adding the new sink.

by **Jeff Gorton**

Before

Your laundry room doesn't have to be a dingy, disorganized place full of cobwebs and dust bunnies. In this article, we'll show you the first steps for converting an unfinished laundry area into a finished room. We'll focus on the most useful upgrade—replacing your old laundry tub with a new, tidy countertop and sink. It involves rerouting plumbing in the walls and installing new cabinets. However, we won't go into detail about cabinet installation, lighting, wall finishing, flooring or moving electrical outlets. Look for details about these subjects in other stories posted on our Web site, thefamilyhandyman.com.

A total laundry room makeover is an ambitious project, since it involves both electrical and plumbing skills. It's not for a beginner. Altogether it'll take four to five weekends to finish.

If your plumbing system is all plastic, you'll only need basic carpentry tools. If you have copper water supply lines, you'll need a tubing cutter and soldering tools. A hole saw might be required to drill 2-1/2-in. holes through studs.

The cost of materials for this 8 x 12-ft. room was about $2,000. This includes about $1,000 for cabinets, countertops and shelves, and $500 for the vinyl floor tiles.

Planning

Replacing the freestanding laundry tub with a drop-in sink frees up space and makes it easier to install a usable length of countertop. Adding a washing machine outlet box at the same time allows you to tuck the washing machine's water supply and drain hoses neatly out of sight when you cover the bare studs with drywall. If possible, leave the dryer in about the same spot so you don't have to move the dryer vent and electrical or gas connection. Also keep the washing machine and the new sink on the same wall as the existing plumbing. You can easily move the sink and washing machine drains several feet, but relocating them to a different wall will sharply increase the difficulty (and cost) of this project.

Measure your laundry room and draw a floor plan showing the new cabinets, sink and appliance locations (**Figure A**). Use the plan to determine the location of the drains and supply lines. Center the sink plumbing on the sink base. Locate the plumbing box for the washing machine slightly below the top edge of the machine.

Draw a sketch of your proposed piping layout, including pipe sizes, and show it to the inspector when you apply for the permit. Use **Photo 4** to help with the drains. Remember to call for an inspection before you cover the pipes with drywall.

While the wall cavities are still open, add countertop outlets and new lighting. The electrical code requires a separate 20-amp circuit for laundry outlets and GFCI protection for outlets within 6 ft. of the sink. Put all light fixtures on a separate circuit.

For the tidiest appearance, rework the dryer vent to fit within the wall. Use 4-in.-diameter aluminum or galva-nized metal ducting, not the flexible kind.

Start by disconnecting the washer and dryer and moving them out of the way. If you have a gas dryer and you're unsure how to safely disconnect it, call the gas company or a plumber for help. Use a hacksaw or a reciprocating saw fitted with a metal-cutting blade to cut the old drain and vent pipes (**Photo 1**). Cut the drainpipe about 2 in. above the bottom wall plate. Cut the vent pipe at 50 in. from the floor. Don't worry if your drain and vent pipes are metal rather than plastic. Just choose the appropriate size transition coupling (**Photo 2**) to join the metal pipe to the new plastic pipe.

Shut off the main water valve before cutting the hot and cold water lines. Be prepared with a bucket and rags to catch any water that's left in the pipes.

Install the plastic drain and vent pipes

Start by laying out the pipe route. Here are a few plumbing code requirements and tips to guide your plan:

- Run a 2-in.-diameter drain to the washing machine.
- Slope drainpipes down 1/4 in. for every foot they travel horizontally.
- For 1-1/2-in. drainpipe, limit the distance from the P-trap to the vent to 42 in. For 2-in. pipe, limit the distance to 60 in. (**Photo 4**).

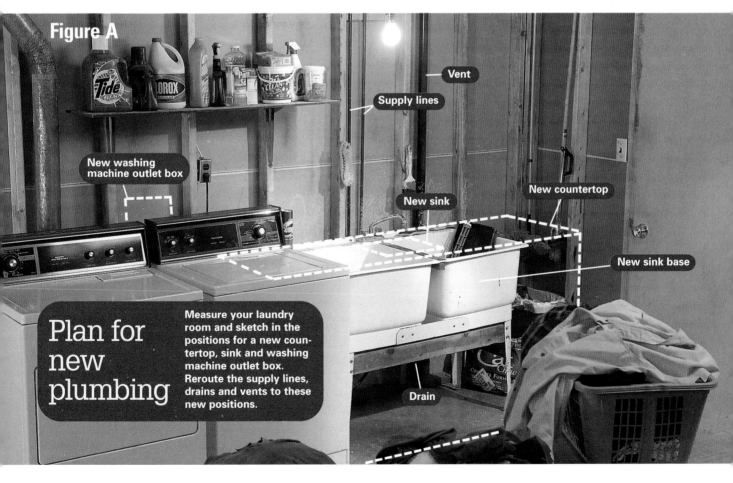

Figure A

Vent

Supply lines

New washing machine outlet box

New sink

New countertop

New sink base

Plan for new plumbing

Measure your laundry room and sketch in the positions for a new countertop, sink and washing machine outlet box. Reroute the supply lines, drains and vents to these new positions.

Drain

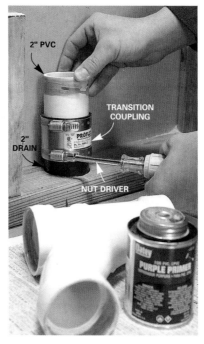

1 SHUT OFF the main water valve and open the laundry tub valves to drain the water. Cut out the old water supply lines. Disconnect the old trap and cut the drain and vent pipes with a hacksaw or reciprocating saw.

2 MARK the drain and vent pipe route and notch or drill the studs for the drain and vent pipes. Cut a short length of plastic pipe and attach it to the drainpipe with a transition coupling.

3 CUT, PRIME AND GLUE together the plastic piping and fittings to fit between the existing drain and the vent. Connect the new pipes to the existing pipes with transition couplings.

- Install any horizontal section of a vent pipe at least 6 in. higher than the overflow level of the fixture it's venting (for laundry sinks, this is the top edge).
- Slope vent pipes slightly downward toward the drain.
- Position the sink drain about 3 in. below the bottom of the sink. In most cases, a height of about 16 in. from the floor will work.
- Locate the top of the washing machine outlet box just below the top edge of the washing machine, usually 42 in. from the floor.
- Before you buy your plastic fittings, note the subtle differences in the types required—sanitary tee, cleanout tee, etc. (**Photo 4**).

Mark the pipe route on the studs. The easiest way to run drains is to notch the 2x4 studs for the new plumbing pipes. Then add 2x2 strips to reinforce the studs later (**Photo 5**). But don't notch the studs if your laundry room wall is a "bearing" wall—that is, if it supports a floor or roof above it. If you're not sure, consult a building contractor or architect. If your walls are 2x6s, you can skip the notching; it's generally easier to drill holes in the center of each stud for the pipes. You'll need a 2-1/2-in. hole saw or auger bit and a powerful drill. One disadvantage of the hole method is that you may have to cut long horizontal pipes into shorter lengths and join them with couplings to fit them in. Install metal nailing plates to protect any plastic or copper pipe that is within 1-1/4 in. of the face of a stud.

Start the drain and vent pipe installation by cutting and gluing the pipe and fittings that fit between the existing drain and the vent pipes (**Photo 3**). Begin at the drain and work up. At the top joint, roll the rubber sleeve on the transition coupling back onto itself to provide clearance for the vent line connection (**Photo 3**). Then roll the rubber sleeve down onto the plastic pipe, slide the metal band over the sleeve and tighten the band clamps. Complete the drains and vents by cutting, priming and gluing the remaining pipe and fittings (**Photo 4**).

Run the supply lines

Start by planning the route of the supply pipes and drilling 3/4-in. holes through the studs. For serving the sink and washing machine, 1/2-in. pipes will do. Cut and solder in copper lines and fittings. (Glue CPVC pipe.) Mount a copper strap, available at home centers, about 4 in. below the stubbed-out sink drain (**Photo 6**). Then solder the stubbed-out copper pipes to the strap to support them. To avoid melting the plastic washing machine outlet box with the torch, solder the vertical lengths of copper tubing to the laundry valve before mounting the valve in the box. Leave the pipes long and cut them to fit later (**Photo 5**).

When you're done with the copper water piping, close the laundry valve and open the main water valve to check for leaks. If there are no leaks, you're ready to call for a plumbing rough-in inspection. At this point, complete the wiring. When the plumbing and electrical rough-in work is complete and approved by the inspectors, hang and finish the drywall and install the base cabinets.

Install the sink cabinets

Before you install the sink base cabinet, lay out the positions of the water and drain stub-outs on the back of the sink base. Drill clearance holes for the stub-outs, working from the inside of the cabinet so any splintering will be hidden. Then install the cabinet.

When you're done installing the base cabinets, cut the countertop to length and fit it to the walls. Then mark the sink cutout on the countertop following the instructions included with the sink. Some sinks include a cutout template. Otherwise use the sink as a template. Mark around the perimeter. Then draw a second line about 1/2 in. inside the first. This will be the cutting line. Drill 1-in. corner holes and cut the hole with a jigsaw. Support the cutout to prevent it from falling as you finish the cuts. Put the countertop back onto the cabinets and attach it from below with screws. Make sure the screws aren't too long or they'll pop through the top of the counter!

Next, shut off the main water valve and cut the capped ends of the stubbed-out copper pipes. Install compression-type shutoff valves ("angle stops," Photo 7).

Install the faucet on the sink according to the manufacturer's directions and attach the water supply tubes before you mount the sink in the countertop (Photo 8). The plastic sink we used did not have any faucet holes. We drilled them with a hole saw to fit our faucet.

Test-fit the sink. Then place a bead of tub-and-tile caulk around the perimeter of the sink cutout before you set the sink permanently in place. Attach the supply tubes to the stop valves. Then trim the length of the tailpiece and the waste arm as needed to connect the sink trap (Photo 9). If either the tailpiece or the waste arm is too short, you can buy longer ones or add extensions. Turn on the water and test for leaks.

Reconnect the washer and dryer

Connect the washer to the new valve with hoses (Photo 10). (For an extra measure of security, we recommend you buy "no-burst" laundry hoses.) Use a sharp utility knife to cut out the plastic cover over the drain hole in the laundry

4 CUT AND GLUE the remaining drain and vent parts. Slope drains about 1/4 in. per foot downstream. Position the laundry P-trap so that the washer box will fit flush with the finished wall.

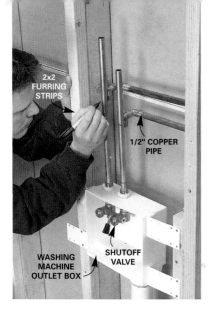

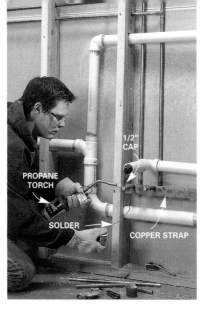

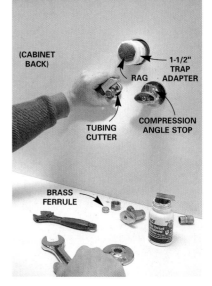

5 SCREW the laundry box to 2x2 furring strips. Solder copper pipe to the shutoff valves and mount the valves in the laundry box. Solder the remaining copper supply lines and fittings.

6 STUB OUT the copper water lines about 6 in. and cap them. Solder them to a copper support strap. Call for a plumbing inspection. Then cover the walls with drywall.

7 FIT the sink base over the stub-outs. Then cut the copper pipes about 2 in. beyond the cabinet back and install the angle stop valves. Cut back the PVC drainpipe and glue on a 1-1/2-in. trap adapter.

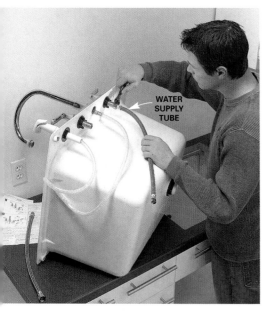

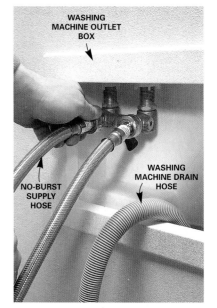

8 MAKE the sink cutout in the countertop with a jigsaw. Mount the faucet, the supply lines and the drain on the sink. Then lay a bead of caulk around the cutout and drop in the sink.

9 CONNECT the sink to the drain with a plastic trap assembly. Hand-tighten the slip-joint nuts. Then tighten them an additional quarter turn with large slip-joint pliers. Connect the supply lines.

10 CONNECT the washing machine to the shutoff valves with "no-burst" hoses. Set the drain hose into the drain opening in the washer box. Use the gasket or clamp provided with the hose to hold it in place.

box. Then place the end of the drain hose from the washing machine about 3 in. down into the drain hole. A new washing machine may include a clamp or gasket to secure the drain hose to the washing machine outlet box. Otherwise, drive a self-tapping sheet metal screw into the plastic box and wrap a zip tie or wire around the screw and hose to keep the hose from falling out.

At this point, you've done the hardest part. Finish wiring the electrical outlets and lighting, install flooring and hang your wall cabinets and shelves. 🏠

HomeCare&Repair

TIPS, FIXES & GEAR FOR A TROUBLE-FREE HOME

INSULATE RIM JOISTS AND CUT HEAT LOSS

1 CUT rigid foam insulation into strips with a table saw or a circular saw. Cut the strips to fit between floor joists using a box cutter.

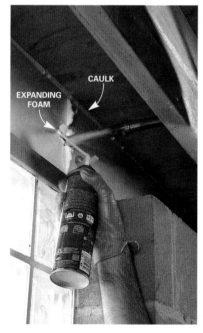

2 RUN a bead of acrylic caulk around each section of foam to form an airtight barrier. Fill gaps larger than 1/4 in. with expanding foam sealant.

In just a couple of hours, you can seal and insulate your rim joists, which are a major source of heat loss in many homes. Properly insulating and air-sealing rim joists takes patience, so most builders simply stuff in some fiberglass and walk away.

If you have an unfinished basement, you can properly insulate the rim joists in two or three hours. (This will also block tiny passages where spiders and other insects enter your basement!) The materials will cost about $1 per foot of rim joist. Call your local building inspections department before you begin this project. The inspector may require you to cover the new insulation with drywall (as a fire block) or leave some areas uncovered to allow for termite inspections. You can insulate second-floor rim joists following the same steps shown here if you happen to tear out a ceiling during remodeling.

Rigid foam is the best insulation for rim joists. We chose 2-in.-thick (R-10) "extruded polystyrene" ($20 per 4 x 8-ft. sheet). Don't use "expanded polystyrene," which is a less effective air and moisture barrier.

Cut the foam into 8-ft.-long strips 1/8 in. less than the height of the rim joist. A table saw is the fastest way to "rip" these strips, but you can also use a circular saw. Then cut the strips to length to fit between the joists, again cutting them 1/8 in. short (Photo 1). A heavy-duty box cutter ($6) is the best knife for making short cuts and trimming foam; the long blade slices cleanly through the foam (a utility knife blade is too short). Use long sections of foam to cover the rim joists that are parallel to the floor joists (Photo 2). Don't worry about cutting the foam for a tight fit around

pipes, cables or other obstructions; you can seal large gaps with expanding foam sealant later.

It's important to create an airtight seal around each section of foam using caulk or expanding foam (Photo 2). Otherwise, moist inside air could condense on the cold rim joist. The resulting dampness can lead to mold and rot. If you have a solid concrete foundation, also run a bead of caulk where the sill plate meets the concrete. If you have a concrete block foundation, also seal the openings on top with expanding foam. Stuff a wad of fiberglass insulation into each opening to support the foam as it hardens (see Figure A).

**Figure A
Insulated
rim joist**

Airtight insulation reduces heat loss through the rim joist. Fiberglass insulation and expanding foam seal the open top of hollow concrete blocks.

HomeCare&Repair

CONVERT WOOD CABINET DOORS TO GLASS

A pair of glass doors can add a designer touch to any kitchen. They can turn an ordinary cabinet into a decorative showcase or simply break up an otherwise monotonous row of solid doors. We recommend this alteration only for frame-and-panel cabinet doors (see **Figure A**), where you can replace the inset wood panels with glass. Converting the two doors shown here took about two hours.

To get started, remove the doors from the cabinets and remove all hardware from the doors. Examine the back side of each door; you might find a few tiny nails where the panel meets the frame. If so, gouge away wood with a utility knife to expose the nail heads and pull the nails with pliers. Look carefully; just one leftover nail will chip your expensive router bit.

Cut away the lips using a router and a 1/2-in. pattern bit (**Photo 1**). A pattern bit ($25) is simply a straight bit equipped with a bearing that rolls along a guide. Most home centers and hardware stores don't carry pattern bits. To find a retailer, check the yellow pages under "woodworking" or order one at pricecutter.com (888-288-2487). Be sure to choose a bit that has the bearing on the top, not at the bottom.

Use any straight, smooth material (solid wood, plywood or MDF) to make two 3-1/2-in.-wide guides. To allow for the 1-in. cutting depth of our pattern bit, we nailed layers of plywood and MDF together to make 1-3/8-in.-thick guides. Position the guides 1/2 in. from the inner edges of the lips and clamp them firmly in place over the door. Support the outer edges of the guides with strips of wood that match the thickness of the door to keep them level (**Photo 1**). Before you start routing, make sure the door itself is clamped firmly in place.

Set the router on the guide and adjust the cutting depth so that the bit just touches the panel. Cut away the lips on

Figure A: Panel door profile

Most cabinet doors are made like this one: A raised or flat panel fits into grooves in the rails-and-stile frame. To remove the panel, just cut away the lips on the back side of the door.

STILE

PANEL

LIP

RAIL

PATTERN BIT

BEARING

GUIDE

SUPPORT STRIP

LIP

1 CLAMP router guides to the back side of the door. Run a pattern bit along the guides to cut away the inside lips.

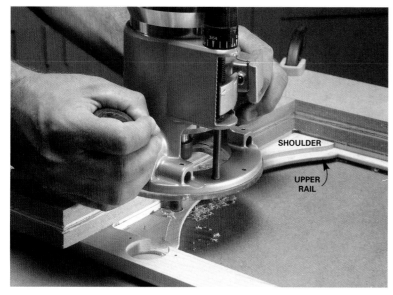

SHOULDER

UPPER RAIL

2 LOWER the router bit and cut away the shoulders on the back side of an arched upper rail to create a square recess for the glass.

GLASS CLIP

3 SET the glass into the frame and secure it with glass clips placed no more than 12 in. apart. Then reinstall the doors.

two sides, then reposition the guides to cut away the other two. With the lips removed, lift the panel out of the frame. If the panel is stuck, a few light hammer taps will free it.

If your door frame has a rectangular opening, it's now ready for glass. If it has an arched upper rail, cut a square recess above the arch (Photo 2). This allows you to use a rectangular piece of glass rather than a curved piece (curved cuts are expensive). Then simply lay the glass in and anchor it with glass clips (Photo 3). Clips are available from the glass supplier or at woodworkershardware.com, (800-383-0130; item No. LAH264; $4 for 20 clips).

GLASS CLIPS

If the glass rattles in the frame, add pea-size blobs of hot-melt glue every 12 in.

Buying glass

Most hardware stores carry clear glass ($3 per sq. ft.) and will cut it for free or a small fee. Ask for 3/16-in.-thick "double strength" glass. Order glass panels 1/8 in. smaller than the recess in the frame. To find tempered, textured or colored glass ($5 to $15 per sq. ft.), check the yellow pages under "glass." We bought clear textured glass and paid the supplier an extra $60 to have the two panels tempered. Building codes require tempered glass for locations within 5 ft. of the floor.

HEATED FLOORS

Heated floors are luxurious and affordable. We'll tell you how to select the best floor-warming system for your home.

by **Gary Wentz**

O nce you shed your fuzzy slippers and discover the comfort of warm floors, you'll be sold. Heated floors, often called radiant floors, offer benefits beyond foot comfort. They keep entry and bathroom floors dry and provide space heating in cold rooms. You can even turn down the thermostat for your central heating system and still keep some rooms warmer.

In this article, we'll walk you through the types of radiant floor systems you can install in your home. We'll tell you the pros and cons, and show you key installation techniques. This will help you decide whether to take on the project yourself or hire a professional. These heating systems are most often installed under ceramic tile in bathrooms, but keep in mind that you can add heat under any type of flooring material (see "Floor Coverings and Heated Floors," p. 69). All floor heating systems warm the floor with either electricity or hot water.

Electric systems are simple and affordable

Electric floor systems work just like an electric blanket: Electricity runs through "resistance" cable and creates heat. Because electricity is fairly expensive, relatively few homes are entirely heated by in-floor electric systems. However, these systems are great for making especially cold floors foot-friendly. They also boost the temperature in

an otherwise chilly room by a few degrees. The warm floor in a bathroom makes getting out of the shower a cozier prospect on a cold day. That's the payoff.

Electric systems have three components: heat cable, a thermostat and a temperature sensor (**Figure A**). The thermostat is connected to the home's power supply and turns the heat on and off according to the floor's (not the room's) temperature. A sensor installed in the floor along with the cable tells the thermostat how warm the floor is. (Most people prefer a floor temperature of 80 to 90 degrees F.) The thermostat and sensor are packaged together ($50 to $100); cable is usually sold separately. Don't use a thermostat from one manufacturer with cable from another.

The electrical connections require only basic wiring know-how, and laying the floor cable is a DIY-friendly project. Because of this easy installation— and the lower cost of materials—an electric system is usually the best choice for small-scale projects like

Tip When you estimate the square footage of a room, include only the areas where you can walk; it makes no sense to heat the floor under appliances or behind the toilet.

heating a kitchen floor or warming up a cold bathroom. Adding electric heat to a typical bathroom when you install a new floor adds only $200 to $300 to the cost of the project. Operating costs are typically about a half cent per square foot per day.

Often the biggest challenge is "fishing" electrical cable through finished walls to the thermostat and cable. Since these systems generally draw only 10 to 15 watts per sq. ft., you can usually connect them to an existing circuit to heat a typical bathroom. For a larger room, you may have to run a new cable to the main panel and pay an electrician about $120 to connect the new circuit there. For wire-fishing howto, go to thefamilyhandyman.com and type "fishing wire" into the search box.

If you're installing heat over a wood-framed floor, place fiberglass insulation between the joists to drive the heat upward. The system will work fine without insulation but will be more efficient with it. Before you install an electric system over a concrete floor, check the manufacturer's instructions—they may require a layer of foam insulation over the concrete before the heat cable is installed.

Floor coverings and heated floors

Any flooring material can cover a heated floor, but some work better than others.

- **Ceramic and stone tile** are the most common. Heat doesn't harm them and they hold and conduct heat best.
- **Solid wood floors** can develop gaps if they dry and shrink when heated. If you opt for solid wood, leave the installation to an experienced pro who will test the moisture content of the wood to avoid shrinkage.
- **Floating floors** made from wood or plastic laminate don't develop gaps because they're not fastened directly to the subfloor. But you'll have to limit the floor temperature. Flooring warranties often limit the temperature to 85 degrees F.
- **Vinyl floors** have similar temperature restrictions, whether they're sheet vinyl or tile.
- **Carpet or rugs** can go over a heated floor, but they act as insulators and reduce heat flow to your feet and to the room as a whole. If you choose electric heat under hard flooring and plan to use an area rug, consider installing the cables only under the flooring that won't be covered by the rug.

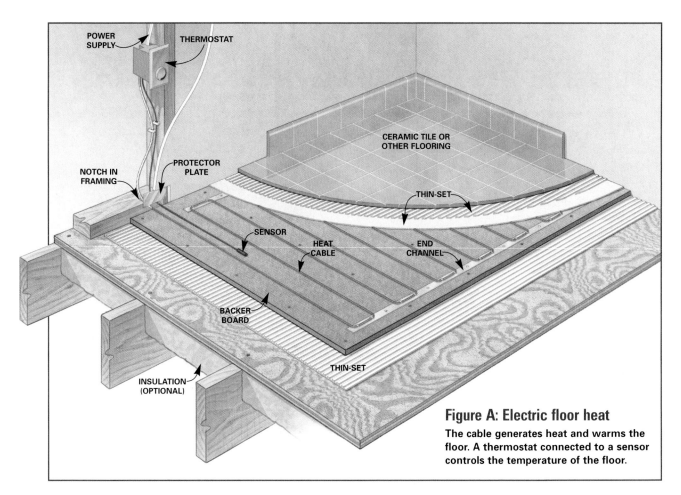

Figure A: Electric floor heat
The cable generates heat and warms the floor. A thermostat connected to a sensor controls the temperature of the floor.

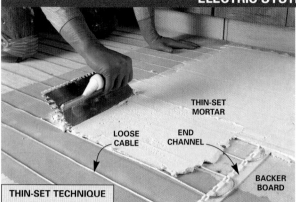

THIN-SET MORTAR

LOOSE CABLE

END CHANNEL

BACKER BOARD

THIN-SET TECHNIQUE

String cable between end channels and fasten the cable to the floor. Screed thin-set over the cable to create a flat surface.

PLASTIC LATH

SELF-LEVELING COMPOUND

LOOSE CABLE

SELF-LEVELING TECHNIQUE

Install plastic lath and loose cable. Pour self-leveling compound to embed cable and create a perfectly flat, smooth surface.

3 types of electric heat

1. Loose cable: $3 to $7 per sq. ft.

The cable comes on a spool, just like any other wire. Loose cable is by far the cheapest way to heat a floor and it's just as effective as the other systems. The drawback of loose cable is installation time; you have to position the cable in a serpentine pattern, fasten it with lots of hot glue or staples, and then "embed" it.

Most loose cable systems include end channels that guide spacing (left photo, above). You can place cables close together to make the floor heat up faster and reach a higher temperature or farther apart to use less cable. Manufacturers offer various cable lengths to suit the floor's square footage. You can't splice sections of cable together to serve a larger room or repair damaged cable (this is true of all electric systems). Fasten the cable every 6 in. so it can't shift or float while you embed the cable. **Caution:** Work carefully with your trowel. If you nick the cable, the entire system won't work.

There are two ways to embed cable: You can install the cable over tile backer board and then cover it with "thin-set," the mortar adhesive used for ceramic tile (left photo, above). The thin-set shrinks as it cures, so you may have to add a second layer after the first hardens to level it out. But creating a perfectly flat, smooth surface with thin-set is difficult. You can make it smooth enough for ceramic tile or a floating floor but probably not smooth enough for vinyl flooring. For a faster, smoother surface, install the cable without backer board and pour on "self-leveling compound," or SLC (right photo, above). SLC is a cement-based powder that you mix with water and then pour over the cable. It becomes rock hard in a few hours. Reinforce the SLC with plastic lath; metal lath can cut the cable. Covering your floor with a 1/2-in.-thick layer of SLC costs about $2 per sq. ft., including the lath. You can then lay tile, carpet, vinyl or a floating floor directly over the SLC.

2. Mesh mats: $10 to $12 per sq. ft.

The cable comes already woven into a plastic net. The prepositioned cable installs quickly—in less than half the time for loose cable. You simply staple or hot glue the mesh to the floor. As with loose cable, you then embed the cable and mesh.

Mats are available in lots of different dimensions. You can cut the mesh into sections to cover your floor or fit around corners (photo below). But you can't cut or splice the cable itself. Some manufacturers recommend combing thin-set directly over the mesh and setting tile all in one operation. But this is difficult. Most tile setters prefer to embed the mesh first with thin-set or SLC just as with loose wire. The mesh tends to "float" as you embed it, so fasten it to the floor every 6 in.—even if the instructions recommend less fastening. After embedding it, you can lay tile, carpet, vinyl or a floating floor.

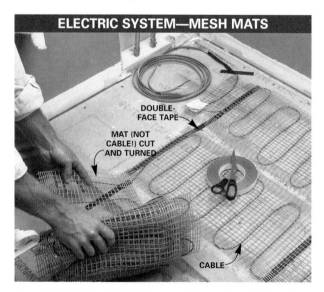

ELECTRIC SYSTEM—MESH MATS

DOUBLE-FACE TAPE

MAT (NOT CABLE!) CUT AND TURNED

CABLE

Cut mesh mats to fit the floor. Position mats with double-face tape and fasten with glue or staples. Cover the mesh with thin-set or self-leveling compound.

3. Solid mats: About $10 to $20 per sq. ft.

Solid mats are often the most expensive electric system, but they're also the easiest to install. The cable is completely enclosed in synthetic fabric, plastic sheeting or metal foil. The big advantage is that you don't have to embed it as you do loose cable or mesh mats. With some versions, you simply smooth the mat onto a bed of thin-set (**top photo at right**). Then you spread more thin-set over the mat and set ceramic or stone tile as you normally would. Some solid mat systems are even easier to install; you just roll out the mats, tape them together and you're done (**middle photo at right**). You can then lay a floating wood or laminate floor directly over it.

Mats are available in various dimensions, and you can combine mats of different sizes to cover your floor. Some mats are sized to fit between joists, so you can heat the floor from below as shown at right, **bottom photo**—a big advantage if you don't want to replace an existing floor. However, don't install electric heat under a subfloor unless the system is specifically intended for that method.

Hydronic systems heat space as well as your toes

In a hydronic system (**Figure B**, p. 72), heated water from a boiler or a water heater runs through loops of flexible plastic tubing called "PEX." (PEX can be used for household water supply lines too.) The hot tubes then heat the floor. The main advantage of hydronic systems is that they generally deliver more heat at a lower operating cost than electric systems. That's why hydronic heat is usually a better option than electric systems to heat large floor areas or even an entire house. However, because they usually involve a boiler, a pump and gas lines, hydronic systems are more complex than electric systems. You can install hydronic floor heat yourself, but you need basic electrical and plumbing know-how as well as professional design help. The materials for a small-scale hydronic project will cost at least $600.

The easiest—and least expensive—way to install PEX is to run it under a subfloor between joists using transfer plates and insulation (**top left photo**, p. 72). This method costs less than $2 per sq. ft. for tubing, plates and insulation. To install PEX on top of a wood-framed or concrete floor, you need to lay a grooved channel system over the floor (**top right photo**, p. 72) or embed the tubing in self-leveling compound (see **Figure B**). Covering PEX requires more SLC than you can mix yourself; leave that to pros who have special mixing and pumping equipment (at least $2 per sq. ft. for the SLC only). With a concrete floor, you may have to lay foam insulation over the slab before installing PEX. In new construction, the tubing is often installed over insulation and the concrete slab is poured over it.

ELECTRIC SYSTEM—SOLID MATS

Lay the mat over thin-set and force it firmly into the thin-set with a grout float. After it hardens, comb more thin-set over the mat to set ceramic tile.

UNDER TILE — BACKER BOARD, THIN-SET, GROUT FLOAT, MAT

Lay mats over an existing floor and duct-tape them together. Lay a floating wood or laminate floor directly over the mats.

UNDER A FLOATING FLOOR — THERMOSTAT BOX, DUCT TAPE, LAMINATE FLOORING, MAT

Staple mats between joists to heat the floor above. Then insulate the underside of the mat with R-13 or thicker fiberglass batts.

UNDER-FLOOR TECHNIQUE — MAT, INSULATION

A hydronic system requires several expensive components. But several rooms share the components, so the more area you heat, the lower the cost per square foot. If you want to heat 200 sq. ft. or more of floor, a hydronic system may cost less to install than electric heat.

The heat source for a hydronic system can be a boiler or a standard water heater. If your home is already heated by hot water radiators or baseboard units, there's a good chance that your existing boiler can handle the hydronic

PEX TUBING

HEAT
TRANSFER
PLATE

UNDER-FLOOR TECHNIQUE

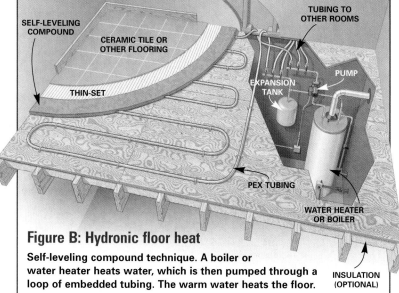

TUBING TO
OTHER ROOMS

SELF-LEVELING
COMPOUND

CERAMIC TILE OR
OTHER FLOORING

PUMP

EXPANSION
TANK

THIN-SET

GROOVED
PLYWOOD

PEX TUBING

WATER HEATER
OR BOILER

SUB-
FLOOR

PEX
TUBING

Figure B: Hydronic floor heat

Self-leveling compound technique. A boiler or water heater heats water, which is then pumped through a loop of embedded tubing. The warm water heats the floor.

INSULATION
(OPTIONAL)

CHANNEL TECHNIQUE

Install a channel system over a wood or concrete subfloor. Press tubing into the grooves. Install a wood or floating floor or add backer board for tile.

system as well. If you don't have a boiler, a water heater can heat one room or several, depending on the size of the water heater. If you're building an addition, you may find that installing a water heater–powered hydronic floor is less expensive than extending your existing central heating system.

Aside from PEX, a heat source and a pump, a hydronic system may require components such as electric zone valves. It may also require additional pumps. You can install these components yourself, but don't try to design a system yourself. Look for a company that specializes in helping homeowners plan and install hydronic systems (see the Buyer's Guide, right). Before you choose to install a system yourself, get bids from professionals. It will help you decide whether the money saved is worth your time and effort. 🏠

Buyer's Guide

■ **NUHEAT:** (800) 778-9276. nuheat.com. Solid mats for tile (top photo, p. 71) or floating floors.

■ **RADIANT FLOOR CO.:** (866) 927-6863. radiantcompany.com. Hydronic supplies, design services and technical support for do-it-yourselfers.

■ **RADIANTEC:** (800) 451-7593. radiantec.com. Hydronic supplies, design services and technical support for do-it-yourselfers.

■ **SUNTOUCH:** (888) 432-8932. suntouch.net. Loose cable, mesh mats and solid under-floor mats (bottom photo, p. 71).

■ **THERMOSOFT:** (800) 308-8057. thermosoftinternational.com. Mesh mats for tile and tape-together solid mats for floating floors (center photo, p. 71).

■ **UPONOR:** (800) 321-4739. uponor-usa.com. Information on hydronic systems and help finding professional installers in your area.

■ **WARMLYYOURS:** (800) 875-5285. warmlyyours.com. Mesh mats for ceramic tile and solid mats for carpeted floors, plus online planning and calculating tools.

10 TIPS FOR SMOOTHER DRYWALL

Simple tricks for fast, flawless drywall finishing

by **Gary Wentz**

1 Use mesh tape, not paper

Pros use paper tape to strengthen joints. But in less-skilled hands, paper tape can ripple, slip out of place or trap air bubbles. If you push too hard as you embed paper tape, you'll squeeze out all the joint compound behind it and the tape will peel off later. Adhesive-backed mesh tape eliminates all those glitches. Just stick it in place and it stays put, leaving you free to concentrate on spreading a smooth coat of mud. And since it doesn't require an underlying layer of compound, mesh allows for a thinner buildup over butt joints and repairs. You can use mesh anywhere except inside corners.

But mesh tape has one weakness (literally): It's not as strong as paper. To compensate, you have to cover it with setting-type joint compound, which is stronger than premixed compound. Apply mesh tape no more than a few hours before you're ready to cover it. Left uncovered, it will eventually fall off.

Apply adhesive-backed mesh tape to avoid fussing with paper tape while you spread joint compound.

2 Flatten bumps and bulges between coats for less sanding later

Everyone hates the dust cloud raised by sanding drywall. And the best way to minimize sanding later is to knock down high spots between coats. Left alone, these high spots will grow higher and wider (and harder to fix) with each coat. Don't worry about low spots; subsequent coats will fill them.

If you used setting-type compound, inspect the joints before the compound has hardened completely. Run a 12-in.-wide knife over every joint. The blade will scrape off small ridges and nubs. More important, it will act as a straightedge, revealing larger bumps and bulges. When the compound is about the consistency of a bar of soap, you can easily shave down bulges without gouging. You can sand and scrape setting compound after it's completely hard, but that's more work.

With standard joint compound, however, it's best to let each coat dry completely before inspecting, scraping and sanding. The surface of partially dry standard compound may be firm while the underlying material remains soft and easy to gouge.

Shave off high spots in setting-type compound before it hardens. Allow standard joint compound to dry completely before you scrape and sand.

3 Fill joints faster with setting-type compound

Mixing up setting compound is a messy nuisance, but it's worth it. Setting compound has three key advantages over premixed versions: It allows you to use mesh tape, it hardens fast and it shrinks much less. Quick hardening and low shrinkage make setting compound perfect for deep filling. A thick layer of premixed compound takes days to dry and shrinks. You'll need several coats to fill the depression, and the more layers you add, the harder it is to get smooth results.

For small repair jobs, you can mix setting compound with a paint paddle. For larger jobs, use a corded drill with a mixer attachment ($10 for a 12-in.-long version). Don't  buy a 24-in. mixer unless you have a powerful 1/2-in. drill. The key to a smooth, chunk-free mix is to let it stand for about five minutes after the initial mixing. That lets the chunks absorb water before final mixing. Setting compounds have different hardening times, ranging from 5 to 210 minutes. The 45- or 90-minute versions are best for most jobs.

MIXER

SETTING COMPOUND

CORNER BEAD

Mix setting compound with water for deep filling around corner bead, tapered joints and gaps in drywall.

Be sure to choose a "lightweight" setting compound. Other versions become so hard that sanding away mistakes is nearly impossible. Even the lightweight versions are harder to sand than premixed compound, so it's best to use setting compound for the first coat and premixed compound for later coats. Be sure to clean tools before the setting compound hardens.

4 Eliminate as many hard-to-hide butt joints as you can

To hide "butt joints" (where two non-tapered ends of drywall meet), you have to build up a hump of joint compound that's very thin and wide. This is time consuming and difficult to do well. So if you're a novice drywall finisher, avoiding butt joints is smart.

The best way to avoid butt joints is to use sheets of drywall that are long enough to cover entire walls and ceilings. As a result, you'll have only tapered joints to finish. Drywall sheets are commonly available in 8- and 12-ft. lengths, and specialty suppliers carry 14-ft. sheets (in the yellow pages under "Drywall").

If your ceiling is longer than 14 ft., you can't avoid butt joints. But you can avoid butt joints on a wall that exceeds 14 ft. Simply hang the sheets vertically rather than horizontally. That way, you'll have several tapered joints to cover, but no butt joints. Hanging drywall vertically is slower than hanging it horizontally because you have to make sure the tapered edges fall at the centers of studs. Cut the first sheet to width so the tapered

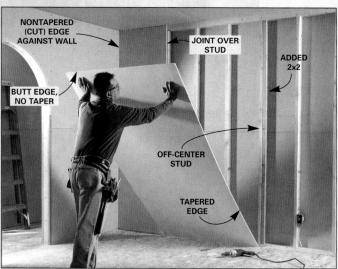

NONTAPERED (CUT) EDGE AGAINST WALL

JOINT OVER STUD

ADDED 2x2

BUTT EDGE, NO TAPER

OFF-CENTER STUD

TAPERED EDGE

Hang drywall vertically on walls to eliminate butt joints. Nail 2x2s to studs that don't align with the edges of the sheets.

edge lands on the center of a stud. After that, the edges of each sheet should fall perfectly on studs. If you run into misplaced studs, nail 2x2s to them. If you have 9-ft. ceilings, call a drywall supplier to find 10-ft.-long sheets.

Tear paper tape to length and wet it. Pull the tape between your fingers to squeegee off the excess water.

5 Dunk paper tape to avoid bubbles and bulges

Paper tape can ripple, slip, bulge and bubble. But you can minimize these problems by dropping it into a bucket of water. Wet paper tape is more pliable than dry tape, so it traps fewer air bubbles behind it. Water also makes the paper slick, so your knife slides over the tape without creating ripples or creases. Wetting doesn't eliminate the squeeze-out problem, so you still have to be careful to leave a thin layer of mud between the tape and the drywall. Don't let the tape soak—that will soften the paper and make it more susceptible to scuffs and tears.

6 Keep crumbs out of your mud to prevent scars

You can't create a smooth surface using joint compound that has crumbs of hardened compound in it. One tiny chunk clinging to your knife will leave a scar across the whole joint. Cleanliness is the key to keeping your mud free of chunks. Scrape down the insides of the bucket every time you scoop out mud. Then wipe the sides clean with a wet rag. At the end of the day, cover the compound with a thin layer of water. The water will remain on top of the compound, so you can pour it off before you use the remaining mud.

Never dump leftover compound from your mud pan back into the bucket; just throw it away. To keep the pan and tools clean between uses, scour them with an abrasive sponge or immerse them in water. Setting-type compound will continue to harden even under water, so wash tools as soon as you're done. Never send large amounts of setting compound down the drain—it can plug pipes.

Prevent crumbs of dry compound from forming in the bucket. Wipe the inside of the bucket clean and cover the leftover compound with water.

7 Keep corners straight with reinforced tape

Inside corners are tough to keep neat and straight. Unless you have a very steady hand, your knife can wander as you embed the tape. And if you create a wavy corner with the first coat of mud, creating a straight corner with subsequent coats is almost impossible.

The solution is to use tape that's backed with metal or plastic strips ($12 for 100 ft. at home centers). This tape is especially helpful on odd-angled corners, which are very hard to keep straight. It's still possible to create a wavy corner if you push too hard, so apply light, even pressure as you smooth the joint compound. The strips reduce ripples and bubbles too, so there's no need to wet the tape. Don't overlap the tape where inside corners meet the ceiling. Instead, cut the tape short to avoid a triple-thick buildup of tape.

Embed reinforced tape at inside corners to provide a straight guide for your knife. Be careful not to kink the metal strips.

REINFORCED CORNER TAPE

KNOCKDOWN
KNIFE

RUBBER BLADE

Smooth out ridges with a knockdown knife. Press lightly as you drag the knife over joint compound.

8 Create a smooth surface with a knockdown knife

Feathering out a butt joint or skim-coating a whole wall is difficult because your knife leaves ridges on the broad surface—and touching them up often creates even more ridges. The solution is a "knockdown" knife. With its soft rubber blade, this squeegee-like tool floats over the surface, flattening ridges without creating new ones.

A knockdown knife won't scrape down big bulges or fill wide depressions, so make the surface as flat as you can with a 12- or 14-in. metal knife first. Then drag the knockdown knife gently over the surface in one continuous pass. Apply light, even pressure and don't stop or hesitate. On a butt joint, you'll have to make two or three passes to smooth the whole surface. You can make more passes if necessary, but stop before the compound starts to harden. Although the rubber blade is soft, it can still make a mess of partially hardened compound. Knockdown knives (about $20) are available in 18- and 22-in. widths at drywall suppliers and some home centers and hardware stores. A 22-in. version is best for butt joints. To order one online, go to amazon.com and search for "knockdown knife."

9 For smooth walls faster, finish with topping compound

Any type of joint compound can hold tiny air or water bubbles that leave pockmarks on the surface. But you'll get fewer pockmarks with "topping" compound. Topping compound looks just like other versions of premixed joint compound, but it has a creamier texture. That smooth consistency makes it easier to feather out and creates a glossy surface with very few pockmarks. It also shrinks less as it dries. With all these advantages, topping compound helps you get to the final sanding stage with fewer coats and fewer fixes between coats. And when the time comes, you'll find that topping compound is the easiest compound to sand. Topping compound has poor bonding strength, so don't use it for the first coat.

10 Coat inside corners faster and smoother with a corner knife

It takes a steady hand to embed tape in inside corners with a standard drywall knife. One little slip of the knife and you'll gouge one side while you're smoothing the other. An inside corner knife ($10) not only eliminates that problem but does the job faster. Outside corner knives are also available, but we don't recommend them, since corner bead makes smoothing outside corners almost foolproof.

Apply compound and place the tape as usual. Then load some mud onto the corner knife to lubricate the knife and leave a thin coat of compound over the paper. Start at the top of the corner and drag the knife down to about 16 in. from the floor. Then start at the floor and drag upward. Ease off when you reach the area that's already smooth. You may have to repeat this process two or three times to fully embed the tape and create a smooth, straight corner. A corner knife doesn't ensure straight corners, so reinforced corner tape is a good idea (see p. 75). Use a corner knife for the first coat only; after that, coat one side at a time, allowing one side to harden before you coat the other.

RIDGE

CORNER
KNIFE

Smooth both sides of inside corners at once with an inside corner knife. Scrape off the ridges with a taping knife.

2
Electrical & High-Tech

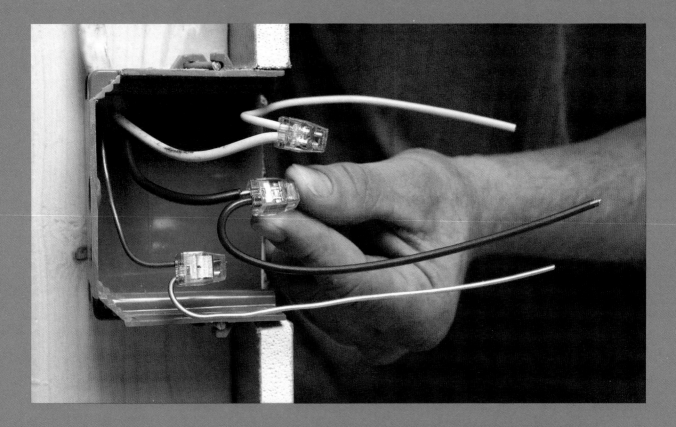

IN THIS CHAPTER

Home Care & Repair 78
*Wireless, battery-free switch,
disposing of old computers, and more*

Top 10 Electrical Mistakes 82

Ask TFH 87
*Sensitive circuit breakers,
universal remotes and more*

**Everything You Need to Know
About CFLs** 89

New Products 94
*Portable cell phone charger,
smart outside light switch
and more*

HomeCare&Repair

WIRELESS, BATTERY-FREE, FINGER-POWERED SWITCH

Putting in a switch for an overhead fan, switching an outlet, or converting a two-way switch to a three-way switch can be a nightmare if you have to fish new wire through old walls and floors. With wallpapered walls and textured ceilings, it can be impossible. Until recently, the only way around the problem was to buy a clunky battery-powered transmitter/receiver.

An entirely different type of switch is available: It converts the energy of a human finger pushing a switch into a radio signal strong enough to be picked up by a receiver in a light fixture or outlet up to 150 ft. away. Only 1/2 in. thick, the switch can be mounted on walls or woodwork or even glued to glass. The receivers come in two different types—one that's hidden inside the light box or outlet and one that plugs into the outlet.

Although the range is reduced by walls and ceilings, one switch can control an unlimited number of receivers, and one receiver can respond to up to 30 switches (30-way switch, anyone?).

First, turn off the power at the main electrical panel. To install the receiver, open the light or outlet and wire the receiver between the power source and the light. Then push the "Learn" button on the receiver and click the switch so the receiver recognizes the signal. (Or buy a plug-in–type receiver.) Plastic electrical boxes work best—metal boxes can interfere with the signal. Install the receiver and try the switch a few times before you attach it to the wall to make sure it's within range.

The switches are available in either the square European style shown here or the traditional rocker style. The switch and receiver are available separately or as sets. Prices start at $60.

RECEIVER

TO FIXTURE

SWITCH

Buyer's Guide
- EnOcean wireless switches: (801) 225-2226. adhocelectronics.com
- Lightning transmitter/receiver: (888) 954-4486. lightningswitch.com

THAT OLD GFCI MAY NO LONGER PROTECT YOU

By detecting dangerous current flow and instantly shutting off power, ground fault circuit interrupters save hundreds of lives each year. But after 10 years or so, the sensitive circuitry inside a GFCI wears out. And usually the test button on the GFCI doesn't tell you there's anything wrong: When you press the button, it shuts off the power as always. So the only reliable way to check an older GFCI is to use a circuit tester that has its own GFCI test button ($10 at home centers and hardware stores).

Plug in the tester and push its test button. If the power goes off, the GFCI is working. Press the reset button to restore power. If the power doesn't go off, replace the GFCI.

Your new GFCI ($9) will never require a circuit tester. All GFCIs manufactured after mid-2006 are designed to tell you when they fail. The vast majority indicate failure by shutting off power permanently. So someday your GFCI (and any other outlets connected to it) will simply stop delivering power and you'll have to replace it.

TEST BUTTON

RESET BUTTON

TEST BUTTON

DOES YOUR TV SIGNAL NEED A BOOST?

A video signal amplifier does exactly what its name implies: It strengthens the signal coming from your antenna or cable company to produce a better TV picture. Here are some common situations where an amplifier can help:

- If you have an outdoor antenna (rather than cable or satellite TV) and live far from the towers that transmit TV signals.
- If your reception suddenly went bad after you installed a new TV, VCR or DVD player.
- If you have several TVs connected to an antenna, cable or satellite dish. Each TV shares signal

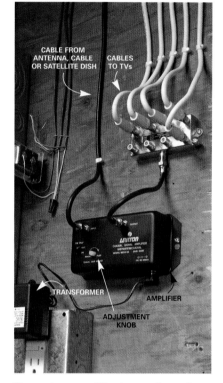

CABLE FROM ANTENNA, CABLE OR SATELLITE DISH — CABLES TO TVs

TRANSFORMER

AMPLIFIER

ADJUSTMENT KNOB

Connect an amplifier to your incoming cable and to a splitter, which distributes the signal to several TVs.

power with the others, so a greater number of TVs means a weaker signal share for each. Usually, three or four TVs isn't a problem. Beyond that, picture quality can worsen.

Amplifiers start at less than $20 at home centers and electronics stores. But spend more than that and you'll get a more powerful boost, amplification of a wider range of channel frequencies and "cleaner" amplification with less "noise" in the signal. The model shown here lets you adjust the level of amplification and costs about $50 at home centers and online at broadband-utopia.com. (Type "video amplifier" into the search field.)

Save your receipt so you can return the amplifier if it doesn't help. Lots of factors

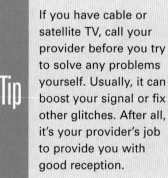

Tip

If you have cable or satellite TV, call your provider before you try to solve any problems yourself. Usually, it can boost your signal or fix other glitches. After all, it's your provider's job to provide you with good reception.

other than signal strength can cause poor reception, and an amplifier may do you no good—it can even make reception worse in some cases.

Home Care & Repair

KEEP COMPUTER KEYBOARDS AND SCREENS CLEAN

Computers seem to be a magnet for dust, lint and sticky fingers, but unlike with household appliances, you can't just douse them with all-purpose cleaner and scrub them clean. However, you can get them sparkling in just a few minutes with the right products and techniques.

The first step is to turn off the computer and disconnect the power. If you're cleaning a laptop, take out the battery. Moisten part of a soft, lint-free cloth (not a paper towel) with water and gently wipe the screen, first with the damp part, then with the dry part. After you're finished with the screen, wipe the keys and the housing down. Some manufacturers also offer or recommend special wipes or cleaning solutions, but check first at the manufacturer's Web site or the place you bought the computer before using any product that's not specifically recommended for your type of computer.

Next, clean the keyboard (**Photo 1**). Tip the keyboard up and shake out the crumbs, then blow out the keys with a can of compressed gases

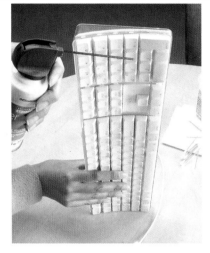

1 USE compressed gases to remove dirt and lint from the keys and the keyboard housing.

($5 or less at office supply or hardware stores). The compressed gases aren't just air, so keep the cans away from children.

Use a 50/50 solution of isopropyl alcohol and water to clean tough spots. Dip a cotton swab in the solution, then pat off the excess water on a paper towel so it doesn't drip between the keys. Wipe the surface and edges of the keys, changing

2 CLEAN greasy dirt off the computer keys with cotton swabs and a solution of alcohol and water.

swabs frequently (**Photo 2**).

Some types of desktop computers with wired keyboards have keys that can be pried off one at a time (gently) with a letter opener. But don't do this with laptops or wireless keyboards. Always check with the manufacturer first, because if you do this with the wrong keyboard you could destroy it. And then snap a photo before you start so you know where the keys go.

ONLINE ENERGY SAVINGS ESTIMATOR

Energy costs keep rising every year, but blowing in more insulation or buying an energy-efficient refrigerator is expensive too. The Department of Energy has created a Web site where you can find out if those big upfront costs really do save you money—and how long the payback period is before you start seeing savings. Just type in your zip code and some basic information about your house and your appliances, and the site creates a customized profile of what energy is costing you now and how much each energy-saving upgrade could reduce that cost. It also generates a list of recommended improvements you can make, with approximate costs.

The site (http://hes.lbl.gov/hes/) also has links to state energy-saving programs, construction and home building information, solar how-to sources, product information and other government resources.

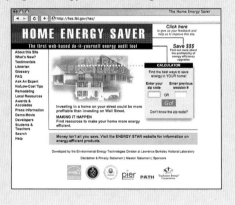

GET RID OF YOUR OLD COMPUTER FOR FREE

Old computers, monitors and other accessories contain toxic materials and must be disposed of properly, not just tossed into the trash. Local recycling programs can be expensive—$40 and up for a desktop monitor and computer.

However, there are a few ways to get rid of old equipment for free (including shipping) or at minimal cost:

- Dell will recycle any brand of computer at no cost when you buy a new Dell computer. The company recycles all Dell products for free even if you're not buying a new unit. Non-Dell products can be recycled for $10.
- Apple also provides free recycling, including shipping, for any old computer when you buy a new computer from an Apple store.

- Hewlett Packard charges about the same as local recyclers, but then reimburses you with a coupon good toward a new HP computer.
- Many computer retailers offer trade-in deals or will put you in touch with companies that buy and sell used computer equipment.
- If your computer equipment is still in good working condition, with the original software, and is less than five or six years old, you can donate it to the National Cristina Foundation. The foundation arranges donations to nonprofits and schools and will find organizations in your area that need computer equipment. Go to its Web site (cristina.org) for more information.

No matter how you get rid of your old computer, remember to delete all personal data first.

For more information about manufacturers' policies on recycling, contact the manufacturer or a local computer store.

NEVER MISS A PHONE CALL

If you can't hear your phone ring when you're in your shop or the backyard, take 30 seconds to plug in a phone amplifier. In addition to a louder ring (up to 95 decibels), some models include a strobe light. Some home centers and electronics stores carry one or two models (prices start at about $20). For a wider selection, do an online search for "phone ring amplifier."

GreatGoofs®

DECEPTIVE DETECTOR

After a power outage, I heard beeping every 30 seconds. It was driving me nuts! I tried pushing the reset button on my smoke alarm—it still beeped. I replaced the battery—it continued to beep. I took it down and went at it with a screwdriver, prying off part of the innards and breaking the circuit board in two. Believe it or not, the stupid thing still beeped! That's when I noticed a red light glowing down the hallway. The hard-wired CO detector was dutifully beeping away, alerting me to the previous power outage. I held in my hands the broken parts to a perfectly good smoke detector.

TOP 10
ELECTRICAL MISTAKES

How to recognize and correct wiring blunders that can endanger your home

by **Jeff Gorton**

<u>CAUTION:</u> **Turn off the power at the main panel when you're doing electrical work.**

mistake | no electrical box

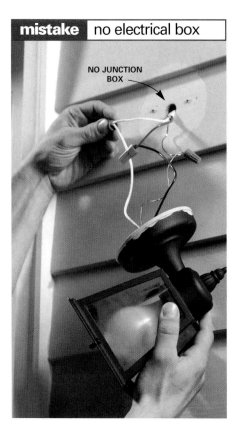

NO JUNCTION BOX

MISTAKE 1

Making connections outside electrical boxes

Never connect wires outside of electrical boxes. Junction boxes protect the connections from accidental damage and contain sparks and heat from a loose connection or short circuit.

Where connections aren't contained in an electrical box, install a box and reconnect the wires inside it. The photo at right shows one way to do this for an exterior light mounted on wood siding.

solution
add a box

REMODEL BOX

CUT-IN BLOCK

MISTAKE 2

Reversing hot and neutral wires

Connecting the black hot wire to the neutral terminal of an outlet creates the potential for a lethal shock. The trouble is that you may not realize the mistake until someone gets shocked, because lights and most other plug-in devices will still work; they just won't work safely.

Always connect the white wire to the neutral terminal of outlets and light fixtures. The neutral terminal is always marked. It's usually identified by a silver or light-colored screw. Connect the hot wire to the other terminal. If there's a green or bare copper wire, that's the ground. Connect the ground to the green grounding screw or to a ground wire or grounded box.

solution
identify the neutral terminal

NEUTRAL TERMINAL   HOT TERMINAL

MISTAKE 3

Cutting wires too short

Wires that are cut too short make wire connections difficult and—since you're more likely to make poor connections—dangerous. Leave the wires long enough to protrude at least 3 in. from the box.

If you run into short wires, there's an easy fix. Simply add 6-in. extensions onto the existing wires. The photo below shows a type of wire connector that's easier to install in tight spots. You'll find these at hardware stores and home centers.

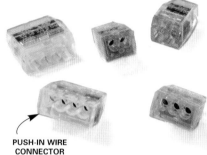

PUSH-IN WIRE CONNECTOR

mistake | wires too short

6" EXTENSION

PUSH-IN WIRE CONNECTORS

SHORT WIRE

solution | extend wires

MISTAKE 4

Leaving plastic-sheathed cable unprotected

It's easy to damage plastic-sheathed cable that's left exposed between framing members. That's why the electrical code requires cable to be protected in these areas. Cable is especially vulnerable when it's run over or under wall or ceiling framing, as shown here.

Protect exposed plastic-sheathed cable by nailing or screwing a 1-1/2-in.-thick board alongside the cable as shown on the far right. You don't have to staple the cable to the board.

mistake | unprotected cable

UNPROTECTED CABLE

solution | install a 2x2

ADDED 2x2

PROTECTED CABLE

MISTAKE 5

Poor support for outlets and switches

solution | add rigid spacers

Loose switches or outlets can look bad (**photo above**), but worse yet, they're dangerous. Loosely connected outlets can move around, causing the wires to loosen from the terminals. Loose wires can arc and overheat, creating a potential fire hazard.

Fix loose outlets by shimming under the screws to create a tight connection to the box. You can buy special spacers like we show here at home centers and hardware stores. Other options include small washers or a coil of wire wrapped around the screw.

PLASTIC ELECTRICAL SPACER

MISTAKE 6

Installing a three-slot receptacle without a ground wire

If you have two-slot outlets, it's tempting to replace them with three-slot outlets so you can plug in three-prong plugs. But don't do this unless you're sure there's a ground available. Use a tester to see if your outlet is grounded. A series of lights indicates whether the outlet is wired correctly or what fault exists. These testers are readily available at home centers and hardware stores for $7 to $10.

If you discover a three-slot outlet in an ungrounded box, the easiest fix is to simply replace it with a two-slot outlet as shown.

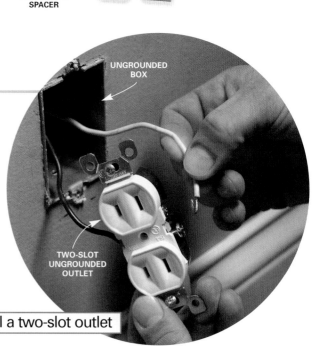

solution | install a two-slot outlet

MISTAKE 7

Recessing boxes behind the wall surface

mistake

exposed combustible material

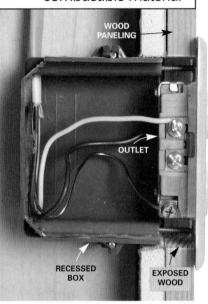

WOOD PANELING

OUTLET

RECESSED BOX

EXPOSED WOOD

PLASTIC BOX EXTENSION

SCREWDRIVER

ELECTRICAL & HI-TECH

Electrical boxes must be flush to the wall surface if the wall surface is a combustible material. Boxes recessed behind combustible materials like wood present a fire hazard because the wood is left exposed to potential heat and sparks.

The fix is simply to install a metal or plastic box extension. If you use a metal box extension on a plastic box, connect the metal extension to the ground wire in the box using a grounding clip and a short piece of wire.

---

mistake missing clamp

MISSING CABLE CLAMP

MISTAKE 8

Installing cable without a clamp

Cable that's not secured can strain the connections. In metal boxes, the sharp edges can cut the insulation on the wires. Single plastic boxes do not require internal cable clamps, but the cable must be stapled within 8 in. of the box. Larger plastic boxes are required to have built-in cable clamps and the cable must be stapled within 12 in. of the box. Cables must be connected to metal boxes with an approved cable clamp. Make sure the sheathing on the cable is trapped under the clamp, and that about 1/4 in. of sheathing is visible inside the box. Some metal boxes have built-in cable clamps. If the box you're using doesn't include clamps, buy clamps separately and install them when you add the cable to the box (**photo above**).

solution install a clamp

CABLE CLAMP

MISTAKE 9

Overfilling electrical boxes

Too many wires stuffed into a box can cause dangerous overheating, short-circuiting and fire. The National Electrical Code specifies minimum box sizes to reduce this risk. To figure the minimum box size required, add up the items in the box:

- **1** - for each hot wire and neutral wire entering the box
- **1** - for all the ground wires combined
- **1** - for all the cable clamps combined
- **2** - for each device (switch or outlet—but not light fixtures)

Multiply the total by 2.00 for 14-gauge wire and by 2.25 for 12-gauge wire to get the minimum box size required in cubic inches. Then choose a box with at least this much volume. Plastic boxes have the volume stamped inside, usually on the back. Steel box capacities are listed in the electrical code. Steel boxes won't be labeled, so you'll have to measure the height, width and depth of the interior. Then multiply to find the volume.

mistake | box too small

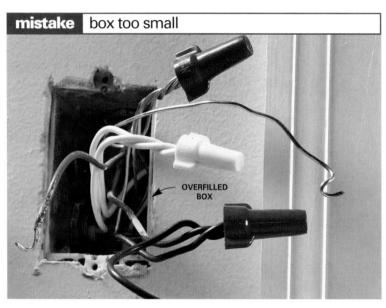

OVERFILLED BOX

solution | install larger box

DOUBLE REMODEL BOX

MISTAKE 10

Wiring a GFCI backward

GFCI (ground fault circuit interrupter) outlets protect you from a lethal shock by shutting off the power when they sense slight differences in current. They have two pairs of terminals. One pair, labeled "line," is for incoming power for the GFCI outlet itself. The other set is labeled "load" and provides protection for downstream outlets. You'll lose the shock protection if you mix up the line and load connections.

NEUTRAL "LOAD" TERMINAL

HOT "LOAD" TERMINAL

NEUTRAL "LINE" TERMINAL

"LOAD" TERMINALS UNDER TAPE

HOT "LINE" TERMINAL

solution
connect power to the "line" terminal

AskTFH ™

The Family Handyman

SENSITIVE CIRCUIT BREAKERS

The AFCI circuit breaker that serves all our bedrooms keeps shutting off. I can't figure out the problem. The house is just two years old!

Arc fault circuit interrupters (AFCIs) are prone to "nuisance tripping," which is probably what you're experiencing. AFCIs are designed to sense an arc, which is an electrical "leak" caused when a hot wire touches a neutral or ground but doesn't trigger the circuit breaker. Although current-sensing circuitry enables AFCIs to detect arcing conditions, unintended trickles of current may also cause the breaker to shut off (AFCIs are very sensitive!).

To solve the nuisance tripping problem, start with things you can do yourself. Unplug or turn off surge protectors plugged into bedroom outlets, fluorescent lights with electronic ballasts, and lighting controls with LED displays that are on the AFCI circuit. They sometimes allow current "leakage" that can trip the AFCI. Damage or deterioration to wires or cords (which can happen when furniture is pushed against plugs in an outlet) also causes arcing faults and will trip the circuit. If you identify one of these sources, you'll have to either replace the electrical item or leave it unplugged.

If unplugging electrical and electronic devices doesn't solve the problem, hire an electrician to install a new AFCI breaker in the electrical panel. There's no reliable method for testing AFCIs (the test button isn't always accurate). If the nuisance tripping stops, then the old one was probably defective.

AFCIs protect against fires caused by arcing faults and are now required in new or remodeled bedrooms.

If the breaker still trips, the electrician then needs to track down the cause by going into each switch, receptacle and light box to look for a wiring problem. Wires are often folded (jammed) into boxes quickly, and if the wrong two wires make contact, they can trip an AFCI.

The National Electrical Code required AFCIs for receptacle outlets in bedrooms beginning Jan. 1, 2002 (local jurisdictions may have additional requirements). Don't confuse AFCIs with ground fault circuit interrupters (GFCIs), which are designed to protect against shocks (not arcs).

ARC FAULT CIRCUIT INTERRUPTER

EASY WAY TO TEST HOLIDAY LIGHTS

Last December, you showed how to test for bad bulbs in Christmas lights. Is there a way to test (and fix) the entire string of miniature lights without testing each bulb individually?

Try the LightKeeper Pro (847-729-4004, lightkeeperpro.com). It'll identify and oftentimes fix most problems in miniature and icicle light sets (but not the sets of larger lights or LED lights) with a few squeezes of the trigger (**Photo 1**).

The trigger sends an electric charge through the circuit to repair internal bulb failures. (The "shunt" in the bulb is supposed to act as a bypass if a filament fails to complete the circuit. If the shunt fails, it knocks out the lights in the section. The electricity sent by pulling the trigger locates and fixes the defective shunt.)

If that doesn't work, hold down the black button on top of the tester and move the tip along the string so it beeps (**Photo 2**). Note where the beeping stops, then replace the previous bulb.

The tester is available at home centers and some hardware stores for about $20 (find retailers on the company's Web site).

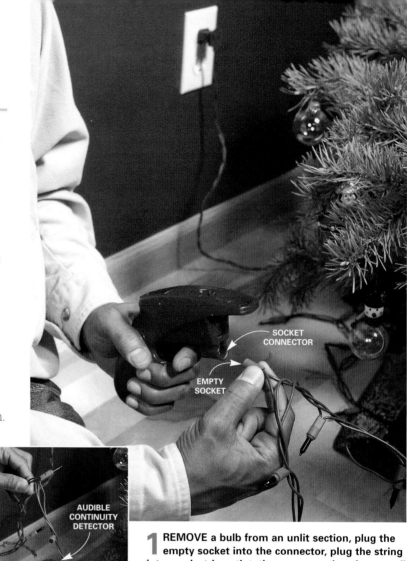

SOCKET CONNECTOR

EMPTY SOCKET

AUDIBLE CONTINUITY DETECTOR

1 REMOVE a bulb from an unlit section, plug the empty socket into the connector, plug the string into an electric outlet, then squeeze the trigger until the lights turn on.

2 PRESS DOWN the black button, hold the tip about 1/2 in. from the string, and move it along the cord until it stops beeping (at the defective bulb).

UNIVERSAL REMOTE CONTROL

We just splurged on a new TV and a universal remote. Before we try to set up the remote, do you have any advice?

To program a universal remote control, you have to locate program codes from the owner's manual of each of your A/V accessories. This is a task you'll only want to do once. Write the codes on a piece of tape and stick it to the inside of the remote's battery cover. This will save you a paper hunt in case a dead battery causes the memory to fail and you need to reprogram the remote.

EVERYTHING YOU NEED TO KNOW ABOUT **CFLs**

10 common questions, 10 commonsense answers

by **Spike Carlsen**

Compact fluorescent bulbs—usually referred to by the initials "CFL"—have come a long way. Early versions were expensive (as much as $15 apiece) and plagued with problems (they appeared dim, flickered, didn't come on instantly and burned out sooner than promised).

But that was then. New technology has solved most of the old problems. Today, using CFLs is one of the easiest and most effective ways to save money on energy. It's as easy as screwing in a bulb and flipping a switch. Many CFLs can be purchased for about $3, and some utility companies offer discounts or rebates to customers who buy them.

That said, buying and using CFLs can still be confusing. The answers to these common questions will help you put these great energy-saving bulbs to best use.

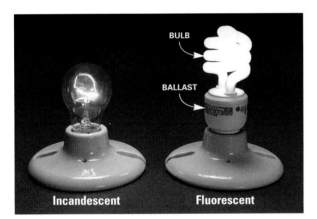

Incandescent   **Fluorescent**

CFLs vs. incandescent bulbs

Q How do compact fluorescent lights work and how do they differ from standard bulbs?

A Standard incandescent bulbs work by using electricity to heat up a thin filament inside the bulb. As the filament heats up, it glows, producing light. The drawback to standard bulbs is that most of the energy consumed—over 80 percent—goes into creating heat, not light.

CFLs work on a totally different principle. They consist of two basic parts: a gas-filled tube (what many of us would call the "bulb") and a ballast that contains the electronics. In simple terms, electricity from the ballast excites phosphors on the inside surface of the bulb; these phosphors in turn glow, producing light. Since CFLs don't waste as much energy creating heat, they're much more energy efficient. You see the savings when you compare the wattages; a 15-watt CFL provides about as much light as a 60-watt incandescent bulb.

Best (and worst) places to use them

Q Are there some places where using a CFL makes more sense than others?

A Since many CFLs last up to 10 times as long as incandescents, consider placing them in difficult-to-reach fixtures. It may mean climbing the ladder once every five years instead of every year. It also makes sense to use CFLs in light fixtures that are continuously "On" more than three hours per day.

CFLs save energy in any location, but there are some circumstances that can reduce their life span:

- Frequent on-off switching, as in a hallway.
- Excessive vibration near doors or stairways.
- High-humidity areas such as a damp basement.
- A CFL that's not rated for use in an enclosed light fixture might burn out prematurely if enclosed.

Plugging electrical leaks

Even when your appliances and electrical equipment are turned "Off," the truth is, they're still "On." One-fifth of the energy used by televisions, stereo equipment, computers and even answering machines is consumed while they're in standby mode. One solution to the leaking electricity problem is to physically unplug appliances or turn them off via a power strip when they're not in use.

How to choose CFL bulbs

Q I've looked at compact fluorescent bulbs at the home center, but I'm not sure what to buy. How do I know which provides as much light as a regular 60- or 100-watt bulb?

A Look at the lumen rating, not the bulb wattage, to compare real light output. Then buy a CFL with 20 percent more lumens than the incandescent bulb you want to replace has. For example, to replace a 60-watt incandescent bulb that has 870 lumens, buy a CFL with at least 1,050 lumens. If you follow wattage guidelines on the package, you may not be satisfied with the light output. Be wary of CFLs that don't list the lumens on the packaging. Their claims that the light output matches a certain incandescent wattage are sometimes misleading or wrong.

Another reason you need more lumens is that a CFL will dim over time. It will lose 20 to 25 percent lumen power after 4,000 hours (40 percent of a CFL's 10,000-hour-rated life). Incandescent bulbs also lose lumens, but the life of these bulbs is extremely short compared with that of CFLs.

Some CFLs have screw-on covers so they look much like standard incandescent bulbs.

Payback: How long? How come?

Q CFLs cost five or six times as much as regular bulbs. How long do I need to use them before I recoup my investment?

A Although CFLs have come down dramatically in price, their electronic ballast and other features do make them more expensive to manufacture than incandescent bulbs. The payback period will vary with the cost of electricity in your area. However, based on a cost of 10¢ per kWh, a 15-watt CFL will cost about $12 to operate over its 8,000-hour projected life span. Burning a 60-watt incandescent bulb with equivalent light output for the same length of time will cost about $48; a cost difference of $36 (and you'll need to buy four to eight bulbs since they have a much shorter life span). Based on those numbers, a CFL will pay for itself in about 500 hours (in about four months if the bulb is used four hours per day).

Incandescent bulb
- PURCHASE PRICE: 50¢
- ENERGY USAGE COST OVER PROJECTED LIFE SPAN: $48

CFL bulb
- PURCHASE PRICE: $2.50
- ENERGY USAGE COST OVER PROJECTED LIFE SPAN: $12

What a watt costs

The cost of electricity in the United States ranges from less than 10¢ per kilowatt hour to nearly 40¢ per kilowatt hour. The more expensive your electricity, the faster you'll recoup the extra money you pay for CFLs.

The "quality of light" factor

Q I stopped buying CFLs because the first few I bought years ago seemed dim and the color of the light was weird. Are CFLs more like "normal" incandescent bulbs these days?

A Because CFLs last so long, some of the first-generation bulbs are still burning and giving people the wrong impression of the newer CFLs.

The newer bulbs flicker less, make less noise, start up faster and emit light very similar to that of standard ("Type A") incandescent bulbs. The spiral shape, which is often used in CFLs, casts light more like a standard incandescent bulb. The color of the light has improved dramatically. If you couldn't see the bulb, you wouldn't know whether the light was incandescent or fluorescent. "Daylight" bulbs (**photo right**), which broadcast a whiter light, are available for those desiring a cooler, less yellowish light.

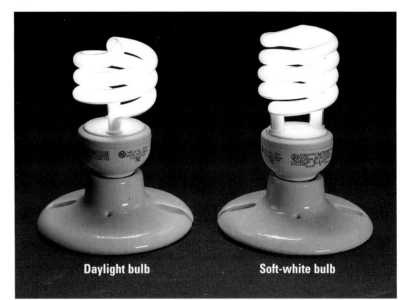

Daylight bulb   **Soft-white bulb**

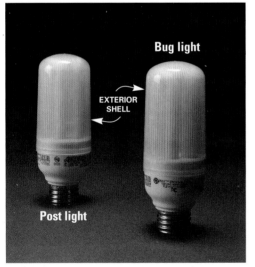

Bug light

EXTERIOR SHELL

Post light

Outside in the cold

Q Can I use CFLs outside and in my garage during the long, cold winter?

A Yes, they're great energy savers outdoors, but beware. Older fluorescent lights—both compact and tubular—are powered using magnetic ballasts. The lower the temperature, the more difficult it is for these bulbs to "get up to speed" and operate evenly. However, most CFLs made today have electronic ballasts that are much less sensitive to the cold.

If you're planning to use a CFL in an area exposed to the elements, purchase one designated for "exterior" or "outside" use. These usually have an extra translucent shell surrounding the fluorescent bulb for additional protection. Specialty bulbs like the "bug light" shown and exterior floodlights are also available.

CFLs reduce cooling costs, too

Since CFLs generate less heat than standard incandescent bulbs, your air conditioner won't have to work quite as hard in the summer.

New CFLs on the block

Q I've seen smaller fluorescent bulbs that don't screw in. What's the story on pin-type fluorescent bulbs?

A The pin-type fluorescent bulb familiar to most of us is the classic circular kitchen bulb (**photo below**). These aren't considered true CFLs since the ballast is in the fixture, not built into the bulb itself.

But there is a new generation of pin-type bulbs, like the modular bulb shown at right. These are true CFLs, but they have a base designed to fit only into fixtures made specifically for these pin-type bulbs. Another unique feature of these bulbs is that the ballasts and tubes are separate. One of the reasons behind this modular design is that a typical ballast can last 30,000 hours, while a typical CFL bulb lasts 10,000. Because the parts are independent, you only need to change the bulb part that fails. These bulbs also meet the strict energy code in California.

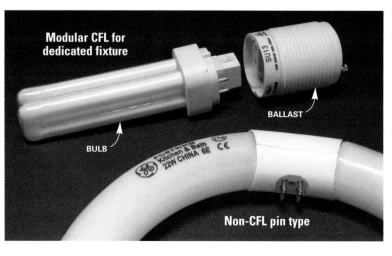

Modular CFL for dedicated fixture

BULB

BALLAST

Non-CFL pin type

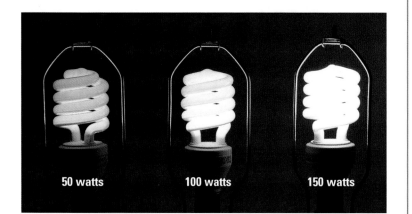

50 watts

100 watts

150 watts

Three-way bulbs

Q Are there three-way CFL bulbs, and if so, do they require a special lamp or light fixture?

A Yes, three-way CFLs are available, and no, you usually don't need a special lamp. The three-way bulbs that ramp up to the equivalent of a 150-watt incandescent can be either circular or spiral. Both shapes are quite large. For bulbs in that range, check to be sure they'll fit the harp and shade of your lamp.

Also make certain your three-way bulb is screwed in snugly. Unless the contacts on the bottom of the bulb make solid contact, your three-way bulb may work like a single-output bulb.

Dim the lights

Q Can I install CFLs in fixtures that operate on a dimmer switch?

A Yes—but only if you buy the right ones. Look for CFLs that are labeled "dimmable" on the package; they have special ballasts that allow them to be operated using a standard incandescent dimmer switch. Expect to pay $3 to $4 more for a dimmable CFL than for a regular CFL. We found dimmable CFLs at a local discount department store, but they're relatively new, so you may have to search around town (or on the Internet) to find them.

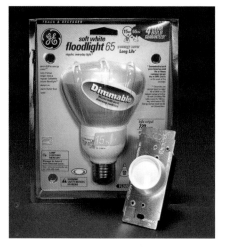

Lights out

There is a small power surge and a small spike in electrical usage when most lights are turned on, but as a rule of thumb, you'll save money by turning off lights that will remain off for more than five minutes.

Disposing of CFLs

Q What's the best way to dispose of a spent or broken CFL bulb?

A Manufacturers have reduced the amount of mercury in CFLs, but they still contain a small amount—on average, about 5 milligrams (roughly equivalent to the size of the tip of a ballpoint pen). Special steps should be taken when disposing of CFLs. You can try these recycling options:

- Many municipalities have hazardous waste facilities that accept broken or spent CFLs. You can find information on sites near you by visiting earth911.org. Type in or select "fluorescent bulbs" from the list and then enter your zip code to find facilities in your area. Note that most facilities accept hazardous waste only during certain business hours and/or on certain days. Also call 877-EARTH911 for local disposal sites.

- Some retail stores offer a fluorescent bulb collection service. You may find some in your area by visiting the Web site listed above. In our area, we found a number of Ace Hardware stores and other hardware stores that serve as collection sites. Many IKEA stores also take back spent CFLs.

- There are a number of national organizations that can help. The U.S. Environmental Recycling Hotline (877-327-8491) can help you find local collection centers. Additional information for businesses and homeowners can also be found at lamprecycle.org.

- Never send a CFL or other mercury-containing product to an incinerator. If a CFL breaks, sweep up the glass fragments and place them in a sealed plastic bag, along with the wet paper towel you use to pick up stray shards. Don't use a vacuum. Open windows to air out the house. ⌂

CAUTION: Do not put CFLs in with your trash!

Special CFLs for special uses

If every American household replaced just one standard incandescent bulb with one high-efficiency compact fluorescent lightbulb, enough energy would be saved to light over 2-1/2 million homes for an entire year! There used to be only a few types of CFLs, but now there are dozens. Here are a few:

GE

TUBE CFLs have one of the smallest overall sizes and are available in a wide range of wattages. Some have a rated life as long as 15,000 hours.

REFLECTOR CFLs are available in a variety of beam spreads for indoor and track lighting applications. Some are dimmable and/or rated for use in recessed light fixtures.

GE

DECORATIVE CFLs are available for fixtures where bulbs are exposed, such as bathroom strip lights or chandeliers. They're available in "candle," "globe," "bullet" and other shapes.

GE

LARGE-LOOP CFLs are ideal for ceiling fixtures and torchiere lamps. Many are modular with independent ballasts and bulbs.

GE

NewProducts

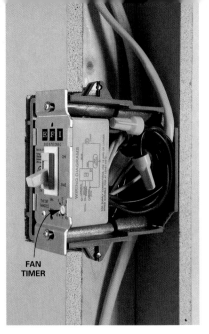

PORTABLE CHARGER FOR CELL PHONES

CARRYING CASE

ADAPTER TIPS

CORD

CHARGER

The new Sidewinder cell phone charger ($25) ensures your cell phone always has power. Compact and weighing only 2.5 ozs., it provides six minutes of talk time with two minutes of hand cranking— great when you're away from a power source and need to make a call, but your phone is dead. It's perfect to take along on those "wilderness" experiences (wherever you still have service). The Sidewinder works for most cell phones (check with the charger manufacturer to make sure it'll work for yours).

The LED light on the charger can be used as a flashlight and runs for more than five minutes with 30 seconds of charging. Buy it online.
IST Designs, (888) 478-6565. sidewindercharger.com

FAN TIMER

SWITCH FOR LONGER VENTING TIME

This new fan time delay switch ($40) turns on the bathroom light and fan simultaneously. When you flip the switch off, the light turns off, but the fan continues to run for a preset time up to 60 minutes. The company says it usually takes 25 minutes to clear a bathroom of moisture after a shower.

The switch replaces the light and the fan switches and can be installed in an electrical box. Buy it online.
Energy Federation Inc., (800) 962-7015. efi.org

SMART OUTSIDE LIGHT SWITCH

Enter your longitude and latitude (coordinates are included in the instruction manual), the day of the year, and the time in Aube's Solar Timer Switch (T1035 model) and it will automatically turn your outside incandescent, halogen or fluorescent lights on at dusk and off at dawn (or any other period you choose). You'll only have the light on when you want it, so you don't waste electricity. Unlike other light-switch timers, this one doesn't have to be reprogrammed as the seasons change.

The memory is protected so you don't have to redo the settings after power outages. You can also operate the switch manually, if desired. The LCD screen shows the time, day and load status. Find retailers on the company's Web site or buy from energyfederation.org for $36.
Aube, (800) 831-2823. aubetech.com

3 Plumbing, Heating & Appliances

IN THIS CHAPTER

Ask TFH 96
  *Never lose power again, cold air
  in dryer vent and more*

Install a New Shower Faucet 98

Stop Sink Leaks 102

Handy Hints 107
  Faucet handles, soldering and more

Plumbing with PEX 108

Flip a Switch, Save $200 112

Great Goofs 115

Do's & Don'ts 116
  Soldering copper

10 Pitfalls of Sink Replacement 118

The Family Handyman

NEVER LOSE POWER AGAIN

What's involved in installing a generator for backup power for my house? Is a gas model the best option?

When the electricity goes out, a backup generator is a good way to keep your house running. But keep in mind that most generators will only power part of your home's electrical load. So first determine how much backup power you'll need. An 8.5-kilowatt generator (which starts at $3,500) will power your essential electric appliances, such as the furnace, refrigerator, freezer, sump pump, lights, and even the TV and computer. A 30- or 35-kilowatt liquid-cooled unit (which starts at $15,000) will provide enough electricity for everything in your house, including the air conditioner. Forget gasoline-powered units. They're not a long-term solution.

Buy a unit that uses the same fuel as your furnace, usually natural gas or propane. Both types of generators are relatively maintenance-free and start automatically.

The generator sits outside on a mounting pad (some have an attached pad), just like an air conditioner. In addition, you'll need a transfer switch, which allows you to select the circuits you want powered. It's connected to the generator and the main electrical circuit panel, and it monitors utility power. When it senses a power failure, it starts the generator to restore electricity to the house. When power resumes, it turns itself off. The generator can run for days or weeks, if needed, so you'll never be without power. These units make very little noise when they're running (they're quieter than a typical vacuum cleaner).

Installation is complicated and must be done right. It requires a building permit and you may need to add a sub-panel to your circuit panel. A do-it-yourselfer can mount the pad, install the transfer switch and run the conduit that goes from the transfer switch to the circuit panel (usually in the garage or basement). Hire a licensed electrician to handle the connections in the circuit panel and to make the fuel connection. Or, a pro can handle the entire installation for about $1,500.

The generators are sold at home centers (sometimes by special order), some electrical suppliers and manufacturers' dealers. Two companies that make backup generators are Kohler (800-544-2444; kohlerpowersystems.com) and Generac (888-436-3722; generac.com).

KOHLER (2)

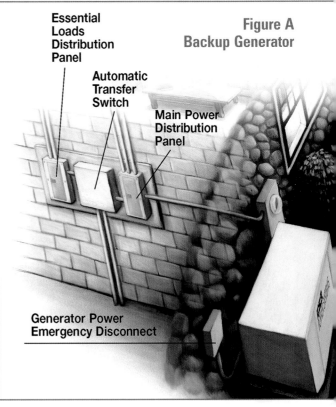

Essential Loads Distribution Panel

Automatic Transfer Switch

Main Power Distribution Panel

Generator Power Emergency Disconnect

**Figure A
Backup Generator**

COLD AIR IN DRYER VENT

Cold air comes in through our dryer vent, making our laundry room very cold. What can we do to stop it?

The vent should have a flap (or flaps) at the end to stop air infiltration (see photos). Go outside and make sure there's a flap and that it's not stuck open. If the flap works well, check the caulking. If it's cracking and peeling away, it's probably allowing cold air to leak in. Cut away the old caulking, make sure the vent is flush against the siding, and apply new latex caulk.

If the flap doesn't close on its own, try cleaning it and then spray silicone on the pivot point. If the flap still won't close, replace it. A new vent costs about $5 at home centers, and installing it will only take about 15 minutes.

Start by cutting away the caulking around the vent on the siding with a utility knife, remove any screws and unclamp the duct leading to the dryer. Slide the old vent out of the wall, slip in the new one and reattach it to the duct. Caulk around the vent flange.

SINGLE-FLAP DRYER VENT

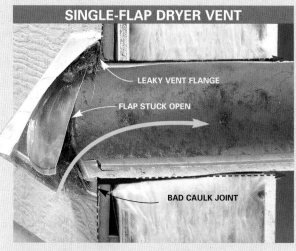

- LEAKY VENT FLANGE
- FLAP STUCK OPEN
- BAD CAULK JOINT

Check that the flap (or flaps) is closed, the vent is flush against the house, and the area around the vent is properly caulked.

THREE-FLAP LOUVERED DRYER VENT

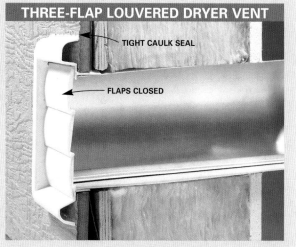

- TIGHT CAULK SEAL
- FLAPS CLOSED

The vent flaps are completely closed and the flange is caulked to stop air infiltration.

- 5" VENT
- REDUCER
- 4" VENT

WATER HEATER VENT QUANDARY

I need to replace my gas water heater. Most of the new ones have 3- or 4-in. vent openings, but my current vent is 5 in. Do I have to replace my entire vent as well?

If you can't find a unit that has the same size vent opening as your current water heater (or you just want a smaller unit), buy one with a vent opening that's just 1 in. smaller, then use a "reducer" to connect to the vent as shown. Use clamps or sheet metal screws and aluminum tape to connect the reducer. Install it on the horizontal part of the vent, at least 12 in. away from the elbow. Reducers are available at home centers for about $5.

Be sure to check building codes (this project requires a permit) and manufacturer's specifications for any additional venting requirements.

INSTALL A NEW
SHOWER FAUCET

3 common problems, 3 simple solutions

by **Kurt Anderson**

If your bath or shower faucet drips, you can fix it with a few inexpensive replacement parts. But if it's a new style you're after or features like preset temperatures or anti-scald protection, it's time for replacement. Installing a new shower faucet is a straightforward process of connecting the new valve to the old pipes. Sometimes all you need are the manufacturer's instruc-

tions and some basic plumbing know-how. But it isn't that easy very often. This article will focus on three complications that installation manuals and plumbing books ignore.

1. There's no access to the inside of the wall.
2. The old pipes are galvanized steel.
3. You want to replace a two-handle faucet with a single-handle model.

1 PUNCH a hole into the wall behind the faucet
to mark the location of the access panel. Just slip a
long screwdriver alongside the tub spout nipple and push.

2 CUT a hole 3 in. smaller than the access panel so you can see the exact
pipe locations. Then mark and cut the full-size access hole.

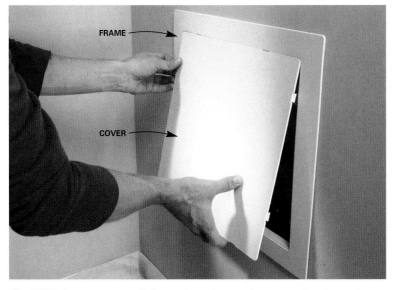

FRAME

COVER

3 GLUE the access panel's frame into place and snap on the cover after
you've installed the new faucet. You can paint the panel to match the wall.

PROBLEM 1:
NO ACCESS PANEL

To replace the faucet, you have to work *inside* the wall. Some homes have a removable panel in the next room behind the faucet. If you don't have an access panel, you might be able to replace the faucet by cutting a hole in the shower surround, but the best solution is to install a paintable plastic panel behind the faucet. You'll find them in various sizes at plumbing suppliers, some home centers or online (search for "access panel"). Buy a panel that's at least 14 x 14 in. ($25). If you don't want to install a panel because it would be an eyesore, an oversized cover plate inside the shower surround is another option (see Problem 3 on p. 101). If you already have an access panel but it's too low to provide easy access to the faucet, you can install a second panel above the existing one.

Don't try to position the access hole by taking measurements. Instead, remove the tub spout or faucet handles and punch a marker hole through the wall (**Photo 1**). If the wall is plaster rather than drywall, use a drill and a long bit instead of a screwdriver. Before you cut a hole sized for the access panel, cut a smaller hole (**Photo 2**). That way, you can see exactly where the pipes and valves are located and position the full-size hole for best access to them. Use the access panel frame as a template to mark the full-size hole. To avoid damaging the frame of the panel, install it after you've replaced the faucet (**Photo 3**).

Tip

More help online. To find articles on fixing a dripping tub or shower faucet, search for "tub faucet."
For tips on working with copper or plastic plumbing, search for "pipe."
thefamilyhandyman.com

PROBLEM 2: **GALVANIZED STEEL PIPE**

Unlike copper or plastic, steel pipes are joined with threaded, screw-together connections. So you can't simply cut the hot and cold supply pipes. That would remove the threaded ends and you'd have no reliable way to connect new pipe.

To preserve those threaded ends, unscrew the union fittings that connect the supply lines to the faucet (**Photo 1**). You can leave the spout nipple connected to the faucet and remove it along with the valve. If the faucet is connected to a showerhead, cut the "shower riser" pipe

(**Photo 2**). This pipe isn't under constant pressure, so you can reconnect it with a special coupler later.

Connect the new faucet as shown in **Photo 3**. To connect the cutoff shower riser, use a special compression coupler designed for galvanized steel pipe (called a "Dresser" coupling). For a better seal and easier installation, apply Teflon pipe sealant to the coupler's threads and rubber seals. Run the shower and check the coupler for leaks. If you find one, tighten the coupler's nuts.

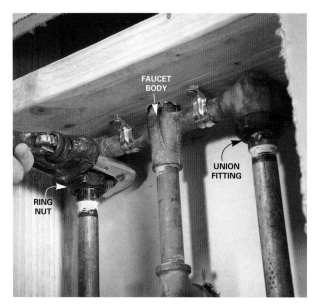

1 UNSCREW the ring nuts that fasten the union fitting to the faucet body. Then unscrew the union fittings from the supply lines.

2 CUT the shower riser with a reciprocating saw or jigsaw. Cut slowly and gently so you don't loosen the connections above.

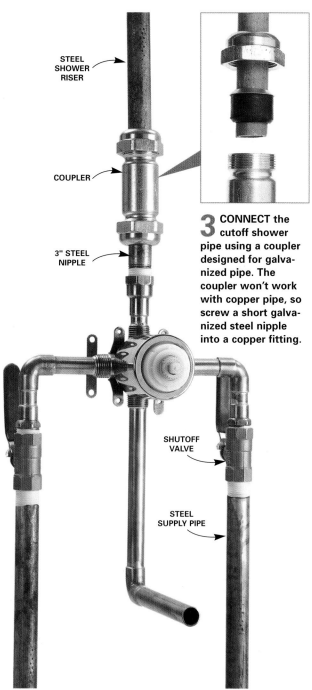

3 CONNECT the cutoff shower pipe using a coupler designed for galvanized pipe. The coupler won't work with copper pipe, so screw a short galvanized steel nipple into a copper fitting.

PROBLEM 3: REPLACING TWO HANDLES WITH ONE

If you have a two-handle faucet, it's easiest to replace it with another two-handle model. If you want the convenience of a single handle, you'll have to hide the two holes left by the handles. An oversized cover plate does just that. Plus, it covers an access hole, possibly allowing you to skip adding an access panel (as shown on p. 99). Keep in mind that replacing a faucet using this smaller hole can be difficult if not impossible—a large access panel makes the job much easier. You'll find oversized cover plates ($23) at plumbing supply stores or online (search for "renovation cover plate").

To install a single-handle faucet, you'll have to cut a hole into your shower surround. If your surround is fiberglass or acrylic, cut the hole using a jigsaw and a fine-tooth blade (a coarse blade causes more vibration, which can crack the surround). Apply strips of masking tape to the surround to avoid scratching or chipping the surface. Run the saw at full speed, but push it slowly and gently along the cut mark. If you feel the blade hitting a pipe inside the wall, stop immediately and continue past the pipe using a hacksaw blade.

To cut tile, use a rotary tool ($30) equipped with a tile-cutting bit (**Photo 1**). Set the cutting depth of the bit at 1/4 in. and make the first pass. Make more passes, setting the bit 1/4 in. deeper each time until you've cut completely through the surround. If you don't own a rotary tool, you have a few other options: You can try a jigsaw and ceramic tile blade ($5). These blades cut softer tile well. If you find that your tile is too hard, drill a series of 1/4-in. holes through the tile and wall using a carbide ceramic tile bit ($5). Drill the holes close together so there's little or no space between them. Then cut any material between the holes with the ceramic tile jigsaw bit. 🏠

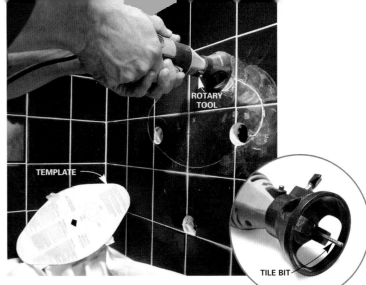

1 CUT a hole for the new valve using a rotary tool equipped with a tile-cutting bit. Mark the cutout using the cover plate's paper template and a crayon.

2 SOLDER in the new valve. Use the paper template to make sure the valve is centered in the cutout.

3 MOUNT the oversized cover plate. Install the faucet's standard cover plate over it.

STOP SINK LEAKS

Sink rim leaks

Sink rim leaks allow water to seep under the rim or the base of the faucet. They will gradually destroy your cabinets and countertops in kitchens and bathrooms.

Signs of trouble:

■ Puddles, dampness or water stains inside the cabinet.

■ Loose plastic laminate near sink.

■ A loose faucet base.

■ Deteriorating caulk around sink.

How to find the source:

■ If you have a plastic laminate countertop, examine the underside of the countertop using a flashlight. Look for swollen particleboard or other signs of water damage.

■ Dribble water around the sink rim and look for leaks (photo, right).

How to fix it:

■ Tighten the faucet base by turning the mounting nuts underneath it.

Test for rim leaks: **Dribble water around the sink rim and faucet base with a sponge. Then look for leaks below using a flashlight.**

■ If the sink rim is caulked, scrape away the old caulk and recaulk.

■ Tighten the clips under the sink rim that clamp the sink to the countertop.

Figure A: Sink leaks

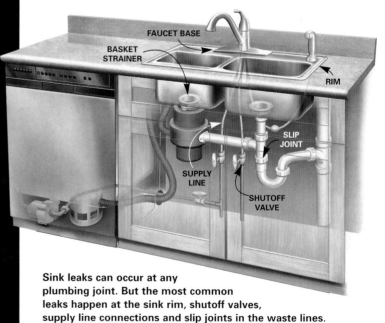

Sink leaks can occur at any plumbing joint. But the most common leaks happen at the sink rim, shutoff valves, supply line connections and slip joints in the waste lines.

STOP LURKING LEAKS

Find and fix minor drips before they cause major damage

by **Eric Smith**

Tiny leaks that go unnoticed for years can do just as much harm as big, sudden leaks. By keeping walls and floors constantly damp, these lurking leaks rot framing, destroy walls and ceilings, ruin flooring and feed mold. Given enough time, a tiny drip will cause hundreds or even thousands of dollars of damage.

This article will show you how to recognize and find the most dangerous slow leaks. We'll also outline the solutions to these leaks. For detailed leak fixes, go to thefamilyhandyman.com.

Supply leaks

Supply leaks under the kitchen sink or bath vanity can go unnoticed for a long time since they're usually at the back of the cabinet. Water can run down the pipes into the floor or subfloor, rotting the sink base, the floor and the framing.

Check for supply leaks: Don't rely on your sense of touch to find tiny leaks. Wipe each connection with a dry tissue. Then look for a wet spot on the tissue.

Signs of trouble:

- Puddles, dampness or water stains inside the cabinet.
- Stains on the ceiling below.

How to find the source:

- Dab shutoffs and connections with a dry tissue or paper towel and look for wet spots (**photo, above**).
- Run the dishwasher and check for leaks under it.

How to fix it:

- If the valve stem on a shutoff valve drips, tighten the packing nut. If the leak doesn't stop, replace the valve.
- For other leaks at the shutoff valve or at the faucet, try tightening the compression nut first. If that doesn't stop the leak, disassemble the fitting, coat the ferrule or gasket with Teflon joint compound (available at home centers and hardware stores) and reassemble the connection.

Drain leaks

Drain leaks in kitchens and bathrooms usually occur at the drain or at the slip joints in the drainpipe. Hidden behind boxes and bottles, these leaks can damage flooring, cabinets and even ceilings below before you notice them.

Signs of trouble:

- Puddles, water stains or a dank odor in the cabinet.
- Loose or damaged flooring in front of the sink.

How to find the source:

- Fill the sink bowls, then as they drain check all joints from the sink to the wall with a dry tissue (**photo, above**).
- Run and drain the dishwasher and check the waste hose connection.

How to fix it:

- For a slip joint leak, first tighten the slip nut. If that doesn't work, disassemble the joint, coat the washer with Teflon joint compound and reassemble.
- For a leak from the basket strainer, tighten the ring nut under the sink. If the leak continues, disconnect and remove the basket strainer. Reassemble it using plumber's putty as a sealant under the basket's rim.

True stories from readers

"The caulk around my cast iron sink was in bad shape, but I didn't worry about it until the plastic laminate in front of it began to loosen. The particleboard under the sink rim was black and swollen. I had to replace all my countertops at a cost of $800. I'm glad the old countertop warned me—with a few more months of rot, that 100-lb. sink could have fallen into the cabinet below."

STOP LEAKS **AROUND THE HOUSE**

Test for hidden leaks

The vast majority of leaks occur at or near plumbing fixtures like tubs, sinks and toilets. But if you suspect a leak in the water supply system, there's a simple way to check it— even if the pipes are hidden inside walls. First, turn off all your faucets.

If you have drippy faucets or a toilet that runs between flushes, close the shutoff valves. Then go to your water meter and check the position of the "1-cubic-foot" dial (**photo, right**). Check the dial again two hours later. If the dial has moved, you have a leak in the water supply.

Turn off all the faucets and check the 1-cu.-ft. dial on the water meter to test for hidden leaks.

Two slow leaks that signal catastrophe

If you notice puddles near your water heater, check the pressure relief valve and the drain valve. If either is dripping, replace the valve. If not, the tank is leaking and you need a new water heater. Don't delay. Tank leaks often start slow and then suddenly burst days or weeks later, causing a major household flood.

The same goes for washing machine supply hoses. If you notice a tiny leak in the hose itself or at the crimped metal fittings at the ends, replace the hose. Otherwise the hose may eventually burst, releasing a continuous flow of water.

STOP **TUB AND SHOWER LEAKS**

Splash leaks

Splash leaks are simply water escaping past a shower curtain or a shower door. Plumbers tell us it's the most common type of bathroom leak. Although it may sound minor, this leak causes major damage when water seeps into the subfloor where flooring meets the tub or shower. Before long the vinyl flooring or tiles begin to loosen. Even worse, the plywood subfloor delaminates and rots, requiring a huge, expensive tearout and replacement project.

Signs of trouble:

- Curling vinyl flooring or loose tiles next to the tub.
- Peeling paint or flaking, chalky-looking wood finish near the shower.
- Water stains on the ceiling or joists below.
- Mold spots on the wall or floor near the tub or shower.
- If you use a curtain, look for standing water on the floor after you shower.

How to find the source:

- If you have a shower door, splash water all around the door and frame. Leaks around the frame may take five minutes or longer to show up.
- If the door has rubber gaskets or a rubber door sweep, check them for gaps.
- Also check for any gaps in the caulk where the shower or tub meets the flooring.

How to fix it:

- Be sure to overlap sliding doors correctly when you close them. The inner door should be closest to the faucet.
- If you have a shower curtain rather than a door, make sure you close it completely when you shower, or add a splash guard.
- Seal a leaking frame by running a small bead of caulk around the inside of the frame. Force the caulk into any gaps between the frame and the shower surround. Quickly wipe away all the excess caulk. When the caulk dries, test for leaks again.
- Replace any worn gaskets or door sweeps. Bring the old one to a home center or plumbing supply store and look for a matching replacement.
- If the old caulk along the floor shows gaps, scrape it out and run a new bead.

OVERFLOW

DRAIN

GAP ALONG SHOWER CURTAIN

CAULK JOINT

Figure B
Tub and shower leaks

The most damaging tub and shower leaks occur when water splashes out of the enclosure. Tile and drain leaks can also cause major damage.

Test a shower door: Splash water all around a shower door. If water seeps out from behind the frame, caulk the frame on the inside. Run a new bead along the floor/tub joint.

SHOWER DOOR

FRAME

Drain leaks

Drain leaks allow water to sneak around the outside of the drain where it's connected to the tub or shower. This is especially common with plastic or fiberglass tubs and shower pans, since these materials flex slightly when you stand on them, often breaking the seal around the drain. These leaks can stain or destroy the ceiling below or rot floor joists. In the case of a tub set on a concrete slab, the leak will ruin flooring in the bathroom or adjoining rooms.

WALL FRAMING

GROUT

CAULK

Signs of trouble:
- Water stains on the ceiling or joists below.
- Loose flooring near the tub or damp floors in adjoining rooms (if the tub is on a concrete slab).

How to find the source:
- If you can see the underside of the drain through an access panel or open ceiling, partially fill the tub and then release the water. In a shower, plug the drain with a rag and then release the water. Check the drains and traps for leaks from below through the access panel.
- If you don't have access to the underside of the drain, plug the drain and add enough water to form a small puddle around the drain (**bottom photo**). Mark the edge of the puddle by setting a bottle of shampoo next to it. Then wait an hour. If the puddle shrinks, the drain is leaking. Don't rely on your tub stopper for this test; it may leak. Remove the stopper and insert a 1-1/2-in. test plug ($5 to $10 at home centers). Remove the grate and use a 2-in. plug for a shower.

Test a drain: Plug the drain with a test plug and add water. After an hour, check to see if the water level has dropped.

TEST PLUG

DRAIN GRATE

How to fix it:
- To repair a tub drain, unscrew the drain flange from above. Then clean the flange and apply silicone caulk. Also remove the rubber gasket that's under the tub's drain hole and take it to a home center to find a matching gasket. Slip the new gasket into place and screw in the drain flange. For more, go to thefamilyhandyman.com and search for "bathtub drain."
- If you have access to a shower drain from below, tighten the ring nut that locks the drain to the shower pan. If that doesn't work, replace the drain assembly ($15). If you don't have access beneath the drain, cut a hole in the ceiling below or replace the drain assembly with a WingTite drain ($65; plumbrite.com).

Tile leaks

Tile leaks occur when water seeps through deteriorating grout or caulk and gets into the wall behind the tile (**Figure B**). Depending on the materials used to set the tile, this can lead to tile falling off the wall, severe rotting of the wall framing, and damage to the subfloor, joists or ceiling below.

Signs of trouble:
- Loose tiles.
- Persistent mold.
- If the shower is against an exterior wall, you may find an area of peeling paint outside.
- Stains on the ceiling under the shower.

How to find the source:
- Examine the grout and caulk joints for gaps. You almost always find mold here.
- If you have loose tile behind the tub spout or faucet, open the access panel behind the faucet and look for dampness or stains.

How to fix it:
- Remove the old grout, caulk and loose tiles.
- If the surface behind the tile is still solid, you can reattach tiles, regrout and recaulk.
- If more than a few tiles are loose or if the wall is spongy, you'll have to install new backer board and tile, or a fiberglass surround.

> **True stories from readers**
> *"I noticed the floor tile along the tub was coming loose. I pushed on it and it crunched down into the underlayment, which was totally rotten. We ended up replacing all of the tile and part of the subfloor."*

STOP **TOILET FLANGE LEAKS**

Toilet flange leaks

These leaks occur where the toilet meets the waste pipe below. They allow water to seep out at every flush, which will wreck flooring, rot the sub-floor and joists, and damage the ceiling below (**right photo**).

Signs of trouble:

- Water seeping out around the base of the toilet.
- Loose or damaged flooring.
- Stains on the ceiling below.
- A toilet that rocks slightly when you push against it. This movement will eventually break the wax seal between the toilet and the closet flange.

How to find the source:

If you have ceiling stains, measure from stacked walls (**right photo**) before you go through the hassle of removing the toilet. If the stain is near the toilet, a leaking flange is the most likely source. Remove the toilet (**far right photo**) and look for these leak sources:

- The flange is level with or below the surrounding floor surface.
- Cracks in the flange.
- Bolts or the slots they fit into are broken.
- The flange is loose, not screwed solidly to the subfloor.

How to fix it:

- If you don't find any of the problems listed above, reinstall the toilet with a new wax ring.
- If the flange is too low, install a plastic flange riser over the existing flange.
- If the flange or bolt slots are broken, install a metal repair flange.
- If the toilet rocks because the floor is uneven, slip toilet shims under the toilet when you reinstall it. 🏠

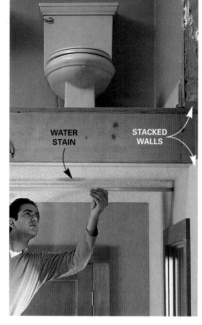

WATER STAIN

STACKED WALLS

Locate the source: Take measurements from stacked walls to find the source of a ceiling stain. In most cases, the stain occurs close to the source.

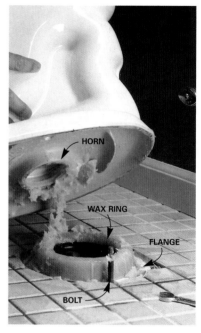

HORN

WAX RING

FLANGE

BOLT

Check for flange leaks: Unscrew the toilet bolt nuts and remove the toilet. Scrape away the wax and look for leaks. Also check for cracks around the toilet's horn.

FLANGE

WAX RING

Figure C
Toilet leaks

Toilet leaks can come from the water supply or tank, but the most damaging leaks occur at the flange and wax ring.

True stories from readers

"I had noticed the toilet rocking slightly for a few years, but I kept putting off the repair. Then one day the ceiling under the toilet fell in. It turned out that the wax ring had been leaking for years. The subfloor around the toilet was rotted, and the more it rotted, the more the toilet rocked and the more water leaked out with every flush."

Handy Hints ®

NO-SEIZE FAUCET HANDLES

Corrosion can "weld" faucet handles onto valve stems, making future repairs a headache. A dab of plumber's silicone grease will prevent this.

AQUARIUM TUBING

SIPHON BEFORE SOLDERING

Before soldering water pipe that you can't drain, use aquarium tubing to siphon the excess water out of a vertical copper pipe between the plumbing shutoff valve and the faucet. Once the water is out, you can solder the joint with ease.

NEW TRAP

EMPTY THE TRAP

Before you remove a sink trap, give the drain a few plunges with a toilet plunger. This will push most of the water out of the trap, lessening the mess when you pull the trap. If you have a double sink, be sure to plug the other drain to contain the air pressure. If the strainer isn't a screw-down style, you'll have to hold it down while you plunge the drain.

PLUMBING WITH **PEX**

This new water supply pipe is easy to install and may just show up in your home. Here's how to work with it.

by **Kurt Anderson**

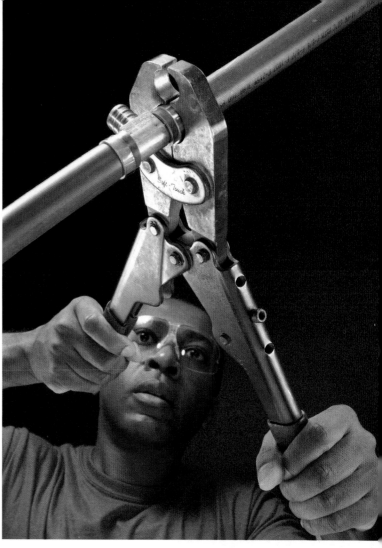

Step into just about any house built in the past 50 years, and odds are, you're going to see one of three materials used for the water supply lines: copper, steel or CPVC. While these three materials are reliable and fairly easy to work with, a new flexible tubing called PEX ("cross-linked" polyethylene) has become popular with many plumbers. PEX has been used for many years for in-floor heating systems but only more recently for supply lines. You may find it in a newer home, and, since it's easy to work with, you might consider it as an alternative to traditional materials when running new water lines. It's now available at many home centers. In this article, we'll introduce you to PEX and show you the basic techniques for working with it.

THE **ADVANTAGES** OF PEX

PEX, a flexible tubing that comes in long rolls, offers several advantages over traditional piping. First, you can usually make long continuous runs, eliminating most elbows and joints. You can snake long runs through joists and studs (**Photo 1**, p. 111). Second, PEX doesn't sweat under high humidity conditions, and it's also resistant to bursting, even if the lines freeze solid. Third, joints are easier. You add fittings simply by crimping metal rings over barbed fittings using a special crimping tool. Crimping takes seconds and is virtually error-free, avoiding the hassle of soldering (copper) and the fumes and mess of cementing (CPVC).

However, PEX has a couple of drawbacks. First, the crimper is expensive, about $100. You can sometimes rent one (about $15 per day), but each manufacturer wants you to use its proprietary crimping tool for its tubing. The rental store might not carry the right one. A second drawback is a somewhat sloppy appearance. And third, the fittings are more expensive than for copper and CPVC systems. The overall cost of materials is about the same as for other systems.

Some home centers may stock more than one brand of PEX. Buy the same brand of pipe, fittings and tools to ensure proper installation and fulfill warranty conditions.

Check with a local plumbing inspector for local requirements and read the manufacturer's directions, which may vary slightly from what we show here.

 **Tip**

Mark the barbed fitting with a permanent marker once you've made the crimp. Before turning the water back on, go through and check for the mark on each fitting to make sure it's been crimped.

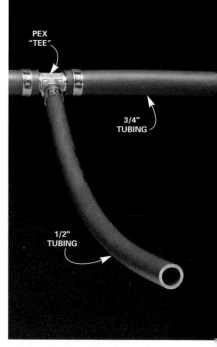

PEX "TEE"

3/4" TUBING

1/2" TUBING

PEX is a somewhat flexible plastic pipe that you can run for water supply lines much like copper or CPVC.

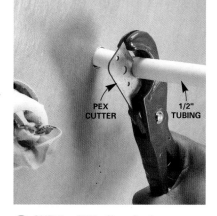

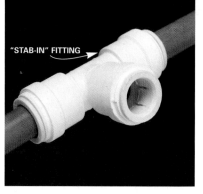

1 MAKE connections with special crimp fittings in which you clamp a copper ring around an inner fitting sleeve.

2 CUT the PEX off perfectly square for leakproof joints. This special PEX cutter costs $15.

3 USE stab-in fittings only where you have access to the joint. These fittings don't require a special tool. You simply push the pipe into the openings. Press the outer ring onto the fitting to release the pipe.

MAKE **CRIMPED JOINTS** AT FITTINGS

The heart and soul of the PEX system is the barbed fitting/ crimping ring combination (**Photo 1**, above). There's no need for solder, glue or pipe wrenches—just position the crimping ring over the end of the PEX pipe, slide the pipe over the barbed fitting and use the special crimping tool to compress the ring. Just be sure to center the ring over the barb and depress the crimping tool's handles completely. Fittings cost $1 to $3.

That's it. The resulting seal is watertight. The crimping tool shown can be used for both 3/4-in. and 1/2-in. crimps, important when you're running several sizes of pipe. If you make a mistake in crimping, you can use a special decrimping tool ($40) to remove the ring and then reuse the fitting. A clean, square cut is essential for a proper seal; the PEX cutter ($15) shown in **Photo 2** (above) works great and is available anywhere PEX is sold.

Another type of fitting for joints is the "stab-in" fitting ($4 to $7; **Photo 3**, above). You simply push the ends of the PEX into the fitting, where it locks in place. These fittings are available for most situations, including joining PEX to copper and to CPVC. However, we don't recommend them unless you have easy future access to the joint.

PLAN FOR **STUB-OUTS** IN ADVANCE

There are a couple of options for bringing PEX out through a wall (stub-outs). If the piping is going to be exposed, say for a pedestal sink or a toilet, buy a copper stub-out and crimp it onto the PEX (**Photo 1**, right). Then use standard shutoff valves. If the stub-out will be hidden, inside a cabinet, for example, or you don't mind the look of exposed PEX line, use a barbed PEX shutoff valve (**Photo 2**, right).

Whichever method you use, be sure to add a couple of extra fasteners next to the stub-out to increase stability.

1 USE special copper stub-outs for more visible locations. Cut off the tube and mount a standard shutoff valve.

2 MAKE tight turns with 90-degree angle fittings. For hidden stub-outs, use shutoff valves designed for PEX.

FITTINGS FOR A **SHOWER VALVE**

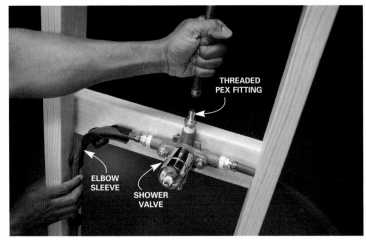

Most shower valves have threaded ports for the supply lines. Tighten the threaded fittings into the shower valve before crimping on the PEX line. Then run the lines through the studs (**Photo 1**, left), make 90-degree turns with a plastic or metal elbow sleeve, or crimp in right-angle fittings in tight quarters. Splice in shutoff valves as well (**Photo 2**, left).

Then, install "drop-ear elbows" to stabilize the spouts and/or showerhead assemblies, just as you normally would (**Photo 3**, left). Once you've secured your drop-ear elbows and threaded fittings, run the PEX line between the valve and the drop-ear elbows and crimp each joint.

1 USE threaded fittings for shower valves. Tighten the fittings before crimping the PEX. A plastic bracket forms the sharpest 90-degree angle permitted for this brand of PEX.

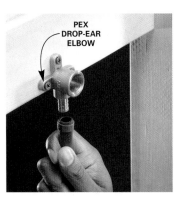

2 CRIMP PEX shutoff valves into the hot and cold lines.

3 USE drop-ear fittings designed for PEX for the shower arm and tub spout.

Precautions
Although PEX can be used for hot water supply and in-floor heating, it can melt if run next to exhaust vents on water heaters. Use special 18-in. copper extensions if you run PEX near these vents.

Since PEX won't burst when it freezes, you might be tempted to use it for seasonal dwellings, such as cabins. PEX is soft, however, and rodents could chew through exposed lines.

TRANSITIONS TO OTHER TYPES OF PIPE

If you're adding a guest bath or finally getting to that laundry tub you've been promising for the past five years, you'll have to join PEX to the existing system. Make sure you shut off the main water supply, then drain the lines. Use the special transition fittings shown (right) to transition from copper, CPVC or steel. Solder, glue or thread on the transition fitting, then crimp PEX line on the barbed fitting.

Note: Plumbing codes vary on allowing brass/steel connections. If they're allowed, be sure to apply liberal amounts of both Teflon tape and pipe joint compound to prevent reaction between the two metals.

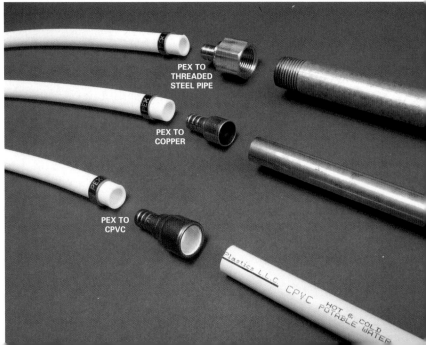

RUN THE LINE WITHOUT JOINTS

You can run PEX line a couple of different ways. Most often, you run PEX as you would in a conventional plumbing system, with 3/4-in. main lines and 1/2-in. branch lines (**bottom photo**, p. 108). You can also use a "manifold" system, where you run a 1/2-in. line to each fixture from a central spot. But we won't show that system here.

Run your main lines first—don't worry about cutting in your branch lines yet. If you're running PEX through joists or studs, drill 3/4-in. holes for 1/2-in. piping and 1-in. holes for 3/4-in. piping. You don't have to drill holes in an exact straight line; there's enough flex in the pipe to feed it through misaligned holes. Have a helper feed the line to avoid kinks and snarls (**Photo 1**, right). Where the pipe runs along a surface, be sure to support it every 16 to 24 in. to reduce sag and give the piping a neat appearance (**Photo 2**, right). Some manufacturers recommend adding "suspension clips" (not shown) at each hole to prevent abrasion. You must use suspension clips for PEX that goes through metal studs, and nail protection plates when the tubing runs within 1-1/2 in. of the face of a stud or joist.

Once you've run your main line, mark the location of each branch line with a marker, leaving a 1-in. gap for the barbed tee. Cut the 1-in. gap out of the main line, crimp your tees into place and run your branch lines to the appropriate fixtures (**bottom photo**, p. 108). This eliminates the need to measure each section of main line and makes installation faster and easier.

You can generally flex PEX into gradual bends without risking a kink (**Photo 2**, right). When you need to turn a corner, many times you can bend the pipe manually and eliminate the need for an elbow. But different brands of PEX have different "kinking" points, so always read the manufacturer's guidelines. Buy special plastic or metal elbows (**Photo 1**, p. 110) to make the tightest recommended turns virtually kink-proof.

If you need to make a really sharp turn, cut the line and use a copper 90-degree ell (**Photo 2**, bottom, p. 109).

1 SNAKE a single length of PEX through joists and between floors. It doesn't require joints unless you have tight turns. Have a helper feed it to avoid kinks in the plastic.

GRADUAL BEND

PEX SUPPORT CLAMP

2 SUPPORT PEX every 24 in. and at turns with special clamps.

FLIP A SWITCH, SAVE $200

*8 quick furnace fixes
you can do yourself*

by **Eric Smith**

Look for simple solutions first

A furnace can be intimidating—especially when it's not working. However, there is good news from furnace repair pros. Roughly a quarter of all service calls could be avoided with easy fixes that cost little or nothing.

In this article, we'll focus on the common culprits and show you what to do about them.

SAFETY NOTE: Always turn off the shutoff switch (see No. 2 on p. 114) and turn the thermostat off or all the way down before changing the filter or working on the thermostat or furnace.

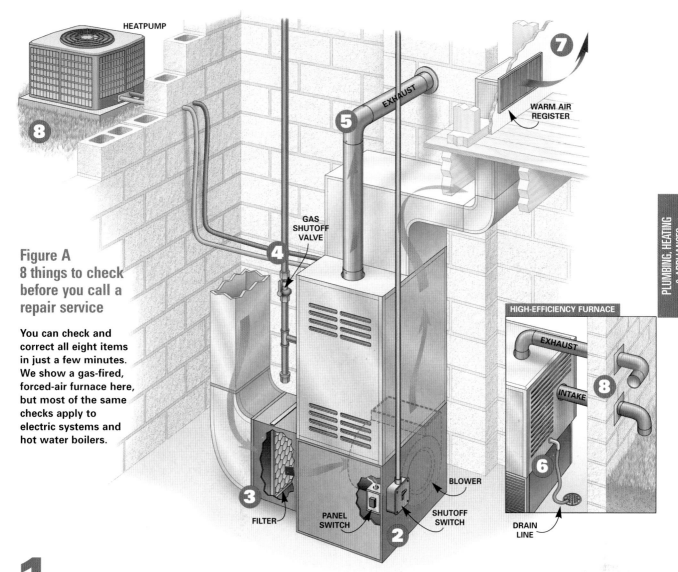

HEATPUMP

EXHAUST

⑤

⑦

WARM AIR
REGISTER

GAS
SHUTOFF
VALVE

④

**Figure A
8 things to check
before you call a
repair service**

You can check and
correct all eight items
in just a few minutes.
We show a gas-fired,
forced-air furnace here,
but most of the same
checks apply to
electric systems and
hot water boilers.

HIGH-EFFICIENCY FURNACE

EXHAUST

INTAKE

⑧

⑥

③

BLOWER

FILTER

PANEL
SWITCH

②

SHUTOFF
SWITCH

DRAIN
LINE

⑧

1 Check the thermostat to make sure it's on

THERMOSTAT

Before you assume you have a furnace problem, check the
thermostat to make sure it's actually telling the furnace to
come on. Thermostats, especially programmable ones, can
be complicated, and the more options a thermostat has,
the more that can go wrong.

■ Make sure the
switch is on
"Heat" rather than
on "Cool."
■ Check the tempera-
ture setting.
■ Compare the tem-
perature setting to
the room temperature. Set the temperature five degrees
higher than the room temperature and see if the furnace kicks on.
■ Make sure the program is displaying the right day and
time, as well as a.m. and p.m. settings.

Tip Lost your owner's
manual? Most major-
brand manuals are
on the Web—just go
to the manufacturer's
Web site.

■ Trace the thermostat wires back
to the furnace to check for
breaks, especially if you've done
any remodeling recently. If you find
a break in one of the thin wires, splice
the line back together and wrap it with electrical tape.
■ Replace the battery. If you have a power outage with a
dead battery, you'll lose your settings and the thermostat will revert to the default program.
■ Open the thermostat and gently blow out any dust
or debris. Make sure it's level and firmly attached on
the wall, and that none of the wires coming into it
are loose.
■ If you can't make the program settings work, you can
bypass them altogether. Simply punch in the temperature you want with the up/down control and then press
the hold button. That will switch on the furnace if the
thermostat programming is the problem.

2 Check shutoff switches and breakers

It sounds unbelievable, but furnace technicians often find that the only "repair" a furnace needs is to be turned on. Look for a standard wall switch on or near the furnace—all furnaces, no matter what age or type, have one somewhere. Check the circuit breaker or fuse for the furnace as well. Make sure the front panel covering the blower motor is securely fastened—there's a push-in switch under it that must be fully depressed for the furnace to operate.

3 Make sure the chimney exhaust flue is clear

Drawn by the warmth, birds sometimes fall into the chimney exhaust flue. Turn the furnace off and the thermostat all the way down, then dismantle the duct where it exits the furnace and check for debris. Be sure to reassemble the sections in the same order and direction that you took them out.

4 Change filters

Dirty filters are the most common cause of furnace problems. Dust and dirt restrict airflow—and if the filter gets too clogged, the heat exchanger will overheat and shut off too quickly, and your house won't warm up. If the blower is running but no heat is coming out, replace the filter. A dirty filter also causes soot buildup on the heat exchanger, reducing the efficiency of the furnace and shortening its life.

The owner's manual shows where the filter is and how to remove it. Change inexpensive flat filters at least once a

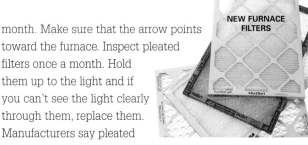

month. Make sure that the arrow points toward the furnace. Inspect pleated filters once a month. Hold them up to the light and if you can't see the light clearly through them, replace them. Manufacturers say pleated filters are good for three months, but change them more frequently if you have pets, kids or generate lots of dust.

5 Clean away leaves and debris from heat pumps or intake and exhaust valves

If you have a furnace that vents out the side of the house, make sure nothing is blocking the intake or exhaust. If either of the pipes is covered with screen mesh (like window screen), replace it with 1/2-in.-mesh hardware cloth. If ice is clogging one of the pipes, you have a bigger problem somewhere in the system. Clear it off and call a technician to find out why it's happening.

If you have a heat pump, clear away grass and leaves from the fins of the outdoor compressor unit. Before heating season starts, hose it down gently from the top to rinse dirt and debris out of the housing.

6 Flush out drain lines

High-efficiency furnaces can drain off several gallons of water a day in heating season. If the drain lines become restricted by sediment or mold growth, the furnace will shut down. If the drain hose looks dirty, remove the hose, fill it with a mixture of bleach and water (25 percent bleach), then flush it after several minutes.

7 Make sure the gas is on

Just as with switches, someone may have turned off a gas valve and then forgotten to turn it back on. Trace the gas line back from the furnace to the meter, and if you see a handle that's perpendicular to the gas pipe, turn it so it's parallel.

If you have an old furnace or boiler, you may have a pilot light. Remove the front panel and the burner cover and check to make sure it's lit.

8 Look for blocked or leaky ducts that can restrict airflow

If your furnace comes on but one or two rooms are cold, first make sure all the room registers are open. Then examine any ductwork you can get access to and look for gaps between sections or branching points. Seal any gaps between sections of duct with special metal duct tape. Don't use standard cloth duct tape—it quickly deteriorates, and it may also cause ducts to leak if it was used to seal sections in the past.

Also check for handles protruding from the ductwork. These are dampers or air conditioner bypasses—make sure they're open.

GreatGoofs®

Attention-getting dryer

I was installing a new, quieter dryer in a client's high-end house. The power cord was unattached and had exposed connectors at one end. Like an idiot, I pushed the plug into the 240-volt outlet to see if the prongs fit. Well, the connectors at the other end were all touching one another and—WHAM!

The loose ends shorted out and knocked me clear over. This in turn set off the house alarm system, alerted the police and set every dog in the neighborhood barking.

It's bad enough to goof—it's far worse to have to explain your screwup to your client and your boss, a crowd of curious onlookers and the police.

No free lunch

I decided to save the price of a plumber and replace the kitchen faucet myself. After installing a new faucet, I treated myself to lunch out with all that money I had saved.

I returned two hours later to about an inch of standing water on the first floor. Apparently, I had neglected to properly tighten a compression fitting at the supply valve under the sink.

After replacing the carpet and having all the wood floors sanded and refinished (ouch!), I now hire a plumber and watch him work while I eat lunch in.

Housewarming gift

My wife and I had just moved into our first house and a few days later decided to celebrate with a night out on the town. When we got home, I slipped into the dimly lit bathroom, lifted the toilet lid and slammed it back down in horror! How much beer had I had?

I turned on the lights, brought in my wife and we confirmed that yes, that indeed was a huge, very dead squirrel floating in the bowl.

I guess when a home inspector suggests you put a critter guard over the end of the plumbing vent on the roof, he means now. We'd planned on getting to that little task soon, but apparently not soon enough.

Even with the critter guard securely in place, we still have a houseful of squirrels, as friends and relatives send us lots of ceramic and stuffed varieties to remind us of our first houseguest.

Do's&Don'ts

SOLDERING **COPPER**

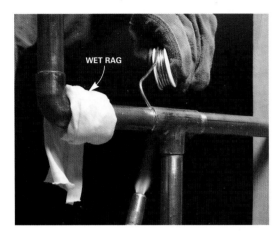

WET RAG

Do keep nearby soldered joints from melting by wrapping a wet rag around them. Wet and wring out a 2-in.-wide strip of cloth and wrap it around the fitting you want to protect. The wet rag absorbs the heat and prevents the solder in the existing joint from melting.

Do use MAPP gas to speed up the job. Lead-free solder melts at a higher temperature than the now-banned lead-based solder. MAPP gas torches burn hotter than propane, making them a better choice for modern solder. Five to 10 seconds of heating with a MAPP gas torch is all that's required before you can feed solder into most 1/2- to 3/4-in. pipes and fittings. Be careful, though. It's easier to overheat a joint with MAPP gas. If the flux turns black and the solder won't flow into the fitting, the joint is overheated.

Don't solder close to wood or other flammable material without protecting it from the flame.

Do use a flame protector. These small flame-retardant blankets are available for $15 each at hardware stores and home centers. You hang one behind the joint you're working on to insulate the flammable material and help prevent fires. In a pinch you could use a piece of sheet metal instead. Wetting the area around the soldering job with a spray bottle of water also helps prevent fires. Keep a fire extinguisher handy as a precaution.

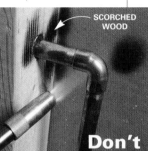

SCORCHED WOOD

Don't

FLAME PROTECTOR

Do

Don't reuse old fittings. Recycle them instead. It's time consuming and difficult to take apart and clean old fittings. And there's a good chance they'll leak.

Do buy new fittings instead. You'll get better results in less time.

Don't feed too much solder into the joint. It's tempting to melt a few inches of solder into a joint as extra insurance against leaking. But excess solder can puddle inside pipes, restricting water flow, and can form small balls that break loose and damage faucet valves.

SOLDER BUILDUP

Do use about 1/2 in. of solder for 1/2-in. pipe and 3/4 in. for 3/4-in. pipe. Here's a tip. Bend the end of the solder at a right angle, leaving a few inches below the bend. The bend makes it easier to gauge how much solder you've used.

Do use tinning flux. Tinning flux works just like standard flux but contains a bit of silver solder powder that melts when heat is applied. The resulting thin layer of solder helps ensure a leak-proof joint. Tinning flux is available at most hardware stores and home centers and only costs a little more than standard flux.

FLUX BRUSH

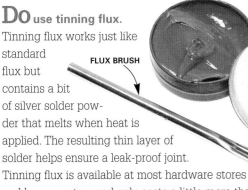

Do cut, flux and assemble a section of pipes and solder them all at once. Soldering one joint at a time is inefficient. Use pipe straps to support the pipes if necessary. Be careful to clean and flux the end of every pipe and the inside of the fittings before assembling them. Then just before you start soldering, press the pipes firmly into the fittings to make sure they're fully seated. Start soldering at one end of the assembly and move methodically from one joint to the next.

SOLDER

Don't get solder on threaded fittings. It can clog the threads, making it difficult to get a good seal when you screw on the matching part.

SOLDER ON THREAD

Do follow these steps to avoid the problem. If the threaded fitting is positioned so that solder will run down onto the threads, solder the pipe and fitting at a workbench instead so you can keep the fitting pointed up. If you have to solder a threaded fitting where the solder will flow onto the threads, make sure to wipe excess flux from around the joint after you assemble the pipe and fitting. Extra flux can run down onto the threads, causing the solder to follow it.

THREADS UP

VISE

Don't solder pipes with water in them. When you're repairing or tying in to existing copper pipes, it's common to find a small amount of water even after you close the valve and drain the pipes. Soldering a joint in pipes that contain water is nearly impossible. Most of the heat from the torch goes into turning the water to steam, so the copper won't get hot enough to melt the solder.

Do stop the trickle of water with a pipe plug. Push the plug into the pipe with the applicator tube provided. When you're done soldering, dissolve the plug by holding the torch under the spot where the plug is. A pack of plugs for 1/2-in. or 3/4-in. pipe costs from $8 to $10. You'll find the plugs at home centers and hardware stores.

An old trick was to stuff a wad of soft white bread into the pipe to stop the trickle of water temporarily. This works but you run the risk of clogging aerators and valves with the partially dissolved bread.

HOLDS WATER BACK

PLUG PUSHER

PIPE PLUG

10 PITFALLS OF
SINK REPLACEMENT

Read on to learn how to avoid hassles when replacing a sink

by **Brett Martin**

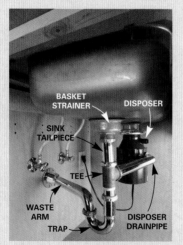

Replacing a sink and faucet is a quick, easy way to spruce up your kitchen. In most cases, the whole job takes less than a day. But there are problems that can sneak up if you haven't planned ahead and aren't sure what to watch out for.

In this article, we'll show you the most common problems that could turn your project into a nightmare—and tell you how to avoid them.

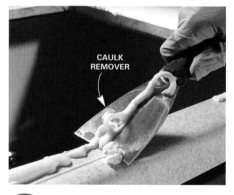

CAULK REMOVER

1 Got your eye on a deeper sink? Measure the tailpiece first!

You can choose a new sink with a deeper basin than the existing sink has, but if it hangs down too low, it won't drain properly and you'll have to lower the sanitary tee connection in the drain line inside the wall. You'll definitely want to avoid this task if the connection is metal and ends up being behind base cabinets. Plastic pipe is easier—if you can get to it easily. The actual tee connection may be several studs over from where the waste arm enters the wall.

Measure the sink tailpiece between the basket strainer and the tee. That measurement is the extra depth that can be added to the sink bowl without lowering the drainpipe going into the wall. Also

BASKET STRAINER | DISPOSER
SINK TAILPIECE
TEE
WASTE ARM
TRAP
DISPOSER DRAINPIPE

be aware that a new disposer may have a lower drainpipe than your existing one—but it can't be lower than the tee. If the disposer drainpipe will be too low, consider a sink with different depth bowls. You'll have a deep bowl for dishes and a shallow one for the disposer.

2 Remove ALL the old caulk

The caulk around your new sink is all that'll stand between your countertop and water damage. For a lasting, watertight bond with the countertop, you have to completely remove the old caulk.

Remove the old sink, then scrape off the caulk (or plumber's putty) with a putty knife. Apply a caulk remover ($10 at home centers) to stubborn caulk. Let the caulk remover sit for a couple of hours, then scrape off the softened caulk. Finally, use rubbing alcohol or nail polish remover to wipe off residue, and then clean the surface with a sponge and water.

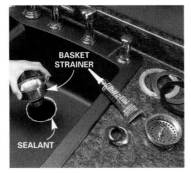

STEEL DRAINPIPE • CORRODED THREADS • TRANSITION COUPLING • PLASTIC TRAP ADAPTER

3 Seal with caulk, not putty

Plumber's putty has long been the standard sealant for sink baskets and sometimes even sink rims. The problem with putty is that it eventually dries out, cracks and causes leaks. Worse, it can damage some plastics, including some of the plastics used to make sinks. Avoid drips and disasters by using a silicone caulk instead.

Use a kitchen-and-bath 100 percent silicone that requires solvent cleanup. A tube costs $4 at home centers. Apply a bead around the sink opening when you set in the sink and around the drain opening when you set the disposer drain and basket strainer. Wipe away excess caulk.

SINK CLIP • SEALANT

BASKET STRAINER • SEALANT

4 Rusty old pipe? Cheat!

Corroded steel drainpipes are a bear to work with, since the slip nuts are almost impossible to loosen or retighten. You can easily bypass those rusty old threads by adding a section of plastic pipe.

If the slip nut attached to the drainpipe in the wall won't come off, spray on WD-40 and try a bigger wrench. If that doesn't work, cut off the drainpipe with a hacksaw (save as much of the threaded area as possible). Then buy a plastic trap adapter, a transition coupling and a piece of plastic pipe (PVC or ABS) and cement ($10 altogether at home centers). Cement the adapter to a 4-in. section of pipe, then place the coupler over the other end of the pipe and over the steel drainpipe.

5 Make sure the new sink will cover the old hole

SQUARE CORNER • OLD SINK

A sink that's too small for the countertop opening will leave ugly gaps along the sides (or even fall right through the hole!). Before removing the existing sink, measure the opening from underneath. Measure all four sides because the cutout may not be square. Pay special attention to the corners. Contractors often cut them at 90-degree angles (instead of rounding them off) because it's faster.

Take the measurements with you when buying the new sink and make sure it'll cover the opening, including any square corners. If you can't find a sink that'll fit, buy a larger one and enlarge the opening.

6 Swollen countertops spell trouble

WATER STAIN

Leaks around a sink rim can soak the particleboard under a plastic laminate countertop. A little water damage is normal and won't interfere with your new sink. But severe swelling will prevent the new sink from sitting flat on the countertop. And crumbling particleboard won't provide a solid base for the clips that fasten the sink to the countertop.

Look at the countertop surface around the sink. Check for bulges or areas where the laminate has loosened from the particleboard. Then look at the countertop from under the sink for areas that are too spongy to support sink clips or support the sink itself. If you find any of these problems, replace the countertop.

Get the gunk out

Working on the water lines always shakes sediment loose. The last thing you want is for these deposits to clog your new faucet. Avoid this problem by purging the lines before hooking up the new supply lines.

Once the entire project is complete and the new supply lines are attached to the faucet, fasten the old supply lines to the shutoff valves. Next, turn the water all the way on for a full minute to wash away any debris in the lines. Then attach the new lines to the shutoff valves. After three days, take the aerator off the faucet and rinse away any sediment that has seeped through.

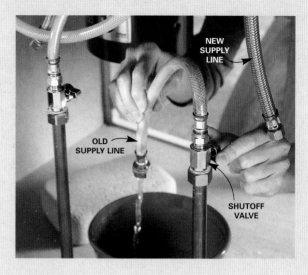

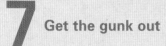 **Make sure you have enough holes**

Most sinks have three holes for the faucet and a fourth for an accessory, such as a sprayer or a soap dispenser. But some faucets require only one or two holes, and you may not want enough accessories to use the rest. You can buy plugs for unused holes, but they usually don't match the sink. If the sink doesn't have enough holes, cutting an extra hole in stainless steel or cast iron is often difficult or impossible.

To avoid these hassles, choose the faucet and accessories first, then buy a sink with a matching number of holes. Some sinks have "knockouts" that you  can drill to provide extra holes. You can also special-order a sink with the number of holes you need.

9 Trash all the old parts

Resist the temptation to save a few bucks by reusing the old drainpipes. The threads are probably corroded and won't form a tight connection. A new drain assembly is easier to install and less likely to leak.

Instead of shopping for each individual part for the drain, buy a kit at a home center that has everything you need. A sink kit ($30) includes drainpipes, fittings, shutoff valves, supply lines and new basket strainers.

10 Test the shutoff valves first

If the shutoff valves under your sink don't work or you don't have any, you'll have to turn off the water supply to the entire house while replacing the sink. This could cause domestic strife, especially if the job turns into a half day or longer project, so make sure the valves work before going to the home center.

To test the valves, close them and turn on the faucet. The faucet may drip for a minute or two, but if the drip continues, the shutoff valves are leaking. Repair or replace old valves. If you're buying new ones, use quarter-turn ball-type shutoff valves. They're more reliable and less likely to leak at the packing nut. ⏏

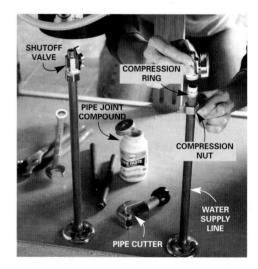

120

4 Woodworking & Furniture Projects, Tools & Tips

IN THIS CHAPTER

Workshop Tips 122
*Space-saving cutting and finishing
bench, flashing shield for sanding
and more*

Classic Arch-Top Bookcases 126

Summer Lounge Chair 132

Charging Station 136

Wordless Workshop: *Bathroom
Reading Rack* 138

WorkshopTips™

CHOPPING BOARD AND SERVING TRAY

Slice, dice and serve in style on this easy, cutting-edge project. We'll show you a simple way to dry-fit the parts, scribe the arc and then glue the whole works together. We used a 4-ft. steel ruler to scribe the arcs, but a yardstick or any thin board would also work. Be sure to use water-resistant wood glue and keep your tray out of the dishwasher or it might fall apart. And one more thing: Keep the boards as even as possible during glue-up to minimize sanding later.

MATERIALS LIST

ITEM	QTY.
20-in. x 3-1/2-in. maple boards	3
23-1/2-in. x 1/2-in. x 3/4-in. walnut strips (handle strips)	2
5-in. x 1/2-in.-diameter dowels (handles)	2
3/4-in. x 3/4-in.-diameter dowels (for feet)	4

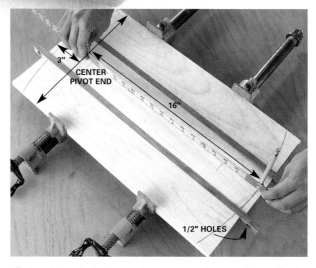

1 DRILL 1/2-in. holes centered 3/4 in. in from the ends of the walnut strips. Then lightly clamp all five boards together so you can scribe the arcs on the ends.

2 TAKE the boards out of the clamp, saw and sand the arcs on each board, and then glue the assembly together, leaving the dowel handles unglued.

3 UNCLAMP, sand both sides and drill a 1/4-in.-deep, 3/4-in.-diameter hole at each underside corner. Glue in the feet and dowel handles, then wipe on a couple of coats of Butcher Block Oil ($6.99 at rockler.com). That's it—chop some veggies!

CATCH BLOCK

SPACE-SAVING CUTTING AND FINISHING BENCH

Save space and make plywood cutting easier by building this hinged, flip-up, open-web bench. It'll take some care and patience to cut the interlocking joints, but after that, assembly is a cinch. Make everything from 1x4s. The bench shown is about 3 x 5 ft.— a good size for nearly any plywood cut. Keep the screws at least 1/4 in. from the top edge. Get it out of the way by tipping it up against the wall and locking it into place with a wooden turnbuckle, turned behind a 1x2 catch block that's mounted with the thin side against the front board.

The web provides solid, even support for sawing or finishing. But make sure to set your saw to cut only 1/8 in. into the table so you don't hit any of the assembly screws or weaken the table.

HINGE

1x4 WEB

INTERLOCKING JOINTS

1x2 CATCH BLOCK

1x4 SUPPORT FRAME

LEG PIVOTS UP

WorkshopTips™

FLASHING SHIELD FOR SANDING

Careful! When you're sanding in the corner of that next masterpiece, your vibrating or random orbital sander can dig some nasty scratches or dents with the sander body and the sandpaper on adjoining surfaces. And they're nearly impossible to fix.

Try this bulletproof tip. Hold a small sheet of metal flashing or plastic laminate between the sander and the surface you don't want dinged up, and then sand as close as you want with no worries. Scratches go on the metal, not on the wood.

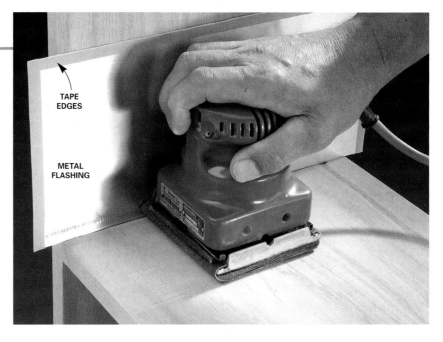

TAPE EDGES

METAL FLASHING

IN-THE-BAG WOOD FILLER

Mix up your own perfectly matching wood filler in a disposable sandwich bag dispenser. First, put a couple of squirts of two-part epoxy into a plastic bag and add some sanding dust from the project (to match the wood). Knead the dust and epoxy with your fingers. Add more dust or epoxy as needed to create the right color. Protect the surrounding wood with masking tape, then nip off one corner of the bag and squeeze out the filler like toothpaste. Smooth off excess filler with a putty knife and let it dry to form an unshrinkable, rock-hard patch. Even better, you'll walk away without epoxy smeared all over your workpiece—or your fingers!

FILLER DUST

EPOXY GLUE

EPOXY GLUE

FENCE-STRADDLING PUSH BOX

This little three-sided, handled box keeps your fingers a lot safer when you rip boards on a table saw. And you can make it in about 30 minutes.

Cut a 10-in.-long piece of 3/4-in. plywood the same width as your saw's fence, and then saw out and screw on a comfortable handle.

Cut a notch on the front end of the 1/4-in. plywood sides a little deeper than the board you're sawing, then screw the sides to the top piece. Mount the push box on the fence. As you saw, the notches lock down on the end of the board to hold it flat on the table. You can further ensure safety and accuracy when you cut narrow boards by using a second push stick in the opposite hand to lightly press the board against the fence.

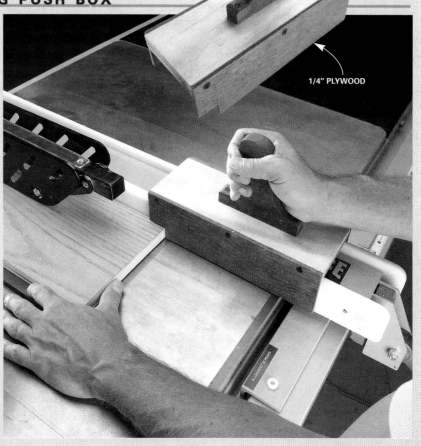

1/4" PLYWOOD

PENCIL SANDING AID

Here's a great old tip that's worth revisiting. Can't tell where you've sanded and where you haven't? Scribble light pencil lines over the surface, and then sand away until they're gone. You'll sand the entire surface without missing a spot, even out hard-to-see high and low areas, and know when to switch to a finer grit of sandpaper. The finer the grit, the lighter the pencil lines should be. It'll take forever to sand off dark lines with fine grits.

PENCIL SWIRLS

CLASSIC ARCH-TOP BOOKCASES

Molded millwork, off-the-shelf cabinets and inexpensive MDF make these classic-looking bookshelves a snap

by **Spike Carlsen**

Arches can be stunning in any room—both in how they look and in how difficult they are to build. But the bookcases you see here are stunning only on the first count. Why? The curved top sections and other decorative moldings are made of high-density polyurethane and come just as you see them; all you do is cut them to length and install them.

The rest of the bookcase is designed to go together simply too. It's basically a big box with a store-bought cabinet for the bottom, a pair of upright "sandwiches" for the sides and a pair of frames for the top. The exposed surfaces and shelves of the bookcases are made of 1/2-in.-thick medium-density fiberboard (MDF), a material that's inexpensive, easy to work with and a dream to paint.

This is a project even those with moderate do-it-yourself skills can tackle successfully. And if you stick with it, you can build and install both bookcase units in a weekend. We used a power miter saw and pneumatic nailer, but

you could use hand tools. If you have access to a table saw, you can save time by using it to cut the MDF panels to width instead of the circular saw method we used. All said and done, each of our bookcases cost about $400, not including the base and cornice moldings.

Working with polyurethane moldings

As a carpenter, I love working with real, honest-to-goodness wood. But even I grew fond of polyurethane moldings the more I worked with them. Crafting the arches from wood would have required advanced woodworking tools and skills or writing one very large check. But the premade arches we used installed quickly and were reasonably priced. Each pair of arches, along with the center keystone, cost about $90; the end blocks, plinth blocks and moldings used to finish the vertical legs cost an additional $115 per bookcase.

Polyurethane moldings cut like butter. We used a power miter saw equipped with a 60-tooth carbide "finishing" blade, but you can use a miter box and fine-tooth handsaw with equally good results.

Just as with wood, you need to fill the nail holes with putty, and lightly sand the surface to remove excess putty and small irregularities. But once properly prepared, they accept paint smoothly and evenly.

There are drawbacks. Rigid polyurethane moldings aren't as hard or as capable of taking a hit as wood moldings. If you have kids who like to play floor hockey or a spouse who likes to vacuum enthusiastically, the base moldings may eventually dent and scratch. Window and door moldings may also take it on the chin when banged by a heavy object.

But for decorative uses, where the millwork is going to be painted, they're a great alternative to wood.

Plan the project and order the pieces

The size of the bookcase is determined by the size of the cabinet it's built around. We chose "ready-to-assemble"

Figure A: Bookcase details

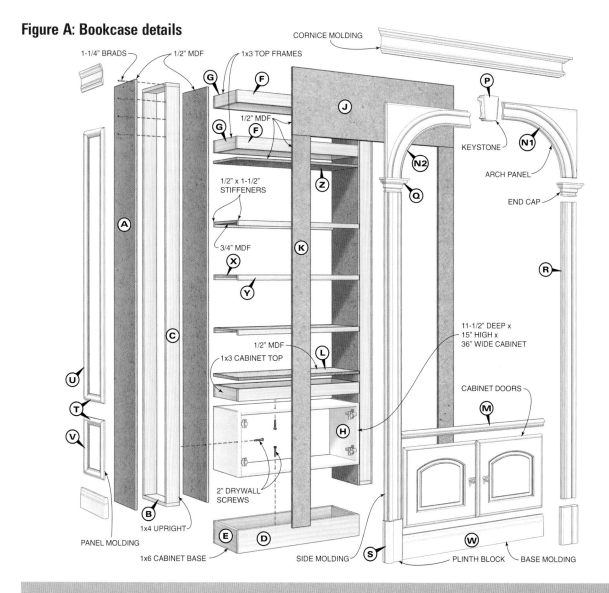

CORNICE MOLDING

1-1/4" BRADS 1/2" MDF 1x3 TOP FRAMES

G F

G F

1/2" MDF

1/2" x 1-1/2" STIFFENERS

3/4" MDF

X

Y

1/2" MDF

1x3 CABINET TOP

A

C

U

T

V

B

1x4 UPRIGHT

PANEL MOLDING

1x6 CABINET BASE

E D

SIDE MOLDING

S

J

Z

K

L

H

2" DRYWALL SCREWS

P

KEYSTONE

N1

N2

Q

ARCH PANEL

END CAP

R

11-1/2" DEEP x 15" HIGH x 36" WIDE CABINET

CABINET DOORS

M

W

PLINTH BLOCK BASE MOLDING

WOODWORKING & FURNITURE PROJECTS, TOOLS & TIPS

CUTTING LIST (PER BOOKCASE)

KEY	PCS.	SIZE & DESCRIPTION
A	4	1/2" x 11-1/4" x 94" upright side panel
B	4	3/4" x 3-1/2" x 10-3/4" upright base and top
C	4	3/4" x 3-1/2" x 92-1/2" upright front and back
D	2	3/4" x 5-1/2" x 36" cabinet base, front and back
E	2	3/4" x 5-1/2" x 10" cabinet base, sides
F	6	3/4" x 2-1/2" x 36" cabinet top and upper frames, front and back
G	6	3/4" x 2-1/2" x 10" cabinet top and upper frames and sides
H	1	11-1/2" x 15" x 36" cabinet

KEY	PCS.	SIZE & DESCRIPTION
J	1	1/2" x 13-1/2" x 45" top face panel
K	2	1/2" x 4-1/2" x 80-1/2" MDF upright face panels
L	1	1/2" x 11-3/4" x 36" cabinet top
M	1	9/16" x 1-9/16" x 37" cabinet top front molding
N1	1	22" façade right arch
N2	1	22" façade left arch
P	1	façade keystone
Q	2	façade end caps
R	2	1-3/16" x 3-3/4" x 62-1/4" façade legs
S	2	1-9/16" x 3-3/4" x 7-1/2" façade plinth blocks

KEY	PCS.	SIZE & DESCRIPTION
T	8	9/16" x 1-9/16" x 9-1/4" side molding horizontals
U	4	9/16" x 1-9/16" x 60-1/4" side molding verticals (upper frame)
V	4	9/16" x 1-9/16" x 13-1/4" side molding verticals (lower frame)
W	1	1" x 4-3/8" x 37" front base molding
X	6	3/4" x 10-3/4" x 35-7/8" MDF shelves
Y	12	1/2" x 1-1/2" x 35-7/8" shelf stiffeners
Z	1	1/2" x 11-1/4" x 36" bookcase ceiling

frameless cabinets 36 in. wide, 15 in. tall and 11-1/2 in. deep (see the Buyer's Guide, p. 131) at a home center. You can modify the design to fit different-size cabinets. Since room heights vary and exact cabinet sizes differ by manufacturer, you may need to modify our dimensions. As you do, remember:

- Build your bookcases 2 in. shorter than your room height; otherwise you can't tilt them up into place.
- Make sure the back of the cabinet is slightly inset from the back of the uprights; otherwise you'll have gaps where the uprights meet the wall.
- Cabinets with protruding face frames need to be shimmed out on the back side to keep things square.
- You can create side-by-side bookcases by using "double width" end caps.

Most stock cabinet widths are based on 3-in. increments, and the uprights add another 9 in. to the overall bookcase dimension. Before you buy anything, make templates to represent the "footprint" of each bookcase and experiment with their positions (Photo 1). Adjust the size of your cabinets as needed.

If you cover an outlet, you'll need to either install a box extender so the face of the outlet winds up even with the back of your cabinet, or cut an oversize hole that allows you to plug in items without risk of the cord rubbing on the edges.

If you have wall-to-wall carpeting, you'll need to peel back the carpet and pad while installing the bookcases, then restretch the carpet when you're done. See "Restretch a Carpet," June '04, p. 92, for more information. To access this article online, go to thefamilyhandyman.com.

Measure from floor to ceiling, then subtract 2 in. to determine the overall height of the bookcases. This will allow you to build the rough boxes in your shop or garage, then carry them inside and tilt them up into place.

A wide range of high-density polyurethane moldings can be ordered by mail or through retailers (see the Buyer's Guide, p. 131). Order well in advance so you have all the materials you need before you start.

Build the framework

Begin by building the 1x4 frames (Figure A, p. 127) for the uprights. Build them 2 in. shorter than the floor-to-ceiling measurement and 3/4 in. narrower than the cabinet is deep. We built 10-3/4-in.-deep frames for our 11-1/2-in.-deep cabinet. Then cut the 1/2-in. MDF panels for the sides of the 1x4 frames, making them 1/2 in. wider than the uprights; ours were 11-1/4 in. wide. In addition to hearing protectors, wear a dust mask; MDF dust is superfine and easily inhaled. See "Circular Saw Cutting Guide," Oct. '04, p. 18, for more information. To access this article online, go to thefamilyhandyman.com.

1 PLAN ahead. Lay paper templates on the floor to help you envision the best positions for the bookcases. Measure the ceiling height; you'll build the bookcases 2 in. shorter so you can tilt them into place.

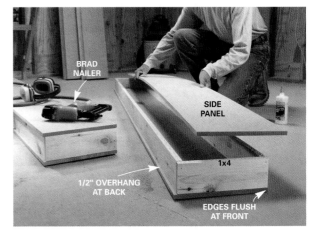
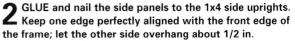

2 GLUE and nail the side panels to the 1x4 side uprights. Keep one edge perfectly aligned with the front edge of the frame; let the other side overhang about 1/2 in.

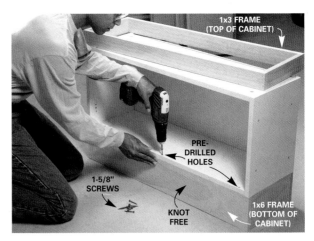

3 SECURE the 1x6 frame to the bottom of the cabinet and the 1x3 frame to the top. When you're prebuilding the frames, use knot-free 1x3s and 1x6s for the front pieces (they'll be exposed).

Secure an MDF panel to each side of the 1x4 frames (**Photo 2**) using yellow glue and 1-1/4-in. brads. Set the uprights aside.

Build two boxes—one from 1x6s, the other from 1x3s—the same dimensions as the top of the cabinet. Drive drywall screws through predrilled holes to secure the 1x6 frame to the bottom of the cabinet and the 1x3 frame to the top (**Photo 3**).

Next secure the uprights to the cabinet using clamps, screws and construction adhesive (**Photo 4**). Keep the front edge of the uprights 1/2 in. back from the edge of the face frame; use a 1/2-in. piece of MDF to ensure proper spacing and shims to hold the parts in proper alignment.

Build two more 1x3 frames the same size as those you built for the top and bottom of the cabinets. Secure one between the tops of the uprights and the other one 12 to 14 in. down (or whatever height you wish the lower edge of your arches to be) as shown in **Photo 5**. Cut and nail MDF to the lower 1x3 frame to create the "ceiling," and across the width of the upper bookcase to create the front surface and "lock" everything together. Finally, install 4-1/2-in. MDF strips to finish covering the fronts of the uprights.

Install the bookcases

With a helper, carry the completed boxes into the room. Measure carefully, then cut out the backs of the cabinets to accommodate any outlets. Tip the bookcases up into place (**Photo 6**).

Use a level and shims to level the bookcases. You'll cover any gaps along the floor later with baseboard

Easy drywall arches

We arched the top of the existing door opening so it would look more "at home" with the new bookcases. For ease of construction, we used prebuilt arched corners (see the Buyer's Guide, p. 131).

The corners we purchased were 4-3/4 in. thick—wide enough to accommodate the standard 4-1/2-in. wall thickness plus the thickness of the metal corner bead around the opening.

To install each arch, apply drywall compound to the back surfaces, "smoosh" it into position, then use four 2-in. drywall screws to fasten the arches into place. Once the drywall compound has set, apply self-adhesive mesh tape to the seams, Then apply two to three coats of drywall compound to the seams so they blend in with the existing wall surface.

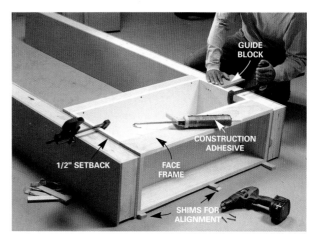

4 GLUE and screw the uprights to the cabinet. Use a scrap piece of 1/2-in. MDF as a guide for maintaining the proper 1/2-in. setback between the front of the uprights and the face of the cabinet.

5 BUILD two more 1x3 frames. Secure one frame to the very top of the cabinet with drywall screws, and the other one at the desired "ceiling height" for the cabinet. Sheathe the face, "ceiling" and legs with MDF (Figure A).

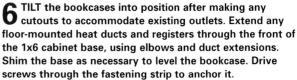

6 TILT the bookcases into position after making any cutouts to accommodate existing outlets. Extend any floor-mounted heat ducts and registers through the front of the 1x6 cabinet base, using elbows and duct extensions. Shim the base as necessary to level the bookcase. Drive screws through the fastening strip to anchor it.

molding. Check to see how the uprights fit against the wall. If there are gaps less than 1/8 in., fill them with caulk. If there are gaps wider than 1/8 in., either apply a small molding to conceal the gap or scribe and trim the back flanges of the uprights to fit. For more information, see "Scribing for a Perfect Fit," Nov. '02, p. 29. To access the article online, visit thefamilyhandyman.com.

Once you're satisfied with the fit, secure the bookcases in place by driving 3-in. drywall screws through the fastening strips and into the wall studs (shown in **Photo 11**).

Install the arched facade

As you install the moldings, keep in mind that the adhesive does the real work; brads or nails only hold the molding in place until the adhesive sets. There are two types of adhesive: Decofix Pro is used to secure the moldings to MDF, drywall or other substrate. OracFix Extra is used for molding-to-molding connections.

You can hand-nail the moldings, but you risk damaging them with any errant hits. A pneumatic nailer allows you to hold the moldings in place with one hand while driving the fasteners with the other.

Draw a level line above the opening in your bookcase (**Photo 7**) so that when the tops of the arches are aligned with it, the lower edge protrudes into the opening about 1/4 in. Also mark the center of the bookcase. Hold the top edge of one of the arch halves on the line, center the lower leg of the arch on the front of the upright, then mark the horizontal leg of the arch 1/2 in. shy of your center mark.

Use a miter saw to cut the arch on the mark you just made; the keystone will eventually cover the small gap. Apply the special adhesive to the back edges of the arch, then use your brad nailer to secure it in place. Repeat the same procedure for the other arch half. When both sides of the arch are in place, install the keystone.

Center an end cap below the vertical legs of each arch, then use adhesive and brads to secure them in place (**Photo 8**). Cut the plinth blocks to the desired height (we made ours 3-1/2 in. taller than our baseboard molding), then use adhesive and your brad nailer to attach them to the uprights. To complete the arches, measure the distance between the end blocks and the plinth blocks, then cut the moldings that go between a hair longer to ensure a tight fit (**Photo 9**). Secure them into place.

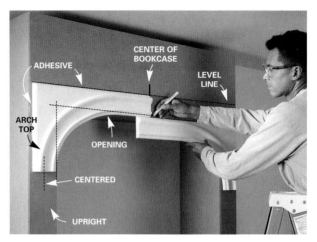

7 DRAW a level line for aligning the tops of the arches. Center the vertical leg of the arch on the upright, then mark the horizontal leg 1/2 in. shy of the center point of the bookcase. Cut the arch to length, then glue and nail.

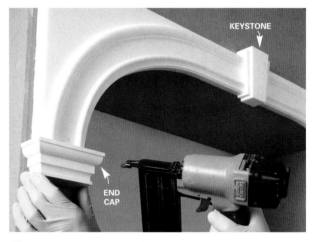

8 GLUE and tack the keystone in place, then install the end caps, centered on the fronts of the uprights. Use molding-to-molding adhesive to secure the end caps to the arches (wear gloves when using this). Then use molding-to-substrate adhesive to secure them to the uprights.

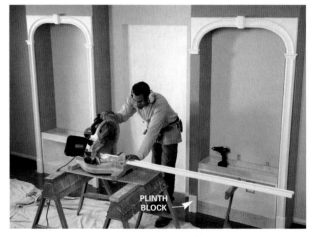

9 CUT the vertical moldings to fit tightly between the lower plinth blocks and the upper end caps. Support the ends of the longer, floppier moldings while handling them. Then glue and nail them into place.

5 POSITION the legs and clamp them to the frame using Figure B as a guide. Drill and fasten them with carriage bolts. Nail the rear storage tray slats to the sides.

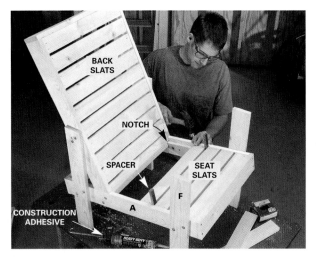

6 CUT the seat and back slats to length. Glue and nail them with 4d galvanized finish nails. Use two spacers to ensure consistent gaps.

7 NOTCH the arms to fit around the seat back frame. Then predrill and fasten the arms to the front and rear legs with 2-in. deck screws.

8 SOAK the legs overnight in a wood preservative or an oil-based deck stain to slow water absorption. Once the legs are dry, prime and paint.

sides overhang the legs 1 in. We painted our chair rather than stain it. But no matter what finish you choose, be sure to soak the legs in a preservative or deck stain to keep water from wicking up and ruining the finish or causing rot (**Photo 8**). If you paint, we recommend that you use an oil-based primer followed by two topcoats of a high-quality gloss or semigloss acrylic paint.

Book? Binoculars? Sunscreen? Phone? Whatever you need to keep within reach, you can stash behind you in the handy built-in tray.

Buyer's Guide
You can find chair cushions at Home Decorators (877-537-8539) or online at homedecorators.com. Choose from simple seat cushion No. 26106 or full seat and back No. 26107 in a wide variety of patterns and colors. Two other sources are Domestications (800-826-8240; domestications.com) and Cushion Source (800-510-8325; cushionsource.com). Cushion Source will make custom cushions in any size.

CHARGING STATION

Park, power and organize your rechargeable gadgets

by Brett Martin

This charging station provides the perfect platform for charging gadgets and taming the tangling cords. A narrow gap along the front of the lid lets the cord ends through to plug into the devices, or you can run the cords over the back side.

We'll show you how to build this charging station in a few easy steps. With a table saw and a miter saw, you can knock this project out in one morning, including the finish. You'll need 8 ft. of 1/2-in.-thick, 5-1/2-in.-wide wood for this project. Most home centers carry common species like oak and maple. For a wider selection, shop online at rockler.com. We used cherry, which cost $80. To get the project into the $20 range, use oak instead.

You can make the charging station any length you want, but be sure it works with one of the standard sizes of power strips. The height shown here works for most cell phones, cameras and iPods. If the height of your charger plug and power strip exceeds 3-3/4 in., make the charging station a little taller. (Measure the height of the power strip and transformer, and add any height difference over 3-3/4 in. to the height of the front and side pieces.) Place the dividers on the lid wherever they work best for your gadgets.

Get started by sanding the lumber with 100-grit sandpaper to remove any rough spots. Then cut the front, back, bottom and rail approximately 17 in. long, and cut the rest of the pieces to size, following the Cutting List. Cut the lid 1/8 in. shorter than the front so it can easily slide in and out. Cut the cleats, dividers and stop from the scrap.

If you're planning to set the charging station on a counter, drill a 1-1/4-in. hole in

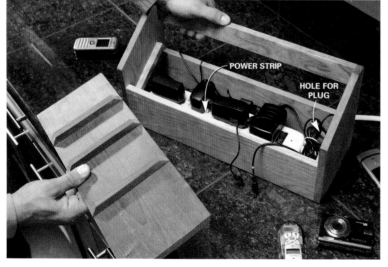

POWER STRIP

HOLE FOR PLUG

The lift-off lid hides a power strip and bulky transformers.

Figure A: Charging station

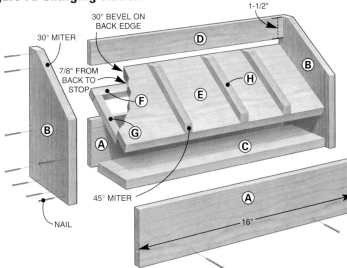

1-1/2"
30° BEVEL ON BACK EDGE
Ⓓ
30° MITER
Ⓑ
7/8" FROM BACK TO STOP
Ⓗ
Ⓕ
Ⓔ
Ⓑ
Ⓐ
Ⓖ
Ⓒ
45° MITER
NAIL
Ⓐ
16"

KEY	PCS.	SIZE & DESCRIPTION
A	2	1/2" x 4" x 16" front and back
B	2	1/2" x 5-1/2" x 8-1/2" sides with 30-degree angle
C	1	1/2" x 4" x 16" bottom
D	1	1/2" x 1-1/2" x 16" rail
E	1	1/2" x 5-1/2" x 15-7/8" lid with 30-degree bevel
F	1	1/2" x 1/2" x 15-7/8" stop
G	2	1/2" x 1/2" x 4" cleats
H	3 or 4	1/2" x 1/2" x 5-1/2" dividers with 45-degree angle at ends

CUTTING LIST

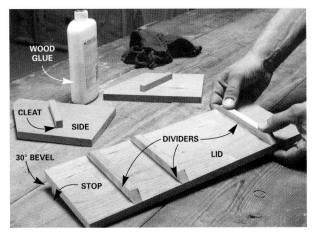

WOOD GLUE
CLEAT
SIDE
30° BEVEL
STOP
DIVIDERS
LID

1 FASTEN the dividers without nails or clamps. Just spread a little glue on each piece and hold it in place until the glue grabs (about one minute). Wipe away any excess with a damp rag. Use the same technique to attach the stop and the cleats.

SPRING CLAMP

2 GANG-CUT parts so they're precisely the same length. Clamp the front, back, bottom and rail together, then cut one end. Flip the boards around and cut the other end to size. Gang-cutting eliminates any slight length differences.

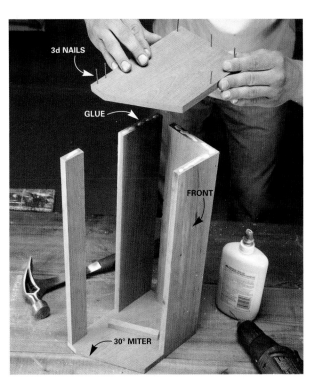

3d NAILS
GLUE
FRONT
30° MITER

3 ATTACH the ends to the sides. Hold each joint together and predrill 1/16-in. nail holes. Then start the 3d finish nails and apply glue to the joints. As you drive the nails home, they'll align the joints perfectly.

the back with a spade bit for the power strip plug (keep the hole away from the corners to avoid hitting nails). If you'll wall-mount it by screwing it through the back, just run the cord through the slot in the bottom.

Once the charging station is assembled, lightly sand it with 180-grit sandpaper. Don't brush on a finish! Spray on a coat of lacquer (a can of spray lacquer costs $6). Or use a wipe-on finish. We wiped on Watco Golden Oak finish ($13 per qt.).

WordlessWorkshop™

by Roy Doty

BATHROOM READING RACK

5 Exterior Maintenance & Repairs

IN THIS CHAPTER

Handy Hints 140
   *No-slip ladder tip, trash-can cement
   mixer, easy-off hose and more*

Sprinkler System Fixes 142

Ask TFH 148
   *Rid your home of pests, repainting
   stucco and more*

Deck Rescue 151

Add an Outdoor Faucet 156

Home Care & Repair 159
   *Replace damaged vinyl siding,
   raise sunken patio pavers and more*

Roof Tear-off 162

New Products 167
   *A ladder for uneven surfaces and
   a screen door alternative*

Installing an Outdoor Handrail 168

HandyHints®

A HELPER UP HIGH

Working up high with lengths of gutter or lumber can be tough, especially if you're working alone—or if you only have one ladder! To make the job easier, use one-hand bar clamps to quickly connect a sawhorse to two 8-ft. studs. Then use C-clamps to position a 1x4 cross member at the desired height. For the best holding power, set the C-clamps at an angle with the jaws up. You can use heavier material for bigger jobs, but be careful: Top-heavy loads are tippy!

NO-SLIP LADDER TIP

Don't let your ladder slip out from under you. Brace the bottom feet with a plank and your lawn tractor. Be sure to set your tractor's parking brake.

NO-SLIP TOOLS

When you're working on the roof, wrap rubber bands around tools to help them stay put. The rubber will grip on roofs with up to a 6/12 slope.

ON-THE-LEVEL TOOL BUCKET

To keep a gutter debris bucket from sliding off the roof, drill an angled 4x4 block into the underside of the bucket. Staple a rubber mat underneath to make everything stay put.

TRASH-CAN CEMENT MIXER

Dump a bag of concrete mix into a garbage can and add a little water. Tilt the can and twirl it back and forth as if you're steering a big truck. Add more water as needed. When the concrete is mixed, just roll the can to its destination and dump out the concrete.

EASY-OFF HOSE

A single wrap of pipe thread tape ($1 at hardware stores and home centers) on outdoor faucet threads makes it easier to thread the garden hose on and off.

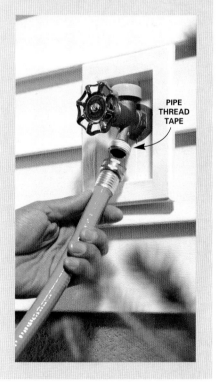

PIPE THREAD TAPE

SPRINKLER SYSTEM FIXES

Do-it-yourself solutions to irritating irrigation problems

by **Brett Martin**

An automatic lawn irrigation system is the best way to keep your lawn looking fresh and green. Correctly designed and programmed, it'll deliver the right amount of water to your yard—no more moving the sprinkler! But like any other system, it occasionally breaks down or requires maintenance.

The good news is you can handle 90 percent of the repairs yourself, even without in-depth knowledge of the system. We'll show you how to identify and fix the most common problems.

Calling in a professional could cost at least $100, even for a simple problem you can fix yourself in 10 minutes.

Don't be intimidated by the prospect of working on a system that involves both plumbing and electricity. The pipes are plastic and much simpler to repair than the plumbing in your house. The electrical lines are low voltage, so they're not hazardous.

You don't need special skills to make the repairs, but you'll need a multimeter ($30) to diagnose electrical problems. See the Buyer's Guide on p. 147 for sources for replacement parts.

PROBLEM:
LOW WATER PRESSURE

Solution 1: Turn on valves at backflow device

Low water pressure will result in the sprinkler heads barely shooting water. In extreme cases, many of the heads won't even pop up. Start with the easiest solution. Make sure the valves at the backflow device are fully open. The backflow device is located above ground, with the valve at least 12 in. above the highest sprinkler head in the yard. Most backflow devices have a valve on the horizontal and vertical pipes. Turn the valves to their open positions as shown. The valve is open when the handle is parallel with the pipe.

BACKFLOW DEVICE

VALVES

Check the valves on the backflow device to make sure they're open. Turn the valve on the horizontal pipe first, then the vertical pipe valve.

Solution 2: Find and repair leaks

Then check for leaks in the water line. Look for a series of sprinkler heads that aren't watering properly. The water line problem is always located between the last working head and the first nonworking head.

Look for signs of leaking water, such as water bubbling up from the soil when the sprinklers are running, a depression in the ground, or a very wet area. If you find running water, follow the water to the highest point to find the source.

Once you locate the approximate leak site, dig straight down to the water line. Then enlarge the hole along the line, following the flow of the leaking water until you find the break or crack. Before making the repair, make sure the system is turned off at the controller.

Use a slip coupling to repair the leak. This special coupling contracts to make insertion easy ($5 at irrigation supply stores).

To fix the leak, use a hacksaw to cut out a 4-in. section of line at the leak. Place a clamp on one of the line ends, insert the coupling, then tighten the clamp.

Place a clamp on the second pipe end, expand the coupling while inserting the nipple into the pipe, then tighten the clamp. Backfill the hole with dirt and replace the sod.

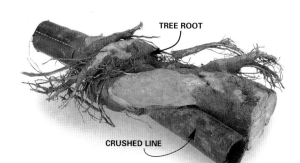
TREE ROOT

CRUSHED LINE

Solution 3: Check for crushed pipes

If you can't locate a leak, the water line may be crushed or obstructed. Sometimes, roots wrap around the line and squeeze it closed over the course of several years (**photo above**). Or vehicles may have compressed the soil and collapsed the line. These problems are harder to find and often require a lot of digging. Again, look for the problem after the last working head. Dig along the water line until you find the damaged section. If the line runs near a tree, start your digging there.

Once you locate the damaged section, cut it out with a hacksaw. If the line was damaged by tree roots, reroute the line by digging a new trench away from the tree.

Cut a new section of pipe to replace the damaged one. Then replace the section of pipe, connecting it at each end with regular couplings and band clamps (**photo below**).

SLIP
COUPLING

A slip coupling easily expands and contracts to replace a damaged section of line.

WATER LINE

SLIP COUPLING

BAND CLAMP

Cut out the damaged section of line and replace it with a slip coupling. Secure the coupling with band clamps.

COUPLING

DAMAGED LINE

Cut out the damaged section of line. Replace it with a new section of line, making connections with standard couplings and band clamps.

PROBLEM:
SPRINKLER HEADS NOT WORKING

Solution 1: Replace a broken sprinkler head

Broken sprinkler heads are easy to identify. Simply look for cracked or broken plastic casing on the heads, heads that don't pop up, or water that sprays wildly or not at all. It's common to find the top of the head completely broken off. This typically happens to heads that are set too high and are run over by vehicles or hit by lawn mowers.

Replacing the head is one of the simplest fixes. Replacement heads are available at home centers and online, starting at $5. Be sure to buy the same type of head that you're replacing.

To change a broken head, turn off the system and dig a 2-ft.-diameter hole around the head. Using a square shovel, slice the sod into easy-to-remove pieces. Set the sod on a tarp so you can set it back into place at the end of the job.

Dig down to the "riser" (the vertical pipe that branches off the main line) which is connected to the sprinkler head. Dig with a light touch to avoid damaging the plastic water line, which is 8 to 12 in. underground.

Turn the head counterclockwise to remove it from the riser. While the head is off, take care not to spill dirt into the riser. Sprinkler heads are installed only hand-tight, but after being in the ground for several years, they may require the use of wrenches to unscrew. If the head doesn't turn easily, hold the riser with slip joint pliers to keep it from twisting loose from the fittings below.

Attach the new sprinkler head by placing it on the riser and turning it hand-tight (**photo right**). Don't use Teflon tape or joint compound on the riser threads.

Sprinkler heads are factory tested to make sure they work. As a result, they're often packaged still wet, so don't be surprised to see water in a new head.

Before filling in the hole and replacing the sod, set the desired sprinkler pattern (see "Reset the Spray Pattern," p. 145).

> **CAUTION:** Before you start digging to access the underground water lines, electrical wires or spray heads, call to have your underground utility lines identified and marked. Visit the Common Ground Alliance site (call811.com) to find the phone number for your area.

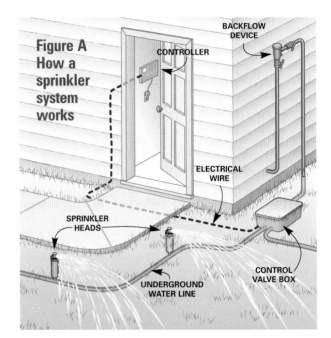

Figure A — How a sprinkler system works

The controller sends a signal to the control valves in the control valve box. The valves open, sending water through the underground water line, which causes the sprinkler heads to pop up and spray.

Dig around the sprinkler head to expose the riser. Unscrew the broken sprinkler head from the riser. Install the new head, turning it tight with your hands.

Solution 2: Clean clogged sprinkler heads

Dirt sometimes gets inside sprinkler heads, causing them to clog up. Clogged heads may rise but fail to spray, not lower after watering, or produce an erratic spray pattern.

To clean the head, dig it out and remove it from the riser (see p. 144). Take the head apart by holding the bottom of the canister and turning the top of the head counterclockwise. Once it's unscrewed, lift it out of the canister (**Photo 1**).

Remove the plastic screen basket, which serves as a filter, at the base of the head. If you can't pop the basket out with your fingers, pry it out with a flat-head screwdriver or pull it free with pliers. Rinse the basket in a bucket of clean water, washing out the debris (**Photo 2**). Clean the rest of the sprinkler head by rinsing it with water. Replace the head on the riser. If it still doesn't work, replace it with a new head.

1 DISASSEMBLE the sprinkler head by unscrewing the top from the canister. Rinse away soil and debris in a bucket of water.

2 REMOVE the screen basket from the bottom of the head, then clean it with water.

Reset the spray pattern

When putting on a new sprinkler head or using the same head after cleaning, you may need to adjust it to water a specific area. Adjustment methods vary. You can adjust some head types by turning a slot at the top with a screwdriver. Others require a special key that you insert into the head and turn (**Photo 3**). Some heads also allow you to adjust the spray pattern by turning a tiny screw located next to the nozzle.

Adjust the heads before installing them, then fine-tune them once they're in place with the sprinkler running.

First, turn the top clockwise until it stops. That nozzle location is the starting point (the head will turn counterclockwise from there). Adjust the head to set the watering rotation anywhere from 40 degrees to 360 degrees counterclockwise from the starting point.

Set the head in the canister. Standing behind the head, align the nozzle with the right edge of the area you want to water, such as along a driveway. Tighten the head in the canister. Carefully backfill the hole and replace the sod.

> ### Note
> In areas of the country that experience freezing temperatures, polyethylene (poly) pipe is used for the irrigation water lines. PVC pipe is used in areas that don't freeze.

3 ADJUST the watering range of the sprinkler head before installing it. Place the head in the canister so the nozzle is at the edge of the area to be watered. Make final adjustments with the water running.

Turn on the sprinklers at the controller. Allow the head to make a few rotations, then make additional adjustments while the system is running.

PROBLEM:
ONE OR MORE ZONES NOT WORKING

Solution 1: Check for voltage to the bad zones

Your watering system is divided into a series of zones. Each zone has an electrically activated valve that controls the heads for a designated area.

Generally, if you have a zone that's not turning on, you have an electrical problem. To solve the problem, make sure the zone wires are firmly attached to the terminals in the controller, the transformer is plugged in, and the circuit breaker at the main panel is on.

Next, test for voltage to the nonworking zone, using a multimeter ($30 at home centers and hardware stores). Turn on the nonworking zone at the controller. Turn the multimeter dial to voltage and place one lead on the common terminal (marked "c" or "com"). Place the other lead on the terminal of the zone that's not working (**photo below**). It doesn't matter which lead goes to which terminal.

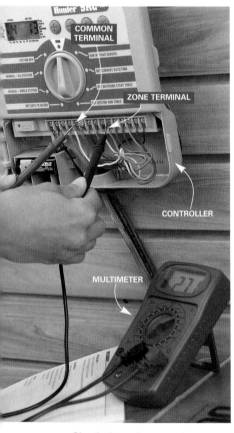

Refer to your owner's manual to see whether the voltage reading falls within the required range (usually 24 to 28 volts). If it doesn't, the controller needs to be replaced. (If you don't get any voltage reading, see "Check Fuse and Transformer," right.)

Fortunately, controllers rarely go bad unless struck by lightning. New ones start at $175 and can cost upward of $400. Replace a damaged controller with the same brand and model as you currently have. To replace it, label each wire that's connected to the controller with a piece of tape. Unhook the wires, then attach them to the new controller in the same sequence.

Check the voltage to the nonworking zone using a multimeter. Touch the leads to the common terminal and zone terminal. If the voltage is too low, replace the controller.

Solution 2: Check fuse and transformer

If no zones will turn on, first turn the controller to the manual setting to see if the system will run. If it turns on manually, the controller is good but the rain sensor may be stopping the automatic programmed watering, which is what it's designed to do.

Rain sensors conserve water by preventing the system from running when the ground is already saturated and doesn't need additional watering. Some states require rain sensors on all new systems. (Your rain sensor is bad if the system runs when the ground is already wet.)

If the system doesn't run in the manual position, check the controller for power. If it has a fuse, make sure it's not blown. Or, if it has a circuit breaker reset button, press the button, then try the system again. If the system is plugged into a GFCI receptacle, press the GFCI reset button.

If it still doesn't turn on, make sure the outlet that the power transformer is plugged into is working by plugging in a power tool. If it's working, plug the transformer back in, turn the system off and test the transformer for voltage. Using a multitester, place a lead on each of the two transformer terminals. It doesn't matter which lead goes to which terminal.

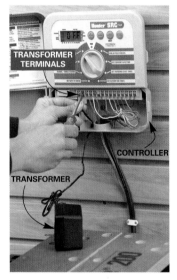

The transformer terminals are marked "24 vac." A 24-voltage transformer should normally test between 24 and 28 volts. If the voltage falls below the manufacturer's range, replace the transformer ($25). Simply unscrew the terminals that hold the two transformer wires in the controller and remove the transformer (**photo right**). Insert the wires on the new transformer through the designated opening in the controller. Attach the wires to the controller terminals marked "24 vac" by placing the wire ends under the screws, then tightening them.

Test the transformer voltage by placing the multimeter leads on the transformer terminals marked "24 vac" with the transformer plugged in. If the reading is less than 22, replace the transformer.

Solution 3: Replace defective valve

If the controller, fuse and transformer check out OK, test the resistance "ohms" between the common terminal and the nonworking zone. Turn off the system, turn the multimeter to test for ohms (the omega symbol), and place the leads on the common terminal and zone terminal, just as you did to test for voltage.

Compare the ohms reading with the range listed in your owner's manual (usually 20 to 60 ohms). If the ohms fall below the required amount, the switch (solenoid) that operates the control valve for that zone is defective and needs to be replaced. The defective solenoid will be connected to the same color wire as the zone wire at the controller. (If the reading is too high, see "Repair Damaged Wires, right.")

Control valves are typically grouped with three to six valves in one box (**Photo 1**). The boxes are located in the ground with a cover that simply lifts off. They can be located anywhere in the yard but are usually close to the main water supply.

Although valves themselves rarely need to be replaced, solenoids do occasionally fail. Replacing them is quick and easy.

Be sure the controller is in the off position (you don't need to shut off the power) and the water valves on the backflow device are turned off (see **bottom photo**, p. 142). Inside the control valve box, remove the wire connectors and disconnect the two wires on the

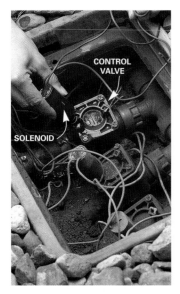

1 DISCONNECT the wires and unscrew the defective solenoid from the control valve. Insert a new one and turn it until it's finger-tight.

defective solenoid from the common and field wires. Turn the solenoid counterclockwise to unscrew it from the valve (**Photo 1**). Water will slowly seep out of the valve opening, even with the water turned off.

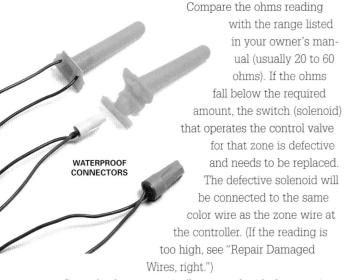

2 CONNECT the two wires on the new solenoid to the common wire and a field wire, using waterproof connectors.

Place a new solenoid in the valve and turn it until it's finger-tight.

Twist the ends of the new solenoid wires onto the same common and field wires that the old solenoid was attached to (**Photo 2**). It doesn't matter which solenoid wire goes to the common and which one goes to the field wire. Twist a new waterproof wire connector over each connection (**Photo 2**). To make waterproof connections, use a silicone-filled "direct bury" connector, available at home centers for $15 for a package of 10.

Repair damaged wires

If the ohms reading between the common terminal and nonworking zone terminal is too high (it's sometimes an infinity reading), the problem is a severed or bad wire to the control valve. If only one zone isn't working, the field wire is damaged. If none of the zones in a control valve box is working, the common wire is damaged, although the field wires could also be bad.

To find a bad wire, bypass each in turn by temporarily substituting a 14-gauge wire for the original that you run above ground. Make the wire connections with the controller turned off. Then turn the controller back on. Test the field wire first. If the zone turns on, the old field wire is bad. Replace it with an 18-gauge wire rated for underground burial. Bury the wire at least 8 in. underground. Follow the same procedure to test the common wire. ⌂

RID YOUR HOME OF **PESTS**

WASPS MOVE IN

We have cedar shingle siding on our home, which the previous homeowner painted. Yellow jackets and bees are highly attracted to the shingles. How can we get rid of them?

The magic bullet for getting rid of wasps (yellow jackets) and bees is to destroy their nest. This is easier said than done. Bees and wasps are notorious for hiding their nests inside walls or high under shingles and eaves, where they're difficult to get at.

YELLOW JACKET

The trick to finding the nest is to observe their movements closely. You'll soon spot where they zoom into the wall of your house. Once you locate the nest, spray it with an insecticide that's formulated for killing bees and wasps. Pick one up at a hardware store or nursery. The best time to spray is at night when the bees are less active and inside the nest.

Be aware that these insects can be extremely aggressive, especially when their home is under attack. Some can sting repeatedly, and those stings can cause severe reactions if you're allergic. If you're on a ladder or on the roof, the last thing you want is an angry storm of bees coming after you!

In difficult situations, have the nest professionally removed. If you decide to spray the nest yourself, make sure to wear protective clothing, including face protection, to guard against stings.

WOODPECKER HEADACHE

Woodpeckers are making holes in the wooden shingles on our home. I think their hammering is even splitting some shingles. How can we stop them?

The first thing to know is what you can't do. The Federal Migratory Bird Treaty Act, as well as some state laws, protects woodpeckers, which means it's unlawful to harm them. (So don't go for the pellet gun!)

The woodpeckers are making holes in your shingles because either they're looking for food, or more likely, "drumming" to mark their territory. Unfortunately, there's no simple way to get rid of them. Your best option is to harass the birds into leaving.

First, fasten sheet metal over the areas the birds are pecking. Also hang mirrors and Mylar tape nearby, for example, from the fascia (or tuck it under the next row of shingles). Shiny lights and reflections sometimes scare woodpeckers away, as do owl decoys. Frankly, however, these remedies don't always work, and the longer the woodpeckers have been at your house, the harder it will be to get them to leave.

To further harass the birds, shoo them away with a broom. If you're persistent, the birds will eventually move on.

PILEATED WOODPECKER

HORDE OF THE FLIES

Every fall I have flies, big and small, on my upstairs windows. There are no flies downstairs. At first I thought the flies came from a dead mouse in the furnace ducts, so I tried blocking the duct openings to keep them out. No luck. How do I stop them?

The good news is the flies probably aren't attracted to a dead animal in your house. If they were, they would disappeared after a few days. You probably have cluster flies. They're about 5/16 in. long and have yellow hairs on their abdomens.

Cluster flies, also known as attic flies, are attracted to light and warmth. They gravitate to second-floor windows, which are usually the warmest spots in the house. The flies breed outside in the ground during late spring and early summer and have a life span of 27 to 39 days. In the fall, they find a way indoors through small cracks around doors, windows, soffits and siding.

The best time to stop cluster flies is before they come indoors. Caulk cracks around the foundation, siding, exterior trim and other potential entry points. Replace weather stripping as necessary to seal around doors and windows. If that doesn't work, spray an insecticide formulated for flies around the outside of your doors and windows, soffits, eaves and cracks in the siding.

If large numbers still come in, an insecticide suitable for use indoors is the only effective way to eradicate them. Or call a professional exterminator to handle the problem.

CLUSTER FLY

REPAINTING STUCCO

I've been told repeatedly that we can't repaint our stucco exterior unless the existing paint is sandblasted off. Is that true?

Whether you can repaint depends on the condition of the existing paint. If it has performed well without bubbling or peeling, then you can paint over it. First, clean the exterior with a power washer, then scrub any flaking areas with a wire brush. Paint the stucco with a 100 percent acrylic paint that's formulated for stucco. If your stucco has cracked (but the crack hasn't opened), ask for a special elastomeric acrylic paint that's designed to bridge and hide the cracks. Elastomerics are available at most paint stores and some stucco supply stores ($120 for 5 gallons) and will last 20 to 25 years. Apply it with a 3/4-in.-nap roller.

If your existing paint is chipping or peeling, a new coat probably won't last, even with thorough prep work. In this case, sandblasting away the old paint is the best solution. Then have pros apply a thin "dash coat" of stucco, tinted to the shade you want. Then the color will last as long as the stucco.

CAUTION: If your stucco was painted before 1978, check the paint for lead. Call your public health department for instructions on how to check it. Don't scrape the stucco because doing so will release lead dust, the primary cause of lead poisoning in children. For more information on lead paint, visit hud.gov/offices/lead or call (800) 424-LEAD.

CRACK FILLER

SQUEEGEE

PATCHING MATERIAL

AskTFH™
The Family Handyman

SEAL BLACKTOP

Should I seal my blacktop driveway? Some folks say no, claiming it needs to breathe. Others say yes. Also, is there a good crack filler?

Without question, sealing blacktop makes it last longer. Sealer protects driveways from the sun's ultraviolet rays, which cause the asphalt in the blacktop to harden and become brittle. You'll know this hardening is occurring when you see your driveway begin to turn gray. Once the asphalt loses its flexibility, it cracks from the weight of your car, especially when frost causes the ground to heave in cold climates.

Let a new driveway cure for a year before sealing. Then fill any cracks and holes before applying the sealer. The filler (available at home centers) will keep out water, which could otherwise get into the crack, freeze and make the crack even larger.

Unfortunately, no filler is permanent, so plan to make crack filling an annual chore. For cracks less than 1/2 in.

wide, use the type of filler that comes in a caulking tube or gallon jug. First clean out the crack using a broom or vacuum, then apply a bead of filler as shown. If necessary, work the filler into the crack with a putty knife. For cracks wider than 1/2 in. and for holes, use the type of patching material that comes in a can. Apply it directly to the crack or holes, then smooth it with a squeegee.

Sealers only last about three years. Although latex sealers may last a bit longer than oil-based, latex sealers eventually crack and peel. You'll have to scrape them before applying a new coat several years down the road. And that's a tough job. We recommend an oil-based sealer, available at home centers and at companies that specialize in driveway sealing.

LEAKING FAUCET

My outdoor faucet leaks around the handle when I turn it on. How do I repair this?

You either have a loose packing nut or a bad packing washer. First try tightening the nut with a wrench or pliers. (The size and type of nut varies a bit with faucet styles.) If the nut is tight but the leak persists, shut off the water to the faucet inside the house, remove the faucet handle from the outside faucet and unscrew the nut. You should be able to pull off the old packing washer and take it to a hardware store to find an exact replacement. Older faucets may have a wad of string, called valve packing, instead of a packing washer. If so, pick up new packing (graphite-coated string) at the hardware store, unwind the old packing and wind on the new clockwise. The packing nut should compress it tightly. You may have to wind on one layer, tighten the nut and then repeat the process to fill the space around the stem completely with packing string.

BEST PAINT FOR EXTERIOR DOORS

I'm looking for help on painting a new steel exterior door that I just installed. I purchased TSP substitute to clean it off, but I'm hesitant about the best paint for the job, for both the outside and the inside faces of the door.

One hundred percent acrylic latex paint works well for both exterior and interior surfaces. It's easy to apply, performs well and is available at paint stores and home centers. Choose a semigloss or satin sheen for durability and easy cleaning.

However, avoid using a dark color on the outside face if the sun hits it. Dark colors absorb heat from direct sunlight, causing the metal to expand and bow the door. This "thermal bow" sometimes makes the door difficult to latch and compromises the weather strip seal.

Prime the door with a latex primer before painting. Most steel doors have a thin coating of primer applied at the factory, but it's basically to keep the door from rusting before it's sold. Since the door is new, you probably don't need to wash it. Simply wipe it down with a clean cloth, prime it again and then paint it.

The only difficult part about painting the door is avoiding brush marks, which is nearly impossible. Spray painting is the best way to solve this problem. But a good spray job takes practice, so we recommend hiring a painting contractor for that perfect coat of paint without runs or brushstrokes. Contractors charge about $75 per door.

DECK **RESCUE**

Make your old, shabby deck look like new!

by **Brett Martin**

If you've been putting off renewing your deck because you think it requires a lot of time, tools and know-how, take heart. In this article, we'll show you how to clean it up fast with the help of a pressure washer and special products that help remove dirt, mildew and old finishes. We'll also show you how to apply a fresh finish, using a foam applicator pad that glides along the wood and quickly applies a nice, even coat. No more messy rollers and brushes.

This process will work on any wood deck, including redwood, cedar and pressure-treated lumber (but not on composite decks). The only special tools you need are a pressure washer (see p. 152) and a foam applicator pad. The project doesn't require any special skills. Just set aside at least four hours on one day to clean your deck, and another four hours several days later to stain it.

The cost of rejuvenating an average-size deck is about $250, including tools, materials and the pressure washer rental. You'll save several hundred dollars by doing the work yourself. Having your deck professionally cleaned and stained will cost $500 to $1,000.

1 PRESSURE-WASH the railings with stripper. Keep the tip 6 to 10 in. from the wood and work from the top down. Spray balusters at the corners to scour two sides at once.

Rent a pressure washer

A pressure washer will scour away dirt and contaminants ingrained in the wood at the same time it sprays on a deck stripper to clean off previous finishes.

Rent a pressure washer from a home center or rental center (about $40 for four hours, or $70 per day). A pressure setting of 1,000 to 1,200 psi is ideal. Too much pressure will damage the wood and make the wand harder to control.

Rent a unit that allows for the intake of chemical cleaners (deck stripper and wood brightener) so you can spray them on through the wand. Most pressure washers have an intake hose that draws in cleaners from a separate bucket. (Use a plastic bucket. Chemicals in the cleaners can react to metal buckets.)

We used sodium hydroxide as the deck stripper. You probably won't be able to find straight sodium hydroxide, but you can find a deck stripping product with sodium hydroxide as the active ingredient in almost any home center or paint store (see Buyer's Guide, p. 155).

We diluted our stripper to a 50/50 mix with water. Some sodium hydroxide–based strippers are premixed and don't require adding water. More commonly, you need to dilute the stripper with water. Read the label on the container to find out what's suggested for your stripper.

Protect your house and plants

Before you begin cleaning, make repairs to your deck, such as replacing cracked or split boards and broken balusters.

Then heavily douse the plants or grass under and around your deck with water and cover them with plastic. Although most strippers aren't supposed to harm vegetation, it's still a good idea to protect plants and it only takes a few minutes. Once you've finished cleaning the deck, immediately remove the plastic.

Also spray down the siding with clean water to ensure that any stripper that splashes onto the house will easily wash off.

Scour away the old finish

With a 25- or 30-degree tip in the wand of the pressure washer and a psi of 1,000 to 1,200, apply the stripper to the deck, starting with the top rails and working down the balusters (**Photo 1**). Spray the rails with a continuous, controlled motion. Keep the wand moving so you don't gouge the wood.

Once you finish the railings, start on the deck boards. Wash along the length of the boards (**Photo 2**). You'll see the grime washing off the wood.

Go over stubborn mildew or other stains a few times rather than turning up the pressure or trying to heavily scour the wood. Later we'll tackle tough stains that won't come out with the stripper.

2 SPRAY one deck board at a time, using a gentle sweeping motion. Avoid sudden stops. Work from the end of the deck toward the exit. Then rinse the entire deck with a garden hose.

3 DIG out trapped debris from between deck boards with a putty knife. Spray the deck lightly with a mixture of oxalic acid and water to brighten the wood.

4 RINSE the siding and windows with clean water at low pressure to remove chemical residue.

This stripping process washes away a small amount of the wood's lignin, which is the glue holding the wood fibers together. As the lignin washes away, the fibers stand up, giving the wood a fuzzy appearance. Don't bother sanding off the fuzzy fibers. They will gradually shear off and blow away.

After you've power-washed the entire deck, rinse all of the wood with plain water to dilute and neutralize the stripper. If there's still debris trapped between deck boards, such as leaves or twigs, remove it now (Photo 3).

Brighten the wood

A deck brightener will return the wood to its newly sawn color and make it more receptive to the stain. Use an oxalic acid–based brightener, which is available at home centers and paint stores (see Buyer's Guide, p. 155). It works fast, won't harm the wood and is environmentally safe in the diluted solution that you'll use.

Like strippers, some deck brighteners come premixed and some need to be diluted with water. Read the label for the manufacturer's recommendations. We mixed our oxalic acid with an equal amount of water and ran it through the pressure washer's intake hose.

Change the tip in the wand of the pressure washer to a fan tip with a 40- or 45-degree angle. Then set the pressure to about 1,000 psi and spray the deck, once again starting with the top rails and working down to the deck boards. Apply just enough brightener to thoroughly wet the wood.

Oxalic acid will brighten the wood in a matter of minutes and does not require rinsing. But your siding does. Rinse off your siding with clean water at very low pressure (about 500 psi) to wash away any stripper or brightener overspray (Photo 4).

If your wood is cedar or redwood, you'll see a dramatic difference as the wood brightens to its fresh sawn color. Our deck is pressure-treated pine, so the brightening of the wood is less noticeable.

Inspect the whole deck

With the deck clean, it's easy to spot any areas that need additional maintenance. Drive any nail heads that are popping up until they're flush with the deck boards. Look for missing or loose screws, and replace them with corrosion-resistant screws that are slightly longer than the original (Photo 5). Replace missing nails with corrosion-resistant "trim head" screws, which are screws that have a small head and resemble a large finish nail.

If lag screws or bolts are loose in the ledger board, rails or posts, tighten them. Inspect the flashing between your deck and house to ensure it's still firmly in place.

CORROSION-RESISTANT DECK SCREWS

5 SINK any raised nails and screws. Replace loose and missing fasteners with screws at least 1/2 in. longer than the original.

6 REMOVE mold, mildew or algae using non-chlorine bleach. Scrub the area with a nylon brush, then rinse with water. For tougher stains, repeat the process with a TSP substitute.

RUST STAINS FROM NAILS

7 DRIVE the heads of stain-causing fasteners below the wood surface. Then sand out the stains using 80-grit sandpaper. Also sand rough or splintered areas.

Attack stubborn stains

Although the sodium hydroxide in the deck cleaner will remove most stains and mold, particularly stubborn ones require extra attention.

Use a non-chlorine laundry bleach to remove the stain. (This works especially well if the stain is from mold, mildew or algae.) Apply it to the affected area, then scrub with a nylon brush. Rinse the area with water.

For tougher stains, use trisodium phosphate substitute. Mix the TSP substitute with water and apply it to the stain. Let it sit for a minute or two, then scrub with a nylon brush and rinse with water (**Photo 6**).

To remove deep stains that don't come out with TSP substitute, let the deck dry. Sand the stains out, using 80-grit sandpaper and concentrating only on the affected areas. Some stains may be too deep to sand out. Spot-sand rough or splintered areas, working in the direction of the wood grain until the surface is smooth (**Photo 7**).

Wear a dust mask, and sand only if the stain bothers you. After all, imperfections are part of an outdoor deck.

Apply the finish—finally!

The deck will need a minimum of 48 hours to dry after the cleaning. If it rains, wait two more days for the wood to dry. Avoid staining in high heat, high humidity and in direct sunlight. Perfect conditions are an overcast day with the temperature in the 70s and no possibility of rain.

Start by staining the top rails and working down the balusters and posts (**Photo 8**). Run the applicator pad down the length of the wood, applying the stain in a steady, uniform manner. Don't go back over areas that are already stained. Unlike paint, stain gets darker with each coat.

If stain drips onto the deck, smooth it with the applicator pad to avoid spotting. Once the railings are complete, stain the deck boards. Load the pad with plenty of stain, yet not so much that it drips. Start by carefully "cutting in" stain along the house. If stain drips onto the siding, promptly wipe it off using a clean cloth and mineral spirits or paint thinner.

Attach a broom handle to the applicator pad. Glide the pad along the length of the deck boards, staining with the grain (**Photo 9**). Stop only at the end of a board. Otherwise, the overlap where you stopped and started could be noticeable.

Once the deck is finished, apply stain to the stair treads, working your way down the stairs.

Finally, use a paintbrush or spray bottle to work stain into tight areas that the applicator pad couldn't reach, such as lattice and crevices between balusters and the rim joist (**Photo 10**).

Allow the stain to dry at least 48 hours before walking on it. Feel the deck to make sure the stain is completely dry. Likewise, check the bottom of your shoes before walking back into the house. ⌂

8 APPLY stain to the top rail, then the balusters and the posts. Work from the top down. Stain one section at a time, using a foam applicator pad. Brush out drips as you work.

9 STAIN the deck boards using a foam applicator pad with an extension handle. Stain the full length of two or three boards at a time, working with the grain.

10 SPRAY on the finish in hard-to-reach areas or surfaces that are difficult to cover with a paintbrush. Use a wide spray to avoid streaks. Work stain into crevices and narrow areas between balusters and posts with a paintbrush.

Choosing the best stain

You have two basic stain choices: oil-based and water-based. Oil stains are easier to apply, penetrate the wood grain and require less work when you reapply them. However, they only last two to four years.

Water-based (latex) stains last four to six years, but they'll eventually peel and require more prep work before recoating. Opaque latex stains generally last longer than semitransparent versions.

When possible, test the stain on an inconspicuous section of the decking. We used a cedar color that worked well since the wood was pressure treated and somewhat dark in color. For a darker color, a redwood-colored stain is available, while a honey color is an option for a lighter, natural wood look.

Be careful not to choose a light color stain if your deck was previously covered with a dark stain or is pressure treated (green). The light stain will not cover the dark wood or darker stain, and it will turn gray within a few weeks.

If you want a natural gray or silver deck, use a clear finish. It will protect the deck from mildew and algae, but not from the sun, allowing the deck to start graying in a month or two.

Pressure washer safety

To use the pressure washer:
■ Wear appropriate safety gear and clothes. Rubber boots and gloves will protect your hands and feet. Safety goggles will keep the chemicals from splashing into your eyes, and a disposable respirator or dust mask will filter fumes.

■ Keep the exhaust from the pressure washer at least 3 ft. away from any objects, including your house.
■ Practice spraying the water until you find an appropriate power setting.
■ Never point the wand at anything you don't want to spray.
■ Cover electrical outlets.

HomeCare & Repair
TIPS, FIXES & GEAR FOR A TROUBLE-FREE HOME

STIFFEN WOBBLY DECK RAILINGS

Deck posts and railings screwed to a single rim joist feel wobbly because the rim joist flexes whenever you lean against the railing. Adding blocking will stiffen the rim joist and make the railing feel much more solid.

First, tighten any loose bolts and screws. If the post doesn't have bolts, add them—carriage bolts work best.

Cut pressure-treated 2-by blocking (the same width as the floor joists) to fit tightly between the rim joist and the next joist. Place the blocking directly behind the post and toe-screw it into both the rim joist and the neighboring joist. Fasten additional blocking every 4 ft. along the rim joist.

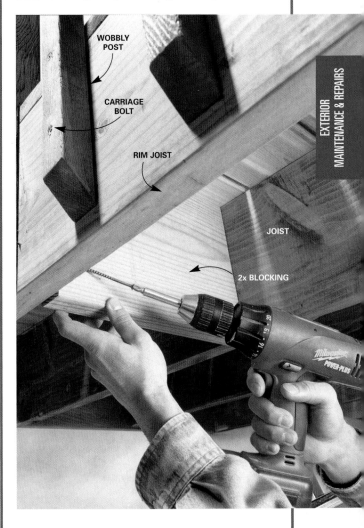

WOBBLY POST

CARRIAGE BOLT

RIM JOIST

JOIST

2x BLOCKING

EXTERIOR MAINTENANCE & REPAIRS

ADD AN
OUTDOOR FAUCET

And stop dragging that hose around!

by **Kurt Anderson**

If you have to stretch out a 50-ft. hose every time you water plants or wash the car, a new outdoor faucet in the right spot could make your summer chores a lot more convenient. To install one, all it takes is a few hours of your time and a little know-how.

This article will provide that know-how, showing you how to drill a hole in an exterior wall, mount the new faucet and connect it to an existing water line inside your home. If you have some plumbing experience, it's an easy project. If you're a plumbing novice, don't let that stop you. Our Web site covers the basics, which aren't included in this article (see p. 158). The steps we show apply to a house with a basement or crawl space. If your home is built on a concrete slab, the process is different. We show copper pipe here, but the job is almost identical if you have plastic pipe. Connecting new pipe to old galvanized steel pipe requires extra steps that we won't cover here, though the rest of the project is similar. For help working with plastic or galvanized pipe, see p. 158.

Everything you need is available at home centers and hardware stores. You'll need basic plumbing tools and a drill (a hammer drill if you have a brick exterior). If you use copper pipe and a brass ball valve, this project will cost about $50. If you use plastic (CPVC), you'll spend $30 or less. A professional plumber would charge at least $120 to complete the simple installation shown here. Before you start work, call your local inspections department and ask if you need a permit for this project.

Choose the "tee-in" point first

To install an outdoor faucet, you need to cut an existing water line, install a "tee" and run a new branch of pipe to the new faucet (**photo below**). In a home with an unfinished basement or crawl space, the exposed plumbing and open joists make this a straightforward plumbing project that takes less than a day. If your home is built on a concrete slab or you have a finished basement, you'll probably have to cut into walls or ceilings. This is a bigger, more difficult job and the repair work can add a day or two to the project.

If you have easy access to several water lines, choose the one that offers the most convenient path for the new

ELBOW

BALL VALVE

DRAIN PORT

FEMALE FITTING

FAUCET VALVE

FAUCET PIPE

VINYL FAUCET BLOCK

VACUUM BREAKER

RIM JOIST

TEE

← WATER SUPPLY

branch, usually the line closest to the new faucet. You can tee into a 1/2-in. pipe, but a larger (3/4-in.) line will deliver higher pressure to the new faucet (and some codes require 3/4-in. pipe). If you have a water softener, it's preferable to tee into your water supply before it reaches the softener; this avoids wasted salt and an unnecessary load on the softener. Be sure to choose a cold water line! Either trace the pipe back to the water meter or water heater to make sure. Or turn on a faucet to run water through the pipe—if the pipe feels warm, choose a different pipe.

Choose a frost-proof, vacuum-breaker faucet

When you've determined the best tee-in point and the pathway of the new pipe, make up a shopping list. You'll need pipe that matches the diameter of the existing water line, an elbow fitting for each turn in the new branch, a tee and a "slip" coupler. Also buy a ball valve that has a drain port so you can easily shut off the water when the time comes to repair the faucet (hopefully never!). Choose a faucet (aka "hose bib" or "sill cock") that's connected to a long pipe. The long pipe on a "freeze-proof" faucet places the faucet's valve far inside house. That way, the pipe empties each time you shut off the water, so it won't freeze and burst the pipe in winter. If the store carries several lengths, choose the longest one and be sure it matches the diameter of your existing pipe (1/2 or 3/4 in.). The faucet must include a vacuum breaker (photo, p. 156) to prevent water from flowing backward into the house and contaminating your water supply.

Before you leave the store, measure the diameter of the faucet pipe's threaded end and buy a spade bit that's about 1/8 in. larger. If screws aren't included with the faucet, buy two No. 10 x 2-in. stainless steel screws. If you have a brick exterior, buy No. 8 x 1-in. screws and 1/4-in. plastic wall anchors.

Drill a hole in your house

Begin by drilling a 1/4-in. hole through the rim joist and wall from inside to mark the faucet location outside. If you have brick or stucco, drill with a standard bit first and finish with a masonry bit. For brick, you'll need a masonry bit at least 6 in. long. Then drill a full-size hole from outside using the 1/4-in. hole as a pilot hole. If you have wood, hardboard or fiber cement siding, simply drill through the siding and rim joist with a spade bit (Photo 2).

Here's how to handle different exterior materials:

Vinyl siding: Cut a rectangular hole for a faucet block ($10 at home centers) by making several passes with a sharp utility knife. "Unzip" the lower edge of the siding with a zip tool ($5) and slip the block into place (Photo 1). Reattach the siding and drill the faucet hole with the spade bit, using the hole in the block as a guide.

Stucco: Mark a circle on the wall slightly larger than your spade bit. Drill a series of holes (without space between them) around the perimeter of the circle using a 1/4-in. masonry bit. Chip out the stucco with a 1/2-in. masonry chisel and cut the metal lath with wire cutters. Then drill through the rim joist with the spade bit.

Brick: Using a hammer drill, bore holes in a circle just as with stucco. Also drill several holes inside the circle. Then chip out the hole with a masonry chisel. Finally, drill through the rim joist with the spade bit.

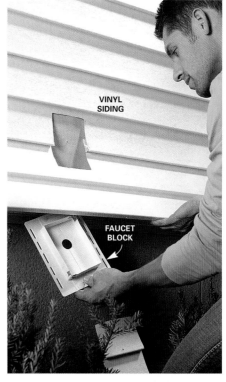

1 DRILL a 1/4-in. hole through the wall from inside to mark the faucet location. "Unzip" vinyl siding and slip the faucet block under the siding. Then drill a full-size pipe hole from outside.

2 RUN a heavy bead of silicone caulk around the back of the faucet flange and insert the pipe. Drill pilot holes and screw the faucet into place.

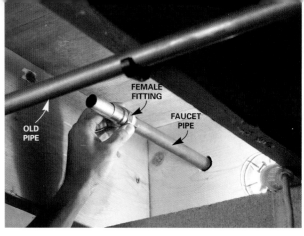

Install the faucet and run pipe to it

With the hole complete, insert the faucet and fasten it with mounting screws (**Photo 2**). If you have overlapping siding (wood, hardboard or fiber cement), be sure to use the tapered plastic shim that comes with the faucet. Slipped behind the faucet flange, the shim prevents the faucet pipe from tilting downward inside the house. The pipe must be level or tip slightly toward the outside so the water drains out.

Solder a section of pipe to a female threaded fitting. The pipe can be short or long, depending on where you want to locate the ball valve later. Screw the fitting onto the faucet pipe (**Photo 3**). For a leak-proof connection, wrap the threaded end of the faucet pipe with Teflon tape and then coat the tape with pipe thread compound. When you tighten the fitting, be sure to hold back the faucet pipe with a second wrench—otherwise you'll turn the spout outside.

Next, slip the ball valve onto the pipe and extend the new branch line toward the existing water line. If you're building a short, simple branch with copper pipe as we show here, it's usually fastest to "dry-fit" the parts first. When the whole branch is complete and connected to the old pipe, disassemble it, clean and flux the parts, then reassemble and solder it all at once. A longer or more complex branch may fall apart as you add parts to it, so you'll have to solder some of the joints as you go.

When the new branch reaches the existing water line, shut off the water at the main valve to your home and drain the line by turning on the lowest faucet in the house (usually a basement or outdoor faucet). Leave this faucet on until you're done soldering.

Mark the old pipe and cut out a 6-in. section. Keep a bucket handy to catch any water trapped in the line. For successful soldering later, it's vital that you drain all the water out of the pipe. If necessary, remove the pipe supports and tilt down the cut ends to drain water out.

Slip the tee onto one of the cut ends of the old pipe (**Photo 4**) and slide a "slip" coupler completely onto the other. Then cut and install a short section of "patch pipe" to span the gap between the tee and the old pipe (**Photo 5**). Slide the coupler halfway over the patch pipe. You must use a slip coupler in order to insert the short patch pipe.

Solder all the joints, starting at the slip coupler and working toward the ball valve. Let the solder joints cool and then turn on the water at the main valve and check for leaks. Turn on the outdoor faucet and let it run for two minutes to flush any sediment out of the pipes. From inside, use silicone caulk to seal around the faucet pipe where it passes through the rim joist. Don't leave a garden hose connected to the faucet in freezing temperatures. The hose won't allow the faucet pipe to drain, and it could freeze and burst. ⌂

3 SOLDER a section of pipe to a female threaded fitting and screw it onto the faucet pipe. Hold the faucet pipe with one wrench while you turn the fitting with another.

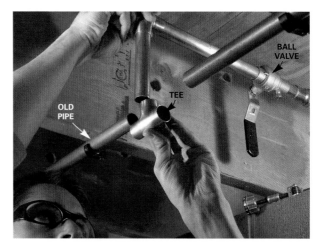

4 ADD a ball valve and run new pipe to the existing water line. Cut out a 6-in. section of the old pipe so you can add a tee.

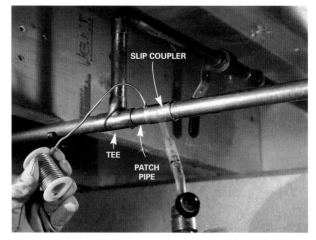

5 CONNECT the tee. Add a short "patch pipe" and connect it to the old pipe with a slip coupler. Solder all the connections, turn on the water and check for leaks.

Tip

Get more help online. Go to our home page and search for "solder copper pipe," "plastic pipe," "steel pipe," and "vinyl siding tools." thefamilyhandyman.com

HomeCare & Repair

TIPS, FIXES & GEAR FOR A TROUBLE-FREE HOME

PROTECT YOUR DECK FURNITURE WITH A CLASSIC WOOD BOAT FINISH

If you'd like to preserve the natural wood appearance of your wood entry door or your outdoor furniture, take a lesson from boat builders. Boat builders and restorers use multiple coats of epoxy and spar varnish to protect wood—instead of spar varnish alone—because the combination is much stronger than either finish is separately. Epoxy creates a tough, flexible moisture barrier; spar varnish adds depth and UV protection, which keeps the epoxy from yellowing and eventually disintegrating.

The epoxy, a special type for clear-coating wood, is sold at woodworking suppliers, hobby shops and marine supply stores (see Buyer's Guide, at right). It's expensive—the 2 quarts we used for our project cost $70—but when fully cured, the finish is very tough and will last for years.

To begin, sand and clean the wood, then stain it if desired. Mix the resin and hardener thoroughly in a disposable container. A batch will start to harden in about 30 minutes, faster if it's hot out, so just mix a small quantity the first time to see how far you get. Apply the epoxy with an inexpensive natural-bristle brush (**Photo 1**). (You'll need a new brush for each coat.) When the epoxy in the container starts to stiffen and feel warm, discard the container and the brush and mix a new batch.

Allow the epoxy finish to harden overnight, then sand thoroughly and apply another coat. The manufacturer recommends three coats.

Sand the final coat of epoxy after it has cured for at least 24 hours (**Photo 2**), then vacuum the surface and wipe it with a damp rag. Topcoat the epoxy with a minimum of three coats of exterior spar varnish (**Photo 3**). Add coats of varnish every few years to keep the finish looking fresh.

TWO-PART EPOXY
Mix the resin and hardener thoroughly in a clean, disposable container, in the proportions specified by the manufacturer.

1 SPREAD the epoxy, then lightly drag the brush back through to even it out and eliminate bubbles. Work quickly and allow the thick epoxy to flatten without brushing it too much.

2 SAND each coat with 120-grit sandpaper to flatten out any ridges and flaws, then clean and resand with 220-grit to create a smooth, scratch-free surface for the varnish.

3 APPLY three coats of oil-based spar varnish with a high-quality china-bristle brush, brushing with the grain. Sand the varnish between coats.

Buyer's Guide
You can find epoxy for clear-coating wood at local distributors or order online at:
- systemthree.com: (800) 333-5514
- westsystem.com: (866) 937-8797

EXTERIOR
MAINTENANCE & REPAIRS

HomeCare & Repair

REPLACE DAMAGED VINYL SIDING

Vinyl siding is tough, but not indestructible. If a falling branch or a well-hit baseball has cracked a piece of your siding, you can make it as good as new in about 15 minutes with a $5 zip tool (available at any home center) and a replacement piece. It's as simple as unzipping the damaged piece and snapping in a new one.

ZIP TOOL

Starting at one end of the damaged piece, push the end of the zip tool up under the siding until you feel it hook the bottom lip (**Photo 1**). Pull the zip tool downward and out to unhook the bottom lip, then slide it along the edge, pulling the siding out as you go. Then unzip any pieces above the damaged piece. Hold them out of the way with your elbow while you pry out the nails that hold the damaged piece in place (**Photo 2**).

Slide the replacement piece up into place, pushing up until the lower lip locks into the piece below it. Drive 1-1/4-in. roofing nails through the nailing flange. Space them about every 16 in. (near the old nail holes). Nail in the center of the nailing slot and leave about 1/32 in. of space between the nail head and the siding so the vinyl can move freely. Don't nail the heads tightly or the siding will buckle when it warms up.

With the new piece nailed, use the zip tool to lock the upper piece down over it. Start at one end and pull the lip down, twisting the tool slightly to force the leading edge down (**Photo 3**). Slide the zip tool along, pushing in on the vinyl just behind the tool with your other hand so it snaps into place.

It's best to repair vinyl in warm weather. In temperatures below freezing it becomes less flexible and may crack.

The downside of replacing older vinyl siding is that it can be hard to match the style and color, and siding rarely has any identifying marks. The best way to get a replacement piece is to take the broken piece to vinyl siding distributors in your area and find the closest match. If the old vinyl has faded or you can't find the right color, take the broken piece to a paint store and have the color matched. Paint the replacement piece with one coat of top-quality acrylic primer followed by acrylic house paint—acrylic paint will flex with the movement of the vinyl.

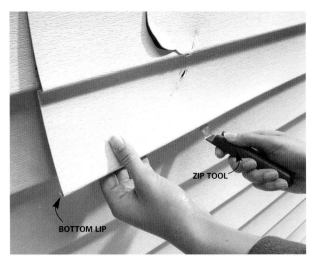

1 SLIDE the zip tool along the bottom edge to release the vinyl siding from the piece below it.

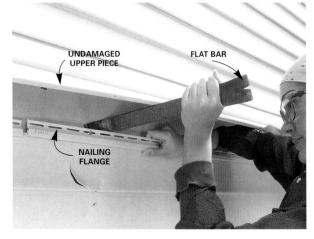

2 SLIP a flat bar behind the vinyl siding and lever out the nails.

3 INSTALL the replacement piece and hook the lip of the upper siding piece into the slot to lock it into place.

RAISE SUNKEN PATIO PAVERS

After a few years, paver block patios and walkways often develop low spots. However, these areas can be brought back up to grade with a few bags of sand, a length of pipe and a screed board.

First, remove the pavers from the low area. If they're packed in tight, use a screwdriver to lever the first paver out, levering each end a little at a time and tapping on surrounding pavers until you can pull out the paver (**Photo 1**).

Make a screed board long enough to rest on the level pavers around it. Then notch the ends 1/8 in. less than the depth of the pavers. If the area is large or against the house or grass, set a screed pipe along one side and level it against the pavers you're matching. If you're trying to match a sloping walk, shim the level at the downhill end to match the slope (**Photo 2**).

Fill the low area with coarse, all-purpose sand, then screed it level (**Photo 3**). Use a trowel like a spatula around the edges to scrape away any excess sand.

Brush any old sand off the sides of the pavers, then set them back into place and drive them down until they're flush with the other pavers (**Photo 4**). Spread dry sand over the pavers, tamping and sweeping until the joints are completely full.

1 PRY up the paver with a thin screwdriver, pounding on adjoined pavers to vibrate packed sand loose.

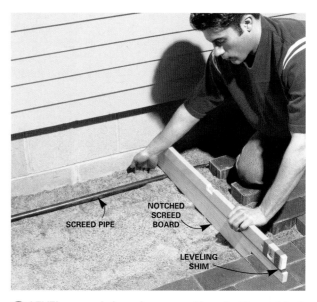

2 LEVEL a screed pipe using a screed board with a notch at one end 1/8 in. shallower than the depth of the pavers.

3 ADD sand to the low area, then level it by pulling the screed board along the pipe and the pavers.

4 REMOVE the screed pipe and set the pavers back, tapping them down level with a board.

EXTERIOR MAINTENANCE & REPAIRS

ROOF
TEAR-OFF

*Conquer the toughest, dirtiest
part of reroofing*

by **Brett Martin**

Don't be intimidated by the toughest part of reroofing—the tear-off. In this story, we'll show you how to remove asphalt shingles quickly, so you can move on to the more rewarding part of the job—laying new shingles. We'll also show you how to "button up" the roof by applying new ice and water barrier and felt paper.

Before you take on this big chore, get a bid from a contractor to make sure the savings are worth the strain. The cost of professional roof tear-off varies widely, depending on where you live, the style of the roof and how many layers of shingles it has. In most situations, you can expect to save at least $1,000 by doing it yourself. In some situations, you'll save $3,000 or more.

Planning

Before starting the tear-off, get a building permit and check local building codes. Keep the time between the tear-off and reshingling to a minimum, and wait until clear weather is forecast. Although the underlayment should protect against water infiltration, the felt paper can easily tear or blow loose, making your home vulnerable to rain damage.

If you're having a contractor apply the new shingles, coordinate the tear-off so the new shingles will be installed right away. If you're tackling everything yourself, work in sections. Rip the old shingles off one area, then reshingle before moving on to the next section.

Roof safety

Working on a roof is dangerous, so take precautions.
- Set roof jacks ($6 each) and a 2x10 about 3 ft. up from the roof edge (**Photo 1**).
- Wear a safety harness ($150), which you can buy at safety equipment stores and some roofing and home centers.
- Wear soft rubber-soled shoes for traction, long pants to protect your legs, work gloves and safety glasses.

Prep for the tear-off

Doing a little prep work on the ground will keep nails and other debris out of the grass and flower beds, reduce cleanup time and preserve the landscaping. Place plywood over the air conditioner (make sure the power to it is turned off) and over doors or windows near the spot where you'll be tossing the debris off the roof. Then cover plants, shrubs, grass and other areas around the house with inexpensive tarps to vastly simplify cleanup.

Rent a trash container (a 20-cu.-yd. size will handle most roofs and costs about $200). If possible, have it dropped next to the house so you can easily throw old shingles directly into it from the roof.

For safety and better footing, nail the roof jacks below the area you intend to strip first (**Photo 1**). Buy the adjustable type designed to hold a 2x10 board. Space the jacks no more than 4 ft. apart. Fasten them with at least three 16d nails driven through the roof sheathing into a rafter.

Strip the roof

Start the tear-off at the section farthest from the trash container. Standing at the peak, use a garden fork or a specially notched roofing shovel to tear away the ridge caps and the top courses of shingles (**Photo 3**). Forks and roofing shovels are available at roofing and home centers, starting at $25. Some roofers prefer forks because they don't get caught on nails, making it easier and faster to remove the shingles. Others like the shovels because they pull out more nails with the shingles.

Work the fork under the ridge caps, prying them loose. As they come loose, allow them to slide down to the roof jacks. Or, if they don't slide down the roof, carry them to the edge of the roof and throw them into the trash container.

Once the ridge caps are gone, slide the fork under the shingles and felt paper and pry the shingles up. Some nails will come up with the shingles. Others won't. Ignore them for now.

Remove shingles in a 2- to 3-ft.-wide section as you work down the roof (**Photo 4**). The shingles will roll up like a ball in front of the fork. Push the shingles down to the roof jacks. Continue tearing off the shingles and underlayment until you reach the roof jacks, then start over at the top of the roof.

Into the trash

As the old roofing material piles up at the roof jacks, carry it to the edge of the roof and toss it into the trash container below (**Photo 5**). If you couldn't get the trash container close to the house, throw the shingles onto a tarp on the ground. Make the pile on a flat area away from flowers and shrubs.

Shingles are heavy. They usually come off in clumps. If you're peeling off two or more layers of shingles, even a small section will be heavy. You may have to pull the shingles apart to make them light enough to carry. Rolling the shingles and felt paper into a ball will also make them easier to handle.

Work with care around roof penetrations

Slow down and work with care when you're next to chimneys, skylights, dormers or an exterior wall. While it's usually best to replace metal flashing, sometimes it's better to preserve and reuse difficult-to-replace types if they're in good shape. But if you see rust and cracks in the metal, replace it. Metal in that condition won't last as long as your new roof.

> **CAUTION:** Watch for soft areas as you walk on the roof. The sheathing may be rotted, and you could break through.

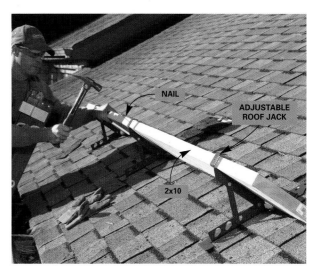

1 NAIL roof jacks to the rafters and then nail on a 2x10 to prevent you—and the shingles—from sliding off the roof.

2 USE a safety harness system to prevent falls. Wear shoes with soft rubber soles for a good grip and long pants to protect against the skin-scraping shingles.

3 TEAR off the ridge caps so you can work the fork under the shingles near the peak.

EXTERIOR
MAINTENANCE & REPAIRS

If you're keeping the old metal flashing, remove nails and bend it upward off the shingles with a pry bar (**Photo 6**). Be careful not to damage the flashing. Once it's out of the way, pull any nails and remove any shingles and underlayment that are underneath. Do the same with step flashing (flashing that's interwoven with the shingles) where the roof abuts a wall (**Photo 7**).

Tip

Heavily tarred areas usually signal a Band-Aid fix for bad flashing underneath. Replace all this flashing.

Tear off shingles along the edge

After stripping the shingles down to the roof jacks, remove the jacks. Work the remaining courses loose with a fork or shovel, but don't pry them completely free or they'll slide off the roof (**Photo 8**).

Loosen the shingles all along the eaves. Then pull off the shingles with your hands, carry them across the roof to the trash container location and throw them in.

Some roofs have a self-adhering ice and water barrier installed along the roof edge. This asphalt membrane usually pulls up with a fork or shovel, although it may require

some scraping. If it refuses to come loose, simply leave it and install your new underlayment over it.

If you don't have time before dark to clean the roof and apply felt, nail down plastic tarps for the night.

Trash old valley and vent flashing

Pry the flashing in valleys and over plumbing vents last. This flashing usually has the same life span as the shingles, so plan to replace it.

Starting at the top of the valley, slip the fork or a flat bar under the flashing and pry the metal edges loose. Continue working down the valley, lifting up the flashing (**Photo 9**). Pry up and toss out old vent flashing as well (**Photo 10**).

Clean the deck

Once a section has been completely stripped, go back and pull out protruding nails. Then use a large broom to sweep the roof deck clean (**Photo 11**). Walk carefully. The shingle granules make the sheathing slippery.

4 WORK from the peak down, tearing off shingles in easy-to-carry sections. Tear off a section all the way down to the roof jacks before returning to the peak.

5 THROW old shingles directly into the trash container as they pile up at the roof jacks. Dispose of the shingles before the pile gets too large and they slide off the roof.

6 PULL nails carefully around flashings you plan to reuse. Skylight and chimney flashings are often worth saving if they're in good condition.

7 PULL nails from any step flashing you want to save, bend it up slightly and pull out the shingles from underneath.

When the roof is clean and bare, inspect the sheathing for damage. Rotted areas and broken boards are the most common problems. Cut out and replace damaged sections as needed. Be sure to use new sheathing that's the same thickness as the old. When removing a damaged section, center the cuts over the rafters so you can nail the new sheathing to the rafters. Also keep an eye out for loose roof sheathing that needs renailing.

"Buttoning up" the roof

Buttoning up the roof is the final prep step before shingling. It consists of installing ice and water barrier ($50 a roll) and 30-lb. asphalt-saturated felt ($10 a roll).

This underlayment acts as a temporary weather barrier to keep rain out. But it won't stop heavy rain and wind, so once you start a section, always try to flash and shingle it by the end of the day.

Ice and water barrier is used at roof edges and other vulnerable areas. To install it, snap a chalk line 36 in. from the edge of the eaves. If you have gutters, you'll want the ice and water barrier to cover all of the gutter flashing that's on the roof (**Photo 12**).

Starting at the rake edge of the roof (**Photo 8**), align the ice and water barrier with the chalk line. Tack it at the top with staples every few feet to hold it in place. Once the entire section is tacked along the chalk line, lift up the bottom part, peel off the backing, then let it fall back into place. The ice and water barrier will immediately stick to the roof.

Flip the top part of the ice and water barrier back over the bottom section (the staples will easily pop out), peel off the backing, then set it back into place on the roof. Work carefully to avoid wrinkles. They're a hassle to get out. Move on to the next section of roof edge, overlapping the vertical seams of the ice and water barrier by 6 in.

Add a second course above the first, if required, overlapping the first by 4 in. Also lay the ice and water barrier in valleys and around chimneys, skylights and other roof penetrations.

Then unroll and staple down 30-lb. felt over the rest of the roof. Use plenty of staples (5/16 in.) to make the felt safer to walk on and keep it from blowing off. This is where a hammer-type stapler ($30) pays off. You can drive a dozen staples in seconds.

8 REMOVE the roof jacks and work the shingles loose along the roof edge with a fork. Then pull them off by hand.

9 PRY up the old flashing in the valleys using a fork. Valley flashing is never worth reusing.

10 PRY flashing loose around vent pipes. Use a pry bar rather than a fork to avoid damaging the pipes. Never reuse vent flashing.

11 SWEEP the roof clean to avoid slips and falls. Watch for any nails you missed earlier and pull them.

Clean up the area

Before climbing off the roof, clean any debris out of the gutters. There will be nails and a lot of granules from the shingles that you don't want pouring out of your downspouts the next time it rains.

Run a broom magnet over the yard to pick up stray nails. You can rent the magnet at tool rental stores for less than $15. Make several passes in different directions. Regardless of how carefully you worked, nails have a way of ending up in the lawn. 🏠

ICE AND WATER BARRIER

12 COVER the roof right away to protect against rain. Cover the lower end with self-stick ice and water barrier. Then staple down roofing felt to protect the rest of the roof.

When are shingles worn out?

The most obvious sign that your roof needs to be replaced is a leak. Since you don't want to wait until that happens, inspect the shingles every year. Most asphalt shingles have a life span of 20 to 25 years, although they can wear out and need to be replaced in as few as 15 years, especially on the south side of the house.

Signs that shingles are failing include cupping along the edges (the edges curl up) and extensive cracking. In severe cases, the shingles will completely deteriorate. Buckling shingles (the shingles develop a bow and lift up from the roof) are an indication that moisture is getting underneath them. If large sections of shingles are coming loose and falling off, it's time for a new roof.

Shingles typically show signs of wear along the edges first. Rounded or curled corners are early warnings that the roof is ready or nearly ready for new shingles.

Replace the roof when shingles show signs of wear such as curling, buckling, cracking, or missing granules.

KEEP RACCOONS OUT

Raccoons will eat almost anything and are always on the lookout for a good nesting site, so our houses, with all their nooks and crannies and overflowing garbage cans and backyard vegetable gardens, are very appealing. Light, water, noise and chemical repellents may work in the short term, but raccoons eventually learn to ignore them. The best way to discourage these pests is to make your house and garden inaccessible.

- Cut back overhanging tree branches and brush so raccoons can't get onto the roof.
- Add chimney caps, or replace them if they're damaged. Fireplace chimneys make great dens for pregnant raccoons. If you hear raccoons in the firebox in the spring or summer, you may need to wait until the fall for the raccoons to leave before capping the chimney, or else call an animal control specialist.
- Block crawl spaces and other possible entry spots with securely nailed 1/4-in.-mesh hardware cloth. Wait until the fall after the babies are out but before hibernation, or until you're sure the raccoons are gone.
- Raccoons eat garbage, pet food, fruits and vegetables, and fish from garden ponds. Make trash cans inaccessible. Cover fish ponds with netting. Don't leave pet food outside.

CORBIS (RF)

- Protect vegetable gardens, especially if you're planting sweet corn, with wire electric fencing (consult the manufacturer's instructions for spacing and wiring instructions). Fencing is available from farm supply stores and online suppliers.
- If raccoons have already made a den in your attic or crawl space, put a radio, flashing lights, ammonia, mothballs or commercially available repellents in it, then give them a few nights to leave. To make sure they're gone, stuff the entry with newspapers. If the paper is still in place after a few days, the raccoons have left.

NewProducts

LADDER DESIGNED FOR UNEVEN SURFACES

Setting up a ladder on uneven ground or stairs can be dangerous, and slipping blocking under one leg to level it isn't safe. Werner's new "Equalizer" extension ladder solves the problem with built-in leg levelers that adjust for uneven surfaces, so you can set it up quickly and work safely. The legs adjust in 3/8-in. increments up to 8-1/4 in. It's ideal for slopes, steps and other unequal surfaces.

Lowe's sells the ladder for $180 to $250, depending on the model.

Werner Ladder Co., (888) 523-3370. wernerladder.com

SCREEN DOOR ALTERNATIVE

Traditional screen doors are prone to sticking. Retractable screens, on the other hand, retract into a housing, so they're less likely to get dinged and banged up, making them easier to operate. Such screens have been available for windows for decades, and now they're being offered for entry doors (starting at $130). When you want to keep out insects, slide the screen closed along the tracks installed at the top and bottom of the door. A magnetic latch secures it. For the several months of the year when the screen isn't needed, it retracts into a housing, where it won't obstruct your view.

The screens are available for swinging and sliding doors and in different heights. They come only in white. Buy the ODL Retractable Screen Door at Home Depot. Detailed installation instructions are included.

ODL, (866) 635-4968. odl.com

INSTALLING AN
OUTDOOR **HANDRAIL**

Add safety and style with a custom railing

by **Jeff Gorton**

A new iron handrail on the front steps will enhance your home's curb appeal, but the real benefit is the added safety it provides. Whether you need to replace a wobbly old railing or add a railing where there isn't one already, we'll show you how to order and install a new one.

Iron handrails range in price from $60 to over $150 per running foot. In addition, most companies charge several hundred dollars to measure for and install the railing. Here's where you can save cash. We'll show you how to measure a simple set of steps so you can order a custom railing and how to bolt the completed railing securely to your concrete steps. If your entry step is curved, has jogs or is an unusual shape, ask the railing company to measure for you.

Order a custom railing

Careful measuring is the key to a successful handrail order. **Photos 1 – 4** show how to take the measurements you'll need to order the railing. Record the measurements on a sketch as we show below, right. Take the sketch to the railing fabricator to place the order.

Most large cities have an iron railing fabricator that will be glad to show you the railing designs it sells. There are a few standard styles, which only require you to choose between straight or twisted spindles, and perhaps whether you want the top rail to start with a "lamb's tongue" like ours (**Photo 8**), or a scroll.

We added a few upgrades to the basic railing to come up with our design. First we chose to install a brass cap rail. Then we added a second rail 4 in. below the top. We also increased the size of the square spindles from the standard 1/2-in. width to 5/8 in. for a heavier appearance. For an easy do-it-yourself installation, ask the railing company to weld 3-in.-square stainless steel plates to the bottom of each post and drill 3/8-in. holes in all four corners.

Then you can simply bolt the rail to the stairs as we show here. Get a quote from your fabricator for the railing design you choose.

After ordering your custom railing, you'll probably have to wait a few weeks for it to be completed. But once you get it home, it'll only take you a few hours to do a top-notch installation. The only special tool you'll need is a hammer drill with a 3/8-in. masonry bit. You can rent a hammer drill for about $30 for four hours, and the bit will cost about $5. Purchase 3/8 x 1-7/8-in. sleeve anchors and 5/16-in. cap nuts for each anchor. Make sure you wear safety glasses and hearing protection when you're drilling.

4 measurements for a perfect fit

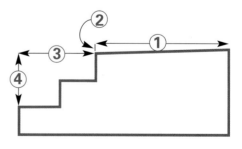

Make a simple sketch and jot down four measurements to help the fabricator build a perfect railing.

1 MEASURE the depth of the landing. If you're installing railings on both sides, make separate sketches and take separate measurements for each side.

2 LAY a level on the landing and shim it until the bubble is centered. Then measure the gap between the level and the landing.

3 HOLD a level against the lowest step and adjust it until the bubble reads plumb. Then measure from the edge of the level to the edge of the landing to determine the total "run" of the treads.

4 LAY a level on the landing and adjust it until the bubble is between the lines. Measure from the bottom of the level to the top of the bottom step to determine the total rise of the steps.

Strong anchors make for a sturdy railing

Sleeve anchors provide strong support in solid concrete. But the pressure the anchors exert as you tighten the nuts can crack or "blow out" concrete that's not structurally sound. Before you order a new handrail, make sure the concrete is solid, that is, free of cracks and surface deterioration. If your steps are covered with brick or stone, materials that may easily crack, you may have to use another anchoring method. A two-part epoxy anchoring system often works better than sleeve anchors in these circumstances. Ask the railing fabricator for advice before you order the rail.

Photos 5 and 6 show how to drill for and set the anchors. Set the railing on the steps with the edge of the plates at least 1-1/2 in. from both the front and the side of

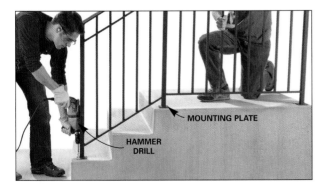

5 POSITION the railing, making sure all the plates are an equal distance from the edges of the steps. Drill one hole at each end and drop in anchors to hold the railing in place. Then mark the remaining holes by drilling 1/2-in.-deep starter holes.

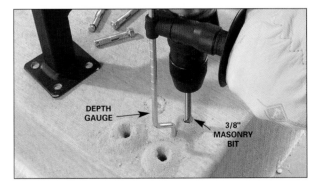

6 SET the railing aside and drill 2-1/2-in.-deep holes. Blow the dust away from the holes.

the step. Adjust the railing position until the mounting plates are parallel with the side of the steps. Then mark the hole locations with the drill while the railing is in place to ensure accurate bolt placement. Start by drilling one starter hole through each of the end brackets and dropping an anchor bolt into the hole. This keeps the railing from

SLEEVE ANCHOR

shifting while you mark the remaining holes. When all the holes are marked, remove the railing and complete the holes by drilling them 2-1/2 in. deep. Drill vertical holes; otherwise, the plate may not fit over the bolts. Set the gauge on your hammer drill for accurate hole depth.

When all the holes are drilled, tap anchor bolts into each one and set the railing in place (Photo 7). Snug up the bolts, but don't fully tighten them until you've checked the posts for plumb (Photo 8).

Shim posts for a perfect installation

Out-of-level steps can cause the handrail posts to lean. Photo 8 shows how to check for and solve the problem. We used stainless steel washers because they won't rust and are thinner than galvanized washers. They're readily available at hardware stores and home centers. As an added precaution against corrosion, spread a layer of polyurethane caulk under each plate before bolting them down. This keeps water out of the bolt holes and provides a little extra strength.

For a neater-looking job, we cut off bolts that were too long and replaced the hex nuts with decorative cap nuts (Photos 9 and 10). The railing company painted the cap nuts to match the railing. 🏠

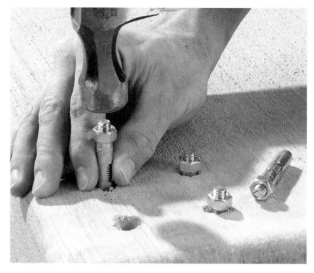

7 TAP in the anchors. Then remove the nuts, set the railing in place and snug up the nuts.

LAMB'S TONGUE

STAINLESS STEEL WASHERS

8 CHECK the posts for plumb with a level. If a post leans, loosen the nuts and slide a thin washer under the side it leans to. Snug the nuts and recheck with the level.

MINI HACKSAW

HEX NUT

9 SAW the bolts flush to the top of the hex nuts with a hacksaw. Then remove the hex nuts.

9/16" WRENCH

5/16" PAINTED CAP NUT

10 THREAD cap nuts onto the bolts and tighten them.

6 Outdoor Structures & Landscaping

IN THIS CHAPTER

Garden Archway .172

Ask TFH 176
   Identifying lumber treatments,
   flashing a deck ledger board and more

Slay the Crabgrass Monster 178

Cast a Concrete Fountain 182

Storage Bench 187

Build a Vinyl Fence 192

Handy Hints 199
   Storing lawn products, locating
   sprinkler lines and more

8 Tips for an Easy-Care Yard 200

Arched Planter 203

New Products 208
   Two-wheel cart, fold-up cart,
   four-wheel dump cart and more

Pour Your First Big Slab 211

Rain Garden 217

Home Care & Repair 221
   Broadcast spreader techniques

Gallery of Ideas .222

GARDEN
ARCHWAY

Make this charming climber from $25 of steel—no welding required!

by **Lucie B. Amundsen**

Looking for a garden feature that's low cost and easy to assemble? Then this archway trellis is perfect for you. We made it from inexpensive steel "rebar" that you can find at any home center. Once the trellis is covered with climbing plants, the steel disappears and you have a dramatic entryway into your garden.

Our design, about 7 ft. high and 6 ft. wide, is made of two 20-ft. lengths of rebar that you bend into arches. You then simply join the arches with rebar circles, lashing them together with wraps of copper wire. No welding needed—and there's no maintenance. The materials for our trellis cost less than $25. For comparison, a welded metal or high-end vinyl trellis costs several hundred dollars.

In this story, we'll show you how to create smooth bends in rebar and how to assemble the trellis. You'll need a few simple tools, including a conduit bender ($30) for tight curves and a hacksaw for cutting the bar to length. In the "fun-to-buy-tools" department, you may want to pick up an angle grinder ($50) and a metal-cutting blade for quicker rebar cuts. And don't forget to buy a pair of heavy leather gloves.

Allow a full day to build your first trellis. Once you've mastered the process, you should be able to build a second one in less than half a day. Rebar itself is relatively inexpensive: A 20-ft. length of 1/2-in. costs about $7 and 3/8-in. about $4. The main problem is getting your 20-ft.

lengths home. Rebar is floppy, not stiff. One trick is to buy a 16-ft.-long 2x4, attach it to your roof rack and then lash the rebar to it. (Be sure to attach a red flag to each end of it.) Otherwise, delivery costs vary from $50 to more than $100.

Create smooth bends with stakes

To create that swooping arch from the 1/2-in. rebar, make a simple bending jig on the ground. Cut the 10-ft. length of 1/2-in. rebar into ten 10-in.-long stakes (**Photo 1**). Drive one rebar stake into the ground and tie a 3-ft. string to it. When you pull the string taut, you create a compass and can mark a smooth arc with chalk (**Photo 2**). Space the other nine stakes evenly in a semicircle around the arc, driving them at least 5 in. deep (**Photo 3**).

The 3-ft. radius makes an arch that will span 6 ft. You can make it larger or slightly smaller if you want. But we found that bending 1/2-in. rebar into a 2-ft. radius is difficult.

Rebar may kink when you bend it, so we inserted a cushion (a 9-ft. length of plastic garage door stop molding; $8 at home centers) between the rebar and the stakes to soften the bend (**Photo 4**). You can use some other firm but flexible item, like vinyl siding or a strip of flexible hardboard to cushion the rebar as well.

Photo 4 shows how to bend the arches. Hold the rebar at the ends while you bend it to keep the arch smooth. Overbend it slightly; the ends will spring back a bit when you release them. Don't worry about that; the arches will form the correct radius when you set them in the ground.

Create circles with a conduit bender

We linked the arches together with circles bent from the 3/8-in. rebar. Cut the rebar into 4-ft. lengths and bend them with a 1/2-in. conduit bender (available in the electrical department of any home center or hardware store). Work on a solid surface and simply fit one end of the rebar into the lip of the bender. Then form the curve by pulling the handle and pressing down on the tool with your foot (**Photo 5**). Shift the bender and continue the bend until

MATERIALS LIST

Two 1/2-in. x 20-ft. lengths of rebar (for arches)
One 1/2-in. x 10-ft. length of rebar (for stakes)
Two 3/8-in. x 20-ft. lengths of rebar (for circles)
18-gauge copper wire
Plastic garage door stop molding or other stiff but bendable material
Conduit bender
Cable ties

**Figure A
Arched trellis**

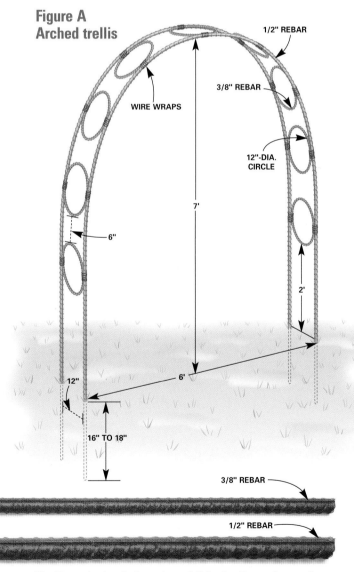

You'll need rebar in two sizes: 1/2-in. for the arches and 3/8-in. for the circles.

1 CUT 1/2-in. rebar into ten 10-in. stakes. Saw about two-thirds of the way through with a hacksaw, then snap off the stake.

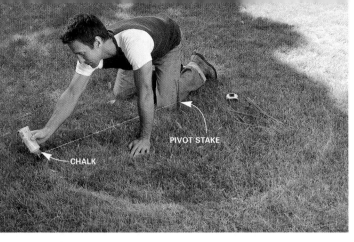

PIVOT STAKE

CHALK

CENTER STAKE

2 DRIVE a stake and tie a string to it. Mark a 3-ft.-radius arc on the lawn using the string to guide the chalk bottle.

3 SPACE nine stakes evenly around the semicircle, and drive them down about 5 in. Mark the middle stake with a string.

OVERBEND

OVERBEND

PLASTIC MOLDING

CENTER MARK

4 LAY plastic molding around the stakes. With a helper, center the rebar on the middle stake and push the ends around the semicircle.

CAUTION: Be sure to have underground utilities marked in your yard. You'll be driving stakes and setting the rebar arches about 18 in. into the ground. Call 811 or visit call811.com.

you have a complete circle. The circle will have a 12-in. diameter. Cut off the extra rebar. Don't worry if the circles aren't perfect. Minor imperfections will be minimized when you wire them to the arches and hidden when your greenery grows.

Assemble the arches

Now find the ideal spot in your yard for the trellis and lay out the footprint (Photo 6). To keep it sturdy and stable, you have to sink each arch end about 18 in. into the ground. Measure up each leg and wrap tape at the 18-in. mark as a depth guide (Photo 7). With a helper, press the ends of the two arches into the ground. Drive a stake partway down to get started, or use a 3/4-in. steel pipe as a holder (see "Solution for Hard Soil," p. 175).

Then add the 3/8-in. rebar circles. Position the first circle about 2 ft. up from the bottom of your arch. Any lower and you may be inviting little feet to use the trellis as a makeshift ladder. Use cable ties to temporarily secure the circles in place, with the cut ends against one arch (Photo 8). Later you'll cover these sharp edges with the wire wrap. Space the remaining circles evenly around the arch. They'll be about 6 in. apart. The cable ties allow you to easily reposition the circles for the best appearance before you wire them into place.

To bind the circles, simply wrap the copper wire around the arch/circle joint. There is no special technique

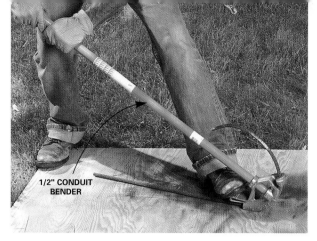

1/2" CONDUIT
BENDER

5 BEND the rebar into a circle with a conduit bender. Cut off the extra rebar. Repeat until you have nine circles.

6 POSITION the anchor holes for the trellis 6 ft. apart and 12 in. between arches. Drive in stakes to start the holes, then pull them out.

MASKING
TAPE
MARK

COPPER WIRE

CABLE TIE

7 MARK the depth with masking tape, position the trellis and push the ends 18 in. deep into the ground.

8 POSITION the circles between the arches with cable ties. Then tightly bind the circles to the arches with 2-ft. lengths of copper wire. Wire down as much of the side of the circle as you can to make the circle stable.

here. About 2 ft. of 18-gauge solid copper wire will do. Just keep the binding tight and extend it about 2 in. along the joint for good stiffness. And tap the wire ends down flat to the rebar with a hammer.

Once you attach the circles to the arches, your trellis is ready to shepherd creeping vines upward, adding height and dimension to your outdoor space. 🏠

Editor's Note

Chances are your rebar arches will look a bit irregular at first. Don't panic. Once you push them into the ground, they'll look more balanced. However, they may never be perfect. Resist the temptation to fix them. A little pressure here, a little push there and the next thing you know, you've got a lopsided mess on your hands. I know; I did it.

It's better to soldier on and attach the rebar circles—the trellis will come together nicely. Bumps that were driving me wild eventually vanished beneath the greenery.

Solution for hard soil

If you have hard soil, you won't be able to push the arches directly into the ground. Instead, you'll have to plant the rebar arches in a pipe. Drive an 18-in. length of 3/4-in. galvanized pipe most of the way into the ground as shown. Pull out the pipe and poke the dirt from the inside of the pipe until it's open. Then push the 3/4-in. pipe back into the hole and drive it down until it's flush with the ground. Now, simply insert the arch ends in the pipe.

AskTFH™
The Family Handyman

PAINT WON'T STICK

A few years ago, I sprayed water onto the exterior of my block walls. Since then, I can't get paint to stick. What's causing this and how can I fix it?

Block walls naturally have moisture in them and they're also very porous, so spraying them allowed water to soak into the blocks. The paint you used sealed in the moisture, which eventually caused the peeling.

To fix the problem, first scrape off the loose paint. Then paint the blocks with an exterior latex paint that's formulated for use with brick or stone. The paint will allow the blocks to "breathe" so moisture won't build up inside the blocks and cause peeling.

IDENTIFYING LUMBER TREATMENTS

I was shopping for lumber for a new deck and noticed preservation treatment levels of .21. This seems low. Is it good enough?

It depends on the chemical preservative used in the treatment. Every treated board carries a label. Check it to find the type of preservative used. The preservative retention for both CCA- and ACQ-treated lumber is .25 for above-ground applications and .40 for ground contact. CCA use has been reduced, so you're more likely to find ACQ when buying treated lumber.

However, the preservation retention is different for another common treatment, called CA-B. The CA-B treatment level of .10 corresponds to an ACQ of .25 and a CA-B .21 to an ACQ of .40.

When a project calls for a certain preservation rate, it's usually for ACQ unless otherwise specified. Lumberyards don't always carry each type of treated wood at each level of retention. The cost for a .25 ACQ-treated deck board is about the same as for a .40, so some lumberyards and home centers don't want the hassle of carrying both. Instead, they often carry only ACQ .40.

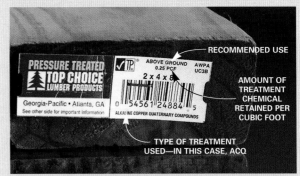

When you're buying treated lumber, look at the tag on the end to find out the type of chemical treatment and the preservation retention level.

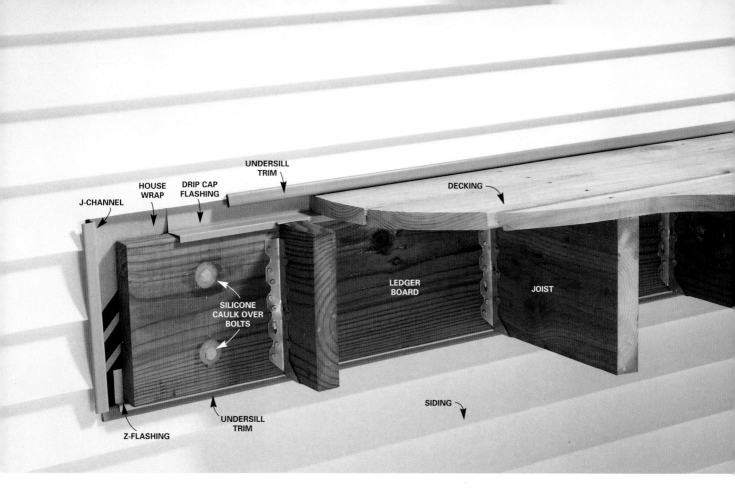

UNDERSILL TRIM

HOUSE WRAP

DRIP CAP FLASHING

J-CHANNEL

DECKING

LEDGER BOARD

JOIST

SILICONE CAULK OVER BOLTS

SIDING

UNDERSILL TRIM

Z-FLASHING

FLASHING A DECK LEDGER BOARD

I plan to add a deck onto my house, but I'm not sure how to flash around the ledger board. What's the best way to do this? I have vinyl siding.

Start by making an outline on the siding where you want to position the ledger board. Make the outline large enough to include space for the deck boards on top, the ledger and any trim boards on the sides. Then cut away the siding.

Nail undersill trim (J-channel will also work) over the bottom cut, using 11-gauge aluminum nails. It's a tight fit to drive the nails into the undersill, but you can gently pull back the siding, then tuck it into the undersill after you nail it. If necessary, remove a few pieces of siding, nail the undersill, then replace the siding.

Tack Z-flashing over the channel, extending it slightly past the cutout on both sides. If you need two or more pieces of flashing, overlap the joints by 4 in. and seal with silicone caulk. Avoid using galvanized flashing with ACQ treated lumber because it can cause corrosion.

Nail J-channel along both sides of the cutout. Then tack the ledger into place with 16d nails. Next, slide drip flashing behind the vinyl so the lip fits over the top of the ledger as shown at right. Install undersill trim along the edge of the vinyl, over the flashing at the top and bottom.

A building inspector we talked to said that incorrectly installed ledgers are the main cause of problems in do-it-yourself decks because the ledger may pull loose from the house. Make sure to get a building permit before starting a deck project so the inspector can check the ledger installation. It's extremely important for the ledger to be firmly attached.

Lag-screw the ledger to the house using the fastener pattern approved in your plan. Finally, caulk around the bolt heads to seal the holes against moisture.

Snap a chalk line, cut out the siding and tack up the ledger board. Then slip flashing behind the siding, covering the top edge of the ledger.

SLAY THE
CRABGRASS MONSTER

4 ways to defend your turf by **Lucie B. Amundsen**

Crabgrass is a relentless yard invader. It grows faster than turf, has incredible tolerance for adverse conditions and will quickly turn a lawn into a weed patch. Fortunately, you needn't call a lawn service to rescue your grass. All you need is a lawn spreader, a pump sprayer and a few turf products. In this story, we'll show you how to head off crabgrass trouble in the spring and how to control plants you spot later in the summer. Wherever you live, you can shut out this grass trespasser and run barefoot through sweet success.

Fight crabgrass with a healthy lawn

The best way to stop crabgrass is to shade it out with a thick, healthy lawn. A thick lawn provides a dark canopy of grass blades over the seeds, so they won't sprout. Follow these good grass-care practices.

■ **Watering:** A thorough watering once a week will encourage the grass's root system to go deeper, making the whole lawn more hardy and heat tolerant. This usually means applying 1 to 2 in. per week at three- or four-week intervals. Avoid short, frequent waterings. These "sips" will promote a shallow, weaker root system in your lawn.

■ **Mow:** As a rule, grass should be mowed to a height of 2 to 3 in. Mowing it shorter than 2 in. will reduce the grass's vitality and give weeds a chance to move in. Be sure to keep your lawn mower blades sharp so they won't tear the grass. Leave grass clippings on the lawn as a natural fertilizer.

■ **Reduce compaction:** Weeds thrive in areas where compacted soil deprives the grass roots of the air and water circulation they need. If your yard is prone to compaction, rent and run an aerator over it every other year, especially if your soil contains a lot of clay.

1 Get 'em before they sprout!

The best weapon you have against this annual weed is crabgrass preemergence herbicide (also called crabgrass preventer). You apply this product in the spring before the crabgrass seed sprouts. This granular herbicide works by creating a chemical barrier at the surface of the soil. As the seeds begin germination, they take in the herbicide and die.

This sounds easy enough, but where you're likely to get it wrong is in the *when*. **Apply too early** and microorganisms and natural processes in the soil break down the herbicide. By the time it's needed, much of the product has lost its potency. **Apply too late** and you've missed the early stage of germination when the herbicide works. There is nothing in preemergence herbicide that kills crabgrass seedlings once they've sprouted. You're just pushing around that spreader for the exercise, not to mention wasting expensive products. As far as prevention goes, you're out of luck until next spring.

Tip

If you're going to err on timing your crabgrass preemergence application, err on the early side. While you'll lose some effectiveness, you'll still probably kill lots of crabgrass. If you go late, you're likely to miss early sprouts.

So how do you select the exact instant for application? Don't depend on the calendar. Pay attention to your grass instead. Fill up the spreader with preemergence granules between **the second and third mowings of the year.** The window is short, only about a week and a half, when the soil hits the ideal temperature—about 52 degrees F.

If you've had a particularly bad crabgrass problem, you're not done for the season. Chances are that the crabgrass will germinate and spring up later in the summer. Preemergence herbicides have a life of about 50 days (check the label; product life spans vary). Once that chemical barrier breaks down, dormant crabgrass seeds, which can remain viable for years, may germinate into seedlings. Or if your yard butts up against property that has a thriving crabgrass crop, you can bet that thousands of seeds will blow into your lawn, just when your herbicide is calling it quits. You don't need to reapply the preemergence herbicide to your whole yard, but hit areas again where crabgrass thrives, like right next to driveways and walking paths. Because they absorb heat, the soil around them gets warmer and encourages the growth of crabgrass.

SECOND MOWING

1 LET grass growth determine the best time for a preemergence herbicide. Apply it after your second regular mowing in the spring.

SPREADER

2 APPLY crabgrass preemergence granules with a spreader, especially around driveways and walks and also alongside the neighbor's crabgrass-infested yard.

■ **Fertilize right:** Avoid lawn fertilizers that say "quick green-up" on the label. These have excessive nitrogen ingredients that will actually weaken your lawn over time, making it more susceptible to weeds. Instead, select a fertilizer product with half of its nitrogen in a slow-release form. For a 1,000-sq.-ft. lawn, use less than 3 lbs. of nitrogen annually.

■ **Reseed:** Weed-damaged or thin areas should be seeded (sometimes called "overseeded") in the fall, when the days are warm, the nights are cool and you have dew in the mornings.

2 Yank 'em while they're young!

OK, your lawn has been growing for a couple of months and you notice light green blades thickening up your Kentucky Blue. Before you think your lawn is having an exceptional season, think again: It's likely to be young crabgrass (see **Photo 1**).

Pulling, at this early stage, is a surprisingly effective way to get rid of crabgrass. But if the weed has pushed up three or four rows of leaves, inspect it carefully before you snatch it. If you spot a slender, green seed head that is still closed and folded up against the leaves of the plant, go ahead and pull it, too (**Photo 3**). However, after the seed head tines have spread out like a fork, leave it alone (**Photo 4**). Otherwise you'll scatter scads of seeds right over that nice big hole you've just created by removing the mature weed. You might as well be trying to cultivate new crabgrass!

Come fall, seed bare and patchy areas (**Photos 1 – 3**, p. 181). With good lawn care practices (see pp. 178–179), you'll soon crowd out those fallen crabgrass seeds.

YOUNG CRABGRASS
(LIGHT GREEN COLOR)

YOUNG
CRABGRASS

1 PULL OUT crabgrass as soon as you spot it. Young plants leave only a small hole in your turf, which desirable grass types will quickly fill.

2 YOUNG crabgrass plants perfect for pulling have two to four sets of leaves but no splayed seed heads.

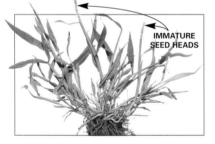

IMMATURE
SEED HEADS

DOZENS
OF SEEDS

SPLAYED
SEED HEAD

3 IMMATURE crabgrass plants have tight, green seed heads. They're more difficult to remove, but it's still OK to pull them.

4 FULLY MATURE crabgrass has splayed seed heads. It's best to leave it alone. Pulling will leave a big hole in the lawn and spread up to 5,000 seeds per plant. The plant will die in the fall. Then hit the area next spring with preemergence granules to keep the seeds from sprouting.

3 Spray stubborn patches

Spray postemergence herbicide directly on crabgrass after it has sprouted (**photo**, far right). Pulling is equally effective, but if the roots are deeply embedded in your lawn, it may be tough to pull them out without pulling grass chunks too. It's not worth spraying a postemergence product on crabgrass that has gone to seed (**Photos 3 and 4**, above). It takes about two weeks for the herbicide to work, which is about how long it takes the plant to finish its seeding process. If it has gone to seed, you're better off waiting for next spring and applying a preemergence product then.

Tip Don't waste your money on a post-emergence herbicide in the fall, when the temperatures are falling. The herbicide won't be effective and the plant will soon die anyway.

4 Kill it all and start over!

While we all admire those who relentlessly defend their turf against crabgrass, there comes a time when the best strategy is to give up. That time is when your lawn only has 30 to 40 percent desirable grass left in a given area and the rest is lost to crabgrass and other weeds.

Begin by killing all the vegetation. On a low-wind day, apply a nonselective herbicide that is approved for lawn use, like Round-Up or Kleen-Up. Follow the label directions exactly. Depending on the product, weeds and grass will die and dry up in five to 14 days following application. Then renovation can proceed.

Thoroughly soak the area to give your new grass its best chance for a good start. Check your watering depth by pushing a spade into the ground and pulling it back to get a deep view of the soil. If the soil is moist to a depth of 6 to 8 in., you're ready.

For patchy bare areas and turf-free areas up to about 8 ft. square, use the spade technique for seeding (**Photo 2**). It's very effective, although it would be slow and tedious on areas that are much larger. Scuff up the dead vegetation with a rake and, using a spade, make 1/4-in.-deep furrows about 2 in. apart. Broadcast your grass seed, then flip a rake upside down and knock the seeds into the furrows. These furrows ensure that the seeds will make good contact with soil; they provide some moisture-retaining shelter as well. Then be sure to keep the seeds and soil moist. Continue to baby your new grass until after its first mowing. Do not apply crabgrass preventer to freshly planted areas. ⌂

1 KILL OFF patches of lawn with non-selective herbicide in the fall if more than half the area is weeds. When it's safe to replant (check the herbicide label), soak the patch with water and rake off dead grass and thatch to bare the soil.

FURROWS

2 CREATE 1/4-in.-deep furrows every 2 in. using a flat shovel. This will give your seeds a better chance to settle into the moist soil.

3 TOSS grass seeds into the patch and keep the soil moist to the touch until the grass becomes established. Mow the new grass when it's 3-1/2 to 4 in. high.

Post-emergence herbicides are most effective when the soil is moist and the plants are dry. Read the label for specific instructions. Typically you apply it with a hand pump sprayer. It's best to apply it on a hot day when there's low wind. If temperatures are too low, the product may be ineffective. Unless the crabgrass is young, you'll probably have to reapply the product a few days later (according to the label) to kill the plant.

After postemergence application(s), keep an eye on the treated area. In extremely dry conditions, water two days after the application to aid absorption. If your grass near the treated area is turning brown, you probably were a little heavy handed. Soak the damaged area with water to dilute the chemical and avoid further damage. Also be on the lookout for new crabgrass sprouts. These will require another herbicide treatment, or if there aren't too many, simply pull them. Be sure to seed these areas in the fall.

CAST A CONCRETE FOUNTAIN

Enjoy the splash and sparkle of water indoors or out—with minimal maintenance and expense

by **Gary Wentz**

If you want to add the sight and sound of moving water to your yard without the heavy work and maintenance of a pond or waterfall, consider a fountain. A freestanding fountain doesn't require hard labor and there's very little maintenance to do later. Best of all, you can place a fountain just about anywhere: among plants, inside a sun porch, or on a deck or patio. You could even build a pair to flank a gateway or path.

This article will show you how to cast a fountain using inexpensive off-the-shelf materials. Our design combines the style of top-selling models found at garden centers with super-simple construction. If you can handle basic tools, you can build it, even if you've never worked with concrete before. Expect to spend about six hours assembling forms and pouring concrete, plus another couple of hours removing forms and setting up the fountain. The materials for this fountain cost about $120. Fountains of a similar size and style (usually made from fiberglass or plastic) cost about $500 at garden centers.

Build forms from foam

To mold concrete, you pour wet concrete mix into a form. You can build forms from wood, but we found that rigid foam insulation is perfect for a small project like this. Foam is lightweight, smooth and easier to cut. Concrete won't stick to foam, so you can reuse the outer form parts to cast several fountains. Best of all, you can assemble sections of foam with the ultimate quick-and-simple fastening system: duct tape! Be sure to use "extruded" polystyrene, not "expanded" polystyrene bead board. A 4 x 8-ft. sheet of 2-in.-thick foam costs about $20 at home centers. Inspect the sheet before you buy, and handle it carefully—deep scratches or dents will show up as bumps on the surface of your fountain. If you can't find extruded foam at your local home center or lumberyard, search for a local dealer at foamular.com or styrofoam.com.

Figures B and C show the dimensions of the column and basin form parts. Cut the tapered parts (A and C) with

a circular saw using a standard wood-cutting saw blade (**Photo 1**). It's difficult to make perfectly straight cuts with a circular saw because the blade can easily wander in the soft foam. But don't worry about slightly wavy cuts; they won't affect the final product. Cut the square and rectangular parts with a table saw or circular saw. Cut the 8-in.-round disc (D) with a drywall saw. Wrap the disc with duct tape to cover the rough edges left by the drywall saw.

Combine basic materials and clever techniques to create a fountain in one weekend.

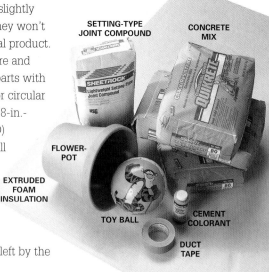

SETTING-TYPE JOINT COMPOUND

CONCRETE MIX

FLOWER-POT

EXTRUDED FOAM INSULATION

TOY BALL

CEMENT COLORANT

DUCT TAPE

Assemble the forms with duct tape

To begin, cut out and assemble the foam parts. Keep in mind that you'll build the column and base forms and pour them in the upside-down position. Also, place the printed side of the foam face out; the ink can stain the concrete.

Tape the seams of the outer column form together and then wrap it with tape. Stretch the tape firmly as you wrap to create tight seams. Assemble the inner form with tape and 3-in. screws (**Photo 2**). Tape the basin form sides (G) to the base (H). Screw one basin block (F) to the base, then screw the second block onto the first. Mark a 4 x 4-in. square on the block to represent the opening at the bottom of the column. Then cut two slits in the foam and insert anchors made from 10-gauge copper electrical wire (**Photo 3**). Leave the legs of each anchor protruding 3/4 in. from the foam. You'll use these anchors later to tie the column and basin together (see **Photo 8 inset**). Be sure to use plastic-coated wire. Copper that's in direct contact with concrete eventually corrodes.

Form the sphere with a plastic ball

To form the sphere, you'll need a toy ball, a plastic flowerpot and a bag of 20-minute setting-type joint compound (which is meant for covering drywall joints). Buy a cheap ball (ours cost $3) made from smooth, thin plastic and make sure it's fully inflated. Don't use a thick-skinned ball like a soccer ball or basketball.

Cover the holes in the flowerpot with duct tape. Mix the joint compound powder with water until it's the consistency of pancake batter. It's OK if the mix is a bit lumpy. Then pour 3 in. of compound into the pot and set the ball into it with the air plug facing straight up. Hold a 3-in. cardboard ring (left over from duct tape) on the ball as you cover the ball with at least 1 in. of joint compound (**Photo 4**). Work fast—the joint compound will start to stiffen after about 10 minutes. You may have to hold the ring in place for a minute or two to prevent the ball from floating up.

Let the compound harden overnight. Then puncture the ball with a utility knife and pull it out through the ring. Slather margarine onto a small rag and coat the inside of the form so the concrete won't stick to it. If your hand won't fit through the ring, recruit a helper with smaller hands.

Fill the forms with concrete

Since the concrete isn't reinforced with wire mesh or rebar, concrete mix that contains tiny threads of fiberglass is best for this project (Quikrete Crack-Resistant concrete is one brand). We used one 10-oz. bottle of Quikrete Cement Color per 80-lb. bag of concrete to pigment the mix. Home centers typically carry three or four colors (we used "buff"). For mixing tips, go to thefamilyhandyman.com and type "mixing concrete" into the keyword box.

Figure A: Cast concrete fountain

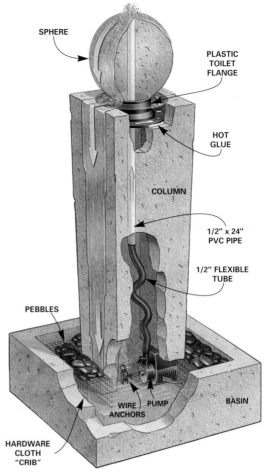

SPHERE

PLASTIC TOILET FLANGE

HOT GLUE

COLUMN

1/2" x 24" PVC PIPE

1/2" FLEXIBLE TUBE

PEBBLES

WIRE ANCHORS

PUMP

BASIN

HARDWARE CLOTH "CRIB"

The fountain consists of three separate parts: a sphere, a hollow column and a basin. A pump drives water up through the sphere, where it bubbles out, cascades down the column and returns to the basin.
- **Overall height: 42 in.**　- **Basin footprint: 20 x 20 in.**

MATERIALS LIST

- One 4 x 8-ft. sheet of 2-in. extruded polystyrene foam insulation
- Four* 80-lb. bags of concrete mix (or five 60-lb. bags)
- Four* 10-oz. bottles of Quikrete Cement Color or equivalent
- 2 ft. of 1/2-in. PVC pipe
- 2 ft. of pump tubing
- 2 ft. of 10-gauge insulated copper wire
- Duct tape, 3-in. screws, 20-minute setting-type joint compound (1 bag), 12-in. plastic flowerpot, 3-in. ABS toilet flange, hot glue, 9- or 10-in.-diameter ball, 1/2-in. galvanized hardware cloth, river pebbles.
- Pump: Select a pump that delivers at least 300 gal. per hour and includes adjustable flow control. Pumps are available at home and garden centers. To find online sources for the pump we used, search for "Beckett M350AUL."

*Three 80-lb. bags of concrete filled our forms, but just barely. Since the amount of concrete in a bag can vary slightly, we recommend you buy four bags and four bottles of colorant.

1 MARK OUT the form parts and cut them with a circular saw. Support the foam with 2x4s. Assemble the column form parts with duct tape.

2 SCREW the disc (D) to the inner form, then screw the disc to the end cap (E). Slip the inner form into the column form and tape it in place.

2" FOAM INSULATION

COLUMN SIDES (A)

BASIN FORM

INNER FORM (C)

OUTER FORM (A)

DISC (D)

END CAP (E)

Figure B: Column form

10"

30"

A OUTER FORM SIDE

12"

B ACCESS HOLE BLOCK (4" x 4")

WIRE ANCHOR (1-1/2" x 3")

C INNER FORM SIDE

2"

28"

3" SCREW

D DISC (8" DIA.)

4"

DUCT TAPE

E END CAP (14" x 14")

Note: The column and basin are formed and cast upside down.

Fill the sphere form first, before the mix begins to stiffen. Shake the form to drive out large air pockets. Then insert a 24-in.-long piece of 1/2-in. PVC pipe (see **Figure A** and **Photo 7**). Cover the end of the pipe with tape to keep out the concrete. Center the pipe and hold a level against it to make sure it's standing straight up.

Fill the column form by dropping in scoops of concrete on all four sides. If you fill only from one side, you'll bend the inner form. When you've dropped in about 6 in. of concrete, tamp it with a 1x2 to fill in large voids. We tamped for about 10 seconds; more tamping will give the concrete a smoother surface, while less tamping will leave more craters and crevices. Whatever surface texture you want, be consistent with your tamping all the way up for a uniform appearance. Continue to fill and tamp in 6-in. incre-

ments until the concrete is 4 in. from the top of the form. Then add the block that creates the access hole and the wire anchors (**Photo 5**).

When you fill the basin form (**Photo 6**), tamp the concrete the same way and be careful not to dislodge the wire anchors you installed earlier. Slide a 2x4 back and forth as you drag it across the form to screed off the excess concrete.

Wait, then remove the forms

Let the concrete "wet cure" for at least a week before you remove the forms. The longer concrete stays damp, the stronger it gets. Cover the column and basin with plastic garbage bags to slow down evaporation. To remove the sphere form, just break it away (**Photo 7**). To remove the outer forms of the column and basin, simply slice the tape

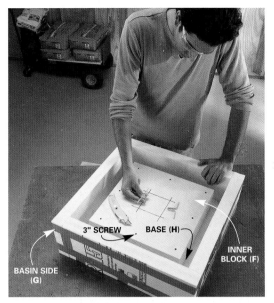

3 TAPE the basin form together and screw in the two inner blocks (F). Mark a 4-in. square in the center and insert wire anchors 1/4 in. inside the square.

3" SCREW — BASE (H)
INNER BLOCK (F)
BASIN SIDE (G)

1-1/2"
3"
WIRE ANCHOR

Figure C: Basin form

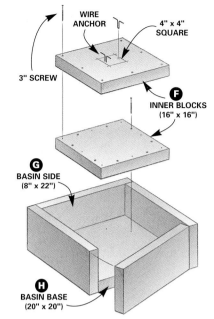

WIRE ANCHOR
4" x 4" SQUARE
3" SCREW
F INNER BLOCKS (16" x 16")
G BASIN SIDE (8" x 22")
H BASIN BASE (20" x 20")

SETTING COMPOUND
3"-DIA. DUCT TAPE RING
PLASTIC FLOWER POT

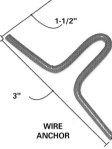

HARDENED COMPOUND
POOR TIGGER

4 CREATE a sphere form by covering a ball with joint compound while holding a tape ring on top. When the compound hardens, puncture the ball and pull it out. Let the compound cure overnight before you fill it with concrete.

with a utility knife. To remove the blocks (F) inside the basin, cut the foam into sections with a drywall saw and break them out. Removing the column's inner form is a slower process; cut the foam with a drywall saw and pry out small chunks with a putty knife, and then cut some more.

Put it all together

Before you assemble the fountain, mount a 3-in. black plastic toilet flange in the recess at the top of the column (see **Figure A** and **Photo 8**). The flange supports the sphere and stands about 1/4 in. above the top of the column. This allows water to fill the recess and spill out over the sides of the column. Cover the screw holes and bolt slots in the flange with duct tape, then set it in place. Apply lots of hot glue over the flange and around it to lock the flange in place and plug all the holes watertight (the tape prevents the glue from dripping through holes).

The column and basin weigh about 100 lbs. each, so you'll need a helper or a mover's dolly to move them. Tie the anchors together with the same wire you used for the anchors (**Photo 8 inset**). Then nudge the column to make sure you twisted the wires tightly enough. It's OK if the column rocks slightly, but it must be

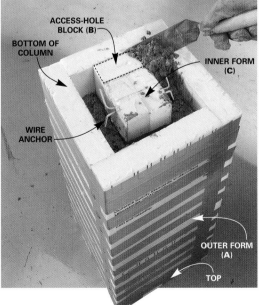

ACCESS-HOLE BLOCK (B)
BOTTOM OF COLUMN
INNER FORM (C)
WIRE ANCHOR
OUTER FORM (A)
TOP

5 FILL the column form with concrete. When it's nearly full, insert the access-hole block (B) and wire anchors. Then finish filling the form.

OUTDOOR STRUCTURES & LANDSCAPING

absolutely tip-proof since the fountain will attract curious kids.

Connect a 2-ft. section of flexible tubing to the sphere's PVC pipe. The vinyl tubing made to fit our pump slipped tightly inside the PVC pipe. If your tubing doesn't fit tightly, use hose clamps or other fittings. Set the ball in place (Photo 8) and position the pump. Trim the tubing to length and connect it to the pump. We filled the recess at the top of the column with smooth black "river pebbles." In the basin, support the pebbles with four "cribs" from 1/2-in. wire mesh (called "hardware cloth"). Cut the mesh into 9-1/2-in. x 12-in. sections, then bend them over a 2x4 block to form cribs 3 in. tall, 3-1/2 in. wide and 12 in. long. Cover the cribs with pebbles. This leaves all the space below the cribs open for water storage. If you simply fill the basin with pebbles, you'll greatly reduce the water-holding capacity.

Fill the basin with water and start the pump (the outlet that powers the pump *must* be GFCI protected). Turn the flow-control knob to adjust the water flow. If water spills down one side of the column but not the others, slip a flat pry bar under that side of the basin. Raise the basin and place shims under it until water flows evenly down all four sides of the column.

The fountain loses water because of splashing and evaporation, so keep an eye on the water level whenever you run the pump. If the basin runs dry, the pump will burn out. On a very hot, windy day, you may need to add water after just a few hours. In a cold climate, freezing water could crack the basin and destroy the pump. Each winter, remove the pump, empty the basin and either move the fountain indoors or cover it with a plastic bag. ⌂

6 FILL the basin form and "screed" off the excess concrete with a 2x4. Let the concrete cure for a week before you remove any of the forms.

BASIN FORM

1/2" x 24" PVC PIPE

SPHERE

TAPE RING

DRYWALL SAW

7 CUT AWAY the plastic pot with a utility knife. Saw deep kerfs in the sphere form and break it open by prying with a stiff putty knife.

ANCHORS

TIE WIRE

24" PUMP TUBE

3" PLASTIC TOILET FLANGE

HARDWARE CLOTH CRIB

PUMP

ACCESS HOLE

8 TIE the column to the base by joining the anchors with wire. Feed the tube into the column and set the sphere in place. Pull the tube through the access hole and connect the pump. Cover the reservoir with hardware cloth and pebbles.

STORAGE **BENCH**

Convenient storage space topped off with comfortable seating

by **Gary Wentz**

At first glance, this bench may look complex. But take a closer look and you'll see that the structure couldn't be more basic. It's just a box made from four frames with legs that wrap around the corners. The panels are plywood with waterproof outdoor fabric stapled over them. Covering the plywood seat with foam and fabric is something even an upholstery novice can manage. This bench is easy to customize, too: You can change the dimensions, choose fabric to complement other patio furniture, and stain the wood to match your deck or paint it to match your house.

Build it from 1x4s and plywood

The wood and hardware for our bench cost about $120. Upholstery supplies can cost $50 to $150, depending on what you select (see "Choosing Upholstery," p. 188).

We built our bench from pine 1x4s. Using a rot-resistant wood like cedar, redwood or teak will more than double the lumber cost. Top-grade pine is expensive too. We used lower-grade pine instead, bought extra material and "harvested" the knot-free sections for the visible bench parts. We used some of the leftovers for the slats (G) that form the floor inside the bench. The upholstered seat and panels are all cut from a single sheet of 3/8-in. BC-grade plywood.

You'll need a table saw, a jigsaw, a sander and a drill to complete this project. A router and chamfer bit are optional (see **Photo 5**). You'll also need a pocket-hole jig (**Photo 2**) or a biscuit joiner to assemble the frames.

Cut curved rails

Each of the four frames that form the box is made from four parts: The vertical frame parts, or "stiles" (C, D), are simply pieces of 1x4 cut to length. The horizontal frame parts, or "rails" (B, E), are ripped to the correct width on a table saw. The Cutting List on p. 188 provides all the dimensions.

Don't cut the curved rails (A) to their final length until the curves are cut and sanded. Instead, start with boards at least 41 in. long. Mark them as shown in **Figure B** and **Photo 1**. Plastic doorstop molding ($3 at home centers) works great in an arc jig, but any thin, knot-free strip of wood will do.

Take your time as you cut the arc with a jigsaw. Don't worry if the cut is a bit wavy. You can smooth it out with a random-orbital or finishing sander and 100-grit sandpaper. Move the sander back and forth across the entire arc using even speed and pressure, to even out minor waves.

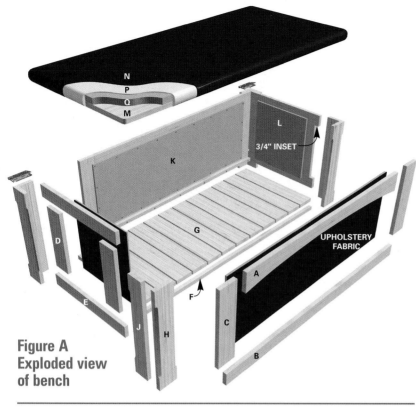

**Figure A
Exploded view
of bench**

Labels within the exploded view: N, P, Q, M, L, 3/4" INSET, K, D, G, E, J, H, F, A, C, B, UPHOLSTERY FABRIC

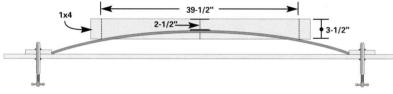

Figure B: Simple arc jig

Labels on arc jig: 1x4, 39-1/2", 2-1/2", 3-1/2"

Make an arc jig by clamping blocks to a 5-ft. board. Bend a 4-ft. strip of wood between the blocks. Adjust the distance between the blocks until the arc is correct.

Choosing upholstery

Craft and fabric stores may carry some outdoor upholstery, but for the best selection and advice, start with an upholstery store (under "Upholstery Fabrics" in the yellow pages). Outdoor fabric costs about $6 to $30 per yard. With batting and foam added, expect your total bill to be at least $45. The standard width of upholstery fabric is 54 in. You'll need a piece at least 90 in. long and an equal amount of batting. We used 1-in.-thick, medium-density foam. Many suppliers will cut the foam to size for you (29 x 57 in.) Here are three things to keep in mind while choosing fabric:

- Most outdoor fabrics are vinyl, but a few other materials are available. Make sure the fabric you choose is waterproof and easy to clean.
- Tell the salesperson how and where your bench will be used. Some vinyl can crack in cold weather or degrade in direct sunlight.
- Solid colors or subtle patterns are easiest to work with. Stripes are the most difficult.

CUTTING LIST

Parts A - J are 3/4-in.-thick solid wood

KEY	QTY.	SIZE & DESCRIPTION
A	2	3-1/2" x 39-1/2" (upper rails)
B	2	2-1/4" x 46-1/2" (lower rails)
C	4	3-1/2" x 14" (front/back stiles)
D	4	3-1/2" x 11-3/4" (side stiles)
E	4	2-1/4" x 19-1/2" (side rails)
F	2	3/4" x 46-1/4" (cleats)
G	13	3-1/2" x 17-7/8" (slats)
H	4	3-1/2" x 18" 1x4 pine (leg fronts)
J	4	2-3/4" x 18" (leg sides)
K	2	13-1/2" x 41-1/2" 3/8" BC plywood (front/back panels)
L	2	13-1/2" x 13-1/2" 3/8" BC plywood (side panels)
M	2	22-1/2" x 51" BC plywood (seat)
N	1	29" x 57" upholstery fabric
P	1	24-1/2" x 53" batting
Q	1	23-1/2" x 52" foam (1" thick)

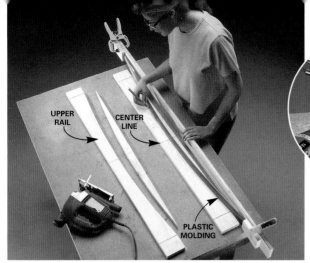

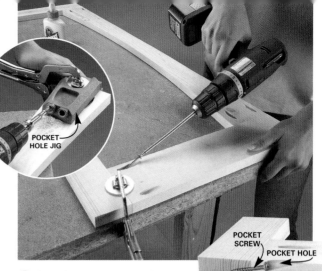

1 MARK a curve on upper rails using the arc jig. Cut the curve with a jigsaw. Don't cut the rails to their final length until you've sanded the curve.

2 CLAMP each joint to a flat surface and add the pocket screws. Be careful not to drive screws too deep in soft wood.

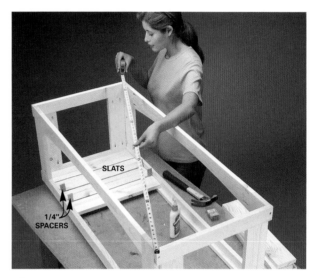

3 GLUE AND NAIL bottom cleats to the front and back frames. Then predrill and fasten the four frames together with 1-5/8-in. screws.

4 GLUE AND NAIL the slats in place, using 1/4-in. spacers to position them. Take diagonal measurements to make sure the box is square.

Assemble frames with pocket screws

You could assemble the frames using biscuits or dowels, but we chose pocket screws because they're fast, easy to master and nearly foolproof. Here's how they work: A stepped drill bit—guided by a jig—bores into the wood at a steep angle to create a pocket (**Photo 2 inset**). Then you simply place a screw in the pocket and drive it into the adjoining piece (**Photo 2**).

In addition to pocket screws, use an exterior wood glue such as Titebond II or Titebond III to strengthen joints. When you assemble the side frames, be sure to position the stiles (D) 3/4 in. from the outer ends of the rails (E). Allow the glue to set for a couple of hours, then sand each frame with an orbital sander.

Join the frames and add slats to complete the box

Before you join the frames to form the box, fasten cleats (F) to the lower front and back rails (B). The frames that form

the box are fastened together only with 1-5/8-in. screws at the corners (**Photo 3**), so the box isn't very strong until you add the legs later (**Photo 6**). Handle the box carefully if you need to move it.

The slats (G) not only form the floor of the box but also hold it square. Take diagonal measurements as you install the slats—equal measurements mean the box is square (**Photo 4**). You have only about five minutes before the glue begins to set, so it's best to have a helper hold the box square as you work. You'll have to rip the final slat on your table saw to fit.

Add the legs

Each leg is made from two parts (H and J) glued together. The final length of the legs is 18 in., but start with pieces that are at least 1/2 in. longer. That way, you don't have to perfectly align the ends when you glue and clamp them together. Scrape away excess glue and let the glue set for at least an hour before removing the clamps. Sand the legs

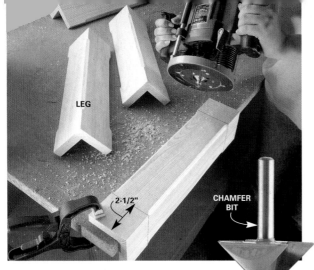

5 CUT 1/4-in.-deep decorative chamfers in the legs with a router. Stop the chamfers 2-1/2 in. from the ends.

6 GLUE AND SCREW the legs to the corners of the box from the inside. Predrill 1/8-in. clearance holes so the screws can draw the legs tight against the frames.

7 GLUE two layers of 3/8-in. plywood together to make the seat. Drive screws every 6 in. through both layers into straight 2x4s and remove the screws after the glue sets.

8 FASTEN the hinges to the box first. Then lay the seat on the floor and position each hinge as shown. Remove the seat to upholster it.

and cut them to length. For a decorative option, we chamfered the three edges of each leg (**Photo 5**). Use eight 1-1/4-in. screws (four on each side) and glue to fasten each leg to the box (**Photo 6**).

Make the seat from two layers of plywood

You could cut the seat (M) from a single piece of 3/4-in. plywood, but we glued two layers together (**Photo 7**) for two reasons: First, this allowed us to buy only a single sheet of 3/8-in. plywood. Second, it gave us a flatter seat. Single plywood sheets are often bowed. By gluing two sheets together (with both bows facing in or out) you end up with a flat sheet. Start with sheets cut about an inch oversize and then cut the seat to final size after gluing. Drill eight 1/2-in. holes in the seat so air can escape from under the upholstery when someone sits on it. Using your jigsaw, round the corners of the seat to about the radius as a nickel. To protect against moisture, we painted both the plywood seat and the panels before upholstering them.

Fastening hinges to the seat is a lot easier before the seat is upholstered (**Photo 8**). Remove the hinges to upholster the seat and finish the bench. With the screw holes established, remounting the hinges later is foolproof.

Upholster the seat

Here's the best thing about simple upholstery work: Most mistakes are no big deal. All you have to do to correct them is pry out the staples and try again.

Cut the fabric, batting and foam to size (see Cutting List) and lay them on your workbench. The foam is easy to cut with scissors or a utility knife. Take the seat outside and coat one side with spray adhesive. Position the seat carefully as you set it on the foam; it will bond immediately and you won't be able to reposition it. **Photos 9 – 12** show the upholstery process. Here are some pointers:

■ Start by tacking the fabric at the middle of all four sides (**Photo 11**). If your fabric has a pattern, flip the seat over to make sure the pattern is properly aligned.

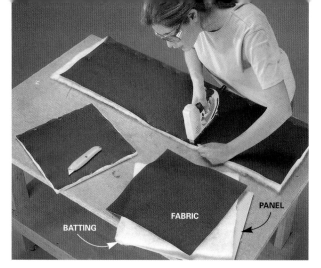

9 STAPLE batting to the panels. Then attach the fabric with staples around the perimeter. Trim off the excess batting and fabric with a utility knife.

10 SCREW the panels inside the frames with 1-in. pan head screws spaced every 6 in.

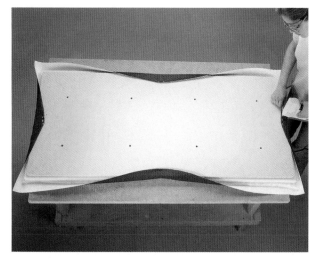

11 LAY OUT the fabric, batting and foam. Lightly coat the plywood seat with spray adhesive and center it on the foam. Staple the fabric to the plywood, starting at the middle of each side and working toward the corners.

12 CREATE small gathers in the fabric, starting about 3 in. from corners. Cut out "V" sections on both sides of the corner. Then fold the fabric inward, pull the corner back and staple.

- Work outward from the middle of one side, then go to the other side and stretch the fabric as you work outward. Tug gently—the fabric doesn't have to be stretched super-tight.
- Stop occasionally and flip the seat over to see if you're creating ripples in the fabric. Usually you can make ripples disappear by prying out a few staples and stretching the fabric more or less.
- Stop stapling about 3 in. from each corner and deal with the corners only after all four sides are done.
- Cut out "V" sections of fabric at corners to avoid creating a thick lump of excess fabric (**Photo 12**). Start by cutting out a small "V" and enlarge it if necessary.
- If your fabric is a stiff vinyl that won't conform well at corners, heat it with a hair dryer to soften it.

Final touches

With the bench stained and the panels covered, screw the panels inside the frames (**Photo 10**). To keep the legs off

the wet patio or deck, screw on 3/4-in. plastic feet. Even with the seat closed, a little rainwater can seep into the box. To minimize this seepage, run weather stripping around the upper edge (**photo right**). We also added a lid support to hold the seat open.

If you store furniture cushions in the bench, you'll create a paradise for mice. To keep them out, staple 1/4-in. galvanized hardware cloth to the underside of the slats. The most important thing you can do to preserve your bench is to maintain the finish. Since the panels and seat are removable, adding a fresh coat of paint or stain is easy. Finally, and most critical of all, if you have children around, don't store yard chemicals inside the bench. 🏠

BUILD A VINYL FENCE

Set the posts right and the rest is easy. We'll show you how.

by **Travis Larson**

If you're thinking about a new fence, consider this: Vinyl fences last practically forever with no maintenance whatsoever. They won't fade or rot or need paint. In fact, the only care they could use is an occasional wash-down, and even that's optional.

This article will show you how to plan and build a vinyl fence. We'll show you how professional installers set the posts in a straight line, perfectly spaced, sturdy and plumb. That is the real key to goof-proof construction. We'll also include some tips on avoiding serious planning missteps

that can cause major headaches down the road.

But use our instructions only as a general guide; your fence may have some different assembly techniques. You'll need standard tools like a circular saw, a drill and an accurate 2-ft. level. With basic carpentry skills and a couple of helpers, you can install 100 ft. of fencing in a weekend. And best of all, you'll save $10 to $20 per running foot doing it yourself. Fence materials will cost $15 to $30 per foot. Ours fell in the upper range.

Easy as building with LEGO toys

If you properly space and set your fence posts, assembling the fence panels is much like snapping together LEGO blocks. Rails snap into the post slots and are held in place with locking tabs. Boards interlock with each other and are held in place with plastic U-channels.

Vinyl fences come in two varieties: "panelized" and board-and-rail systems. A panelized system has panels that hang between posts. Board-and-rail systems have individual boards and rails much like a wooden fence. In this story, we'll cover the installation of a board-and-rail fence. But many of the layout and post-setting tips apply to both, so read on even if you choose a panelized system.

The board-and-rail system shown here was manufactured by Digger Specialties. For information on this company and others, see the Buyer's Guide on p. 198.

Plan your fence (and follow the rules)

Start by picking up a fence permit application from the local building inspections department, along with local fence regulations. They will include setback requirements from your property lines to the fence and maximum heights. These details will likely vary for front and back-

Tip

Plan an accessible spot for a removable section of fence so you can get large equipment or a pickup truck into the yard if it's needed in the future. The fence supplier can provide special hardware just for this.

yard fences and can even be different for houses on corners or busy streets.

If you live in a "planned" community or subdivision, you may also have to submit information to a planning committee. Follow all regulations to the letter. Otherwise you may wind up tearing out and moving your fence.

Draw a dimensioned sketch of your yard that clearly shows your property lines. Then add your proposed fence outline, heights, distances from property lines and gate locations. If you're not sure of your property lines, hire a surveyor to have them marked.

Take photos of each side of your yard, focusing especially on sloped areas and anything that will interrupt your fence, like buildings, trees or retaining walls (and mark

1 STRETCH a string line tightly along the proposed fence run, locate the corner posts and dig 3-ft.-deep postholes. Plumb the posts and fill the holes with concrete.

2 MARK the post locations on the line and then mark each posthole with a stake.

their locations on your sketch too). The photos will also help you and the supplier plan and choose a fence that'll meet local ordinances, so have them with you. With the fence style chosen and the dimensions and layout in hand, apply for and receive your permit before ordering the materials.

As with any other project involving digging, call before you dig (call 811 or visit call811.com) to have underground utilities marked. As a courtesy, discuss your plan with neighbors who may be affected by your fence.

Set the corner and end posts first

With any fence style, set end and/or corner posts first and then fill in between them with the "line" posts. Corner posts have rail holes on adjoining sides, and end posts have holes on only one side. Line posts have rail holes on opposite sides to support fence panels on both sides.

> **Tip**
>
> If you have a big crew and expect to get a big fence installed in a day or two, it's worth renting a cement mixer ($20 to $40 per day) and a power auger ($50 per day) to save on time and labor. Otherwise, just hand-mix the concrete in a wheelbarrow and dig the holes by hand.

3 DIG 3-ft.-deep holes about 8 in. in diameter at each stake. Drop a post into each and adjust the depth to position the bottom rail 4 in. above grade.

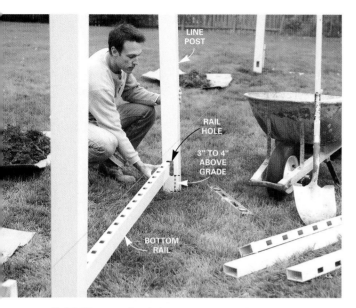

4 DROP a post into place and snap in the bottom rail. Then position it against the string line, plumb it and add concrete.

5 SET the remaining line posts. Cut rails to fit as necessary to fill in shorter spaces.

Start by driving stakes beyond the end or corner positions, and then string a taut line between them even with the outside of the post locations. Then dig and set the end posts (**Photo 1**). (Read the next section for details on setting posts.) Use the rail holes on the posts to determine how deep the holes should be. (Read your fence instructions. The rail holes are usually about 4 in. above grade; see **Photo 4**.) You'll drive all of the posts down to the proper depth later (**Photo 6**), so starting a bit on the high side is best. Never try to lift posts after the concrete is added, because they'll just settle later. If you need to lift a post, add soil and pack it well before setting the post.

Hold each post flush against the string and plumb in both directions as a helper fills around the post with concrete. It'll take about two 60-lb. bags of premixed concrete for each 4-in. post. Mix a fairly sloppy batch so the concrete can ooze into the large holes in the post sides to help lock the post into place. If you want to keep grass from growing around the posts, trowel mounded concrete slightly above grade so water will drain. Otherwise, stop filling the holes with concrete about 4 in. below grade and pack in soil on top of the wet concrete.

Set the line posts

Tie the string to the end posts flush with the outside edges. Hook a tape measure on one of the end posts and mark the string following the manufacturer's post-spacing instructions (**Photo 2**). Then drive stakes to mark the center of each hole (**Photo 3**). Dig holes and set the line posts. Mark, dig postholes and set no more than six posts at a

6 STRETCH the string even with the top of the rail holes on the end posts. Drive each line post down to align the rail holes.

Building on steep slopes

Vinyl fences have a few limitations on steeper slopes. The top and bottom rails have to follow the slope, but the panels have to remain vertical. How much you can angle the rails and still assemble the panels varies with the fence system. Roughly measure the steepest slope that your fence must span (measure the rise for each horizontal foot) and ask your fence supplier for advice. Sometimes you can slightly modify a system so it can handle steeper slopes than it was designed for.

Mark the holes (**Photo 1**, below) and cut them with a jigsaw and then slip in the bottom rail. Then scribe (**Photo 2**, below) and cut the boards to match the slope. Be careful to cut just enough of an angle so the whole board end will nest in the slot 1/2 in. or so. It's OK if there is a small flat area left, as we show. If you cut off the whole angle, the board may be too short. Test the angle and then cut the top angle to match at the right length. Check the fit. When you're satisfied, use that board as a template to mark and then cut the other boards. It's safest to order longer boards for those sections so that after the angles are cut, they'll still be long enough.

1 ELONGATE the rail holes 1/4 in. on slopes, at the top on downhill posts and the bottom on uphill posts.

2 SCRIBE the angle on a board, cut the end and transfer the angle to the other end, adjusting the length as needed to fit between the rails.

time. Then begin using the last post in line to mark and set another group of posts. Otherwise, small errors will accumulate and postholes farther down the line may be misplaced. Drop a post into the hole, fit in the bottom rail and then use the layout mark on the string to exactly space the post. Hold the post plumb in both directions while a helper fills around the post with concrete (**Photo 1**, p. 194). If there are high areas between the posts, you may have to hold the posts up a little more. Use the rail to make sure it'll clear those spots before setting the posts.

Some manufacturers require that posts for fences 6 ft. or higher be filled to some specified point with concrete. If that's required, cap the ends of bottom rails with duct tape before sliding them in. Then pour the concrete in through the post top. A cheap traffic cone (about $10 at home centers) works great as a funnel; just cut the tip shorter for a larger hole.

Frequently check previously set posts with a level as you continue building the fence. You'll be able to straighten posts that get a little out of line just by pushing them around up to a couple of hours after the concrete is added. If you're putting your fence up in especially windy conditions, brace the posts with 2x4s in both directions while the concrete sets. Clamp the 2x4s to the posts and stake them to the ground.

Fine-tune the final post heights

Within two hours of setting the line posts, fine-tune their height by stretching a string between the end posts. Stay on top of this step. Wait too long and the concrete will set up and you won't be able to drive down the posts. Make the string taut and sight it from one end to see how much it sags. Small sags won't be noticeable, but if the string sags more than 1/2 in. or so on long runs, clamp it to a post near the center to keep it straighter. Drive the posts down with a block and maul (**Photo 6**) until the tops are even with the line. If your yard isn't flat, you'll have to follow the contours. Think in terms of sections. String the line between posts at the ends of slopes for those sections and then use the posts at the ends of level areas for them.

Install posts that flank gates with extra care. Make sure the posts are perfectly plumb and spaced. Since the gate is a one-piece unit, there's not much room for fudging. Even though gate hinges are somewhat adjustable (**Photo 13**), the gate won't look good if the posts are out of plumb.

7 DROP metal stiffeners into posts at gates, ends and other locations where required for extra strength.

> **Tip**
>
> If you have hard clay soil or soil that's riddled with rocks, you may not be able to drive down the fence posts to a consistent height later (Photo 6). If that's the case, dig the holes a few inches deeper, then add sand on the bottom and set the posts. Now you'll be able to drive down the posts as needed.

Drop metal stiffeners into posts wherever they're called for (**Photo 7**). They're usually required on end posts (especially ones that might continually get bumped) and on posts that flank gates.

Cutting sections to fit

It's rare to end up with full-width sections of fence for an entire yard. Since the fencing sections are modular and designed for a certain span, each straight run will have at least one odd-size section. Gates, property line limitations and obstructions almost always require you to custom-cut shorter sections. Just cut the rails shorter with a circular saw. Be sure to allow about 2 in. extra on each end to insert into the posts. Since you'll be cutting off the locking tab, secure the rail with a screw (**Photo 6, detail**). You may have to trim a vertical fence board in a solid fence as well. That means cutting off one end of the rails (**Photo 5**) and usually ripping narrower boards for the ends. That's easy with a circular saw and a crosscut blade. But be careful if you're building a picket fence like ours. You may have to cut a little from both ends of the rails to avoid having a picket right next to the post. That looks bad.

8 SLIP pickets into the bottom rail. Snap the top rail into one post, slip it over the picket tops and snap it into the other post.

Assemble the panels

Let the concrete set for at least four hours before you assemble the panels. Simply follow the manufacturer's directions. The system we used required U-channels for the solid panels, which we screwed to the posts at each panel end (**Photo 9**). Then we slid the interlocking vinyl "boards" into place (**Photo 10**).

Place a couple of dabs of PVC cement or clear silicone

9 CENTER and screw U-channels with three evenly spaced screws into fence posts for privacy panels.

OUTDOOR STRUCTURES & LANDSCAPING

10 SLIDE the interlocking vinyl boards into the channel in the bottom rail. Screw them to the U-channel.

11 SLIDE the top rail over the boards, locking the end into the rail hole, and then back into the rail hole at the opposite end.

12 ADD a small dollop of PVC cement or silicone caulk to the tabs at the top of each cap and push the caps over each post.

13 SCREW the hinges and latch to the gate. Then center the gate in the opening and screw a catch to the other post.

on the glue tabs inside the caps where the tabs will rest on the top edge of the post (Photo 12). Next mount the gates and hardware (Photo 13) following the manufacturer's instructions.

Buyer's Guide

- Delgard: (800) 235-0185. delgard.com
- Digger Specialties Inc.: (800) 446-7659. diggerspecialties.com

Editor's Note

Type "vinyl fences" into any online search engine and you'll get about 250,000 results! With so many companies offering fence kits, the selection is a bit daunting, but you can buy your whole fence online and have it delivered directly to your house—with free shipping if the purchase is over a certain amount. It's an option for those who live far from large cities. But do plenty of research. Some companies will help you with your order if you supply a sketch. Others expect you to fill out your own materials list. Doable, but you'd better be extra careful in figuring out exactly what you need. Forgotten, missing or damaged pieces will cause delays and extra shipping charges. Although every Internet source I studied had a phone number you could call for help, go with a local firm if you can. You'll be able to see the product, and it helps to sit down with someone to work out the materials list.

HandyHints®

SAVE YOUR LAWN PRODUCTS

Leave a bag of fertilizer or weed killer open for long and it'll soak up moisture from the air and won't go through a spreader. Even grass seed could use an extra layer of protection from a moisture-wicking concrete floor. Place opened bags of lawn products in large resealable plastic bags ($1 at discount stores). The products will be free of clumps or pests when you need them.

METAL DETECTOR

FISH TAPE

GIANT RESEALABLE PLASTIC BAG

Scotts
Turf Builder
GRASS SEED
QUICK REPAIR MIX

LOCATE SPRINKLER LINES

Before you dig, find your underground sprinkler lines to avoid damaging them. Feed fish tape through an open sprinkler head and locate the line with a metal detector ($20 to $45 for rental).

NYLON SCRUBBER

Put your car-washing sponge inside a pair of old pantyhose for a great nonabrasive, paint-friendly scrubber. The threads act like thousands of little scrapers that rub off insects and gunk with every swipe.

8 TIPS FOR AN EASY-CARE YARD

by **Duane Johnson**

1 Apply a preemergence herbicide to stop crabgrass

The easiest way to stop crabgrass is to nail it before it starts growing. Apply a preemergence herbicide after your second mowing in the spring. Crabgrass grows from seeds scattered in previous years. The herbicide keeps those seeds from germinating. The seeds may remain viable for several years, so it's best to apply herbicide every spring. One springtime application will vastly reduce the need to attack crabgrass later in the year once it has sprouted. For more information on fighting crabgrass, see p. 178.

CRABGRASS PREVENTER

2 Add mulch to protect trees and avoid trimming

Clipping the grass around trees by hand is time-consuming. By adding a 4-in.-deep ring of mulch, you eliminate that chore. You'll also better protect newly planted trees and bushes. Nursery pros report that the most common reason young trees die is that lawn mowers and weed whips damage the bark. For a neater look, surround the mulch with a plastic, metal or brick border.

3 Set your blade at the right height to control weeds

Cutting grass too short weakens it. Longer grass grows stronger and thicker and crowds out weeds. Weed seeds can't germinate easily since they don't get much light. Established weeds have a tougher time competing with the surrounding turf.

Each type of grass has an ideal mowing height to maintain its health and thickness. It's about 2-1/2 in. for most cold-climate species. Cut most warm-climate grasses a bit shorter: 1-1/2 to 2 in. If you're not sure of your grass type, take a sample to a local nursery. Or type "identify grass" into an online search engine for help. Although most lawns contain a mix of grass types, they should have similar ideal cutting heights.

4 Plant hardy ground covers in shady areas

Grass is a sun-loving plant. It typically needs six to eight hours of sunlight daily for good health. While several shade-tolerant species may do OK under trees and in other sheltered spots, it's more likely that you'll end up with weeds, scraggly grass and bare ground. It's much better to plant a shade garden or a shade-tolerant ground cover that in a few years will blanket the area like a green carpet. And you won't have to mow. A local nursery expert will advise you on which plants and ground covers do best in your region.

5 Build paths that you can mow right over

Paths that conform to the landscape require less upkeep than more formal paths that include steps, walls and curbs. The key is to set the stones or pavers no higher than 1 in. above ground level. Then you can mow right over them—no trimming!

OUTDOOR STRUCTURES & LANDSCAPING

6 Install mowing borders

Mowing borders keep grass from growing along flower beds, walls, fences and other obstacles where your lawn mower can't reach. You can run your mower right over the borders and clip off every blade of grass. You'll save time and effort because you won't have to go back and trim later.

For long-term success, follow these two guidelines: (1) Install a border that's at least 4 in. deep. This keeps grass roots from creeping under the border and sprouting in the flower bed or along the fence. (2) Set the top of the border 1/2 to 1 in. above the ground. This keeps grass from creeping over the border.

7 Mulch planting beds for less weeding and watering

A layer of mulch, usually shredded wood or bark, vastly reduces gardening chores. It discourages weeds by shutting out light to the soil and keeping weed seeds from germinating. It reduces the need for watering by slowing evaporation. And it enriches the soil as it breaks down, reducing the need for fertilizer.

WOOD CHIPS   **CYPRESS BARK**

Apply a 4-in. layer of mulch to the bare soil for best results. It'll gradually decompose, so you'll have to replenish it every few years. For more information, search for "mulch" at thefamilyhandyman.com.

8 Fertilize in the fall

If you want the best lawn in town, fertilize four times a year. But you can keep it simple and still have a great lawn if you only fertilize once—in the fall. Choose a fertilizer that's labeled 4-1-2. (Those numbers refer to the percentages of nitrogen, phosphorus and potassium in the fertilizer.) Better yet, ask an expert at a garden center for advice about the best fertilizer blend for your grass type and local soil conditions. Apply the fertilizer about three weeks before the last mowing of the season. Fertilizing in the fall provides energy and nutrients for the grass roots as they multiply in cooler weather before the grass goes dormant. The roots store food for the winter as well, which gives the grass an initial growth spurt when it emerges from dormancy in the spring.

ARCHED **PLANTER**

Bend wood to create this graceful plant stand. You can make it with only two boards!

by **Travis Larson**

With this elegant curved planter, you can have a splash of garden color anyplace you like. Deck it out with flower pots and accent your patio, deck or front steps.

In this article, we'll show you how to build the whole project in a leisurely weekend. Bending wood strips into laminated arches may seem challenging, but we'll walk you through the process step by step. After you build your first planter, you'll have the hang of it, and the next one will be a cinch to build. The key, as you'll see, is a simple plywood "bending" jig that you can use over and over again. You can complete this project if you're handy with basic carpentry tools. However, you'll need a table saw equipped with a thin-kerf blade for ripping the strips and other parts. Sorry, but a circular saw just won't do the job no matter how steady you are. But you'll still need a circular saw, as well as a belt sander, random-orbital sander, and at least four 3-ft. pipe or bar clamps (**Photo 4**). Your total materials cost for each planter should be less than $40. The plywood for the jig costs about $30.

Select wood with small, tight knots

You only need two 8-ft.-long 2x8s for the entire project. Our planter is made from western red cedar, chosen for its beauty and natural decay resistance. But any wood you choose will be fine as long as you select straight boards with small, tight knots. The long thin strips will break at large knots during the bending process. You'll be using nearly every inch of each board, so pick ones without splits or cracks at the ends. It may take some sorting at the home center, but the effort's worth it.

Figure A: Build the whole planter from two 8-ft.-long 2x8s

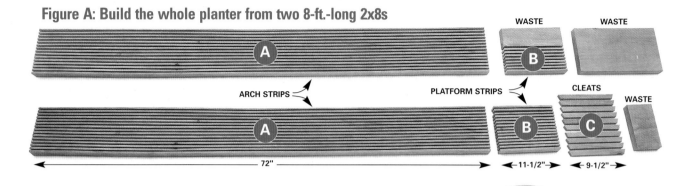

WASTE WASTE

A

B

ARCH STRIPS

PLATFORM STRIPS

CLEATS

WASTE

A

B

C

WASTE

72" • 11-1/2" • 9-1/2"

While you're at the home center, pick up 2 qts. of exterior woodworking glue along with a mini paint roller (**Photo 6**), a 4 x 8-ft. sheet of 3/4-in. plywood and a 10-ft. x 20-ft. roll of "painter's" plastic (3 mil). Also buy a small box of galvanized 1-in. brads if you intend to hand-nail. Or, if you have an air nailer (**Photo 11**), get brads for your nail gun.

Cut the parts

Cut each 2x8 to the lengths called for in **Figure A** and then start the ripping process. Ripping 5/16-in.-wide strips can be hazardous, so be sure to use a push carriage (**Photo 1**). Make your carriage from 1/4-in. and 3/4-in. plywood, custom-sized to match the height of the table saw fence. We were able to cut 15 strips from each board, but you may get fewer depending on the thickness of your blade. Don't worry if you wind up with fewer or unusable ones; you can build each arch with as few as 13 strips. Just make sure to use the same quantity for each arch so they'll match. If any of the strips break at knots, keep the pieces together, because you can still use them (more on this later).

Rip the platform slats next and then the 1/2- x 3/4-in. platform cleats. Rip the pieces first to 3/4 in. wide from a chunk of 2x8, then turn the 1-1/2-in. strips on their sides and rip them into 1/2-in. strips. Cut the cleats to length with decorative 22-degree angles on the ends.

Make the bending jig

Cut the plywood for the bending jig to size (**Photo 2**) and use one of the knot-free strips to form the curve. Use 3-in. screws partially driven into the plywood at the locations we show and push the center of the strip 13-1/2 in. out from the edge while you scribe the curve. Don't beat yourself up striving for a perfect curve; small variations won't be noticeable. It may seem odd to make this curved cut with a circular saw (**Photo 3**), but it's surprisingly easy and safe on a gentle curve like this. The curve will be

smoother than any you can achieve with a jigsaw. Just make sure to set your blade depth at 7/8 in. Any deeper and the blade may bind and kick back.

A

C

B

The two curves on the two sections of the jig are slightly different, and you'll have to recut the top part of the jig to match the bottom. To find this difference, lay 15 strips in the jig and tighten the clamps until the arch is completely formed (**Photo 4**). You'll have to tighten the clamps in "turns" as the strips gradually bend; that is, tighten two clamps until they run out of threads. Then leave them in place while you com-

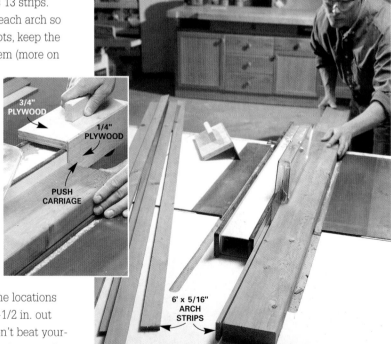

3/4" PLYWOOD

1/4" PLYWOOD

PUSH CARRIAGE

6' x 5/16" ARCH STRIPS

1 CUT the 2x8s to length following Figure A. Rip 5/16-in.-wide strips for the arches and the slats. Build a push carriage sized to fit your fence to safely cut thin strips.

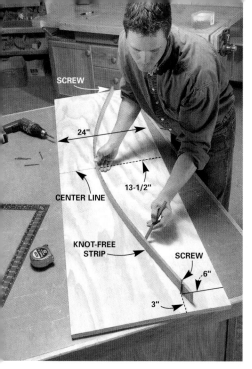

SCREW

24"

CENTER LINE

13-1/2"

KNOT-FREE STRIP

SCREW

6"

3"

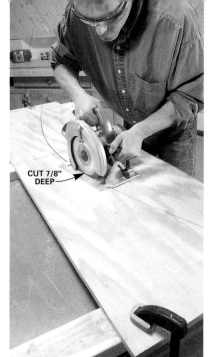

CUT 7/8" DEEP

GAP

3/4" SPACER

2 DRAW the arch on the bending jig plywood using one of the knot-free strips of wood and a pair of 3-in. screws.

3 SET the blade of the circular saw to cut 7/8 in. deep and cut the curve. Clamp the plywood to the workbench and hold your saw with both hands.

4 CLAMP 15 strips in the bending jig and re-mark the top curve with a 3/4-in. spacer block. Then remove the strips and recut that curve only.

pletely unscrew the other two, slide those jaws tight to the jig and continue tightening those. Work on pairs, tightening the outer two, then the inner two. You'll get the feel for the clamping process on this "glueless" dry run and it'll make the actual glue-up easier. When the clamps are tight, the strips will be tight to the jig at the bottom and there'll be a gap between the arch and the jig at the top. Trace around the top with a 3/4-in. spacer to re-mark the top curve (**Photo 4**). Then unclamp everything and recut that part of the jig.

Block up the cauls and glue up the arches

During glue-up, the strips have a tendency to lift away from the clamps while the glue is wet and slippery because of the stresses in the curves. "Cauls" are simply blocks of wood that hold the strips flat and prevent this. Make the cauls from six 2x4s (three on both the bottom and the top) and space them evenly with blocking sized so

the cauls will be flush with the top of the arch (**Photo 7**). Have these ready to go before the glue-up—you won't have time to spare later.

Mark a center line on the strips and keep them aligned with the bending jig center line when you start gluing later (**Photo 6**). Lay painter's plastic directly below the jig to keep your workbench and clamps clean and then start gluing the strips. A mini paint roller greatly speeds up the process, and time is of the essence. Glue both sides of each strip and push the glued surfaces lightly together to delay glue setup. Slip in any broken strips near the middle of the arch, matching up the breaks after they're coated with glue. Use flawless strips for the first and last strips of each arch. After you spread the glue, pull the jig together, bending the strips as far as you can while a helper slides the clamps closed. That'll speed up the clamping process. Then lay plastic over the caul locations, screw the cauls into place, screw the top 2x4s into place and tighten the

Figure B: Cleat template

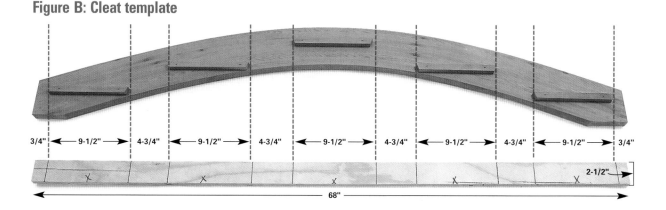

3/4" | 9-1/2" | 4-3/4" | 9-1/2" | 4-3/4" | 9-1/2" | 4-3/4" | 9-1/2" | 4-3/4" | 9-1/2" | 3/4"

2-1/2"

68"

CAUL BLOCKING

2x4

5 SCREW together three clamping cauls, adding blocks as needed so they'll be even with the top of the arch strips (see Photo 7).

6 ROLL glue onto both sides of each strip (one side of top and bottom strips) and position them, keeping the jig and strip center lines aligned.

EXTERIOR WOOD GLUE

MINI ROLLER

CENTER LINE MARK

PAINTER'S PLASTIC

clamps. Again, work on pairs, progressively tightening them. Work quickly. If you still see gaps between any strips, close them by driving a wedge between the jig and the arch or add more bar clamps from above. Ignore the clamping instructions on the glue bottle—leave the clamps in place for at least three hours.

You don't have to wait until you've removed the clamps to start cleaning up glue and flattening the arch. As the glue starts to "gel up" (dry to the touch but gooey beneath the surface, about one hour into clamping), remove the cauls (leave the clamps tightened) and start scraping away the glue from the top side of the arch. A paint scraper works great for most of it; use a small chisel or screwdriver to get into the crevices. The key is to remove as much glue as possible. Hardened glue is nearly impossible to remove and any leftover glue will clog and ruin sanding belts in no time. After you've scraped off the glue, wipe off any other glue smears with a damp (not wet!) rag. Don't worry about the bottom side yet; you can get it after the three-hour clamping period. The glue there will stay softer longer because it's against the plastic.

Flatten the arches and cut the ends

Start belt-sanding diagonally with 60-grit belts to knock off the high spots (Photo 9). After the surface is flat, remove cross-grain sanding marks by sanding following the curve. Then belt-sand with 80- and then 100-grit belts. Finish up with 100-grit paper in a random-orbital sander. Remove the arch from the jig, scrape off the glue, and flatten and sand the opposite side. Then repeat the whole process for the other arch.

But, if you have a benchtop planer, use it for the whole flattening process. Feed in one end and you'll be able to

gently push the arch sideways and follow the curve as it goes through the machine. Make sure all the glue on the surface is removed. Hardened glue will dull the cutting knives.

Mark and cut off the bottom and ends as we show in Photo 10. Cut one end first, then measure over 68 in. and cut the other end. Ease the sharp edges of each arch with a round-over router bit or sandpaper.

Mount the cleats and the platforms

We show you an easy way to mount the cleats on both arches using a mounting template made from plywood (Photo 11 and Figure B). Cut it to 68 in. and lay out the cleat positions as shown. Then position and fasten the cleats (Photo 11).

Separate the arches with temporary platform strips and lightly clamp the arches together (Photo 12). Make sure the arch ends are even, then glue and nail the platforms to the cleats.

If you'd like a finish on your planter, use any stain designed for exterior siding. To further protect your planter against rot, spread exterior wood glue on the feet of each arch. 🏠

7 PULL the jig together as far as possible and snug up the clamps. Then screw the cauls down and finish tightening the clamps.

8 REMOVE the cauls after one hour and scrape off the excess glue from that side. Remove the clamps after three hours and scrape the glue from the other side.

9 BELT-SAND both sides of the arch flat with 60-grit paper, then 80-grit. Smooth the surface with a random-orbital sander with 100-grit paper.

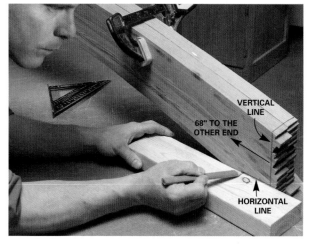

10 CLAMP arches together and draw vertical lines just short of the ends. Scribe the bottom horizontal lines with a 2x4 spacer. Cut the ends with a circular saw.

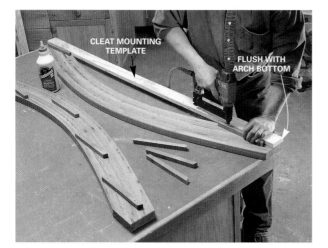

11 LAY the cleat-mounting template (Figure B) flush with the arch bottoms. Then glue and nail the end cleats. Rest the template over the first set of cleats and mount the next two cleats, then move it again to mount the top cleat.

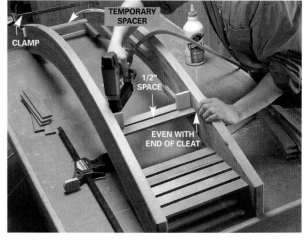

12 SPACE AND CLAMP the arches. Then glue and nail the platform strips on the cleats, keeping them even with the cleat ends and spacing them 1/2 in. apart.

OUTDOOR STRUCTURES & LANDSCAPING

NewProducts

ONE SERIOUS GARDEN TROWEL

You'll feel like a pro when you pull out the Ames True Temper Planter's Buddy. This heavy-duty stainless steel trowel is not only perfect for transplanting flowers, cutting through soil, ripping open bags and pulling up weeds, but also comfortable to use with its ergonomic handle.

It's available at home centers and hardware stores for $15, or $30 for a professional grade model with a heavier-duty handle and leather sheath. **Ames True Temper, (800) 393-1846. amestruetemper.com**

TWO-WHEEL, NO-TIP CART

Two wheels and an ergonomic design give the new EZ Hauler Wheelbarrow ($160) from Ames True Temper greater stability, so it's easier to push and won't tip over under heavy loads. (The company says using it requires one-third less effort than using a traditional wheelbarrow.) The tray sits lower to the ground, making it easier to load. It also dumps the load for you. Find retailers on the Web site. **Ames True Temper, (800) 393-1846. amestruetemper.com**

FOUR-WHEEL DUMP CART

Moving heavy items around your yard or garden is a lot easier when you don't have to actually lift anything. Even wheelbarrows require you to lift the handles, which can be hard on your back. Vigoro's four-wheel garden cart eliminates that problem. It's easy to pull and hard to tip over. Unloading is simple too—pull a lever and the cart dumps its load. It'll haul and dump 300 lbs. per load. The cart is available at Home Depot for $60. **Vigoro, vigoro.com**

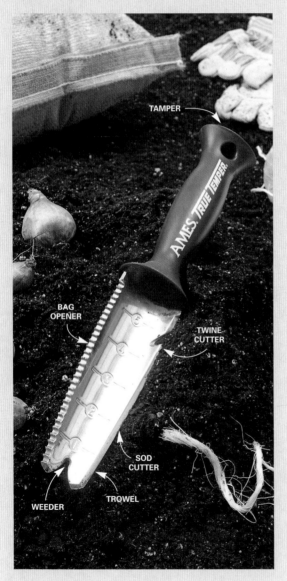

TAMPER

BAG OPENER

TWINE CUTTER

SOD CUTTER

WEEDER

TROWEL

FOLD-UP CART

Garden carts and wheelbarrows often eat up valuable storage space in your garage. The new Fold-A-Cart ($140, plus $35 shipping) saves that space by folding up into just 20 percent of its work size, so you can hang it on the wall, out of the way. Fully opened, the cart holds 6 cu. ft. and 200 lbs. It's available online from the manufacturer.

Fold-A-Tools, (866) 977-3653.

foldatools.com

BETTER WAY TO TRIM AND PRUNE TREES

If cutting and pruning trees is on your to-do list, then get the Alligator Lopper chain saw. It actually makes the chore fun (or at least more tolerable). This electric tool quickly cuts through logs and branches up to 4 in. thick, which is way too big for manual pruners. The clamping jaws grip the branches while the chain slices through.

Weighing less than 7 lbs., the Lopper is easy to handle, even when you're cutting branches overhead. Find it at home centers for $100.

Black & Decker, (800) 544-6986.

blackanddecker.com

OUTDOOR SINK PLUS AUTOMATIC HOSE REEL

How many times have you wished for an outdoor sink for cleaning garden produce or just rinsing off your hands? Now you can have one, and more easily than you think. The ReelSmart outdoor sink station ($100) hooks up to an outdoor faucet for instant water to the 24-in. sink. Just pull the drain plug to let the water in the sink drain off into your yard.

A three-piston engine (run entirely on water—no electricity, fuel or batteries needed) automatically winds up 150 ft. of garden hose. All it takes is the switch of a lever to activate the winding. Find this sink at home centers.

Hydro Industries, (866) 493-7638. hydro-industries.com

NewProducts

3 NO-SWEAT SPRAYERS

Spray as you roll ➤

Forget pumping and heavy lifting. Gilmour's Wheelpump sprayer pumps itself when you push, pull or roll the sprayer back and forth. The wheels pump the tank and carry the weight. It's great in areas where there's room to push the sprayer and for people who can't lift or hold larger sprayers.

The 2-gallon ($65) and 4-gallon ($100) models are available at select home centers, hardware stores and Amazon.com.

Gilmour, (800) 458-0107. gilmour.com

◄ Backpacker

If you don't want to carry a heavy sprayer, then wear it. The Back Pack Sprayer (model 614) fits onto your back with padded shoulder straps. A piston pump is activated by a lever located by your right or left hand, so you can pump it while it's on your back. An adjustable spray nozzle and extra flat-fan nozzle let you control your spray pattern.

The 4-gallon sprayer ($85) stands upright on a metal base for easy filling and storage. You can find it at Home Depot.

Root-Lowell Manufacturing, (800) 748-0098. rlflomaster.com

Battery-powered pump ➤

Eliminating the manual pump is one way to make spraying easier, and that's exactly what Black & Decker has done with its Rechargeable Garden Sprayer ($60). The 14.4-volt battery powers the pump, which will spray up to 5 gallons per charge. You can carry the sprayer with a shoulder strap or an ergonomically designed handle. Even fully loaded, the sprayer weighs just 11 lbs.

A wand trigger controls the spray, and an adjustable nozzle lets you choose a stream or fan pattern. It's available at home centers.

Black & Decker, (800) 544-6986. blackanddecker.com

POUR YOUR FIRST
BIG SLAB

*A pro shows you how to build strong forms, place a solid slab
and trowel a smooth finish*

by **Jeff Gorton**

Forming and pouring a concrete slab can be intimidating. Your heart races because you know that any mistake, even a little one, can quickly turn your slab into a big mess, a mistake literally cast in stone.

In this article, we'll walk you through the slab-pouring process so you get it right the first time. We'll pay particular attention to the tough parts where you're most likely to goof.

Still, pouring a large concrete slab isn't a job for a beginner. If you haven't worked with concrete, start with a small sidewalk or garden shed floor before attempting a garage-size slab like this. Even if you've got a few small jobs under your belt, it's a good idea to find an experienced helper. In addition to standard carpentry tools, you'll need a number of special tools to finish a large slab (see the Tool List on p. 216).

The bulk of the work for a new slab is in the excavation and form building. If you have to level a sloped site or bring in a lot of fill, hire an excavator for a day to help prepare the site. Then figure on spending a day building the forms and another pouring the slab.

In our area, hiring a concrete contractor to pour a 16 x 20-ft. slab like this one would cost $3,000 to $4,000. The amount of money you'll save by doing the work yourself depends mostly on whether you have to hire an excavator. In most cases, you'll save 30 to 50 percent by doing your own work.

Prepare the site

Before you get started, contact your local building department to see whether a permit is required and how close to the lot lines you can build. In most cases, you'll measure from the lot line to position the slab parallel to it. Then drive four stakes to roughly indicate the corners of the new slab. With the approximate size and location marked, use a line level and string or a builder's level to see how much the ground slopes. Flattening a sloped site means moving tons of soil. You can build up the low side as we did, or dig the high side into the slope and add a low retaining wall to hold back the soil.

Your concrete slab will last longer, with less cracking and movement, if it's built on solid, well-drained soil. If you have sandy soil, you're in luck. Just scrape off the sod and topsoil and add gravel fill if needed. If you have clay or loam soil, you should remove enough to allow a 6- to 8-in. layer of compacted gravel under the new concrete.

If you have to remove more than a few inches of dirt, consider renting a skid loader or hiring an excavator. An excavator can also help you get rid of excess soil. Before you do any digging, contact your local utilities to locate and mark buried pipes and wires (call 811 or visit call811.com).

Build accurate forms for a perfect slab

Start by choosing straight form boards. For a 5-in.-thick slab with thickened edges, which is perfect for most garages and sheds, 2x12 boards work best. For a driveway or other slab without thickened edges, use 2x6s. If you can't get long enough boards, splice them together by nailing a 4-ft. 2x12 cleat over the joint. Sight down the boards to make sure they're aligned and straight before nailing on the cleat. Cut the two side form boards 3 in. longer than the length of the slab. Then cut the end boards to the exact width of the slab. You'll nail the end boards between the side boards to create the correct size form. Use 16d duplex (double-headed) nails to connect the form boards and attach the bracing. Nail through the stakes into the forms.

Photos 1 – 3 show how to build the forms. Measure from the lot line to position the first side and level it at the desired height. For speed and accuracy, use a builder's level (**Photo 1**), a transit or a laser level to set the height of the forms.

Brace the forms to ensure straight sides

Freshly poured concrete can push form boards outward, leaving your slab with a curved edge that's almost impos-

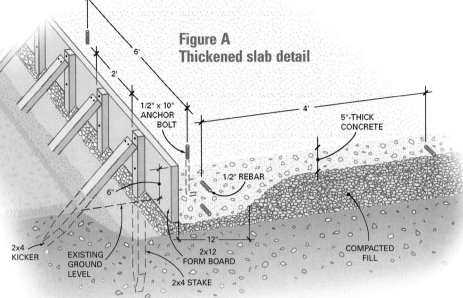

Figure A
Thickened slab detail

1/2" x 10" ANCHOR BOLT — 5"-THICK CONCRETE — 1/2" REBAR — 2x4 KICKER — EXISTING GROUND LEVEL — 2x12 FORM BOARD — 2x4 STAKE — 12" — COMPACTED FILL — 6' 2' 4' 6"

TAPE MEASURE — BUILDER'S LEVEL — CLEAT — 2x12 FORM BOARD — 2x4 STAKE

1 CUT a 2x12 to length (or splice it with a cleat) for one side and nail it to a corner stake. Level the 2x12 and nail it to the second corner stake.

2x4 KICKERS — 8-LB. SLEDGE — 2x4 STAKE — MASON'S LINE

2 STRETCH a mason's line just above the top edge of the 2x12. Align the 2x12 with the string and brace it with pairs of 2x4s spaced every 2 ft. To absorb the shock and make nailing easier, hold a sledgehammer behind stakes and form boards as you nail.

sible to fix. The best way to avoid this is with extra-strong bracing. Place 2x4 stakes and 2x4 kickers every 2 ft. along the form boards for support (Photo 2). Kickers slant down into the ground and keep the top of the stakes from bending outward.

Stretch a strong string (mason's line) along the top edge of the form board. As you set the braces, make sure the form board lines up with the string. Adjust the braces to keep the form board straight. Cut stakes long enough so that when they're driven at least 8 in. into the ground (4 in. more in loose, sandy soil), the tops will be slightly below the top of the forms. Cut points on the kickers and drive them into the ground at an angle. Then nail the top of the kickers to the stakes. If your soil is sandy or loose, cut both ends of the kickers square and drive a small stake to hold the lower end of the kicker in place.

Photo 3 shows measuring diagonally to set the second form board perfectly square with the first. Use the 3-4-5 method. Measure and mark a multiple of 3 ft. on one side. (In our case, this is 15 ft.) Then mark a multiple of 4 ft. on the adjacent side (20 ft. for our slab). Remember to measure from the same point where the two sides meet. Finally, adjust the position of the unbraced form board until the diagonal measurement is a multiple of 5 (25 ft. in this case).

Squaring the second form board is easiest if you prop it level on a stack of 2x4s (Photo 3) and slide it back and forth until the diagonal measurement is correct. Then drive a stake behind the end of the form board and nail through the stake into the form. Complete the second side by leveling and bracing the form board.

Set the third form board parallel to the first one. Leave the fourth side off until you've hauled in and tamped the fill.

Build up fill and pack it well

The key to crack-resistant concrete is a firm base that drains well. Unless you have sandy soil, this means adding a layer of gravel. With the forms in place, you can estimate how much fill you need. To calculate the amount of fill needed, stretch a string across the top of the forms and measure down to the ground. Do this in three or four spots and average the results. Subtract the thickness of your slab. Then use this depth to calculate the cubic yards of fill needed. Look for a supplier under "Sand and Gravel" in the yellow pages. Ask what your supplier recommends for fill under slabs. We used crushed concrete, which compacts and drains well.

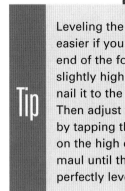

Tip

Leveling the forms is easier if you leave one end of the form board slightly high when you nail it to the stake. Then adjust the height by tapping the stake on the high end with a maul until the board is perfectly level.

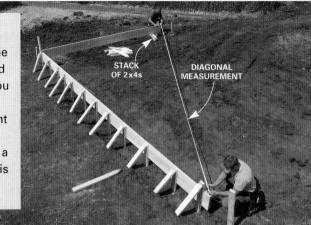

3 CUT a second 2x12 to the width of the slab. Nail one end to the braced form and use the calculated length of the diagonal to set the form at 90 degrees. Drive a stake at the end. Level, straighten and brace the second form board. Add the third side.

4 SPREAD AND TAMP 3-in. layers of granular fill to within 5 in. of the top of the forms. Measure down from a string stretched across the forms. Slope the fill down along the edges to create a thickened edge of concrete.

5 COVER the fill with a layer of 6-mil plastic sheeting if the slab will be beneath a heated structure. Tie two bands of 1/2-in. steel reinforcing rods (rebar) to stakes set about 4 in. from the perimeter of the forms (Figure A).

6 LAY a grid of rebar spaced 4 ft. apart over the plastic and connect the intersections with tie wire. Divide the slab down the middle with a 2x4 nailed to 1x3 stakes. Align the top edge with a taut string.

7 DRAG a straight 2x4 (screed board) across the top of the forms to level the concrete. Make multiple passes if needed to create a flat, evenly filled area. Have a helper add or remove concrete in front of the screed as you pull it.

8 PUSH a bull float across the screeded concrete, keeping the leading edge slightly elevated. When you reach the far side, lift the handle enough to slightly elevate the edge closest to you and pull back to the starting point. Move over and repeat, overlapping the previously floated surface by about one-third.

Spread the fill in layers no more than 3 in. thick and tamp each layer with a rented plate compactor (**Photo 4 inset**). Leave a 12-in.-deep by 12-in.-wide trench around the perimeter for the thickened edge.

If you're building a heated structure on the slab, cover the ground inside the forms with 6-mil polyethylene sheeting. Otherwise you can leave it uncovered.

Strengthen the slab with steel

Concrete needs reinforcement for added strength and crack resistance. It's well worth the small additional cost and labor to install 1/2-in. rebar (steel reinforcing bar). You'll find rebar at home centers and at suppliers of concrete and masonry products ($4 for a 20-ft. length). You'll also need a bundle of tie wires and a tie-wire twisting tool ($5) to connect the rebar (**Photo 5**).

Use a metal-cutting blade or disc in a reciprocating saw, circular saw or grinder to cut the rebar. Cut and bend pieces of rebar to form the perimeter reinforcing. Splice the pieces together by overlapping them at least 6 in. and wrapping tie wire around the overlap. Wire the perimeter rebar to rebar stakes for support. Then cut and lay out pieces in a 4-ft.-on-center grid pattern. Wire the intersections together. You'll pull the grid up into the center of the concrete as you pour the slab.

If you've never poured a large slab or if the weather is hot and dry, which makes concrete harden quickly, divide this slab down the middle and fill the halves on different days to reduce the amount of concrete you'll have to finish at one time (**Photo 6**). Remove the divider before pouring the second half.

Mark the position of the door openings on the forms. Then mark the location of the anchor bolts on the forms. Place marks for anchor bolts 6 in. from each side of doors, 12 in. from corners and 6 ft. apart around the perimeter (**Photo 10**).

Working safely with concrete

Wet concrete on skin can cause everything from mild redness to third-degree, permanently disfiguring chemical burns. You and your helpers should take these steps:

- Wear eye protection. Sandy concrete splashes can wreak havoc with your eyes.
- Wear long pants and long sleeves to protect your skin.
- Wear tall rubber boots if you have to wade in wet concrete.
- Wear gloves (rubber gloves are the safest bet).

If your clothes get saturated with wet cement, remove them, thoroughly rinse your skin and change into clean clothes before going back to work.

Preparation is the key to a trouble-free pour

Pouring concrete is fast-paced work. To reduce stress and avoid mistakes, make sure *everything* is ready before the truck arrives.

Triple-check your forms to make sure they're square, level, straight and well braced. Have at least two contractor-grade wheelbarrows on hand and three or four strong helpers. Plan the route the truck will take. For large slabs, it's best if the truck can back up to the forms. Avoid hot, windy days if possible. This kind of weather accelerates the hardening process—a slab can turn hard before you have time to trowel a nice smooth finish. If the forecast calls for rain, reschedule the concrete delivery to a dry day. Rain will ruin the surface.

To figure the volume of concrete needed, multiply the length by the width by the depth (in feet) to arrive at the number of cubic feet. Don't forget to account for the trenched perimeter. Divide the total by 27 and add 5 percent to calculate the number of yards of concrete you'll need. Our slab required 7 yards. Call the ready mix company at least a day in advance and explain your project. Most dispatchers are quite helpful and can recommend the best mix. For a large slab like ours that may have occasional vehicle traffic, we ordered a 3,500-lb. mix with 5 percent air entrainment. The air entrainment traps microscopic bubbles that help concrete withstand freezing temperatures.

Pour, flatten and bull-float the concrete

Be prepared to hustle when the truck arrives. Start by placing concrete in the forms farthest from the truck. Use wheelbarrows where necessary.

Concrete is too heavy to shovel or push more than a few feet. Place the concrete close to its final spot and roughly level it with a rake. Try to leave it just slightly over the top of the forms. Lift the rebar to position it in the middle of the slab as you go. As soon as the concrete is placed in the forms, start striking it off even with the top of the form boards with a straight, smooth 2x4 screed board (**Photo 7**). Tip the top of the screed board back slightly as you drag it toward you in a back-and-forth sawing motion.

The trick to easy screeding is to have a helper with a rake moving the concrete in front of the screed board. You want enough concrete to fill all voids, but not so much that it's difficult to pull the board. About 1/2 to 1 in. deep in front of the screed board is about right. It's better to make several passes with the screed board, moving a little concrete each time, than to try to pull a lot of concrete at once.

Start bull-floating the concrete as soon as possible after screeding (**Photo 8**). The goal is to remove marks left by screeding and fill in low spots to create a flat, level surface. Bull-floating also forces larger aggregate below

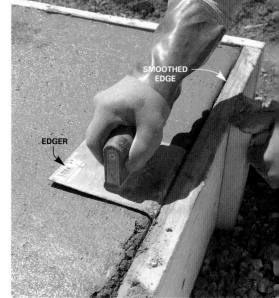

9 ROUND the edges of the slab with an edging tool after any surface water disappears. Work the edger until the edge is solid and smooth.

SMOOTHED EDGE
EDGER

1/2" ANCHOR BOLT
2-1/2"

10 PRESS 1/2-in. anchor bolts into the concrete before it hardens. Place bolts 1 ft. from corners and every 6 ft. Place bolts 6 in. from the sides of door openings. Leave about 2-1/2 in. of the bolts exposed.

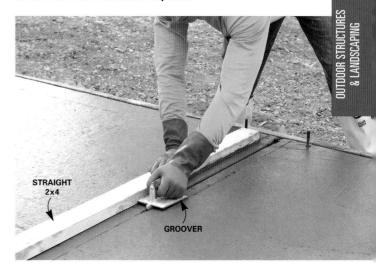

STRAIGHT 2x4
GROOVER

11 FORM control joints to minimize random cracks by running a groover along the edge of a straight 2x4. Work the groover forward and back while making a progressively deeper cut.

OUTDOOR STRUCTURES & LANDSCAPING

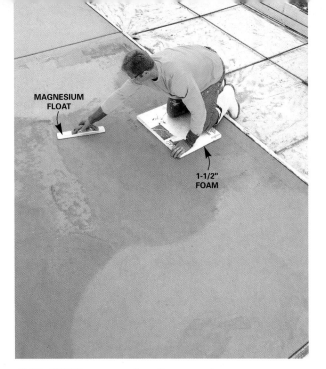

MAGNESIUM
FLOAT

1-1/2"
FOAM

12 SWEEP a magnesium float over the concrete to smooth and flatten the surface when the concrete has hardened enough to support your weight. Then further smooth the surface with a steel trowel.

the surface. Keep the leading edge of the float just slightly above the surface by raising or lowering the float handle. If the float angle is too steep, you'll plow the wet concrete and create low spots. Three or four passes with the bull float is usually sufficient. Too much floating can weaken the surface by drawing up too much water and cement.

Float and trowel for a smooth finish

After you smooth the slab with the bull float, water will "bleed" out of the concrete and sit on the surface. Wait for the water to disappear and for the slab to harden slightly before you resume finishing. When the slab is firm enough to resist an imprint from your thumb, start hand-floating. On cool days, you may have to wait an hour or two to start floating and troweling. On hot, dry days, you have to hustle.

You can edge the slab before it gets firm since you don't have to kneel on the slab (**Photo 9**). If the edger sinks in and leaves a track that's more than 1/8 in. deep, wait for the slab to harden slightly before proceeding.

You'll have to wait until the concrete can support your weight to start grooving the slab. Cut 2-ft. squares of 1-1/2-in.-thick foam insulation for use as kneeling boards. The kneeling board distributes your weight, allowing you to get an earlier start.

Grooving creates a weakened spot in the concrete that allows the inevitable shrinkage cracking to take place at the groove rather than at some random spot. Cut grooves about every 10 ft. in large slabs.

When you're done grooving, smooth the concrete (**Photo 12**) with a magnesium float. Hand-floating removes imperfections and pushes pebbles below the surface. Use the float to remove the marks left by edging and smooth out humps and dips left by the bull float. You may have to bear down on the float if the concrete is starting to harden. The goal is to bring a slurry of cement to the surface to aid in troweling.

For a smoother, denser finish, follow the magnesium float with a steel trowel. Troweling is one of the trickier steps in concrete finishing. You'll have to practice to develop a feel for it. For a really smooth finish, repeat the troweling step two or three times, letting the concrete harden a bit between each pass. At first, hold the trowel almost flat, elevating the leading edge just enough to avoid gouging the surface. On each successive pass, lift the leading edge of the trowel a little more. If you want a rougher, nonslip surface, you can skip the steel trowel altogether. Instead, drag a push broom over the surface to create a "broom finish."

Keep concrete moist after it's poured so it cures slowly and develops maximum strength. The easiest way to ensure proper curing is to spray the finished concrete with curing compound. Curing compound is available at home centers ($18 per gallon). Follow the instructions on the label. Use a regular garden sprayer to apply the compound. You can lay plastic over the concrete instead, although this can lead to discoloration of the surface.

Let the finished slab harden overnight before you carefully remove the form boards. Pull the duplex nails from the corners and kickers and pry up on the stakes with a shovel to loosen and remove the forms. Since the concrete surface will be soft and easy to chip or scratch, wait for a day or two before building on the slab.

RAIN
GARDEN

*It's a beautiful flower bed—
and a reservoir for yard and
roof runoff*

by **Lucie B. Amundsen**

Too much water can undermine your home. If you worry about a wet or damp basement, a busy sump pump, or muddy puddles in your yard after a heavy rainfall, this story is for you. We want to introduce you to a new tool to improve drainage—a rain garden.

A rain garden is basically a plant pond, that is, a garden bed that you plant with special deep-rooted species. These plants help the water rapidly seep into the soil, away from your house and out of your hair. You direct the rainwater from the downspouts to the garden via a swale (a stone channel) or plastic piping. The garden captures the water and, when properly designed, drains it into the soil within a day. You don't have to worry about creating a mosquito haven; the water drains before mosquitoes even have time to breed.

If there's an especially heavy rainfall, excess water may overflow the rain garden and run into the storm sewer system. Even so, the rain garden will have done its job. It will have channeled water away from your foundation and reduced the load on the sewer system. A rain garden also reduces the amount of lawn chemicals and pet wastes that may otherwise run off into local lakes and rivers. In some communities, the runoff problem is so big that homes with rain gardens qualify for a tax break! Call your municipality to learn your local policy.

In this article, we'll tell you how to design, build and plant a rain garden suitable for your yard. We've condensed it to a few handy guidelines. You won't need any special tools or equipment. A shovel and a level will do. But expect to sweat through some heavy digging!

Location and slope

Check the slope of your yard with a level and a long, straight board. You'll need a minimum slope of 1 in. in 4-1/2 ft. (2 percent) for water to flow into your rain garden. If you don't have this slope, you'll have to do major landscaping, both to create the slope and to improve drainage.

- Locate your rain garden where rainwater will feed into it from downspouts, driveways or low points in your yard.

- Lay attractive river rock (1-1/2 in. diameter and, if desired, larger decorative rocks) or run an underground 4-in. PVC pipe to channel water from a downspout to your garden. Use PVC for a better flow if the garden is more than 30 ft. from a downspout.

- Place your rain garden at least 10 ft. away from your home. Otherwise, water may saturate the soil close to the foundation or even back up against it. If you already have water pooling close to your home, channel it with an underground PVC pipe to the garden. This may mean tunneling under a walkway or other obstruction.

- Keep in mind "the big rain," that storm a couple of times a year that will overflow your garden. Create an overflow zone, a slightly lower area on one side with stones that will channel water away once the garden fills. Locate it away from your house and your neighbors' homes as well.

- Do not locate the garden over a septic tank or underground utility lines. Remember to call to have your utilities marked before digging—call 811 or visit call811.com.

FIGURE A:
Rain Garden Details

Gutters

Downspout

Swale

Splash Rocks

Berm

FIGURE B: Depth Profile

Original Grade

Depth of Garden When Full of Water

Berm

Finished Grade

FIGURE C: Plant Selection

Sedges

Cone Flowers

Sedges

Lavender

Asters

Foxglove

Liatris

Iris

Astilbe

Sedum

Artemisia

Sage

Artemisia

Daylilies

☐ Moderate-Moisture Plants
☐ High-Moisture Plants

Drainpipe

Mulch

Berm

Garden depth

You only want to capture as much water as will sink into the soil in 24 hours after a storm—a garden dug in sandy, well-draining soil can be deeper than a garden dug in poorly draining clay. To determine the ideal depth, first test the porosity of your soil.

Dig a hole in your garden area about the size and depth of a large coffee can (8 in. x 8 in. x 8 in.) and fill it with water. Time how long it takes for the water level to drop. If in one hour the water level has dropped by 1/2 in., you can figure the soil drains an inch in two hours. At this rate, the garden soil will handle 12 in. of water in a 24-hour period, making the ideal depth of this garden 12 in.

Garden size

To determine the best size for your garden, estimate the volume of water that would flow off the roof and down the spout that feeds it during a 1-in. rainfall (the rainfall from an average storm). To do this, calculate the rough area of the roof that drains down the spout. For example, in a 2,400-sq.-ft. rectangular home with a downspout at each corner, you'd have approximately 600 sq. ft. of runoff going to each downspout. Multiply by rainfall depth (1 in., or 1/12 ft.) to get the volume of water—50 cu. ft. in this case. If your soil porosity can handle a 6-in.-deep (that is, 1/2 ft.) garden bed, dividing by 1/2 ft. gives you a 100-sq.-ft. (10 x 10 ft.) garden size.

However, it's OK to vary the size. A smaller garden can still yield big benefits. Rain gardens that are 30 percent smaller than ideal still handle nearly 75 percent of the storm water shed from a house. Of course, you can also make it larger. In any case, make sure the size of the garden fits your landscape.

TLC for the first year

- Baby your garden its first year. Mulch with shredded hardwood mulch (not pine bark or wood chips, which will float away) and weed regularly.
- Dig a notch into the berm on the low side to allow about half the water to flow out for the first year. Young plants can't handle a large volume of water.
- Add large decorative rocks at the garden's entrance to prevent heavy rain from washing out young plants.
- Water your new garden about an inch per week during dry spells. If you select native species, you'll find that these plants will be highly tolerant of dry conditions once they mature.

Plant selections

While growing zones and soils vary dramatically throughout the country, plant selections for this type of garden are fairly standard.

Aster, daylily, iris, sedum, coneflower, artemisia and sedge are examples of good rain garden specimens. Talk to your local university extension or other garden experts about other options for your area.

Choose plants that have "average to moist" water requirements listed on their tag. Position them in the deepest parts of your rain garden. On the higher edges of the bed, position plants that thrive in "average to dry" water conditions. While it may seem intuitive to purchase moisture-loving plants for your rain garden, don't do it. Since your garden is designed to drain in 24 hours, the moisture-loving plants will soon be left high and dry.

While almost any plant with the right moisture requirements will do fine in a rain garden, there are some good reasons to select native plants. Native grasses, wildflowers and shrubs generally have very deep root systems, sometimes burrowing down 10 ft. or more. Most native plants also cast off their roots annually, growing new roots and providing more soil aeration and pathways for water to flow. And because they're indigenous, you know these plants will thrive in your zone and soil conditions.

ASTER

DAYLILY

SEDUM

IRIS

BAILEY NURSERIES

NewProducts

Water wand with longer reach

Spraying hard-to-reach areas can be difficult, but that's how Solo's telescoping wand sprayer (model 420-2L, $15) earns it keep. The wand extends up to 23 in. for those high plants. The ergonomic grip on the handle, the thumb trigger and the large pump make the sprayer comfortable to operate. Look for it at hardware stores (find retailers on the Web site) or buy it online.

Solo, (757) 245-4228. solousa.com

HomeCare&Repair

TIPS, FIXES & GEAR FOR A TROUBLE-FREE HOME

BROADCAST SPREADER TECHNIQUE

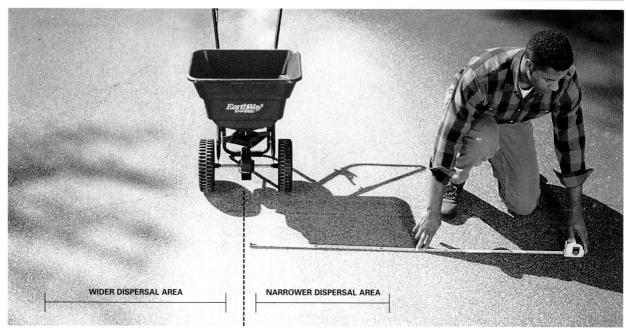

WIDER DISPERSAL AREA   NARROWER DISPERSAL AREA

Walk the spreader up the center of the driveway, then measure the total width and the width on each side.

Broadcast spreaders do a great job of spreading grass seed, fertilizer and weed killer on larger lawns because they throw the material out more consistently over a wide area. However, unless you know how much area they cover for each type of product, you can end up spreading too much or too little and get bad results.

The best way to find out the actual dispersal pattern for your broadcast spreader is to do a test run on your driveway and then measure the results. Clean off a 12 x 20-ft. section of the driveway. Close the flow lever on your spreader and set the controls for the product you're using. Fill the spreader—do this on the driveway or sidewalk to avoid spills on the grass—then open the flow lever and push the spreader several feet down the center of the driveway at your normal pace, continuing for a few steps after you close the hopper.

Measure the average dispersal pattern to the sides and front. (Note: The right side of the dispersal pattern for spreaders is wider than the left side.)

Sweep up the test material and dump it back into the spreader, then apply the material to your lawn, walking back and forth in the long direction on your lawn (**Figure A**). Overlap each course 6 to 12 in., but close off the flow when you make tight turns.

Figure A
Spreader pattern

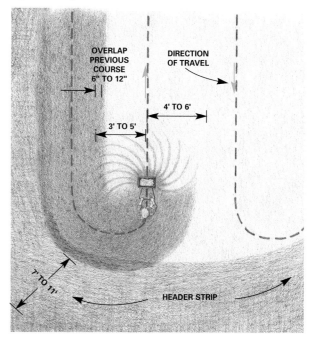

OVERLAP PREVIOUS COURSE 6" TO 12"

DIRECTION OF TRAVEL

4' TO 6'

3' TO 5'

7' TO 11'

HEADER STRIP

Apply a "header strip" around the perimeter of the yard, then fill in the middle. Shut off the spreader when you turn.

Gallery of Ideas

QUICK AND EASY SHED

FROM JULY/AUGUST, 2007, p. 42

If you need more space to store and organize your lawn and garden gear, consider this simple 5 x 12-ft. shed. It's large enough for wheelbarrows, lawn mowers and even a moderate-size garden tractor. We've also included a built-in bench for potting plants. And this shed will look good for years because it's built from durable cedar siding, pressure-treated wood and a 30-year steel roof. You can leave the back of the shed open or install a sliding door.

Project Facts

Cost: Less than $800
Skill level: Intermediate to advanced
Time: Three weekends

STONE PATH AND STEPS

FROM MARCH, 2007, p. 38

You don't have to let the hills and slopes of your yard stop you from enjoying your outdoor space. With a little imagination (and a good bit of sweat!), you can change those negatives into striking landscape features. The heart of this project is a practical path and steps. The bonus is a series of terraces, garden beds and sitting areas that turn largely wasted space into beautiful outdoor living space.

Project Facts

Cost: $4,000 for materials
Skill level: Advanced
Time: 10 full days

BACKYARD OASIS

This shaded outdoor retreat is surprisingly easy to build. Place it next to your deck or anywhere in your yard and it will soon become your favorite place to relax. It's open and airy, yet you'll be shaded from the hot afternoon sun and those passing summer showers.

We've simplified the difficult building steps with goof-proof techniques—like positioning the posts with a 2x4 frame and shaping the ends of the beams with a circular saw. If you've tackled projects like basic deck building or wall framing, you can build this shelter.

Project Facts

Cost: $3,000 for materials (we also show you how you can cut the cost in half by selecting alternative building materials)
Skill level: Intermediate
Time: At least three full weekends

FROM MAY, 2007, p. 36

OUTDOOR STRUCTURES & LANDSCAPING

Gallery of Ideas
CURVED GARDEN ARBOR

A simple arbor is the perfect feature to draw you and your family into your yard. It offers you a semishaded place to relax and take in the view. And if you plant climbing vines, you'll have an inviting green oasis in a year or two. It's also a great way to add a handsome yet inexpensive focal point to an otherwise plain landscape.

We'll show you how to build this arbor, step-by-step, including the graceful curved seat. This project is not difficult—our instructions will walk you through the tricky parts and you'll love the results!

Project Facts
Cost: $300
Skill level: Beginner to intermediate
Time: Two weekends

FROM MARCH, 2007, p. 52

RAISED GARDEN BED

FROM APRIL, 2007, p. 34

If you or one of your family members loves plants and flowers, why not build this natural-stone raised bed? The soil mix can be hand selected to suit your favorite plants and the raised bed is easier on your back because you don't have to bend over as far to tend the plants. The stonework techniques shown here will work for a raised bed of any shape or size.

Project Facts
Cost: $1,300
Skill level: Beginner
Time: One weekend for the 4-ft. x 16-ft. planter shown

To order photocopies of complete articles for the projects shown here, call (715) 246-4521, email familyhandyman@nrmsinc.com or write to: Copies, The Family Handyman, P.O. Box 83695, Stillwater, MN 55083-0695. Many public libraries also carry back issues of *The Family Handyman* magazine.

7 Auto & Garage

IN THIS CHAPTER

Ultimate Garage Wall System 226

Car & Garage 232
  *Replace spark plug wires, fix a
  windshield washer, touch up
  scratches and much more*

Garage Bump-out 240

Handy Hints 247
  *Bumper sticker release, cargo liner,
  trunk lid tie-down*

Car & Garage 248
  *Change your own transmission fluid,
  change your own coolant and much more*

Car Caddy 256

Home Care & Repair 261
  Three garage door fixes

New Products .263
  *Heat and light your work space,
  turn your garage into a screen
  room and more*

ULTIMATE GARAGE
WALL SYSTEM

Convenient work space and storage galore in one weekend

by **Eric Smith**

For most of us, the garage is more than just a parking space. It's also storage space for outdoor toys and gardening gear and a workshop for home projects and hobbies. With its cabinets, open shelves and counter-top, this wall system is designed to suit all those additional needs and still leave room for parking. And because it's built around standard cabinets, installation is simple. If you can screw cabinets to the wall, you can build this system.

You can install the cabinets, countertop and shelves in a single weekend. If you add extras like we did—a fresh paint job, a backsplash shelf, hooks and other hardware—expect to spend a second weekend completing the job. You'll need standard tools like a drill and circular saw. A table saw will come in handy but isn't absolutely necessary. We bought all the materials for our 24-ft.-long wall system at a home center for a total cost of $2,400. That's about $100 per linear foot. If you use inexpensive cabinets as we did, your per-foot costs will be similar.

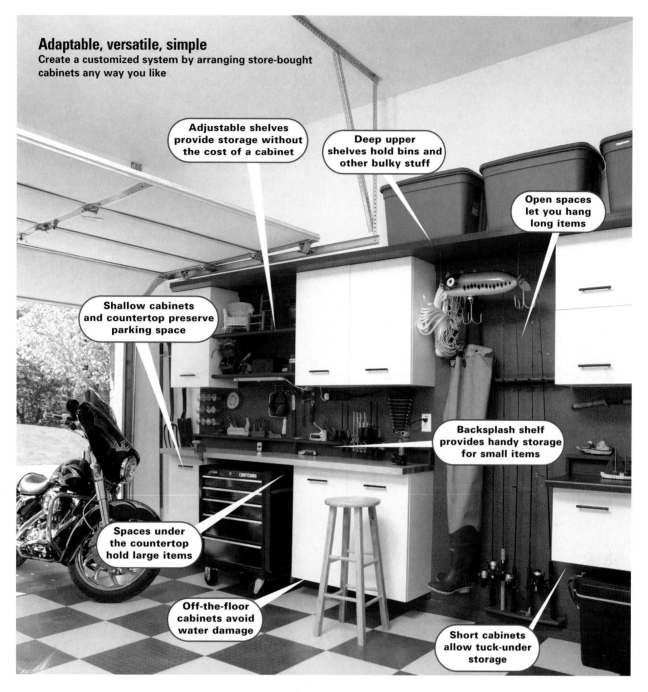

Adaptable, versatile, simple
Create a customized system by arranging store-bought cabinets any way you like

Adjustable shelves provide storage without the cost of a cabinet

Deep upper shelves hold bins and other bulky stuff

Open spaces let you hang long items

Shallow cabinets and countertop preserve parking space

Backsplash shelf provides handy storage for small items

Spaces under the countertop hold large items

Off-the-floor cabinets avoid water damage

Short cabinets allow tuck-under storage

Shop first, then plan and buy

Before you plan this project, check out your cabinet options at a home center. Most home centers carry several styles of inexpensive standard kitchen cabinets. Other options are unfinished cabinets, which you can paint or stain, or "ready-to-assemble" cabinets that you assemble yourself. With either option, ask for a list of available sizes. You'll need only "upper" cabinets, which in a kitchen typically hang above the countertop. Most upper cabinets are 30 in. tall, about 12 in. deep and available in various widths. We used mostly 30-in.-tall cabinets, including two corner cabinets. We also used three short "refrigerator cabinets" (designed to fit above the fridge in a kitchen).

While you're at the home center, also look at countertops. You can choose from a small selection of in-stock colors (about $10 per linear ft.) or order any color imaginable starting at $20 per linear ft. If you special-order, you can have the countertops made to the width you choose and avoid cutting them (**Photo 5**). If you'd like to make your own laminate countertops, go to thefamilyhandyman.com and enter a keyword search for "laminate countertops." We also used butcher block ($35 per linear ft.) as one section of our countertop to provide a heavy-duty work surface.

With your list of available cabinet sizes in hand, you can plan the cabinet layout by making a scale drawing on graph paper. Or you can experiment with different layouts

Figure A

The entire system is based on standard wall cabinets. The countertop and upper shelf rest on the cabinets. Open shelves hang on adjustable shelf supports between cabinets

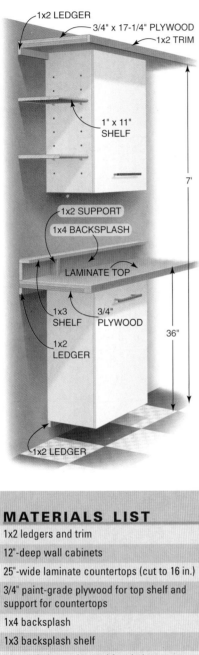

1x2 LEDGER
3/4" x 17-1/4" PLYWOOD
1x2 TRIM
1" x 11" SHELF
7'
1x2 SUPPORT
1x4 BACKSPLASH
LAMINATE TOP
1x3 SHELF
3/4" PLYWOOD
1x2 LEDGER
36"
1x2 LEDGER

MATERIALS LIST

1x2 ledgers and trim

12"-deep wall cabinets

25"-wide laminate countertops (cut to 16 in.)

3/4" paint-grade plywood for top shelf and support for countertops

1x4 backsplash

1x3 backsplash shelf

5/4 x 11" pine stair tread for shelves

Butcher block for workbench

1 lb. of 1-1/4" screws

1 lb. of 2-1/2" screws

Cabinet screws

Cabinet bolts

Shelf pins

Wood glue

right on the wall, using masking tape to mark cabinet locations. Don't space cabinets more than 36 in. apart or the countertop and shelves may sag. You may want to leave out the countertop in one or two spots so you can hang shovels, rakes and other tall stuff on the wall. The countertop can be anywhere from 13 in. to 16 in. deep—just be sure that it won't interfere with parking the car or opening the doors. When your plan is complete, make up a shopping list using our list as a guide (below left).

Start with a straight, level ledger

To get started, locate all the wall studs. Then use a level to draw a continuous line on the wall marking the position of the lower edge of each cabinet. If you make this line perfectly straight and level, your cabinet and countertop installation will go quickly and smoothly. If your cabinets are 30 in. tall, place the line 4-1/2 in. from the floor to end up with a standard countertop height of 36 in. Keep in mind that many garage floors slope for drainage. To deal with the slope of our garage floor, we measured up 4-1/2 in. at the middle of the wall. That gave us a 3-1/2-in. height at the high end and 5-1/2 in. at the low end.

Next, screw 1x2s along the level line to create the ledger that supports the cabinets (**Photo 1**). Fasten the ledger with 2-1/2-in. screws. You can make the ledger continuous, but the final project will look better if you place the ledger only where you'll later place cabinets.

1 LEVEL and screw 1x2 ledgers to the wall to support the base cabinets and keep them off the floor.

Solutions for any garage

Our garage had stud walls covered with drywall, but you can install this system in any garage. Here's how:

If your garage has concrete block walls, follow the same steps we show, but use masonry screws to fasten ledgers and cabinets to the block. You'll have to predrill holes with a hammer drill, so the project will take longer.

If you have bare stud walls, you could install this system as shown. But consider covering the wall with 3/4-in. plywood or OSB. That way, you can fasten ledgers and cabinets to the plywood; no need to locate studs.

If your garage walls are built on a protruding block or concrete curb (shown) that won't allow you to mount cabinets near the floor, you can "fur out" the wall to create a flat surface. Screw horizontal 2x4s to the wall centered 24 in. apart, then screw 3/4-in. plywood to the 2x4s.

FURRING STRIP

3/4" PLYWOOD

CURB

Set cabinets on the ledger

Remove the cabinet doors to make installation easier. Also drill shelf support holes in those cabinets that will support open shelves (**Photo 3**). Then simply rest each cabinet on the ledger and screw them to the wall studs using special cabinet screws (available at home centers). Drive at least two screws at the top and two at the bottom of each cabinet. With narrow cabinets that don't span two studs, use toggle bolts. When a cabinet is screwed into place, hold a level upright against the front. Chances are, you'll have to loosen screws and insert shims behind the top or bottom to make the cabinet plumb (**Photo 2**).

Our plan included cabinets with open shelf spaces between and a few cabinets that were joined together. Cabinet bolts (available at home centers) are the best way to join cabinets like ours (**Photo 4**). Screws would easily pull out of the thin particleboard sides. With face-frame cabinets, you can simply screw the face frames together.

CABINET SCREW

Cut down and beef up the countertops

Cut your countertops to width (**Photo 5**). We cut ours 16 in. wide. The cut doesn't have to be perfect since the backsplash will hide it. Next, cut the countertops to length (or adjust the spacing between cabinets, as we did). If the cut end will be exposed, this cut has to be straight and smooth, so clamp a straightedge to the countertop to guide your saw. For help attaching an end cap to cover the cut end, go to thefamilyhandyman.com and do a keyword search for "install countertop."

The countertop will bridge open spaces between cabinets, so strengthen it with a 3/4-in. plywood backing. The plywood also allows you to form strong "half-lap" joints at mitered corners (**Photo 6 and 7**). You can't join miters as usual using draw bolts

SHIM

LEDGER

2 SET each cabinet on the ledger and screw it to studs. Hold a level against the front of the cabinet and level it with shims.

AUTO & GARAGE

because the bolt slots aren't accessible from inside the cabinets. Before you set the countertops in place, screw 1x2 ledgers between cabinets. To fasten the countertops, drive screws into the countertops from underneath at the front and back of each cabinet.

Hang uppers and add shelves

Mark a level line 18 in. above the countertop. This line marks the bottom of the upper cabinets just as your previous level line marked the lower cabinets. Then build a 17-7/8-in.-tall box from scrap wood to make installing the upper cabinets easier. Set each cabinet on this box and use shims to perfectly align the cabinet with the level line (**Photo 8**). Fasten and level the cabinets just as you did before.

Assemble the upper shelf on top of the cabinets. First

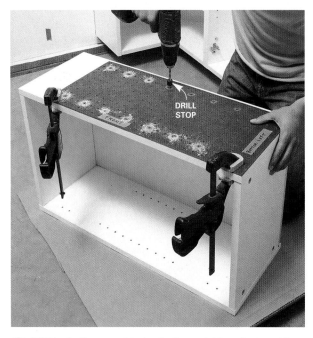

3 DRILL shelf-support holes in the outsides of any cabinets that will support open shelves. Position the holes with a scrap of pegboard.

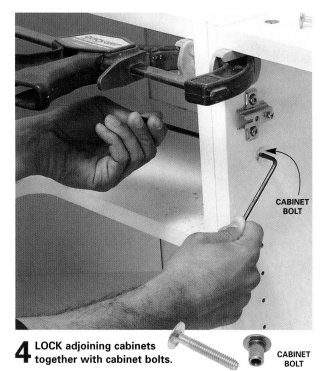

4 LOCK adjoining cabinets together with cabinet bolts.

5 CUT countertops to width with the laminate side down to avoid chips and scratches.

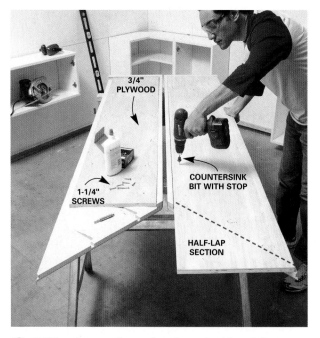

6 GLUE and screw plywood to the undersides of the countertops to strengthen them. Create a "half-lap" at corners by running plywood short on one side and long on the other.

cut 3/4-in. plywood into strips 17-1/4 in. wide. Screw ledgers between the cabinets and set the first layer of plywood over the cabinets with the best-looking side face down. Drive 1-1/4-in. screws up through the cabinets to fasten them. Then add the second layer and screw it to the first (Photo 9).

Cut the shelves that hang between cabinets from pine stair tread stock, which is a full 1 in. thick and won't sag like particleboard shelves. Cut the shelves 1/4 in. shorter than the spaces between cabinets. Your backsplash can be as simple as a painted 1x4 nailed to the wall. To build a backsplash shelf like ours, see **Figure A**. Space the upright 1x2 supports every 4 ft. To avoid damaging the doors, hang them after the entire project is complete. Align the doors using the adjusting screws on the hinges, then attach the door pulls. 🏠

HALF-LAP SECTION

7 SPREAD glue on the half-lap joint and fit the mitered countertop sections together. Fasten the countertops by driving screws up through the cabinets.

LEVEL LINE

SHIM

8 SUPPORT the upper cabinets with a homemade wood box. Adjust the cabinet height precisely with shims and screw it to the studs.

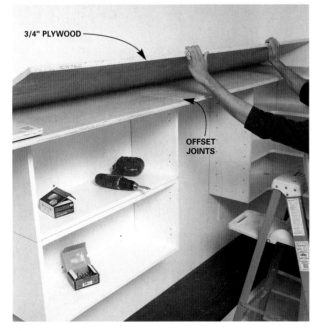

3/4" PLYWOOD

OFFSET JOINTS

9 BUILD the upper shelf from two layers of plywood. Offset the joints and make sure all joints are over cabinets.

1x2 TRIM

10 CUT to fit mitered 1x2 nosing, and glue and nail it in place with 1-1/2-in. brads.

Car&Garage

REPLACE **SPARK PLUG WIRES**
BEFORE THEY WEAR OUT

Worn plug wires and boots can start to leak voltage to nearby engine parts, causing arcing.

Do spark plug wires wear out? You bet. That's because spark plug wires aren't actually made of wire. They're made of delicate carbon fibers. Over time, the carbon breaks down and the fibers separate, causing high electrical resistance. High resistance degrades the spark, resulting in poor combustion, misfires, lousy gas mileage and ultimately a glowing "Check Engine" light. If you let that condition go on too long, the wires can start to leak voltage to nearby engine parts, causing arcing, severe performance problems, and even ignition component failures.

That's why it pays to replace your spark plug wires before they wear out. We recommend changing them during spark plug changes (whenever your owner's manual recommends, or between 60,000 and 100,000 miles). Here, we'll show you which materials and tools you'll need and all the steps required to do a quality job on your own. You'll save about $80 on shop labor charges and ensure that you won't be in for the costly diagnostic fees associated with worn spark plug wires. The whole job is pretty easy and will only take about an hour.

Before you start the job, use a digital camera to

SPARK PLUG BOOT

record how the wires attach to the coil/distributor/coil pack and the path they take to each plug. Notice how each wire wraps around the others and how they are arranged

1 USE your digital camera to record the route of each wire. They have to go back the same way.

in the plastic retaining clips. They're arranged that way for a reason: to prevent cross-firing and interference with other engine sensors. So be sure to put them back in the same manner.

When you're at the auto parts store, we recommend that you buy a premium set of wires. The economy wire set we looked at didn't match the factory connectors, and the individual wires were either too long or too short for our vehicle. The premium set carried a lifetime warranty; the economy set, only two years. Next, invest in a spark plug wire puller tool (**Photo** 3). A wire puller tool makes

ECONOMY BRAND,
$22.99

PREMIUM BRAND,
$41.99

FACTORY

WIRE OPTIONS
The premium replacement exactly matches the factory connectors. The economy wire doesn't.

3 USING a wire puller, twist the boot to break the seal from the plug and then pull off the old plug. Match the old wire length to the new wire.

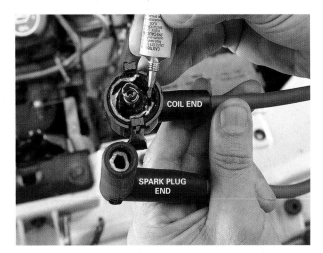

COIL END

SPARK PLUG END

2 UNCOIL the new spark plug wires and sort them by length.

4 APPLY dielectric grease to both the plug and the coil/distributor end of each wire. Route the wire and press it onto the plug/coil tower until it clicks.

removal much easier and saves a lot of busted knuckles. To use it, simply grasp the boot with the rounded jaws, rotate left and right, then pull straight out. This is a tool that's worth the investment.

Some manufacturers precoat the insides of the plug and coil/distributor boots with dielectric silicone grease. The grease prevents the boots from sticking to the plug or coil/distributor. It also provides an additional layer of insulation to prevent voltage from traveling down the inside of the boot. If your set isn't

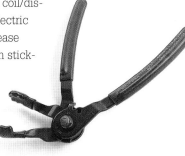

WIRE PULLER
Lisle 51750 Adjustable Spark Plug Wire Puller, $22.95.

precoated, purchase a small tube of silicone grease and run a bead around the inside of each boot.

Then remove one old wire at a time and match it to a replacement wire of the same length. Route the new wire and push the boot onto the plug or coil/distributor until you feel it click. Repeat the procedure for each wire.

DIELECTRIC GREASE
Dielectric grease is available at any auto parts store.

Buyer's Guide
Lisle tools are available at toolsource.com and at CARQUEST Auto Parts stores nationwide.

FIX THAT **WINDSHIELD WASHER** YOURSELF!

Diagnosis and repair are easy, cheap and fast

Windshield washers are fairly reliable. When they fail, it's usually the result of a clogged nozzle or a dead pump. Here's how to diagnose and fix both problems. (Of course, first make sure that you have washer fluid in the reservoir.)

Step 1: Check the fuse

With the car parked in a quiet place, operate the washer and listen for the whirring of the pump. If there's no sound, head right for the fuse box. If the fuse is blown, it's usually a sign of a dead pump motor or one that's ready to check out. If it blows again, replace the motor (see Step 4).

Step 2: Clear clogged nozzles

If you hear the pump going but don't get fluid, you probably have clogged nozzles. Lift the hood and trace the washer hose from the nozzles back to the reservoir. Somewhere along the route, you'll find either a plastic barbed connector or a round one-way check valve. Disconnect the tubing there and try

the washer again. If fluid squirts out, you know the nozzles are plugged. Clean the nozzles by pushing a small pin in to loosen any debris, then blow the clog back down the hose and out the end that you disconnected (**Photo 1**).

Step 3: Clean dirty electrical connections

If you don't hear the pump and the fuse is OK, the problem is usually a poor electrical connection at the pump or a bad pump. Most car manufacturers mount the washer pump near or inside the washer fluid reservoir. To locate your reservoir, simply follow the washer hose. If your reservoir is located in the engine compartment, access is simple. But many are hidden inside the front fender. Remove the wheel and the wheel line fender liner. Then you'll have access to the reservoir and pump. Remove the pump wire connector and have a friend operate the pump switch while

FILLER TUBE

IN ENGINE COMPARTMENT

RESERVOIR

HIDDEN IN FENDER

REAR WINDOW MOTOR

WINDSHIELD MOTOR

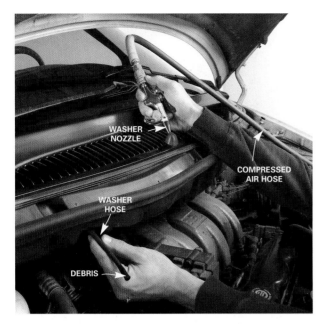

1 CLEAR the clogged nozzle with a pin, then use compressed air to blow the debris backward through the hose.

2 ACCESS a hidden-style reservoir by removing the tire and the wheel well liner.

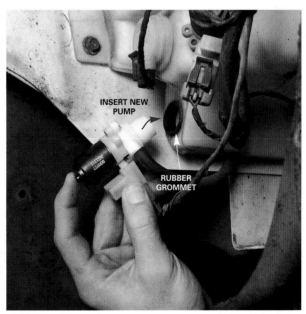

3 IF THE FUSE is good but the pump doesn't run, disconnect the connector at the pump and check for power with a volt meter. With the washer switch on, it should read 12 volts.

4 PULL out the old pump and replace it with a new one, following the replacement procedures packaged with your new pump.

you check for 12 volts with a digital meter at the connector. If you don't have voltage, the problem is probably in the washer switch or the wiring. That's the time to take the vehicle to a pro.

If you have voltage, clean the terminals and coat them with dielectric silicone grease. Try the pump again. If it works, your problem is solved. If it doesn't, replace the pump. The main cause of pump failure is repeatedly running the motor while the reservoir is empty. So try to keep your reservoir full to avoid dealing with replacing a bad one.

Step 4: Replace the washer pump

Check with an auto parts store for a "direct-fit," not a universal-style replacement. If one isn't available, buy directly from the dealer (ours was $49). If your reservoir is located inside the engine compartment, remove the retaining clips and lift out the entire unit and remove the pump. If it's in the wheel well, just remove the pump (**Photo 4**). Some pumps are held in place by a rubber grommet, others with retaining rings or clamps. Follow the instructions included with your new pump for installation advice.

Car&Garage

REPAIR YOUR SIDE VIEW MIRROR GLASS FOR LESS THAN $15

You don't have to replace the entire side view mirror assembly just because the glass is broken. Replacing the mirror glass is a do-it-yourself project that costs less than $15 in most cases.

Several manufacturers offer precut glass mirrors to fit vehicles of all makes and models. One is Dorman Products Inc. Our local auto parts store didn't carry the mirror for our Ford Expedition, so we ordered it from Dorman online for $7 plus shipping. You'll also need a $4 tube of black rubber sealant (Permatex No. 80338), sold at any auto parts store.

Start the repair by picking away as many loose pieces of the broken mirror as you can. Wear leather gloves and eye protection while doing this. You can leave the old adhesive in place. Then clean the remaining glass and the plastic mirror base with glass cleaner.

The new glass comes with adhesive strips on the back, but don't rely on those strips alone to keep the glass in place. Apply a thick bead of black rubber sealant 3/4 in. in from the perimeter of the plastic mirror retainer. Put a few large dollops of the sealant on the honeycomb portion of the plastic base and a few more on the old broken glass. Don't apply the sealant in areas where the adhesive pads will contact the plastic base. The pads must make contact with the plastic base to hold the new glass in place while the sealant sets up. Apply the mirror to the base.

Use masking tape to hold the mirror in place until the sealant cures.

1 REMOVE the loose pieces of glass and clean the remaining glass and the base with glass cleaner.

2 APPLY a bead of black rubber sealant 3/4 in. in from the edge of the plastic base and a few dollops in other locations. Then press the new mirror into place.

3 THE FINISHED project looks just like the original. Total cost: less than $15.

ADD OIL WITHOUT MAKING A MESS

Sometimes it's hard to keep from spilling when you're adding oil. And that oil not only collects dust and dirt but also can get on the exhaust manifold and start an engine fire. (Never a good way to start the day.) Prevent the mess and danger just by wrapping a rag around the oil filler port before adding the oil. It'll soak up all but those Exxon Valdez–size spills.

DON'T CROSS SIGNALS WHEN YOU ROTATE YOUR TIRES

If your car is equipped with a tire pressure monitoring (TPM) system, you may have to reset the TPM system after a tire rotation. Some systems use a pressure sensor that transmits a unique identifier code back to the receiver. If it isn't reset, it will report the wrong location of an underinflated tire. Refer to your owner's manual to see if this step is required. If it is, follow the manufacturer's resetting procedure. If you're having a shop do the work, make sure it does the reset procedure as part of the job.

Buyer's Guide
Check dormanproducts.com to find the part number for your mirror. Then contact your local auto parts store for purchase.
Dorman products are available at CARQUEST Auto Parts Stores nationwide and O'Reilly Auto Parts.

SCRATCH TOUCH-UP

Sometimes the small brushes that come with vehicle touch-up paint slop the paint on and make the repair look worse than the scratch. Try using a toothpick: The tip of the toothpick fills the scratch with just the right amount of paint.

JUMP-START SMARTS

Left your lights on and now your battery is dead? Jump-starting it and driving away may be the worst thing you can do. As soon as you drive away, your alternator starts pumping out maximum amps to recharge the battery. The strain of recharging a dead battery and powering headlights and a blower motor can toast an alternator. The cost for a new alternator and a tow can easily run $600 to $800 (parts and labor).

To avoid that scenario, give your charging system a head start by begging your Good Samaritin to leave the jumper cables on the battery for five to 10 minutes before starting your car. Once it's running, let your car idle for 10 minutes with the lights and blower motor off. Then, when you get home, use a trickle charger to bring the battery back up to full charge.

DRIVE UP YOUR SAFETY FACTOR WITH A WINDSHIELD GLASS TREATMENT

Research has proven that glass treatment products can improve your view through your windshield in rainy weather by as much as 34 percent. The improved vision can increase your response rate by up to 25 percent. That could mean the difference between avoiding an accident or being part of one.

Most glass treatments work by coating your windshield with a water-repellent silicone film. The coating makes water bead up and improves the wiper blade's ability to remove the water. The coating also makes it easier to wipe off ice and bugs.

Most conventional silicone treatments last about one month. But a new glass treatment called Aquapel achieves a much longer service life by chemically bonding with the glass. It should last for six months. Many auto parts stores sell Aquapel for $10. However, if you're willing to buy in larger quantities, you can pay as little as $4 per applicator. Try autobodydepot.com for larger quantity purchases (or $7 for singles).

AQUAPEL APPLICATOR

Application of Aquapel is simple. Make sure the temperature is at least 50 degrees F. Clean the windshield and allow the glass to dry. Then wipe Aquapel onto the glass and wipe it off. Then wipe on a second coat, wipe it off and you're done.

Treated | Untreated

Photo courtesy of PPG Industries

Squeeze the wings on the Aquapel applicator to start the flow of the fluid. Apply to the windshield. Wipe off. Repeat.

PORTABLE POWER STATIONS KEEP YOU AND YOUR TOYS ON THE GO

If you've ever used a portable jump starter on your car, you know how handy they are. But have you taken a look at them lately? Jump starters have morphed into a multifunction tool that belongs in every trunk or garage. In addition to jump-starting capabilities, today's models include an air compressor, lighting, 12-volt DC outlets and even a DC-to-AC inverter for powering plug-in appliances like laptops. All the models can be recharged from receptacles and/or a cigarette lighter. Look for these features and specifications:

- Battery. Minimum 17AH (amp/hour) battery.
- Jump starting. Minimum 350 to 400 amps.
- Air compressor. Minimum 100 psi and an integral pressure gauge.
- DC-AC inverter. 400 watts. That's enough to power most laptops for four hours.

BLACK & DECKER ELECTROMATE 400, $99

AIR PRESSURE GAUGE

AC OUTLETS

DC OUTLETS

Extra features worth having:

- Polarity sensitivity. Alerts you if you've hooked up the battery cables backward. The feature can prevent expensive damage to your car's charging system.
- Keyless on/off. Allows you to hook up the jumper cables and start the jump from inside the car with a wireless transmitter.
- Built-in recharging transformer. Just plug it into the end of an extension cord to recharge; no wall adapter needed.

ASK "BOB THE MECHANIC"

My owner's manual suggests changing the oil and filter every 7,500 miles. But the quick-change stores all recommend 3,000 miles. Is this a scam to grab more business?

The truth is, how often you should change your oil depends on your driving habits, the temperature conditions and the type of oil you use. Oil change intervals of 3,000 miles are critical for severe driving conditions. Short trips and stop-and-go driving are hard on your oil, and thus on your engine, too. Engines need a rich fuel mixture at startup. A certain portion of these rich combustion gases gets into the crankcase. There, the raw fuel and sooty exhaust gases mix with the oil, forming acids and grit. On long trips, the oil gets hot enough to burn off the fuel and acids, but it doesn't on short trips.

If the majority of your trips are less than 5 miles and include stop-and-go traffic, your driving is considered severe service. That's also true if you routinely drive in extreme temperatures (above 90 degrees F or below freezing) or use your vehicle for towing or hauling.

But for some drivers, changes every 7,500 miles are perfectly adequate. You qualify if you take long highway commutes to work (highway speeds for more than 20 minutes). You can also use the 7,500-mile interval if you switch to the newer synthetic oils, even if your driving is considered severe service. Synthetic oils are far superior to conventional oils.

My advice is to use synthetic oil and change it every 7,500 miles along with the filter. That's a safe method for all driving conditions. It saves the hassle of frequent oil changes and costs about the same as using conventional oil and changing it twice as often.

—Bob Lacivita, ASE/GM Certified Master Technician

GOT A CAR THAT REEKS OF CIGARETTE SMOKE?

Forget about those wimpy scent trees—they just mask bad odors. Professional auto detailers can get rid of the smoke smell for about $59 to $79. But you can do it yourself for less than $15. Here's how:

First, clean the inside of all the windows with an ammonia-based glass cleaner. If your vehicle is equipped with a cabin air filter, remove it and purchase a new one.

With the windows rolled up, spray the headliner (ceiling), fabric, carpet and door panels with Dakota Non-Smoke odor eliminator. Keep the spray nozzle at least 14 in. from all surfaces.

Next, set your heating system to the "recirculate" or MAX AC mode and find the return air vent (**Photo 2**). With the fan turned to high, spray a three-second burst into the return intake vent.

Move the vehicle outside and start the engine. Leave the car, close the doors and allow it to run for 15 minutes. Then turn off the engine and open all the windows so the car can air out. Clean the windows again. Finish the job by installing the new cabin air filter.

1 STARTING with the ceiling fabric, hold the can 14 in. away and spray all fabric and carpet.

2 TO FIND the return air duct, set the fan on high and the mode to "recirculate" or MAX AC. Hold a paper towel under the dash. The recirculating air will suck the paper towel toward the return air duct.

Buyer's Guide
Buy Dakota Non-Smoke odor eliminator for $14 from dakotaproducts.com or topoftheline.com.

SPARK PLUG SHOPPING TIPS

Choosing new spark plugs isn't as easy as it used to be —dozens of choices are available. Here's what you need to know:

Tip 1: It's best to stick with the types of plugs you rode in on. The car manufacturer may have originally installed plugs made with precious metals. Platinum, yttrium and iridium plugs are more expensive than traditional plugs, but the coatings provide much better wear resistance and maintain their gap longer. Never downgrade to a less expensive plug. Your savings will be quickly offset by the shorter service life and reduced gas mileage. Consult your owner's manual or ask the auto parts store for the manufacturer's recommended plug.

Tip 2: Some plugs have adjustable-plug gaps and others have a fixed gap, but gap is always important. If the store recommends a fixed-gap plug, check your owner's manual to make sure it's the correct gap. If it isn't, find another brand. If the gap is adjustable, make sure you check (and adjust if necessary) the gap on each plug before installation.

The auto parts store computer showed eight different plug choices for a 1999 Ford Taurus. Prices ranged from $1.79 for a traditional plug to $14.99 for iridium. We chose the $2.79 double platinum type because that's what had been installed at the factory.

SINGLE PLATINUM PLUG $1.79

DOUBLE PLATINUM PLUG $2.79

AUTO & GARAGE

GARAGE
BUMP-OUT

Get more garage space with a simple addition

by **Jeff Gorton**

I s a packed garage keeping you from buying your dream motorcycle? Or maybe you just need a little more space for lawn equipment, bikes or your woodworking tools. A bump-out addition may be the solution to your overcrowded garage. And in this article we'll show you how to build one.

If you have basic carpentry skills and experience building a deck, shed or other structure, then you can build this garage addition. In this article, we'll focus on the tough parts of the project, like installing the beam and building the roof. Study **Figures A – C** for construction details. Then if you need more help with things like footings, deck framing, wall building, drywall or other construction skills, search these topics at thefamilyhandyman.com.

A simple foundation

There's no need to pour concrete. Get off the ground with a simple treated-wood foundation. Build it just like a deck platform. Then add the walls and roof to finish the addition.

Figure A: Bump-out details

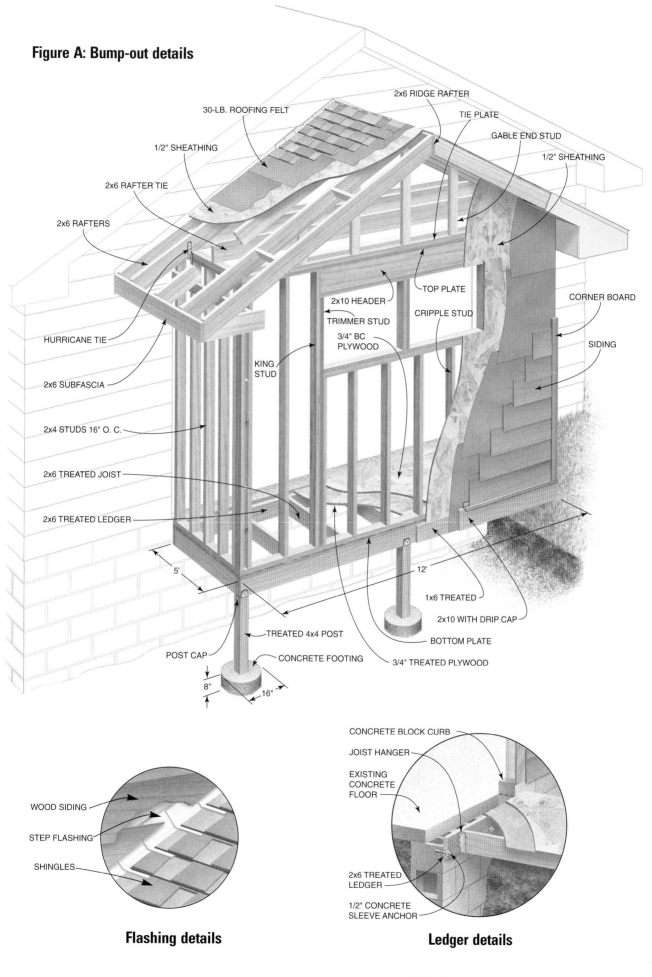

30-LB. ROOFING FELT

1/2" SHEATHING

2x6 RAFTER TIE

2x6 RAFTERS

HURRICANE TIE

2x6 SUBFASCIA

2x4 STUDS 16" O. C.

2x6 TREATED JOIST

2x6 TREATED LEDGER

KING STUD

2x6 RIDGE RAFTER

TIE PLATE

GABLE END STUD

1/2" SHEATHING

TOP PLATE

2x10 HEADER

TRIMMER STUD

3/4" BC PLYWOOD

CRIPPLE STUD

CORNER BOARD

SIDING

5'

12'

1x6 TREATED

2x10 WITH DRIP CAP

BOTTOM PLATE

3/4" TREATED PLYWOOD

TREATED 4x4 POST

POST CAP

CONCRETE FOOTING

8"

16"

Flashing details

WOOD SIDING

STEP FLASHING

SHINGLES

Ledger details

CONCRETE BLOCK CURB

JOIST HANGER

EXISTING CONCRETE FLOOR

2x6 TREATED LEDGER

1/2" CONCRETE SLEEVE ANCHOR

Tools, time and cost

In addition to a basic set of carpentry tools, you'll need a hammer drill to bore holes for the concrete anchors, and ladders or rented scaffolding to finish the roofing and other exterior details. While not essential, a reciprocating saw will simplify the wall tear-out.

We spent about $1,000 for framing and sheathing materials, $600 for siding and roofing materials and $400 for windows for this 5 x 12-ft. garage addition. Your costs will vary depending on the type of siding, roofing and windows you choose.

With a helper, plan to spend about half a day installing the beam and a long weekend framing the addition. Then plan to spend another weekend finishing the exterior. The time it takes to complete the project will depend on whether you finish the inside as we did. Keep in mind that you can hire a siding, roofing or drywall contractor to complete parts of the project you're not comfortable with.

This addition is large enough to accommodate a garden tractor, a large motorcycle, or a workbench and a table saw. If you'd prefer a larger size, contact an architect or structural engineer to specify the size of the header, floor joists and rafters.

Garage additions usually require a building permit. Contact your local building department to see what's needed. Make sure to call 811 or go to call811.com a few days before you dig the footing holes to have underground utilities located and marked.

Support the roof with a new header

Before removing a section of the garage wall, you'll have to add a header to support the weight of the roof above it. The gable end of this truss-framed garage roof doesn't support much weight, so we were able to add the double 2x10 header and remove the wall section without adding temporary supports. Gable end walls that support a second floor or ridge beam will require a larger header and

Figure B: Header details

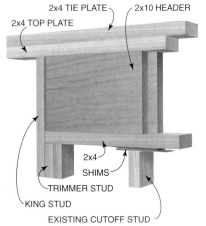

2x4 TIE PLATE
2x4 TOP PLATE
2x10 HEADER
2x4 SHIMS
TRIMMER STUD
KING STUD
EXISTING CUTOFF STUD

1 FRAME the sides of the opening and install the new header. Then support the header with double trimmers on each end.

2 KNOCK out the wall to create the new opening. First cut the sheathing and bottom plate along the framed opening. Then cut the wall into sections and push them out.

3 ATTACH the ledger board to the garage foundation with concrete sleeve anchors. Temporarily support the ledger with wood stakes while you drill holes for the anchors.

temporary support. If you have a second floor above the garage or aren't sure how the roof is framed, contact an architect or engineer to calculate the header size.

Start by locating the center of your addition and marking the size of the opening on the bottom plate of the wall. We centered the bump-out on the garage wall, but this isn't necessary. Remember to make the opening 7 in. narrower than the width of the addition. Next make marks 3 in. beyond the opening marks on each side to locate the inside edge of the king studs. Cut king studs and nail them to the top and bottom plates. For a 12-ft.-wide addition, the distance between the king studs should be 11 ft. 11 in. Cut the 2x10 headers to this length and nail them together with 10d nails. Nail a 2x4 to the bottom of the 2x10s to complete the header (**Figure B**).

Cut out the top section of the wall studs with a reciprocating saw to make a path for the new header. Saw the studs 11-1/2 in. down from the top plate and knock out the short stud sections with a hammer. Then cut off the nails with a nail nipper or reciprocating saw. You may also have to cut off a few sheathing and siding nails so they don't interfere with the header. After nailing in the king studs (**Photo 1**), set the header in place on the cutoff studs. Wedge the header tight to the top plate by driving shims between the cutoff studs and the header at each end. Cut a pair of trimmer studs for each end of the header and nail them in place with 16d nails (**Photo 1**).

Remove the wall

If you have vinyl, aluminum or steel siding, it's probably easier to remove it from the entire garage wall and reinstall it after the addition is built. We cut the wood siding 2-1/2 in. beyond the width of the addition to allow for 1/2-in. wall sheathing and 2-in. inside corner boards. Pry off the siding and remove the wall (**Photo 2**).

In many garages, the walls rest on a block or concrete curb that has to be removed to create a continuous floor. We used an angle grinder fitted with a diamond blade to score the concrete block flush to the cutoff bottom plate on both sides of the opening. Then we broke out the concrete blocks between the trimmers with a sledgehammer. If you have a solid concrete curb, removing it will be a tougher job. Consider renting a concrete saw to score the entire length of the opening before breaking it out. **Photo 6** shows how to patch the concrete after the plywood floor of the addition is in place.

Build the platform

Start building the platform by bolting the ledger to the garage. Position the top edge of the ledger 1-1/2 in. below the garage floor in the center of the opening and level it, using temporary stakes for support. Attach it with 1/2-in.

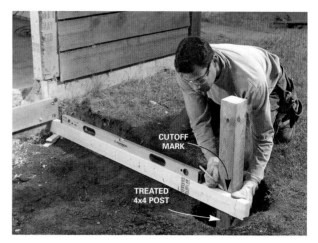

4 MARK the posts level with the bottom of the ledger and cut them off. Put the cutoff posts back in the holes, but don't fill around them until you've built and squared the floor frame.

5 START the floor frame by toenailing the joists to the ledger and nailing through the first rim joist into the floor joists. Then install the second rim joist and nail on the joist hangers. Square the frame and nail the two layers of plywood to the joists.

6 FILL the gap between the garage floor and the plywood bump-out floor with concrete. Drag a scrap of 2x4 over the concrete to level it. Then trowel it smooth when it begins to harden.

concrete sleeve anchors located 12 in. apart. Add two extra anchors at each end.

Next locate and mark the center of the footings (**Figure A**). Dig the footing holes and pour 8-in.-thick concrete pads into the bottom of each. After the concrete hardens, set treated 4x4 posts into the footing holes. At this point, you'll know whether you need to remove soil in the area under the bump-out to make room for the joists. Make sure there are at least a few inches of clearance between the bottom of the joists and the ground.

The next step is to cut the posts to the correct length and build the platform. Use a level resting on a straight board to mark each post level with the bottom of the ledger board (**Photo 4**). Cut the posts at the marks and set them back into the holes. Complete the floor frame by cutting and assembling the floor joists and attaching the frame to the posts with metal post caps (**Figure A**). Finally, pack dirt around the posts and nail one layer of treated plywood and a second layer of BC plywood to the floor framing. If the surrounding soil is above the bottom of the joists, build a three-sided 2x6 dam and pack the soil against it. Don't attach the 2x6s to the joists. The goal is to prevent dirt from getting under the joists while allowing the 2x6s to move with the soil.

Build and stand the walls

Build the walls on a flat surface like the garage floor. Start by cutting the top and bottom plates for the long wall and marking the stud locations on them. Use **Figure A** as a guide. Lay out the window opening to match the rough-opening dimensions provided by your window supplier. Assemble the wall by nailing the studs to the plates with 16d nails. Stand the wall on the platform, straighten the bottom plate and nail it to the rim joist. Plumb and brace the outside corners. Now measure from the new front wall to the existing garage wall at the top and bottom on each side and cut the plates for the short walls accordingly. If the existing garage wall isn't plumb, this procedure will ensure that the short walls will fit correctly.

Build the two short walls and set them in place on the platform. First position the walls and nail through the bottom plate into the floor with 16d nails. With a level, plumb the stud that's against the garage wall before nailing it to the wall. Align the corner studs on adjacent walls and nail them together. Finally, use a level to make sure the corner stud on the long wall is plumb and nail a diagonal brace to the inside of the wall (**Photo 7**). Complete the wall construction by adding the tie plates, making sure to cut them so they overlap the top plate at the corners. Then nail 1/2-in. sheathing to the studs.

7 BUILD the walls on a flat surface like the garage floor. Stand them up on the bump-out floor and nail them to the floor and to the garage wall. Plumb and brace the front wall before installing the sheathing.

8 MAKE a rafter pattern by tacking a 2x6 to the garage wall, parallel to the garage roof, and drawing lines on it to indicate the center of the bump-out, the overhang distance and the bird's-mouth cut. Use the pattern to mark and cut the rafters.

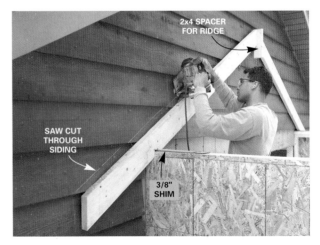

9 TACK a pair of rafters to the garage wall as a guide for cutting the siding. Place a 2x4 spacer between the top ends of the rafters to simulate the ridge. Remove the rafters and pry off the siding.

Figure C: Rafter details

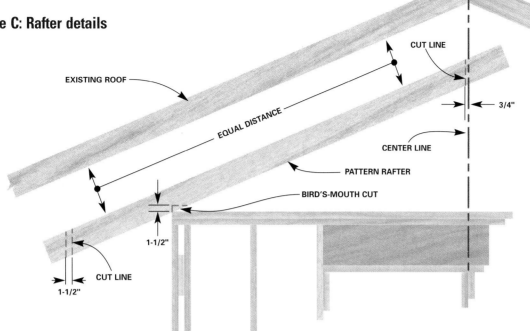

EXISTING ROOF

CUT LINE

EQUAL DISTANCE

3/4"

CENTER LINE

PATTERN RAFTER

BIRD'S-MOUTH CUT

1-1/2"

CUT LINE

1-1/2"

Cut the rafters and build the roof

For the best appearance, match the slopes of the addition and garage roofs. In **Photo 8**, we show a simple method of marking a 2x6 to use as a guide for making a pattern rafter. **Figure C** shows how to modify the marks to create a pattern rafter. Use the pattern to mark the remaining rafters. **Photo 9** shows how to cut the siding using the rafters as a saw guide. We added a 3/8-in. shim under the rafters to allow a 1-3/4-in. gap between the roof framing and the siding cut (**Photo 9**). This provided enough room for 1/2-in. sheathing, two layers of dimensional shingles and a 3/4-in. space for the step flashing to slide into. Adjust the cut in your siding to correspond to the thickness of your roofing and sheathing material. Set the saw just deep enough to cut through the siding. When you're done cutting both sides, remove the rafters and pry off the siding in the area of the new roof.

Frame the roof using **Figure A** and **Photos 10 and 11** as a guide. Nail through the ridge into the rafters and toenail the bird's-mouth to the tie plate. Reinforce the connection between the rafters and the tie plate with metal hurricane ties. Then complete the roof frame by adding the 2x6 subfascia and building the side and end overhangs. Match the overhangs to the overhangs on the garage. When you're done with the roof frame, cut 1/2-in. sheathing to fit and nail it to the rafters.

Finish the addition with trim, roofing and siding

At this point in the project, your garage addition will probably vary considerably from what we show here. In general, you'll start by finishing the trim on the overhangs,

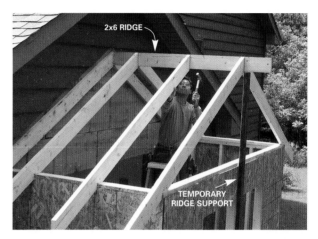

2x6 RIDGE

TEMPORARY RIDGE SUPPORT

10 TEMPORARILY support the ridge while you nail the rafters to it. Nail through the ridge into the rafters and toenail the rafters to the tie plate. Then reinforce the connection between the rafters and the tie plate with metal hurricane ties.

BOXED RETURN

SUBFASCIA

11 COMPLETE the roof frame and fill in the gable end rafters. Then nail plywood over the roof frame.

MATERIALS LIST

ITEM	QTY.
Garage header	
2x10 x 12' spf (spruce, pine or fir) lumber	2
2x4 x 12' spf lumber	1
2x4 x 8' spf lumber	6
Foundation	
Concrete mix	10 bags
4x4 x 10 .60 treated lumber	1
Floor frame	
2x6 x 12' .40 treated lumber (rim and ledger)	3
2x6 x 10' .40 treated lumber (joists)	6
4x8 x 3/4" treated plywood (bottom layer flooring)	2
4x8 x 3/4" BC plywood (top layer flooring)	2
Walls	
2x4 x 12' spf lumber (plates)	3
2x4 x 10' spf lumber (plates)	3
2x4 x 92-5/8" precut studs (wall frame)	33
2x10 x 8' spf lumber (window header)	2
4x8 x 1/2" OSB (oriented strand board; wall sheathing)	7
Roof	
2x6 x 10' spf lumber (roof frame)	12
2x6 x 12' spf lumber (ceiling joists)	2
2x4 x 12' spf lumber (nailers)	5
4x8 x 1/2" OSB (roof sheathing)	4
Siding	
House wrap or building paper	250 sq. ft.
Siding	250 sq. ft.
Roofing	
Ice and water barrier	1 roll
30-lb. roofing felt	1 roll
Shingles	120 sq. ft.
Ridge cap	6 lin. ft.
Galvanized metal step flashing	50
10' lengths of metal drip edge	4
Hardware	
1/2" x 3" sleeve anchors	16
16d common double-dipped galvanized nails	2 lbs.
8d common double-dipped galvanized nails	5 lbs.
Galvanized joist hanger nails	2 lbs.
8d common nails	5 lbs.
10d common nails	2 lbs.
16d common nails	5 lbs.
1" galvanized roofing nail	5 lbs.
4x4 metal post cap	3
Triple 2x6 inverted flange hangers	4
Single 2x6 joist hangers	10
Hurricane ties	8

including the soffit and fascia, with wood or metal to match your garage. Then install the roof shingles according to the manufacturer's instructions. The key to a leak-proof roof is proper step flashing (**Photo 13**). We slid the flashing under the siding. But if you've removed the siding entirely, then simply install the step flashing with the shingles. Then install the siding over the flashing.

Install the window before the siding, being careful to flash around it with building paper or special self-adhesive window-flashing tape according to the manufacturer's instructions (**Photo 12**). Finally, install siding to match your garage.

On the inside we added a few outlets and recessed ceiling lights. Then we insulated the walls and ceiling before hanging and taping the drywall. 🏠

12 INSTALL the windows according to the manufacturer's instructions. Layer self-adhesive flashing over the nailing fins as shown, making sure each layer overlaps the one below and that the final assembly will shed water over the top of the building paper below the window.

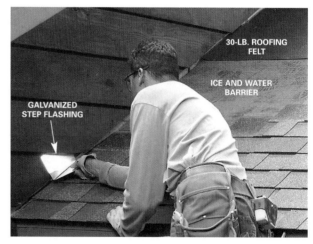

13 SHINGLE the roof. Install building paper and shingles according to local codes and the instructions on the shingle package. Slide galvanized metal step flashing under the siding and position it over the end shingle in each course.

HandyHints®

BUMPER STICKER RELEASE

Heat from a hair dryer softens adhesive, making bumper stickers, price tags and other labels easy to pull off. Start at one corner and pull slowly, allowing the heat to loosen the sticker.

CARGO LINER

Always carry a tarp in your car to protect against messy cargo (or occupants). To make the tarp stay put, use self-adhesive hook-and-loop tape such as Velcro. Apply the hook part of the tape to the tarp. The hook side will cling to most car interiors; there's usually no need to use the loop tape.

TRUNK LID TIE-DOWN

When you're hauling oversize items in your car trunk, there isn't a good place to tie a rope to the trunk lid. Make one by manually engaging your trunk's upper lock latch: Just move it over with your finger until it clicks into place. Insert a 2-in. ring or a small carabiner (available for $1 at home centers) into the latch and run a rope through it and the trunk's bottom hasp for a handy tie-down. To release the ring, pull the "trunk release" lever in your car.

CHANGE YOUR OWN
TRANSMISSION FLUID

Make $200 an hour and add years to your transmission's life

Y ou should change your automatic transmission fluid according to the manufacturer's recommendation—whether that's 30,000 or 100,000 miles. This maintenance task will add tens of thousands of miles—which could be years of service—to a transmission's life expectancy and prevent repairs costing thousands down the road.

A transmission flush-and-fill from a shop will cost you $149 to $199. But you can do it yourself and save about $100. Draining the old fluid has always been a messy, ugly job. That's because it has meant lying under the car, "dropping" the pan—and then getting drenched in fluid. But here's a new way to change your fluid without going under the car and without spilling a drop. The procedure takes less than 30 minutes.

The trick is to work from the top, sucking out the old fluid up through the filler tube. Then refill with fresh fluid. A hand-operated vacuum pump makes the job simple and clean. You can remove one-third to one-half of the fluid from the transmission at a time. The rest

New fluid is bright red.   **This transmission fluid has been working for 60,000 miles. It turns brown as it degrades—time to change.**

LIQUIVAC FLUID PUMP, ABOUT $60

This pump is the key to saving you time and money when you change your transmission fluid.

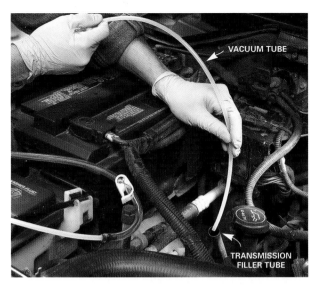

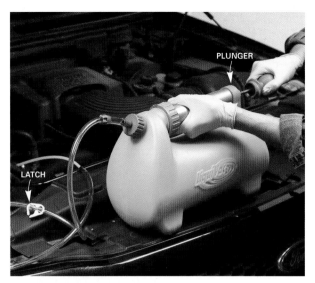

1 REMOVE the dipstick and insert the vacuum tube until you feel it "bottom out" on the bottom of the transmission pan.

2 CLOSE the latch on the vinyl hose and pump up the vacuum tank with 30 to 50 strokes of the plunger.

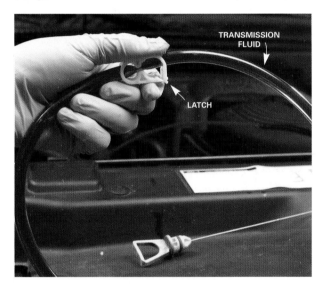

3 RELEASE the latch on the hose and wait while the vacuum draws the old fluid out.

4 READ on the tank the amount of fluid you withdrew and refill the transmission with that amount of new fluid.

Buy the right stuff

Carmakers have made major improvements to transmission fluids in the past two years. Contact the dealership parts department to see if your car requires a newer fluid. Then call auto parts stores until you find one that stocks it. If you strike out, bite the bullet and buy it from the dealer.

will remain in the torque converter and the transmission cooler. So do the procedure three times at one-week intervals to replace nearly all of the old fluid. The little leftover old fluid will be diluted with plenty of fresh new fluid.

Some manufacturers recommend replacing the filter every time you change the transmission fluid. Go with what your dealership recommends. Note: But if your transmission pan is leaking, you should either "drop" the pan and replace the gasket, or take it in for service.

FREE UP A STUCK TRAILER HITCH

When the ball mount on your trailer hitch is rusted in place, don't whack at it with a sledgehammer. Here's what to do instead. Buy a can of CRC Freeze Off penetrating spray ($6) and an air hammer fitted with a "hammer bit." The air hammer will run about $15 and the extra bit will be about $8. Spray the opening to the hitch receiver. This newest style of penetrating fluid chills the metal, causing it to contract to help break the rust seal. Then use an air hammer fitted with

AIR HAMMER

HAMMER BIT

a hammer bit to knock everything loose. The air hammer will break up the rust, spread the penetrant and free up the ball mount. Once it's free, just tap the rusted ball mount out with a hammer. If you plan to reuse the rusty mount, coat it with a rust converter or waterproof marine grease.

HITCH RECEIVER

BALL MOUNT

1 GENEROUSLY spray the opening to the hitch receiver with a penetrating fluid. Then insert the spray straw deep into the corners of the receiver and spray liberally.

2 RAP the sides, top and bottom of the hitch receiver for 15 seconds with blows from the air hammer. Spray again. Repeat the rapping until the ball mount loosens.

NITRILE GLOVES PROTECT YOUR HEALTH AND HANDS

In the old days, guys called you a wimp if you wore gloves when you worked on cars. Aside from the wimp factor, gloves were too clumsy for fine work. But we now know that some automotive fluids contain caustic or even carcinogenic chemicals. That's why most auto techs now wear nitrile gloves, as should you.

Nitrile is a durable synthetic material that protects your skin from the chemicals. The gloves are available at auto parts stores and online for about $7.50 for a box of 100. That's 15¢ a pair—a small price to pay to protect your health.

Buy nitrile gloves by the box and use them for all auto and household repair jobs. They cost about 15¢ a pair.

GREAT WAY TO STORE USED OIL

Storing used oil is a hassle. Here's a tip: Restaurants order liquids such as cooking oil and soy sauce in 5-gallon jugs. Next time you're out to eat, ask if you can have a few empty jugs. Rinse them and use them to store several changes' worth of used oil between trips to the recycling center.

5-GALLON JUG

TRANSMISSION FLUID DILEMMA

I have 105,000 miles on my car and I've never changed the transmission fluid. I was supposed to change it every 30,000 miles. The quick lube shop is now encouraging me to do a transmission fluid exchange. Is this good advice?

Failure to change transmission fluid is the No. 1 cause of expensive transmission problems. When the fluid is neglected, it degrades and loses its ability to lubricate and cool transmission components. Without proper lubrication and cooling, metal parts touch, causing excessive friction and faster wear. The heat generated by this metal-to-metal contact cooks the fluid, leaving charred "varnish" deposits in the clearances. The varnish looks like scorched butter.

In theory, the advice from your quick lube shop to exchange the fluid makes sense. But in reality, it's probably too late. Fresh transmission fluid is highly detergent and it immediately attacks the varnish deposits in the transmission. Some of the deposits dissolve and break away from the wear areas. The varnish that previously filled the clearances is now gone, making for a sloppy fit that causes even more metal wear. The charred grit that breaks away then clogs valves and the filter, causing shifting problems that can literally tear a transmission to pieces.

At this point, it's probably better to leave the old fluid in the transmission. If you develop transmission problems, promptly take your car to a reputable transmission shop. With your next vehicle, be sure you follow the manufacturer's maintenance advice. Good luck.

–Richard Muscoplat, ASE Certified Master Technician

CLEAN YOUR MAF SENSOR AND SAVE $300

A Mass Air Flow (MAF) sensor monitors the temperature and weight of air entering your engine. Your onboard computer needs that information to calculate the right amount of fuel for all engine operating conditions.

The sensor works by heating a delicate platinum wire or plate and measuring the current required to keep it at a constant temperature while air blows past it. Over time, dust and oil particles stick to the hot wire/plate and bake on. Eventually, those baked-on particles insulate the wire/plate from the airstream. This causes starting, idling and acceleration problems, as well as poor gas mileage.

Carmakers recommend that you replace the MAF sensor ($300) at that point. But if you clean your car's MAF sensor regularly, you can avoid that $300 repair and keep your engine running at top efficiency. The cleaner only costs $7! We recommend that you clean the MAF sensor every time you change your air filter. Here's how:

Before going to the store, pull off the air duct between the air filter box and the throttle body to see how the MAF sensor is anchored. If you see Torx screws, buy a Torx tool and a can of CRC Mass Air Flow Sensor Cleaner. Don't use any other cleaners; they can ruin the MAF. Everything you need is available at CarQuest, Advance and O'Reilly auto parts stores.

With cleaner and tools in hand, locate the MAF sensor in the air duct between the air filter box and the throttle body. Before you remove the sensor, use a digital camera to record the sensor setup and connections for reference later. Carefully remove the sensor from the air duct and disconnect the electrical connector.

Spray 10 to 15 spurts of the cleaner onto the wire or plate. Don't scrub the parts; you may break the wire or damage the plate. Allow the MAF sensor to dry completely before reinstalling it in the air duct.

Car&Garage

CHILL OUT WITH A NEW **CABIN AIR FILTER**

Improve your car's cooling and heating and save $70!

About half of all newer cars are equipped with a cabin air filter. If your car has one (check your owner's manual), you're supposed to change it every 12,000 to 15,000 miles, or once a year. But if you're like most drivers, you're still driving with the original filter and it's likely clogged. It's not just a comfort issue. Just as a clogged furnace filter reduces the furnace's efficiency, a clogged cabin air filter reduces the efficiency of the heating and cooling system for the car interior.

A clogged filter can also cause major window fogging problems and contribute to lower gas mileage. And because of the sluggish airflow, eventually you'll have to replace a burned-out blower motor for $150 or more.

The good news is that cabin air filter replacement is a do-it-yourself project. A local service center quoted us $95 for the filter and labor on a 2003 Toyota Camry. We saved $70 by doing the job ourselves. The filter cost only $25 at the dealer, and the job took less than 30 minutes. In most cases, you'll only need a Phillips screwdriver. You can usually find replacement instructions in the owner's manual.

Our Camry's air filter setup is shown. But locations vary depending on the make and model of your car. In fact, some luxury cars are equipped with as many as three different types of filters: one for fresh air, a second for recirculated air and a third made of activated charcoal to remove odors. It's best to replace all three filters at the same time.

Road debris, leaves, dust and pollen all clog cabin air filters.

If your manual doesn't show how to find and replace the filter, ask the dealer parts department for instructions. Many new filters have an instruction sheet—or the instructions may be on the manufacturer's Web site.

Where is it?

1 UNSCREW the glove box hinges. Then press in on both sides of the glove box to tilt it down and pull it free to access the filter tray.

NEW FILTER

2 SLIDE out the filter tray and the old filter. Note the orientation of the pleats and install the new filter in the same direction.

3 SLIDE the filter tray back into place and reassemble the glove box.

NO CABIN FILTER?
ADD AN AIR PURIFIER

If your car isn't equipped with a cabin air filter, you're not out of luck—you can still add an ion purifier. Ion purifiers generate billions of negatively charged ions that attach to viruses, bacteria, dust and pollen. The particles are then attracted to positively charged surfaces like your plastic dashboard. Once they settle, it's just a matter of using a spray cleaner on all the hard surfaces to wipe away the pollutants.

AIRTAMER A400 BY FILTERSTREAM. $49.99. AIRTAMER.COM

We conducted a quick Internet search and found several different types of automotive plug-in ion purifiers. We chose one that plugs into the cigarette lighter. It comes with an extension ion generator that attaches to the louvers on a dash air vent. That feature allows you to direct the flow of ions toward the passenger seat or the backseat—important if you carry passengers with allergies. And because it works with the car's blower system, it doesn't need a built-in blower fan like some other units.

The AirTamer ionic purifier plugs into any 12-volt DC power source. It comes with an extension ion generator that attaches to a dash vent.

DIAGNOSE AND FIX
A LEAKING VALVE STEM

You topped off the air in your tires, but a few days later, you notice that one of them is low again. You may have a hole in the tire, but before you take it in to the garage, first check for a leaky valve stem (Photo 1). If the stem is leaking, you can easily fix it yourself. You only need a valve core tool and a package of new valve cores (total cost: about $5).

The fix is simple. Jack up the wheel. Then remove the old core with a valve core tool, screw in a new core (just snug it up; it's easy to strip the threads), and then refill the tire. But here are a few nuggets of advice. First, be sure to wear safety glasses when you pull out the old core. Debris or even the old core could hit you right in the peepers when the air releases. Second, look closely at the old core threads. If they show any sign of corrosion, clean the interior threads of the valve stem with the tap end of the valve core tool. And last, always use a valve stem cap to keep out the dirt! Dirt around the core is probably what caused the problem to begin with.

A valve core tool is four tools in one. The forked end removes and installs valve cores. The tapping end cleans and restores the interior threads, and the die end cleans and restores the cap threads.

1 SQUIRT soapy water into the valve. If you see bubbles form, you have a slow leak.

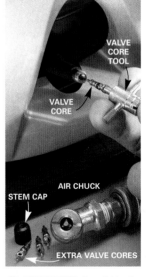

2 UNSCREW the old leaky valve core with a valve core tool. Screw in a new one using the same tool.

Car&Garage

CHANGE YOUR OWN **COOLANT**

A cool way to save $70—

If you're way past due for a coolant change and your cooling system is corroded (see "Do You Need New Coolant?," p. 255), you should take your car in for a professional flush ($90). The same is true if you've mixed different types of coolant in your radiator. But if you're on schedule for a coolant change and your coolant is free of brown, gunky corrosion (extract a little coolant with a baster to examine it), you can skip the flush procedure and perform a simple drain and refill operation yourself and save about $70. Here's how.

Start by buying the type of coolant listed in your owner's manual. If your manual calls for an "extended life" coolant that isn't available at the auto parts store, buy it from the dealer. Don't buy a "universal" coolant. Using the wrong coolant can cause premature component failure and void your warranty.

Raise and safely support the front end of your car on jack stands. Place a large drain pan under the radiator and remove the radiator cap. If your radiator doesn't have a cap, remove the pressure cap from the coolant tank. Then open the drain cock and drain the radiator.

Drain cocks come in several different styles—screw threads, quarter-turn twist, and quarter turn and pull. Plastic drain cocks become brittle with age and can break easily, especially if you try to unscrew a quarter-turn twist style. So, buy a replacement drain cock at the auto parts store before you begin the job (less than $4; return it if you don't need it).

Then remove the lower radiator hose clamp and hose from the engine to drain the rest of the coolant. Use slip-joint pliers to remove spring-style clamps. If you have trouble accessing or releasing the clamps with pliers, buy hose clamp pliers

UNSCREW

QUARTER TURN

UNSCREW AND PULL

QUARTER TURN AND PULL

Drain cocks come in several different styles.

(photo, right). Reconnect and clamp the radiator hose and reinstall the drain cock after draining.

Follow the coolant manufacturer's directions for diluting concentrated coolant. Mix the coolant and water thoroughly in a clean bucket. To prevent mineral deposits on internal engine and radiator surfaces, always use distilled water—never tap water. Leave the car raised while you refill the radiator to reduce the possibility of air pockets forming in the engine.

Slowly fill the radiator or coolant tank with fresh coolant until the coolant is 1 in. below the neck of the radiator or a few inches below the full mark on the coolant tank. Start the engine and let it run. After the engine warms, you'll see the coolant level quickly

ASTRO PNEUMATIC NO. 9409 HOSE CLAMP PLIERS (ABOUT $27 AT AUTO PARTS STORES AND TOOLDISCOUNTER.COM)

drop in the radiator/coolant tank. That means the thermostat has opened and it's time to add more coolant to bring the level to the top of the radiator, or to the "HOT" mark on the coolant tank. Check your owner's manual or service manual to see if your car requires a special air bleeding procedure. Check for leaks, shut off the engine, install the cap, lower the car and go for a spin.

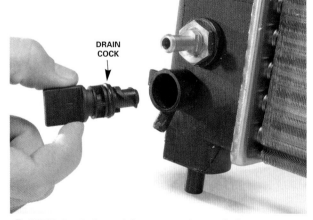

DRAIN COCK

1 OPEN the drain cock by unscrewing, twisting a quarter turn, or twisting and pulling. (The various styles are shown in the photo at left.)

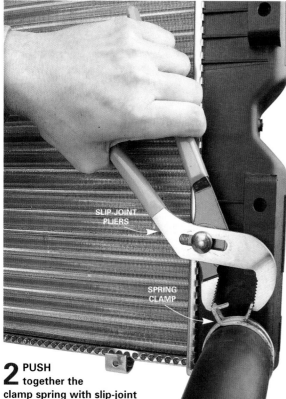

2 PUSH together the clamp spring with slip-joint pliers and slip the clamp away from the neck. Pull the hose free and drain the remaining coolant. If access is difficult, hose clamp pliers save time and bruised knuckles.

3 STIR 1 gallon of full-strength (not premixed) coolant and 1 gallon of distilled water together in a clean bucket before adding the mix to the radiator.

CAUTION: Used coolant is toxic waste. Pour it into a screw-cap plastic container and drop it off at a recycling center. Sweet-tasting coolant is irresistible to pets—and poisonous. Just a small amount can be deadly. So soak up any spills with paper towels or rags immediately if you have pets wandering around.

DO YOU NEED
NEW COOLANT?

Find out with a multimeter

If you think the only job of antifreeze (coolant) is to cool the engine during the summer and prevent freeze-up during the winter, read on. Coolant also plays an important role in preventing corrosion caused by electrolysis. Electrolysis occurs when two dissimilar metals start swapping electrons, causing the metals to corrode. Since an engine has aluminum, copper, cast iron, steel and magnesium alloys, electrolysis will slowly eat away at its innards.

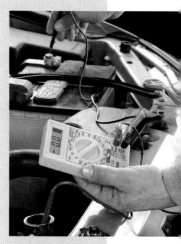

A reading of .4 volts or less means the coolant is good. Replace the coolant if the reading is higher than .4 volts.

Coolant has additives to prevent all of that electron swapping. But, as coolant ages, the additives are depleted and can't do the job anymore. In fact, worn coolant becomes a pretty darn good electrical conductor, accelerating internal electrolysis. The good news is that it's pretty easy to check the conductivity of your coolant with a digital multimeter. If the conductivity is high, it's time for a coolant flush and fill. Here's a quick way to check it.

Begin with a cold engine. Remove the radiator cap and start the engine. Set your digital multimeter to DC volts at 20 volts or less. When the engine reaches operating temperature, insert the positive probe directly into the coolant. Rev the engine to 2,000 rpm and place the negative probe on the negative battery terminal. If the digital meter reads .4 volts or less, your coolant is in good condition. If it's greater than .4 volts, the electrolysis additives are exhausted, and you may be in the market for a new radiator, a water pump or a heater core in the future. All of those are far more expensive than a simple coolant change.

CAUTION: When you work on or around a running engine, wear safety glasses and tight-fitting or short sleeves to keep from being drawn into the moving parts.

AUTO & GARAGE

CAR CADDY

Mobile storage makes car care quick and convenient

by **Travis Larson**

Professional mechanics don't waste time wandering around their shop hunting for tools. Instead, they roll a tool chest right up to the car so all their gear is within reach. That's the idea behind this rolling cabinet. It provides organized, mobile storage for all your maintenance gear, from cleaning supplies to fluids and basic tools.

Even though this project is all about building a cabinet, you don't have to be a seasoned woodworker to build it. The construction is simple. Everything is glued together and end-screwed or nailed together—no fancy joinery here. The whole cabinet is built from 1-1/2 sheets of 3/4-in. plywood and one sheet of 1/2-in. (we chose birch). If you have some experience using hand and power tools, you can build this cart in one weekend for about $100. You'll need a few special tools, such as a self-centering drill bit and a 1-in. Forstner bit. You could drive nails by hand, but a pneumatic brad nailer will speed up assembly. If you don't have a table saw, you can cut the plywood using a circular saw guided by a straightedge.

One-stop shopping

All the tools and materials you need are available at home centers (see Materials List, p. 257). Home centers stock plastic laminate in only a few colors. But at most home

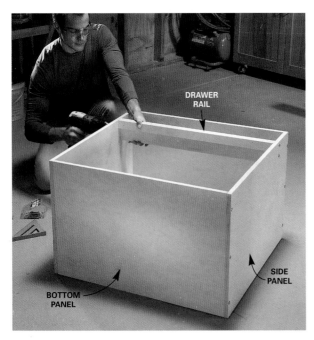

1 ASSEMBLE the cabinet box quickly with glue and brad nails. Then add screws for extra strength.

2 SCREW the drawer slides and shelf standards to the cabinet. A self-centering drill bit makes both jobs easier. Position the standards with a spacer.

Figure A: Car caddy details

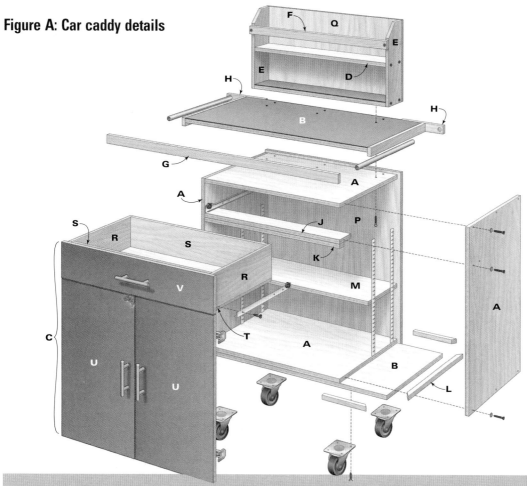

MATERIALS LIST

ITEM	QTY.	ITEM	QTY.	ITEM	QTY.
4' x 8' x 3/4" sheets plywood	2	2" No. 6 screws	1 box	Hinges	2 pairs
4' x 8' x 1/2" sheet plywood	1	1" No. 6 screws	4	Shelf standards	4
3' x 8' plastic laminate	1	1-1/4" No. 6 screws	1 box	Shelf brackets	4
3" swivel casters	4	No. 6 finish washers	1 box	Drawer pulls	3
1-1/2" No. 12 screws	16	1-1/2" brads		Contact cement	1 qt.
4' of 1" aluminum pipe or 1" wood dowel	2	18" under-mount drawer slides	1 pair		

CUTTING LIST

KEY	PCS.	SIZE & DESCRIPTION
A	4	20" x 30" cabinet box sides, top and bottom*
B	2	20" x 40" top and base*
C†	1	30" x 31-1/2" door and drawer fronts*
D	2	5" x 30" rack shelf and bottom*
E	2	5" x 15" rack sides*
F	1	1-1/2" x 31-1/2" rack front rail*
G	1	1-1/2" x 50-1/2" front top edge*
H	2	1-1/2" x 9-1/2" back top edge*

KEY	PCS.	SIZE & DESCRIPTION
J	1	4" x 30" drawer rail*
K	1	1-1/2" x 30" drawer rail*
L	1	3/4" x 40" wastebasket lip*
M	1	10-1/4" x 29-1/2" shelf*
N	1	1-1/2" x 29-1/2" shelf edging* (not shown)
P	1	31-1/2" x 31-1/2" cabinet back**
Q	1	31-1/2" x 15" rack back**
R	2	4" x 19" drawer sides**
S	2	4" x 28" drawer front and back**

KEY	PCS.	SIZE & DESCRIPTION
T	1	19" x 29" drawer bottom**
U	2	15-5/8" x 24" doors**
V	1	31-1/2" x 5-1/2" drawer front**

* 3/4" plywood

** 1/2" plywood

† Cut C as one piece, laminate it, and then cut it into the door and drawer fronts.

AUTO & GARAGE

centers you can special-order almost any color. Some stores will even have it delivered right to your front door for an extra $10 or so.

Cut and assemble the plywood parts

Cut the large cabinet parts to size. **Figure B** helps you get the most out of each sheet of plywood, while the Cutting List on p. 257 shows you the dimensions. Don't cut the trim parts to length yet. It's smarter to measure and cut them to fit after the cabinet takes shape.

Assemble the four cabinet box sides (A) first. Spread a thin layer of glue on the edges. If you have a brad nailer, pin the sides together with a few 1-1/2-in. brads. After all four sides are glued and pinned, drill 1/8-in. holes and screw the sides together with 2-in. screws and finish washers. If you don't have a brad nailer, use screws and glue only. Skip the washers and countersink the screws wherever the screws will be covered by other pieces. Then add the pair of drawer rails, leaving a 5-1/4-in. space for the drawer (**Photo 1**). They're in two parts simply to make the rail thicker to act as a divider between the doors and the drawer.

Install the cabinet drawer slides and shelf standards (**Photo 2**) before you install the back. Space the standards using plywood scraps. Look at the numbers stamped on the standards to be sure you don't install them upside down. Use a self-centering bit set in the screw holes for drilling pilot holes. Then screw on

SELF-CENTERING DRILL BIT

the base panel and anchor each caster with 1-in. No. 12 screws (**Photo 3**).

Laminate the drawer/door fronts and top

Plastic laminate is optional for this project. You could skip it and coat the parts with polyurethane instead. For more help with laminate, do a keyword search for "plastic laminate" at thefamilyhandyman.com. Apply plastic laminate to two pieces of plywood, one for the top and another for the door and drawer fronts (part C). Cut the bottom for the rack and laminate that separately. Cut part C to the exact dimensions given in **Figure A** before laminating. Later, you'll cut part C into three parts to make the doors and drawer fronts. (The width of the saw kerf will give you perfect gaps between the parts.) Rough-cut the laminate to size, about 2 in. larger than the plywood blanks. Do that by scoring the laminate with a utility knife (use a sharp blade!) and a straightedge. Make three or four passes, pressing firmly with the knife. Then carefully bend the sheet over a workbench edge and the pieces will break right at the score. Use a small foam roller to spread the

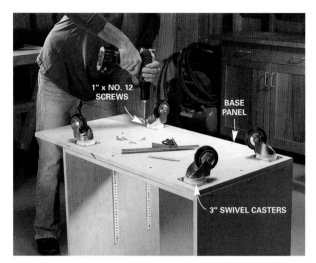

3 ADD the base and casters to the cabinet. Position the casters 1 in. from the edges of the base.

4 CEMENT plastic laminate to the drawer and door blank and to the top. Cut off the excess with a flush-trim router bit.

5 CLAMP the top in place and fasten it with screws from inside the cabinet. Don't drive the screws too deep or they'll break through the laminate.

contact cement on both the plywood and the back of the laminate. After the cement dries to the touch (it should be tacky but not wet), carefully hold the laminate over the plywood so all edges overhang the plywood, then lower it into position. Roll the entire surface with a laminate roller to force out air bubbles and get good contact, especially at the edges. Or, use the edge of a 2x4 to force down the laminate by pushing and dragging. Lastly, trim off the overhanging laminate with a flush-trim router bit (**Photo 4**). Then center, clamp and screw the top to the cabinet from the underside with 1-1/4-in. screws (**Photo 5**).

FLUSH-TRIM ROUTER BIT

Add handles and the rack

Drill 1-in.-diameter holes 1/2 in. deep in both ends of the edge trim using a Forstner bit, then center, glue and nail the front piece in place. Cut the handle tubing (aluminum piping or a wood dowel) a bit on the long side and test-fit it by slipping it into the holes and holding the second edge-trim pieces against the cabinet. Cut a bit at a time off the end until you get a perfect fit. Then glue and nail the second trim pieces (with the handles in place) to the top.

FORSTNER BIT

Assemble the rack using **Figure A** as a guide and mount it as shown in **Photo 7**. Clamp the rack to the top while you screw it to the cabinet from the underside with 2-in. screws. Cut the wastebasket lip to fit and pin it to the base with 1-1/4-in. brads (**Figure A**).

Build the drawer and mount the fronts

Glue and nail the drawer fronts and backs to the sides. Before the glue sets, glue and nail on the bottom to square the drawer box. Then screw on the drawer slides (**Photo 8**) and install the drawer. Make sure the drawer is flush with the cabinet front, then lock it into place by forcing shims between the drawer and the cabinet. Cut the last sheet of laminated plywood into the drawer and door fronts, then center and drill the drawer pull holes in the drawer front. Space the drawer front down from the top with 1/4-in. spacers and screw it to the drawer box with temporary 1-1/4-in. screws (**Photo 9**). Pull out the drawer and screw the drawer box to the front from the back side with four 1-in. screws. Then remove the two temporary screws, finish drilling the drawer pull holes through the drawer box and install the pulls. Most drawer pulls come with screws that are too short to penetrate two layers of plywood. If

6 GLUE and nail the back to the box. Measure the box diagonally to make sure it's square before you drive any nails.

7 SCREW the rack to the top from below. Clamp it in place or have a helper hold it while you drive the screws.

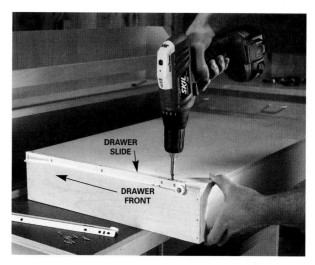

DRAWER SLIDE

DRAWER FRONT

8 BUILD the drawer box and screw on the slides. Make sure the slides are flush with the front of the box.

AUTO & GARAGE

that's the case, drill a second clearance hole for the screw head from the back.

Use the hinge template (included with the hinges) to mark and predrill the hinge screw holes in the doors first (Photo 10). Mount the hinges, then mark and predrill the cabinet hinge holes and hang the doors, spacing them 1/4 in. down from the drawer front (Photo 11). Then add the door pulls.

Carefully mask off the laminate and apply two coats of polyurethane to the outside and one coat to the inside of the cabinet. ⌂

Figure B: Cutting diagram

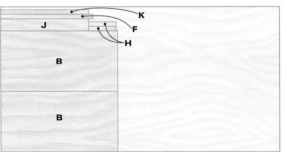

3/4" plywood sheet

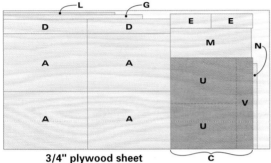

3/4" plywood sheet (half sheet)

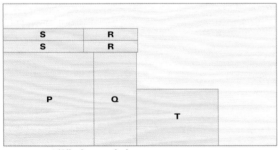

1/2" plywood sheet

Tip

You only need 1-1/2 sheets of 3/4-in. plywood for this project, but you'll pay a premium price per foot for a half sheet of plywood. Get a second full sheet instead and save the rest for your next project.

1/4" SPACER   TEMPORARY SCREW

9 POSITION the drawer front perfectly: First drill the drawer pull holes. Then position the front and drive temporary screws through the holes and into the drawer box. Open the drawer and drive the screws from the inside.

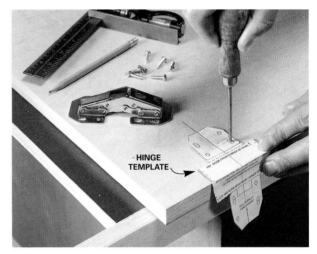

HINGE TEMPLATE

10 DRAW center lines on the doors and mark screw positions using the template. Drill pilot holes and screw on the hinges.

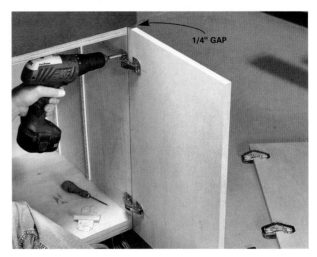

1/4" GAP

11 SCREW the hinges to the cabinet. Fasten each hinge with one screw and close the doors to be sure they're positioned right. Then add the remaining screws.

THREE **GARAGE DOOR FIXES**

1 Replace rotting trim

Wood garage doorjambs and trim often rot near the bottom or get crunched by bumpers.

A good, long-lasting solution is to replace the wood jamb, brick mold trim and doorstop with paintable solid-vinyl pieces that won't crack or decay. Available at home centers and lumberyards, the three pieces cost a total of about $4 per ft.—comparable to clear wood. The vinyl can be cut, nailed and painted just like wood. It's available in white, but you can order brown, bronze and tan. Fill nail holes with white caulk or exterior wood filler, then if desired prime and paint with acrylic latex. Use a light paint color over white vinyl to keep it from overheating.

Remove the old jamb and trim (**Photo 1**), then nail the vinyl jamb to the frame, beginning with the top piece (**Photo 2**). Fasten every 12 to 16 in. with 8d galvanized nails or stainless steel trim screws. Precut the miters on

the top piece of brick mold trim and nail it to the framing every 12 in. with 10d galvanized casing nails. Use 6d casing nails for the stop molding, nailing it at the premarked points on the trim.

If the temperature is below 40 degrees F during installation, predrill nail holes and leave a 1/8-in. gap at the ends of the jamb for expansion.

Glue the brick mold corners with PVC cement (**Photo 3**), then nail them into place after the glue sets. To avoid breaking the joint, wait at least an hour for the glue to fully cure before nailing within a foot of the corner. Splice long runs with glued butt joints.

The edge of the vinyl stop molding should be 2-1/2 in. back from the garage door so the rubber seal fits loosely against the door (**Photo 4**).

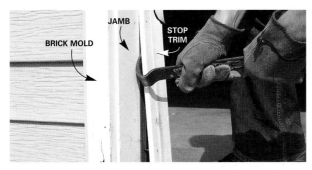

1 CUT through any caulk lines with a utility knife, then pry off the old garage doorstop, brick mold and jamb.

2 USE a clamp to hold up one end of the top jamb, then nail the jamb to the framing with 8d galvanized casing nails.

3 SPREAD PVC cement on both sides of the mitered corners, then hold them together until they bond.

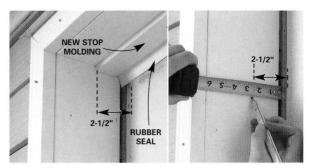

4 MARK the width of the trim piece at several points on the jamb, then nail. Trim the overlapping rubber seal at the corners.

AUTO & GARAGE

2 Clean up rusty door track

Garage door tracks often rest directly on damp concrete floors, where they eventually rust. However, there's no reason they can't be slightly above the floor and stay dry: The garage rafters carry the weight of the track and the angle brackets hold the track in place.

Clean up the tracks and prevent rusting by simply cutting off the bottom 1/2 in. First make sure all the angle bracket bolts are tight, then cut the track bottoms off (**Photo 1**). Use a rag dipped in thinner to remove any lubricant on the first 6 in. of track, then scrape and brush off as much rust as you can. Finally, paint the bot-

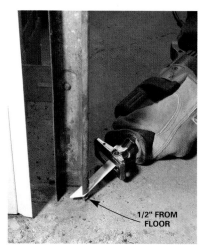

1 MARK the bottom of the track, then cut the metal with a reciprocating saw or hacksaw.

1/2" FROM FLOOR

tom with a metal spray paint that's formulated to bond to rusted areas

2 CLEAN the bottom of the track with mineral spirits, wire-brush the rust, and then paint the area.

(**Photo 2**). Rust-Oleum Rust Reformer is one choice.

3 Install new weather seal

If the weather seal attached to the bottom of your steel garage door is torn or completely flattened, it's time to

1 LIFT the garage door to about 6 ft. high and pull the old weather seal out through the gap behind the door track.

WEATHER SEAL TRACK

2 SCRAPE dirt and corrosion out of the weather seal track with a screwdriver and a stiff brush.

replace it with a new piece. Home centers sell two types: a nail-on style for wood doors and a slide-in "bulb" type for steel doors ($10 to $20).

Lift the door just enough that the garage door track doesn't get in the way of the weather seal, then slide out the old rubber bulb (**Photo 1**). You may need to pry the track ends open with a flat screwdriver if they've been crimped. If it's especially stubborn, cut it and remove it in pieces.

Clean the door bottom (**Photo 2**), then cut the new rubber seal to length with a razor knife. Thread the T-shaped edges into the weather seal track, then slide the seal across the door. Be patient—it takes a lot of pushing and pulling even with a helper.

DISH SOAP HERE

3 LUBRICATE the rubber with a few drops of dish soap, then push and pull the new weather seal into the track.

NewProducts

LASER PARKING SYSTEM

Hanging a tennis ball at just the right spot in the garage is a tried-and-true method for knowing when to stop your vehicle, but now you can have precision parking without a gaudy ball dangling from the ceiling.

    The laser parking system shoots a laser beam across the hood of your vehicle, letting you know when to stop. The control module plugs into an electrical outlet and is mounted to the door opener. When the garage door opens, the vibration activates the laser, guiding you to your stopping point. It shuts off after one minute. You'll never notice the system components since they're installed near the ceiling. The Genie system, shown here, is sold at Lowe's for $40 and comes with two lasers for two vehicles.

Genie, (800) 354-3643. geniecompany.com

LASER BEAM

CONTROL MODULE

LASERS

FINGER-SCAN GARAGE DOOR OPENER

Forget about memorizing four-digit codes to open the garage door. Master Lock's SmartTouch garage door opener ($200) works by reading a finger scan. Just swipe your finger across the sensor and it reads your personal fingerprint (yes, it works even if your finger is dirty!) to open or close the door—no more keys or access codes. The door opener works with any automatic garage door system, stores up to 20 users (as young as 4) and is wireless, so it's easy to install.

    A separate programming module (included) connects to the sensor unit to record finger scans and program the unit, and then is removed. A relay unit is also included to serve as a traditional push button opener inside the garage (and it's needed for the scanner to work). It's wired to the garage door opener. Buy the SmartTouch online at biometrx.net.

Master Lock, (800) 308-9244. masterlock.com

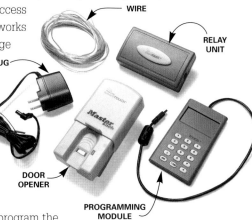

WIRE

RELAY UNIT

PLUG

DOOR OPENER

PROGRAMMING MODULE

NewProducts

TURN YOUR GARAGE INTO A SCREEN ROOM

We've seen several versions of garage door screens that fit over the opening to keep out bugs, but none with Kitty Mac's Fresh Air Screens' great prices—$126 for a single garage door opening (9 x 7 ft.) and $156 for a double door (16 x 7 ft.). Installation only takes about 15 minutes. Nail the screen along the top

(to the outside of the garage door frame so it won't interfere with the garage door), then use the Velcro straps to adhere the frame along the sides and attach the screen. Slide a 3/4-in. plastic pipe or conduit (not included) through the pocket at the bottom of the screen to keep it rigid.

When you want the screen up, simply detach the sides, roll them up, and then fasten the straps along the top. It's a practical, inexpensive way to work in the garage without battling insects. Buy the screens at Menards (in the Midwest) or directly from the manufacturer.

Kitty Mac, (888) 549-0783. freshairscreens.com

RECHARGEABLE WORK LIGHT

I didn't believe this work light would put out enough light to find anything in the dark until I shined it into my trunk at night looking for jumper cables. The LED lights are plenty bright, and they'll never burn out.

The TLW-60 work light ($45) is rechargeable or can be plugged into your car's cigarette lighter socket. It's a great work light to keep on board for car emergencies. A 90-minute charge lasts four hours. Retailers are listed online.

TerraLUX, (866) 498-1564. terralux.biz

CIGARETTE LIGHTER PLUG

ELECTRICAL PLUG

WORK LIGHT

SPECIAL BONUS SECTION

Storage & Organizing

Smart ways to expand and organize your storage space

MUFFIN TIN HARDWARE BINS

Work surface cluttered with miscellaneous nails, screws, hardware, whatever? Clean it up and still keep that stuff at your fingertips, thanks to this tip.

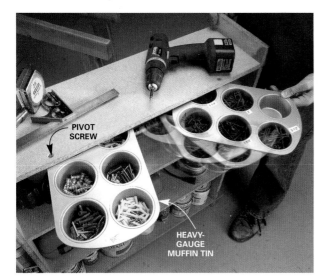

PIVOT SCREW

HEAVY-GAUGE MUFFIN TIN

Attach a muffin tin under a shelf with a single 1/4-in. x 1-1/2-in. flat head machine screw. The tin pivots out from beneath work surfaces to organize and serve up any little doodad you frequently use. And you store all that little stuff without using up a single square inch of workspace. For best results when installing your muffin bins:

- Use muffin tins made from heavier gauge metal.
- Drill and countersink a 1/4-in. hole in the shelf top, so the top of the screw is flush with the shelf.

1/4" x 1-1/2" FLAT HEAD MACHINE SCREW

FENDER WASHERS

- Place 1/4-in. fender washers above and below the rim of the muffin tin.
- Tighten two nuts against each other on the underside so the threads won't loosen.

MOVABLE BIKE RACK

Tired of that darn bike hanging in your way? Build this movable bike rack from a 2x4 and a pair of bicycle hooks. Cut four 3-1/2-in. blocks, stack two on top of each other, and screw them together. Now screw them on the end of a 4-ft. 2x4 and repeat the process for the other side. Drill a hole in the middle of the stacked blocks and screw in the bicycle hooks. Lay the rack across your garage ceiling joists, and hang your bike from the hooks. When you need to get behind the bike, simply slide the entire rack out of the way.

SPECIAL BONUS SECTION

Storage & Organizing

AIR COMPRESSOR CART

Build this mobile home for your small air compressor and roll it to any job, anywhere in the shop, house or yard! The built-in air hose reel and tool bin keep your whole air-powered tool operation together. Measure your compressor before building. You may have to alter the dimensions so yours will fit.

You'll need:

■ Two 2-ft. x 4-ft. sheets of 3/4-in. plywood ($8 each at a home center)
■ One 2-ft. x 4-ft. sheet of 1/2-in. plywood
■ One 1-1/4-in. closet dowel
■ Two 4-in. casters ($8 each at a home center)
■ One air hose reel ($37; part no. 159184 at northerntool.com)
■ Six 3/8-in. x 2-in. hex head bolts, nuts and washers
■ Eight 5/16-in. x 1-in. lag screws

Cut out the plywood parts (see illustration) with a circular saw or a table saw and a jigsaw for the curves. Bore the 1-1/4-in. dowel holes before assembling the cart. Mount casters to the underside of the base with lag screws, then mark and drill holes in the crosspiece for the hose reel and bolt it on. That's it! Organize nail guns, nail packs, nail gun oil and tire inflation accessories in the handy tool pockets and you're ready to roll.

TOOL AND NAIL STORAGE

STUD-SPACE SHELVES

Open wall framing in a basement or garage makes ideal storage space for narrow items like cleaning supplies or small boxes of nails and screws. Simply cut 2x4s to fit between the studs and toe-screw them in to form shelves.

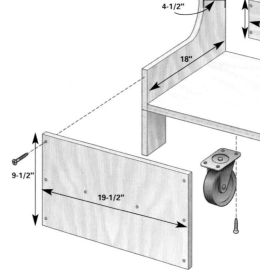

CLOSET ROD
1-1/4" DIA. x 19-1/2"

1/2" PLYWOOD
ALL OTHER PARTS
3/4" PLYWOOD

6-3/4"

11"

5" x 18"
SHELF

33-1/2"

5"

4-1/2"

19-1/2"

18"

4-1/2"

9-1/2"

19-1/2"

5"

4"

SOAP BOX NAIL HOLDER

Use a travel soap holder to store screws, nails and fasteners and protect them from rust. Tape the description from the original box onto the plastic container and you'll have all the information you need on a long-lasting package.

TRAVEL SOAP BOX

STAY-PUT BALLS

Keep sport balls off the floor and out of the way by resting them in flowerpot drip trays (80¢ at home centers). Screw the trays down to an inexpensive shelving unit. The balls will stay put.

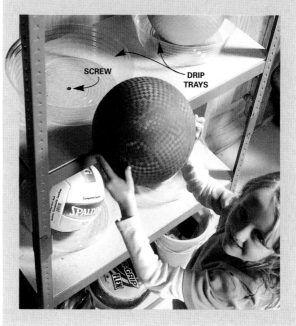

SCREW

DRIP TRAYS

PAINTED PIPE INSULATION

CORD CONTROL

Tame that cord jungle under your desk with a length of 1/2-in. foam pipe insulation. Paint it the color of your wall and it will virtually disappear.

EASY STORAGE FOR USED BATTERIES

Avoid playing the "is this battery good or dead" game by dropping used batteries into a large plastic container. When the container is full, just take it to a battery drop-off site. Many retailers accept used batteries for no "charge"—ha!

Storage&Organizing

HEAVY-DUTY UTILITY SHELVES

Store-bought shelving units are either hard to assemble and flimsy or awfully expensive. Here's a better solution. These shelves are strong and easy to build and cost about $70. We sized this sturdy shelf unit to hold standard records storage boxes ($4 each). If you want deeper storage, build the shelves 24 in. deep and buy 24-in.-deep boxes. If you prefer to use plastic storage bins, measure the size of the containers and modify the shelf and upright spacing to fit.

Refer to the dimensions at right to mark the location of the horizontal 2x2 on the back of four 2x4s. Also mark the position of the 2x4 uprights on the 2x2s. Then simply line up the marks and screw the 2x2s to the 2x4s with pairs of 2-1/2-in. wood screws. Be sure to keep the 2x2s and 2x4s at right angles. Rip a 4 x 8 ft. sheet of 1/2-in. MDF, plywood or OSB into 16-in.-wide strips and screw it to the 2x2s to connect the two frames and form the shelving unit.

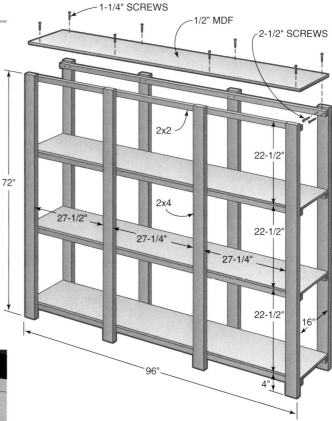

1-1/4" SCREWS
1/2" MDF
2-1/2" SCREWS
2x2
22-1/2"
2x4
22-1/2"
27-1/2"
27-1/4"
27-1/4"
22-1/2"
72"
96"
16"
4"

Build sturdy, simple shelves, custom sized to hold boxes or other storage containers.

SAFE CORD STORAGE

To store elastic cords safely and neatly, pull out the spine of an old three-ring binder. Punch out the rivets and screw the spine to the garage wall. The rings are the perfect spot to hang cords without dangerous tension.

THREE-RING BINDER SPINE

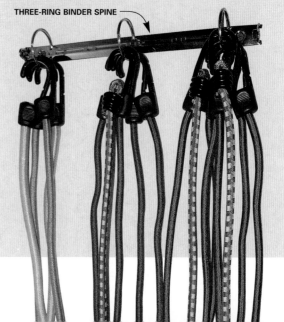

BEHIND-THE-DOOR SHELVES

The space behind a door is another storage spot that's often overlooked. Build a set of shallow shelves and mount it to the wall.

The materials cost about $40. Measure the distance between the door hinge and the wall and subtract an inch. This is the maximum depth of the shelves. We used 1x4s for the sides, top and shelves. Screw the sides to the top. Then screw three 1x2 hanging strips to the sides: one top and bottom and one centered. Nail metal shelf standards to

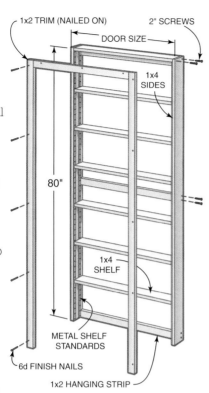

the sides. Complete the shelves by nailing a 1x2 trim piece to the sides and top. The 1x2 dresses up the shelf unit and keeps the shelves from falling off the shelf clips.

Locate the studs. Drill clearance holes and screw the shelves to the studs with 2-1/2-in. wood screws. Put a rubber bumper on the frame to protect the door.

Build shallow shelves to fit behind the door in your laundry room, utility room or pantry.

SERVICE RECORD STORAGE

For easy access to car and tool manuals and service records, screw a closing accordion file onto a board mounted to a garage wall. Keep a pencil with it to quickly track routine maintenance chores.

JOIST-SPACE SPACE-SAVER

Don't waste all that space between joists in a basement or garage. Screw wire shelving to the underside of the joists. An 8-ft. x 16-in. length of wire shelving and a pack of plastic clips (sold separately) costs $21.

Screw a wire closet shelf to the underside of joists to create a shelf that's strong, easy to see through and won't collect dust.

Storage&Organizing

STUD-SPACE CABINET

When you can't find a convenient nook for a set of shelves, you can often create one by recessing the shelves into the wall itself. Choose the location before you build the project to make sure it will fit. Start by looking for a space with no obvious obstructions.

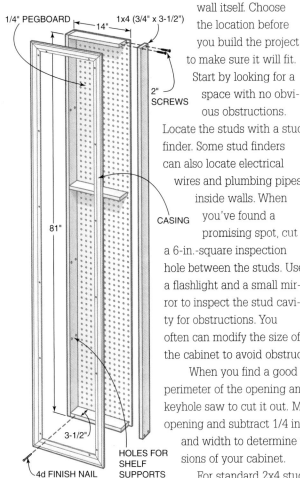

1/4" PEGBOARD

14"

1x4 (3/4" x 3-1/2")

2" SCREWS

CASING

81"

3-1/2"

HOLES FOR SHELF SUPPORTS

4d FINISH NAIL

Locate the studs with a stud finder. Some stud finders can also locate electrical wires and plumbing pipes inside walls. When you've found a promising spot, cut a 6-in.-square inspection hole between the studs. Use a flashlight and a small mirror to inspect the stud cavity for obstructions. You often can modify the size of the cabinet to avoid obstructions.

When you find a good space, mark the perimeter of the opening and use a drywall keyhole saw to cut it out. Measure the opening and subtract 1/4 in. from the height and width to determine the outer dimensions of your cabinet.

For standard 2x4 stud walls with 1/2-in.-thick drywall, build the cabinet frame from 1x4s that measure 3-1/2 in. wide (see illustration). If your walls are different, adjust the depth of the frame accordingly. Then add a 1/4-in. back. We screwed 1/4-in. pegboard to the back so we could hang stuff from pegboard hooks.

Add casing that matches the trim in your house. Drill holes into the sides to accept shelf supports. Shelf supports fit in 3mm, 5mm or 1/4-in. holes depending on the style.

Install the cabinet by slipping it into the opening, leveling it and nailing through the trim into the studs on each side. Use 6d finish nails placed every 12 in. along both sides.

DOUBLE-DUTY LUGGAGE

Put your luggage to use when it's not on vacation. Fill it with off-season clothes and stash it under the bed.

CLOSET NOOK SHELVES

Salvage the hidden space at the recessed ends of your closets by adding a set of shelves. Wire shelves are available in a variety of widths. Measure the width and depth of the space. Then choose the correct shelving and ask the salesperson to cut the shelves to length for you. Subtract 3/8 in. from the actual width to determine the shelf length. Buy a pair of end mounting brackets and a pair of plastic clips for each shelf.

Make the most of the recesses at the ends of your closet with wire shelving.

Remove the drywall from between two studs and construct a shallow cabinet to fit the space.

STACKED RECYCLING TOWER

Five plastic containers, six 2x2s and screws, and one hour's work are all it takes to put together this space-saving recycling storage rack. Our frame fits containers that have a top that measures 14-1/2 in. x 10 in. and are 15 in. tall. Our containers were made by Rubbermaid.

If you use different-size containers, adjust the distance between the uprights so the 2x2s will catch the lip of the container. Then adjust the spacing of the horizontal rungs for a snug fit when the container is angled as shown.

Start by cutting the 2x2s to length according to the illustration. Then mark the position of the rungs on the uprights. Drill two 5/32-in. holes through the uprights at each crosspiece position. Drill from the outside to the inside and angle the holes inward slightly to prevent the screws from breaking out the side of the rungs.

Drive 2-1/2-in. screws through the uprights into the rungs. Assemble the front and back frames. Then connect them with the side crosspieces.

17"
7-1/2"
2-1/2"
ALL SUPPORTS 10-1/2" APART
70"
4"
CROSSPIECE
2-1/2" SCREWS
7-1/2"

Build a space-saving tower for plastic recycling containers with simple 2x2 and screw construction.

SANDWICH-BAG PARTS ORGANIZER

Keep screws, connectors, nails and other small parts in sight and handy with this resealable bag holder. You can build it out of a 3/4-in.-thick scrap of plywood. Start by cutting two pieces of plywood as shown. Draw lines 1 in. apart across the shorter piece with a square, stopping 1 in. from the edge. Now cut along the lines with a jigsaw. Screw the two pieces of plywood together and screw the unit to the wall. Fill resealable bags and slip them into the slots.

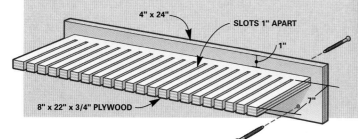

4" x 24"
SLOTS 1" APART
1"
8" x 22" x 3/4" PLYWOOD
7"

Cut slots in a piece of plywood with a jigsaw. Fill resealable bags with small parts, hardware or craft items and hang them from the slotted plywood.

SPECIAL BONUS SECTION

Storage&Organizing

Double the shelf space in your closet by adding a second shelf above the existing one.

TWO-STORY CLOSET SHELVES

There's a lot of space above the shelf in most closets. Even though it's a little hard to reach, it's a great place to store seldom-used items. Make use of this wasted space by adding a second shelf above the existing one. Buy enough closet shelving material to match the length of the existing shelf plus enough for two end supports and middle supports over each bracket. Twelve-in.-wide shelving (about $9 for an 8-ft. length) is available in various lengths and finishes at home centers and lumberyards. We cut the supports 16 in. long, but you can place the second shelf at whatever height you like. Screw the end supports to the walls at each end. Use drywall anchors if you can't hit a stud. Then mark the position of the middle supports onto the top and bottom shelves with a square and drill 5/32-in. clearance holes through the shelves. Drive 1-5/8-in. screws through the shelf into the supports.

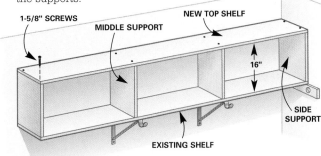

1-5/8" SCREWS — MIDDLE SUPPORT — NEW TOP SHELF — 16" — SIDE SUPPORT — EXISTING SHELF

BACK-OF-DOOR ORGANIZER

The back of a door that opens into a utility room or closet makes a handy hanging space. The trouble is that most doors don't offer a good mounting surface for hardware. The solution is to screw a piece of 3/4-in. plywood to the back of the door. Add construction adhesive for hollow-core doors. Cut the plywood 3 or 4 in. shy of the door edges to avoid conflicts with the doorknob or hinges. Now you can mount as many hooks, magnets and other storage gizmos as you like.

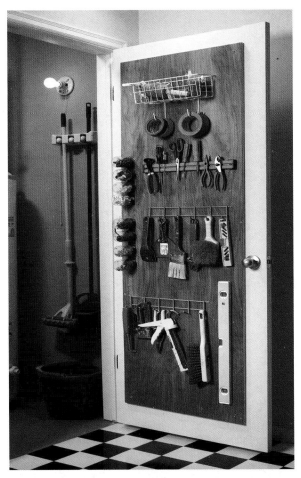

Screw 3/4-in. plywood to the back of a door to provide a solid mounting base for screw hooks, baskets or other storage accessories.

LABELING PLASTIC BINS

If you store things in plastic bins, label the plastic with a wet-erase marker. When it's time to relabel the bin, just wipe away the marks with a damp rag.

GLASS SHOWER SHELF

Tired of the clutter of shampoo and conditioner bottles along the rim of your tub? This tempered safety glass shelf on a cable shelf bracket is an easy solution. The cable shelf bracket requires only two screws for support. If studs aren't located in the right positions, use toggle bolts to anchor the shelf brackets. The glass hangs on the cables. The cable shelf brackets (No. CSB5B) are available online from expodesigninc.com and cost $21 per pair. Order a tempered glass shelf from a local glass company. The 3/8-in.-thick, 12-in.-deep shelf we used cost $64.

Mount a shelf above your tub to store towels, shampoo and conditioner.

DOUBLE-DECKER CLOSET ROD

All you need to gain a lot of hanging space in your closet is two metal closet brackets and a length of closet rod. If your existing closet rod is at least 66 in. from the floor, there's enough space to add a second rod below it and still hang shirts and slacks. We placed the top of the rod 35 in. from the floor, which allowed just enough room to hang two levels of pants.

Locate studs on the back wall of the closet with a stud finder. Then attach metal brackets to the studs. Use a level to align the brackets along the top. Space the brackets no more than 32 in. apart.

Add a lower closet rod to gain extra hanging space in your closet.

SHOE-STORAGE BOOSTER STOOL

Build this handy stool in one hour and park it in your closet. You can also use it as a step to reach the high shelf. All you need is a 4x4 sheet of 3/4-in. plywood, wood glue and a handful of 8d finish nails. Cut the plywood pieces according to the illustration. Spread wood glue on the joints, then nail them together with 8d finish nails. First nail through the sides into the back. Then nail through the top into the sides and back. Finally, mark the location of the two shelves and nail through the sides into the shelves.

Build this double-duty step stool from six pieces of 3/4-in. plywood.

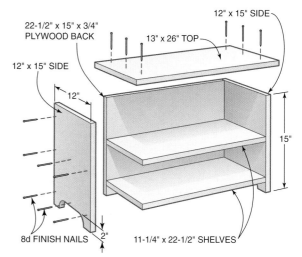

22-1/2" x 15" x 3/4" PLYWOOD BACK

12" x 15" SIDE

13" x 26" TOP

12" x 15" SIDE

12"

15"

8d FINISH NAILS

2"

11-1/4" x 22-1/2" SHELVES

Dirty, Dusty GreatGoofs®

These blunders resulted in big messes. Let's hope your home improvements are much more successful!

Sunken hopes

My son and I built a wooden rowboat in our garage for his high school shop project. It turned out great. We sanded it and got set up to paint. After we rolled and brushed the paint, we were anxious for it to dry, so I grabbed the box fan from the corner of the garage and aimed it toward the boat. Bad idea! The fan had accumulated the sawdust from the project on its blades and blew all of it onto the freshly painted boat. My son looked at me with a long face and requested that I warn him before I had any more clever ideas.

Blown away

After cleaning out the trap under the bathroom sink, I had the brilliant idea to clean the rest of the drainpipe with the high-powered blower feature on my shop vacuum. I opened up the cleanout plug at one end and blew away. Feeling proud, I went upstairs, only to find the less-than-proud results—rancid gunk and drain cleaner all over the walls, counters, sink, floors and even the ceiling. Fortunately, I got the mess cleaned up before it destroyed the wallpaper.

Dust devil

I was feeling like Johnny-on-the-spot to be so promptly vacuuming up dust from the drywall that I'd sanded that morning—at least until my sister started shouting, "Turn it off! Turn it off!" I turned to see a huge cloud of dust in the air. After earlier taking care of a water spill with the wet/dry shop vacuum, I'd forgotten to reinstall the dust filter.

Super-charged blower

One December Sunday, we returned from church and found the house cold. I checked our old furnace and discovered that the electric blower motor was shot. I removed the motor, examined the mounting bracket and noticed that the motor from my table saw could be hooked up as a temporary substitute. Then I could get someone out the next day to replace the motor. After exchanging the motor, I turned the switch on. The motor roared as it started and I soon noticed dust everywhere in the house—so much that I could write my name on the kitchen table. I then shut off the furnace and realized that the table saw motor was 3,600 rpm—twice as fast as the old motor. The squirrel cage had gone into high gear and blown out all the accumulated dust in our ductwork. We kept ourselves warm the rest of the day cleaning every square inch of the house!

Just call me Dusty

Although I'm not a remodeler by trade, I like to think I'm pretty handy. I decided to tackle a remodeling project at home that involved some concrete block and a bit of framing and drywall hanging. The project was going just fine until it came to hanging the drywall. I wasn't sure how to cut it, but I'd cut plywood before, so I thought, "why should this be any different?" I laid my first sheet across the sawhorses outside, marked the piece, set the depth on my circular saw and started to cut the drywall to size. It didn't take long for the dust to completely envelop me. I stopped and wrapped a towel around my face and kept cutting. As I was finishing, I could see my neighbors laughing at me as the huge cloud of dust settled. Later, after telling my friends at work the story, they too broke out laughing and asked me, "Haven't you ever heard of a utility knife?"

Duct tape disaster

My old vacuum cleaner lost its suction, so I took it apart to see what was wrong. The seal between the bag and the hose was broken, so I grabbed my roll of duct tape (my first line of attack for most problems) and wrapped the connection. Happy that the vacuum was now working, I decided to vacuum up the two-day-old ashes in the fireplace in the living room. I stuck the nozzle into the pile and in no time the ashes started to disappear. As I was finishing up, I could smell ashes, but it didn't register until I looked 10 ft. behind me and saw fine ashes blowing out of the vacuum all over the room. Seems the duct tape fix wasn't the right repair for this job!

[Editor's note: Never vacuum up ashes. Put them in a metal container until disposal.]

Dirty, Dusty
GreatGoofs®

Do the 'Mashed Potato'

While moving out of our house, I decided to throw out old packaged food instead of boxing it up and moving it. I ran across some old instant mashed potato mix and emptied it into the garbage disposer. I then ran the water and hit the switch. My disposer groaned as it went into a seizure and in a huge eruption, spouted mashed potatoes all over the sink, cabinets and floor. My husband heard the commotion and came running in and couldn't believe what I'd done. Now we always break into laughter when I ask him if he'd like mashed potatoes for dinner.

Smoker gone bad

Last Thanksgiving, my father prepared a turkey in his smoker. He soaked hickory chips and put them in a charcoal grill along with the turkey. The results were fantastic. The next day he cleaned the grill and threw the burned charcoal into the trash can in the workshop. A day later we walked out to the shop. When we opened the door, a huge billow of black smoke and heat poured out. After a few minutes, the air was clear enough for us to get in and open the large garage door. The entire shop was coated in black soot and in the middle of the floor sat a 3-ft. circle of melted plastic and ash—all that was left of his 35-gallon plastic trash can. He now discards his ashes outside—in the fire pit!

Indoor blizzard

While remodeling our bathroom, I had to remove some drywall from the ceiling and wall to run a new plumbing stack. When I cut through the drywall, a ton of loose-fill attic insulation rained down. I was able to bag most of it, but I thought I'd let my super-duty vacuum suck up the rest. Space was tight in the bathroom, so I set the huge vacuum cleaner in the kitchen, hooked up my extension hose and got to work sucking up every last bit of insulation. I went back into the kitchen to shut off the vacuum. As I entered the room, I was overcome by a huge dust cloud. I'd forgotten to reinstall the filter after cleaning it the last time.

He blew it, all right

Not long ago, our refrigerator was cooling poorly, so I loosened the grille cover on the bottom of the fridge. Sure enough, I'd neglected that cleaning job way too long. The cooling coils were packed with dust. After failed attempts to rig up small tubing to the shop vacuum to clean between the coils, I went to the garage to find a better solution. The leaf blower caught my eye, so I brought it inside, plugged it in and aimed it at the coils and turned it on. Before I could switch to the low speed, a huge cloud of dust had billowed out from behind the fridge and covered the whole kitchen. Luckily, my wife wasn't home at the time. I got out the vacuum and spent more than an hour frantically cleaning. Later that day, she opened the cupboard above the fridge and asked me why there was a layer of dust and soot covering everything inside. I now use the leaf blower for outside work only.

Insulation frustration

My wife and I rented an insulation blower to add insulation in our attic. When I got the unit home, I noticed it had remnants of tape on the hose connection. I checked it out and it seemed to work fine. With my wife feeding bags into the hopper and me up in the attic with the hose, we proceeded to get the nasty job done. Working my way around the attic, I noticed that the hose seemed to be caught, so I gave it a tug. Then nothing was coming out, and finally I heard the machine stop. I squeezed back downstairs to discover the downstairs covered in insulation. After a whole day of cleaning, I figured out what all the tape was for!

OUR BEST CLEANING TIPS

Clever ways to clean up all around your home

CORNER CLEANER

If you find it frustrating to clean all the tight corners in your cabinet doors and windows, go to the store and buy a cheap electric tooth-brush. You can use it to clean all those hard-to-reach places.

PIMPLE PADS FOR PAINT CLEANUP

Facial cleansing wipes aren't just for pimple prevention. The alcohol in them softens latex paint, but won't harm most surfaces (test first to make sure). They work best on paint that's been dry just a few hours.

BLEACH AWAY STUBBORN STAINS

Remove stains from marble, cultured marble or plastic laminate with a bleach-soaked paper towel. Cover the towel with a cup to contain the bleach odor and leave it in place overnight. If the stain has faded but not disappeared, just repeat the process. Test this trick in a hidden area first; it could discolor the surface.

BLAST DIRTY SCREENS CLEAN

If you have an air compressor and an air nozzle, you can clean window and door screens in seconds with-out removing them. Just turn the air pressure to 60 psi and blow away dust, debris and cobwebs.

LINT BUNNIES BEGONE

If you notice that it takes longer
than normal for loads to
dry in your clothes
dryer, it may be
time to clean out
the vent. First
detach the duct
from behind the
unit and then
push a plumbing
snake through your
dryer vent from out-
side. Tie a rag securely to
the snake end. Pull the cloth and snake through a
couple of times and your clean vent will not only
save energy but possibly prevent a fire as well.

DRYER
SHEET

DUSTER FOR THE
VERTICALLY CHALLENGED

Unless you play in the NBA, dusting ceiling fans
and other high, out-of-reach objects is a real
chore. Wrap a dryer sheet around a clean painting
roller and secure the ends with rubber bands.
Attach an extension handle to the roller
and dust away.

MICROWAVE CLEANER

It's easy to clean baked-on food and spills from your
microwave! Partially fill a measuring or coffee cup with
water and add a slice of lemon. Boil the water for a
minute, and then leave the door closed and let the
steam loosen the mess. After 10 minutes, open the door
and wipe away the grime.

WASHING WINDOWS

Try washing windows with a squeegee and you'll never go back to a spray bottle and paper towels. Squeegees get your glass clear and streak free in a fraction of the time it takes with paper towels.

The same high-quality window washing tools the pros use are readily available at home centers and full-service hardware stores. The whole setup costs less than $30 and will last many years. You'll need a 10- or 12-in. squeegee ($6 to $12), a scrubber ($4 to $8), a bucket (a 5-gallon plastic bucket will work), hand dishwashing liquid (we recommend Dawn) and a few lint-free rags or small towels.

Yes, you can use a squeegee inside the house too

The pros do it all the time, even in houses with stained and varnished woodwork. The key is to squeeze most of the soapy water out of the scrubber to eliminate excessive dripping and running. Then rest the scrubber on the edge of the bucket rather than dropping it in the water after each window. Depending on how dirty your windows are, you may be able to wash five or ten windows before

SQUEEGEE

rinsing the scrubber. Keep a rag in your pocket to wipe the squeegee and quickly clean up soapy water that runs onto the woodwork. Use a separate clean rag to wipe the perimeter of the glass. Microfiber rags (top left **photo, p. 281**) work great for window cleaning. They're available at discount stores, home centers and hardware stores.

SCRUBBER

Get your window sparkling clean in less than 30 seconds—

WIPE PERIMETER

MICROFIBER RAG

Use a microfiber rag to wipe up excess water along the bottom edge of the window. Then poke your finger into a dry spot on a separate lint-free rag and run it around the perimeter of the window to remove any remaining suds. Wipe off any streaks using a clean area of the lint-free rag. Change rags when you can't find any fresh, clean areas.

Tips for hard-to-clean windows

Dried paint, sticky labels, tree pitch and bug crud may not yield to plain soap and water. Here are a few tips for removing this tough grime.

■ Scrape wetted glass with a new, sharp razor blade to remove dried paint.

■ Remove tree pitch or bug droppings with a fine (white) nylon scrub pad. Wet the glass first and rub in an inconspicuous area to make sure you're not scratching the glass.

■ Add 1/2 cup of ammonia per gallon of water to help remove greasy dirt.

■ Loosen sticky residue left from labels or tape by soaking it with a specialty product like Goof Off. You'll find Goof Off in the paint department at hardware stores and home centers. Then scrape off the residue with a razor blade.

DIVIDED-LITE WINDOW

NARROW SQUEEGEE

Wash divided-lite windows with a sponge and a small squeegee. If you can't find a small enough squeegee, you can cut off a larger one to fit your glass size. Scrub the glass with a wrung-out sponge. Then use the tip of the squeegee to clear a narrow strip at the top. Pull the squeegee down and wipe the perimeter.

CLEAN STRIP

TOUCHING GLASS

just scrub, squeegee and wipe!

STURDY, SIMPLE
SAWHORSES

Every do-it-yourselfer needs at least one pair of sawhorses. Here are three styles—choose the one that best suits your projects and shop.

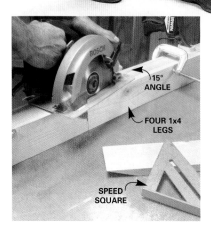

STACKABLE SAWHORSES

We designed these sawhorses for strength, yet they stack compactly. We built them from construction-grade 1x4s (for the legs) and 1x6s (for the top), glue and a handful of screws. They cost only about $6 each.

We made our legs 32 in. long, which put the horse height at about 30 in., the height of a standard table. Adjust the leg length to your own comfort level. The top 1x6 is 32 in. long, but again, adjust its length to fit your needs.

The trickiest part is cutting the sharp (15-degree) angle on the top of each leg. The best method is to clamp at least four 1x4s together and cut them on edge (**Photo 1**). Mark the cutting line on all sides because you have to flip the 1x4s over to complete the cut. A standard Speed square has angle marks that'll help you measure the 15 degrees. Then cut the legs to length at a 75-degree angle (15-degree saw setting) so they rest flat on the floor.

If you don't have a table saw, screw the cleat stock to your workbench, using spacers (**Photo 2**). That'll keep the piece stable while you cut the angles with a circular saw. Note that the narrow side of the cleat is 2-1/8 in. wide. Make sure the legs are perpendicular to the 1x6 when you assemble them (**Photo 3**).

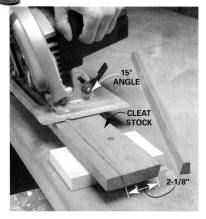

15° ANGLE

FOUR 1x4 LEGS

SPEED SQUARE

1 CLAMP four 1x4s together, mark the 15-degree angle along their edges and cut them all at once. Flip the bundle over and finish the cut from the opposite side.

15° ANGLE

CLEAT STOCK

2-1/8"

2 TEMPORARILY SCREW a 1x4 to your workbench and mark the cleat cuts. Set your saw to 15 degrees and cut the angles. Unscrew the board and cut off 5-in.-long cleats.

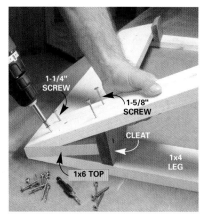

1-1/4" SCREW

1-5/8" SCREW

CLEAT

1x4 LEG

1x6 TOP

3 CENTER AND SCREW the cleats to the 1x6. Predrill, then spread glue and screw the legs to the 1x6 and cleats. Keep the edges flush.

ADJUSTABLE-HEIGHT
SAWHORSES

Every shop needs horsepower. These adjustable horses are easy to build from construction-grade 1x4s and 2x4s. Add the adjustable-height jig and these horses will hold projects at the perfect working height. Use a pair of them as a stand for portable or bench-top power tools, or make a temporary workbench by throwing a piece of plywood on top.

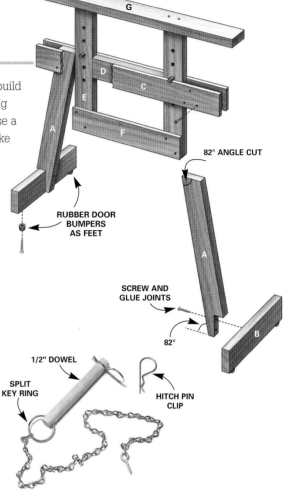

82° ANGLE CUT

RUBBER DOOR BUMPERS AS FEET

SCREW AND GLUE JOINTS

82°

1/2" DOWEL

SPLIT KEY RING

HITCH PIN CLIP

CUTTING LIST

KEY	PCS.	SIZE & DESCRIPTION	KEY	PCS.	SIZE & DESCRIPTION	KEY	PCS.	SIZE & DESCRIPTION
A	2	1-1/2" x 3-1/2" x 25" legs	D	1	1-1/2" x 3-1/2" x 13" spacer block	F	1	3/4" x 3-1/2" x 20" slide support
B	2	1-1/2" x 3-1/2" x 18" footers	E	2	1-1/2" x 3-1/2" x 21" adjustable slides; drill 1/2" dowel holes 2" apart	G	1	1-1/2" x 3-1/2" x 40" work rail
C	2	3/4" x 3-1/2" x 36" top rails						

STRAIGHT-CUT SAWHORSES

1" TO TOP SCREWS

3-1/2" TO BOTTOM SCREWS

32"

I-BEAM

26-1/4"

Need sawhorses right now? You can make a pair from five 8-ft. 2x4s cut into six 32-in. lengths and eight 26-1/4 in. lengths.

Nail or screw the 32-in. pieces into I-beam shapes and, after drilling pilot holes, attach the legs to the I-beams with 3-in. drywall screws. These screws, along with the upper edge of the I-beam, stabilize the legs. They're the perfect horses for holding a heavy load of boards and sheet goods. And when you need another workbench, just screw a piece of plywood on the sawhorses and you'll have a stable table.

INDEX

Visit thefamilyhandyman.com to search five years of article archives.

A

AFCI (arc fault circuit interrupters), 87

Air filters, changing, 252

Air leaks in attic, sealing, 45–49

Air purifiers, for cars, 253
phone ring, 81
video signal, 79

Antifreeze changes, 254–55

Arbor project, 224

Archway project, 172–75

Attic air leaks, sealing, 45–49

Automobiles
air purifiers, 253
bumper sticker removal, 247
cabin air filters, 252
cargo liner, 247

Automobiles, cont.
cigarette smoke removal, 239
coolant changes, 254–55
jump start tips/tools, 237, 238
MAF sensors, cleaning, 251
nylon scrubber, 199
oil changes/filling tips, 236, 238
portable jump starters, 238
scratch touch-up, 237
side view mirror glass replacement, 236
spark plug replacement, 232–33, 239
storage caddy for tools, 256–60
tire rotation, 236
tires with leaky valve stem, 253

Automobiles, cont.
trailer hitches, stuck, 250
transmission fluid replacement, 248–49, 251
trunk lid tie-down, 247
windshield glass treatment, 237
windshield washer repair, 234–35
work light, 264

B

Baseboards, painting, 50

Basements, waterproofing, 57

Bathroom fan time delay switch, 94

Bathroom reading rack project, 138

Bathtubs, leaks, 104–05

Blacktop, sealing, 150

Block walls, painting, 176

Bookcase project, 126–31

Bumper stickers, removal of, 247

C

Cabin air filters (automotive), changing, 252

Cabinets, glass door modification, 66–67

Cable, running, 58, 83, 85

Cargo liner, 247

Carpet, removal of dents in, 21

Cars. *See* Automobiles

Carts, outdoor, 208–9

Caulk removal, 22

Cell phones, portable charger, 94

Cement mixer, 141

CFLs (compact fluorescent lights), 89–93

Charging station project, 136–37

Chimneys, 48

Cigarette smoke, removal from cars, 239

Circuit breakers, sensitive, 87

Computers
cleaning, 80
disposal of, 81

Concrete slabs, pouring, 211–16

Coolant changes, 254–55

Copper pipes, soldering, 116–17

Countertops
gap filler, 24
granite, installation, 52–55
tiling, 59

Crabgrass, 178–81, 200

Cutting board project, 122

D

Decks
  installation of, 177
  lumber choices, 176
  renewal of, 151–55
Doors
  exterior doors, painting, 150
  keyless locks, 10
  paint removal from hardware, 13
  sticking problem, 11
  weatherstripping, 49
Drawers, lubricating, 11
Drill bit guide, 21
Dryer vents, cold air in, 97
Drywall finishing tips, 73–76

E

Electrical
  bathroom fan time delay switch, 94
  cable, running, 58, 83, 85
  CFLs, 89–93
  circuit breakers, fixing sensitive, 87
  electrical boxes, 82, 85, 86
  garage door openers, 94
  generators, 96
  GFCI outlets, 79, 86
  holiday lights, testing, 88
  hot and neutral wire reversal, 82
  outlet installation, 84

Electrical, cont.
  switch installation, 84
  video signal amplifiers, 79
  wireless switches, 78
  wiring mistakes, 82–86
Energy savings
  estimator for, 80
  ideas for, 89, 92
Eye protection, 21

F

Fan time delay switch, 94
Faucets
  corrosion problem, 107
  outdoor, 141, 150, 156–58
  for showers, 98–101
Fence installation, 192–98
Fertilizer, 202, 221
Flies, 149
Floor joists, drilling in, 59
Floors
  grout haze removal, 57
  heated, 68–72
  tile installation, 59
  wood floor restoration, 24–29
Fountain project, 182–86
Front doors. *See* Doors
Furnaces, DIY fixes, 112–14
Furniture, renewal of wood finish, 14–15

G

Garage doors
  finger-scan openers, 94
  rotting trim replacement, 261
  rusty door tracks, 262
  screens, 264
  weatherseal replacement, 262
Garages
  bump-out addition, 240–46
  car care caddy, 256–60
  heating/lighting, 263
  wall organization system, 226–31
Gardens. *See* Landscaping
Garden trowel, 208
Generators, 96
GFCI (ground fault circuit interrupter) outlets, 79, 86
Glass cabinet doors, 66–67
Gloves, nitrile, 251
Goofs, 36–37, 81, 115, 274–77
Granite countertops, installation of, 52–55
Grinders, 42–44
Grout
  haze removal, 20, 57
  regrouting shower, 38–41

H

Handrails, outdoor, 168–70
Hardware, paint removal, 13
Heated floors, 68–72
Hinge screws, stripped, 11
Holiday lights, testing, 88

I

Insulation
  attics, 46–48
  removal of fibers from skin and clothes, 20

J

Jump-starting tips/tools, 237, 238

K

Keyless locks, 11
Kitchens
  countertop gap filler, 24
  granite countertop installation, 52–55
  layout plans, 20
  sink cabinet renewal, 22
  tile countertop installation, 59

L

Ladders, 140, 167
Landscaping
 archway project, 172–75
 fountain project, 182–86
 planter project, 203–7
 rain gardens, 217–20
 raised garden bed
  project, 224
 storage bench project,
  187–91
 tools, 208–9
 vinyl fence installation,
  192–98
Laundry room
 makeover, 60–64
Lawn care
 crabgrass, 178–81, 200
 fertilizing/weed killing,
  202, 210, 221
 product storage, 199
 tips, 200–202

Leaks, plumbing, 102–5
Light
 bulbs, CFLs, 89–93
 switch, 94
Locks
 keyless, 10
 lubricating, 11
Lounge chair project,
  132–35
Lubricants, 11, 22

M

MAF (Mass Air Flow)
 sensors, cleaning, 251
Magnetic paint, 50
Motor oil
 filling tips, 236
 storage of used, 250
Mowing height, 201
Mulching, 200, 202

O

Oil
 filling tips, 236
 storage of used, 250
Outdoor faucets
 easy-off hose, 141
  installation, 156–58
  leaks, 150

Outdoor furniture
 lounge chair project,
  132–35
 wood protection, 159
Outdoor handrails, 168–70
Outdoor shelter project,
  223
Outdoor sinks, 209

P

Paint and painting
 of baseboards, 50
 of block walls, 176
 bucket caddy, 23
 choosing colors, 15
 clean paint-can rim
  tool, 50
 of exterior doors, 150
 magnetic paint, 50
 project reminder
  notes, 24
 roller covers, 23, 51
 spray paint booth, 24
 spray paint caddy, 24
 storage overnight, 51
 of stucco, 149
 tips, 16–19
 waterproofing product,
  57
Path, garden, 223
Patio pavers, raising
  sunken, 161
Pest control, 148–49, 166
PEX systems, 108–11
Phone ring amplifiers, 81
Pipes, soldering copper,
  116–17
Planter project, 203–7

Plumbing
 bathtub/shower
  leaks, 104–5
 laundry room project,
  60–64
 PEX systems, 108–11
 shower faucet
  installation, 98–101

Plumbing, cont.
 sink leaks, 102–3
 sink replacement,
  118–20
 tips, 107
 toilet flange leaks, 106
 water heater vents, 97
 water supply leaks, 103
Pressure washers, 152, 155
Projects. *See* Woodworking
  projects
Push box, 125

R

Raccoons, 166
Rain gardens, 217–20
Raised garden bed, 224
Recessed lighting, 48
Remote controls, 88
Rim joists, insulation of, 65
Roofs
 safety tips, 162
 tear-off process, 162–66
 tool bucket, 141
 tool grips, 141
 when to replace, 166

S

Sanding
 flashing shield for, 124
 pencil lines to mark, 125
Screen doors, retractable,
  167

Scuffs, removal from vinyl
    floors, 20
Shed project, 222
Showers
    faucet installation, 98–101
    leaks, 104–5
    regrouting, 38–41
    tiling project, 31–35
Siding, replacement of, 160
Sinks
    leaks, 102–3
    outdoor, 209
    replacement, 118–20
    trap removal, 208
Siphon, 107
Sliding doors, sticking
    problem, 12
Soldering, copper pipes,
    116–17

Spark plug replacement,
    232–33, 239
Sprayers, garden, 210
Spray paint booth and
    caddy, 24
Spreaders, broadcast, 221
Sprinkler systems, 142–47,
    199
Stain
    for decks, 155
    mixer for, 22
Stone path/step project,
    223
Storage bench project,
    187–91

Stripped hinge screws, 11
Stucco, repainting, 149
Switches,
    outdoor, 94
    wireless, 78

T

Tile
    countertops, 59
    cutting, 42–44
    floors, 59
    grout haze removal,
        20, 57
    regrouting, 38–41
    shower project, 31–35
Tires
    fixing leaky valve
        stem, 253
    rotation of, 236
Toilets, leaks, 106

Tools
    cleaning, 23
    grinders, 42–44
    landscaping, 208–9
    roof work, 141
    storage caddy for,
        256–60
Trailer hitches,
    removing stuck, 250
Transmission fluid
    replacement, 248–49,
    251
Trees, trimming, 209
Trimwork, painting, 17–18
Triple-glazed windows, 58
Trunk lid tie-down, 247
TVs, signal boosters, 79

V

Video signal
    amplifiers, 79
Vinyl fence installation,
    192–98
Vinyl siding, replacement
    of, 160

W

Wasps, 148
Water heaters
    leaks, 103
    vents, 97
Waterproofing paint, 57
Water wand sprayer, 220
Weatherstripping, 49
Wheelbarrows, 208–9
Windows
    films for, 56
    lubricating, 11
    triple-glazed option, 58
Windshield glass treat-
    ment, 237
Windshield washer repair,
    234–35
Wiring. See Electrical
Wood filler, homemade, 124
Wood floors, restoration of,
    24–29
Wood furniture, renewal of
    finish, 14–15
Woodpeckers, 148

Woodworking projects
    bathroom reading
        rack, 138
    bookcase, 126–31
    car care caddy, 256–60
    charging station, 136–37
    cutting board, 122
    lounge chair, 132–35
    planter, 203–7
    storage bench, 187–91
    workbench, 123
Workbench project, 123
Work light, rechargeable,
    264

ACKNOWLEDGMENTS

FOR THE FAMILY HANDYMAN

Editor in Chief	Ken Collier
Senior Editors	Travis Larson
	Gary Wentz
Associate Editors	Jeff Gorton
	Eric Smith
Assistant Editor	Brett Martin
Senior Copy Editor	Donna Bierbach
Design Director	Sara Koehler
Senior Art Director	Bob Ungar
Art Directors	Becky Pfluger
	Marcia Roepke
Office Administrative	
Manager	Alice Garrett
Financial Assistant	Steven Charbonneau
Technical Manager	Keith Kostman
Reader Service Specialist	Roxie Filipkowski
Production Manager	Judy Rodriguez
Production Artist	Lisa Pahl

CONTRIBUTING EDITORS

Lucie B. Amundsen   Jeff Timm
Kurt Anderson   Bruce Wiebe
Joe Hurst-Wajszczuk

CONTRIBUTING ART DIRECTORS

Kristi Anderson   David Simpson
Evangeline Ekberg

PHOTOGRAPHERS

Tate Carlson
Mike Krivit, Krivit Photography
Ramon Moreno
Shawn Nielsen, Nielsen Photography
Bill Zuehlke

ILLUSTRATORS

Steve Björkman   Bruce Kieffer
Gabe De Matteis   Don Mannes
Roy Doty   Paul Perreault
Mario Ferro   Frank Rohrbach III
John Hartman

OTHER CONSULTANTS

Charles Avoles, plumbing
Al Hildenbrand, electrical
Jon Jensen, carpentry
Bruce Kieffer, woodworking
Bob Lacivita, automotive
Dave MacDonald, structural engineer
Costas Stavrou, appliance repair
John Williamson, electrical
Butch Zang, painting and wallpapering
Les Zell, plumbing

For information about advertising in
The Family Handyman magazine, call (212) 850-7226

To subscribe to *The Family Handyman* magazine:
- By phone: (800) 285-4961
- By Internet: FHMservice@rd.com
- By mail: The Family Handyman
                     Subscriber Service Dept.
                     P.O. Box 8174
                     Red Oak, IA 51591-1174

We welcome your ideas and opinions.
Write: The Editor, The Family Handyman
2915 Commers Drive, Suite 700
Eagan, MN 55121
Fax: (651) 994-2250
E-mail: fheditor@readersdigest.com

Photocopies of articles are available for $3.00 each. Call (715) 246-4521 from 8 a.m. to 5 p.m. Central, Monday through Friday or send an e-mail to familyhandyman@nrmsinc.com. Visa, MasterCard and Discover accepted.

CELTIC CROSS STITCH

30 Alphabet, Animal, and
Knotwork Projects

GAIL LAWTHER

THE READER'S DIGEST ASSOCIATION, INC.
Pleasantville, New York/Montreal

A READER'S DIGEST BOOK

Edited and produced by David & Charles Publishers
Photography by Di Lewis
Book design by Christopher Lawther

Library of Congress Cataloging in Publication Data
Reader's Digest and the Pegasus logo are trademarks of The Reader's Digest Association, Inc.

Lawther, Gail, 1995.
    Celtic cross stitch : 30 alphabet, animal, and knotwork projects /
Gail Lawther.
        p.   cm.
    Includes bibliographical references and index.
    ISBN 0-89577-859-9
    1. Cross-stitch—Patterns. 2. Decoration and ornament, Celtic.
I. Title.
TT778.C766L392   1996
746.44'3041—dc20   95-25749

Printed in Italy by New Interlitho SpA

CONTENTS

Introduction   7

KNOTS AND PATTERNS   13

Cross Bookmark   14

Trinket Box   16

Knotwork Greeting Cards   18

Decorated Hand Towel   20

Doll's House Rug   22

Placemats and Napkins   24

Celtic Jewelry   26

Knotwork Picture   28

Embroidered Christening Gown 30

Square Pillow   32

ANIMALS AND PEOPLE   37

Horse Card and Picture   38

Baby's Bib   40

Peacock Vest   42

Lion Picture   46

Serpent Pincushion   48

Stained-Glass Angel   51

Rooster Sweatshirt   54

Curtain Tiebacks   56

Horseman Picture   60

Celtic Rug   64

LETTERING   69

Initial Cards   70

Stitched Nameplate   78

Pincushion and Needle Case   80

Bright Sampler   86

Noel Christmas Decoration   90

Wedding Initials   92

Initial Pictures   100

Tie and Handkerchief   107

Versal Sampler   109

Illuminated Initial   112

PATTERN LIBRARY   115

Knots   115

Knotwork Borders   118

Fret and Key Patterns   120

Animals   122

Letterforms   124

Acknowledgments   127

Suppliers   127

Index   128

INTRODUCTION

When we see a particular kind of interweaving knotwork pattern, we immediately recognize it as a Celtic design, but who were the Celts and why has their art been so influential? "Celtic" usually describes the peoples of western Europe who spoke – or speak – languages similar to those of the ancient Gauls: Breton, Cornish, Welsh, Irish, Manx, and Gaelic. Several Scandinavian countries are also rich sources of Celtic art.

The Celtic period of history is even harder to define, partly because it occurred in different countries or regions at different times. The roots of Celtic art and patterns lie in traditional Anglo-Saxon designs; the jewelry found at Sutton Hoo, an archeological site in Suffolk, England, dates from pre-Christian times but shows knotwork animal patterns similar to the ones associated with later Celtic art. The style found its real flowering, though, in religious books, carvings, and artifacts as Christianity swept across pagan western Europe. Celtic art began in Ireland in the fifth and sixth centuries and continued until at least the ninth century, providing us with a wonderful visual record of the period at the end of the Dark Ages.

MOTIFS IN CELTIC ART

The motifs of Celtic art are many and varied. The wonderful interweaving knots are famous, of course, and were especially popular with Celtic artists, but many other patterns were also worked. Key and fret designs were frequently used, and their borders and panels were often elaborate mixtures of squares, circles, and rectangles. In addition to these, animal and bird forms, both realistic and fantastic, occured

Horse Card and Picture (see page 38)

frequently, while humans and angels were very often the subjects of illuminations.

The letters themselves are rich inspirations for modern artists. The letterforms range from relatively simple uncial and half-uncial forms used for text in books to the opulence of richly illuminated initial letters – sometimes so large they almost fill a page.

For the projects I have taken inspiration from all these different sources, building them into a wide variety of items ranging from samplers and monograms to pincushions, rugs, cards, and pictures. Like Celtic art itself, some of my designs are realistic, while others are highly stylized.

COLORS

There is no such thing as a typical Celtic color scheme; Celtic artists had an instinctive color sense, which included unlikely combinations as well as those we would consider harmonious. A flip through a book of facsimiles of Celtic illuminations takes you from subtle pastels placed side by side through rich, dark combinations of red, brown, and ocher, to lurid yellow/green/red/black mixtures and rainbow combinations of purple/green/red/yellow/jade/pink/orange and blue. Sometimes the colors used are pure and bright; at other times they are toned down by the addition of gray or brown or diluted to pastels with white or beige.

To represent these varied styles in Celtic art, I have chosen many different color schemes. For example, the Initial Cards on page 70 use bright color schemes taken directly from their inspiration, the *Book of Kells*, and the Horseman Picture on page 60 uses a wide range of impure colors, matching the realistic style of the figure and the horse.

ADAPTING THE DESIGNS FOR CROSS STITCH

The flowing lines of most Celtic designs are quite a challenge for the cross-stitch designer because they have to flow realistically while being worked on a regular grid! This is especially difficult for some of the letters, since they rely on carefully weighted and angled lines for their attractiveness. The great benefit, though, is that some of the designs, especially the regular knots, such as the Doll's House Rug on page 22, can be worked out first on a simple formula and then adapted easily to fit a larger, smaller, or differently proportioned rectangle.

If you want to try to work out your own Celtic designs or vary the ones in the book, begin with a simple knot and make a few adaptations. For instance, the example below is very straightforward but lends itself to all kinds of variations once you have worked out the correct relationship of the interweaving lines. Make sure you keep this relationship constant; then you can play around with the shape, size, and number of strands almost ad infinitum, just on one simple knot design!

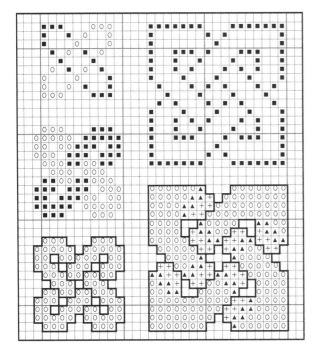

CROSS-STITCH TIPS

If you are an experienced cross-stitcher, you will already have all the skills needed to tackle the projects in this book. If you are a beginner, you will find some of the larger projects more challenging than the smaller, simpler ones, but they should all be within your scope if you follow a few basic guidelines.

Some people prefer to work both parts of each stitch – the bottom diagonal stitch and then the top one – before they move on to the next stitch.

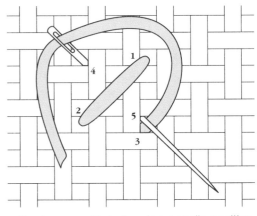

Single cross stitch showing needle position

Others prefer to stitch a row or a column of half-stitches before working their way back along the row and crossing with the top stitches. Either of these ways is satisfactory – there is no "correct" way to stitch – so choose the method you prefer. If you are a beginner, experiment with both techniques and see which gives you the most even tension; the stitches should lie flat so the threads are not distorted, and they should not pull the fabric out of shape.

The main thing to remember is that the top stitch of each cross should always be in the same direction, so that the finished work has an even texture and the stitches all catch the light the same way. While you are stitching, especially if you are working on a large project with lots of repetitive movements, you may find

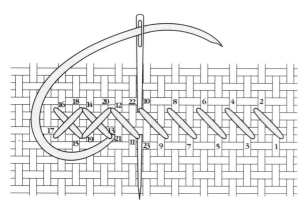

Partly completed stitches – completed on
return journey

that your thread becomes tightly twisted and
keeps knotting back on itself. If this happens,
simply let the needle and thread hang down
loosely from the work so that it can untwist
itself. If you have the opposite problem, and
your thread keeps becoming untwisted so the
strands separate, just make a small twist with
your needle every few stitches so that the
thread maintains a better texture.

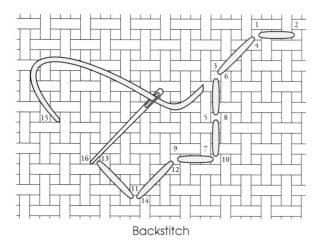

Backstitch

WORKING BACKSTITCH OUTLINES

In addition to cross stitch, you will also need
backstitch for working outlines on some of the
charts. Backstitch outlining is worked by

stitching single backstitches, the width or height
of one cross stitch, around all or some of the
sides of specified cross stitches.

MATERIALS

Cross stitch is generally worked on some kind
of even-weave fabric, which is a fabric that
has strong threads running vertically and
horizontally, with obvious holes between the
threads. Even-weave fabrics are described as
being so many holes per inch (hpi) or threads
(or thread groups) per inch, and vary from fine
fabrics, such as linen and silk gauze, which may
be 25–30 hpi, or threads per inch, to very
coarse fabrics, such as binca, which is often
6 hpi. Because there are obvious holes in
even-weave fabrics, you don't need a sharp
needle – in fact, a sharp needle is a definite
disadvantage because it may split the threads
when you are trying to find the right hole. On
these fabrics, tapestry needles are used; they
come in different sizes, from very fine (sizes
26–28) to very large (sizes 16–18), and have
rounded tips. Each project specifies either a
fine, medium, or large tapestry needle; I have
not specified an exact size, because this is very
much a matter of personal preference.

Other even-weave backgrounds are suitable
for cross stitch. Ordinary canvas is satisfactory
but has the disadvantage of being transparent,
so that you have to cover the whole area that
will show with stitching; with even-weave fabric
such as Aida cloth, you only need to stitch the
design. Cross-stitch paper is also on the market
and is available in a variety of colors; it is best
for small projects, such as Christmas
decorations or cards, because it is not very
durable and becomes worn if you are stitching
on one piece for a long time. Plastic canvas is
available in several gauges and colors; it has a
firm mesh that can be built up into 3-D shapes.

If you want to stitch a cross-stitch pattern
onto a fabric that is not even-weave, such as a

sweatshirt or a T-shirt, you can use the method known as waste canvas. Waste canvas looks like conventional canvas; you cut out a piece and baste it onto your chosen background fabric, then stitch the design over the threads of the canvas and through the background simultaneously. You must have a sharp-tipped needle, such as a crewel needle, for this technique. When the design is complete, dampen the threads of the waste canvas to dissolve the glue holding it to the background fabric; it can then be withdrawn from behind the stitching, leaving the cross-stitch design behind.

YARNS AND THREADS

Cross stitch can be done in virtually any thread as long as you choose the right background, but some threads are more versatile than others. Stranded embroidery floss is always a favorite because it comes in so many shades and can be used in several different thicknesses; pearl cotton has a pleasant sheen and is good for projects that don't require a fine thread. Flower thread is a matte, fine, single-strand cotton thread. Marlitt is a viscose thread that is very shiny but also very slippery; it can be used in several different thicknesses. Many metallic threads are available; some are more successful than others for cross stitch, but if you treat them carefully, it is usually possible to adapt them; they also look good mixed with embroidery floss to provide sparkle. Matte embroidery cotton, tapestry yarn, knitting yarns, and other thick yarns can also be used successfully for cross stitch on larger-gauge backgrounds.

Each project is accompanied by a chart where you will find a color key for the threads used. It is assumed that you will buy one skein of each color listed (although less may be used), unless the key specifies more skeins. Each chart key gives both Anchor and DMC colors; generally these can be intermingled unless the project specifies otherwise.

EXTRA EQUIPMENT

As well as needles, threads, and fabrics, you will also need the usual extra equipment you probably have in your sewing basket: a thimble, if you like using one; small, sharp scissors; a tape measure; and larger scissors for trimming.

FINDING THE STARTING POINT

The best point to start stitching depends largely on the shape of the finished embroidery. It is often wise to begin in the center, working the stitch from the middle of the chart first. In the following projects arrows have been added to the charts which should be started in this way to indicate where the central stitch is. This stitch should be worked in the middle of your fabric. To find this point, fold the fabric in half, and then into quarters. Pinch the folds gently to make light creases and then unfold the cloth again. Mark the point where the creases intersect, using one of the methods described below.

Where it is easier to begin a particular design at one edge, instructions have been given to show you how to find the starting point.

MARKING METHODS

One very useful piece of equipment is a water-soluble pen that makes turquoise marks on the background fabric. The marks disappear when they are wetted, making this pen ideal for marking positions, especially the center point, on your fabrics before stitching. When you dampen the fabric to make the marks disappear, don't iron it until the fabric is completely dry; otherwise you may get brown blotches where the pen marks have been. Fading pens are also available, which make purple marks that disappear in daylight, but the marks last only about 24 hours, which can be frustrating if you need a mark on the fabric to last longer! You can also use basting lines to mark the center point if you prefer.

HOOPS AND FRAMES

If you like using a hoop or frame and find that your tension tends to pull a little too tight without, by all means use one, but there is generally no need to. The background fabric rarely pulls out of shape if you keep the tension of your stitches even. If the fabric is not quite square when you have finished stitching the design, simply dampen the fabric, pull it into shape, then iron on the back with a steam iron.

PRESSING CROSS STITCH

When pressing your completed cross stitch or any other embroidery, lay the design face down on a soft surface, such as a light-colored towel, and iron from the back; this prevents the stitching from being squashed. If you have used a water-soluble pen on a project, it is safe to iron on a steam setting if you have let the fabric dry completely, after sponging out the marks.

USING THE CHARTS

Each square on each chart represents one cross stitch worked in the color specified on the key for that particular square. A thick line around part of a square represents one backstitch, also worked in the color specified on the key. So the chart shown below results in the piece of stitching that is shown next to it.

Each project carries a design size and stitch count at the beginning. The design size describes the dimensions of the finished design when it is stitched on the specified fabric. The stitch count gives the number of stitches across the width and height of the design.

If you want to adapt the design to a smaller or larger gauge of fabric, the stitch count will enable you to work out exactly how much fabric you need. Remember, though, that you may need to adjust the thickness and amount of the threads needed if you are working the design on a larger or a smaller scale.

FRAMING

A wide range of picture frames are available commercially and their method of assembly varies dramatically. However, the following advice should be relevant for most frames.

First take the frame apart. The backing board, which makes up the reverse of the picture frame when it is assembled, may be simply a strong piece of card or it may be adhesive on one side. When you have ironed your work, press it onto the adhesive side of the board, making sure it is straight. Trim the edges of the fabric, and then assemble the frame once again. If the backing board it not adhesive, you will need to stretch your fabric over a strong piece of card (the backing board itself may be too flimsy). To do this, lay the embroidery face down and place the card on top. Fold one of the longer sides of the fabric over the card and push T-pins lightly into the edge of the card. Hold the work taut and repeat this on the opposite side, then on the other edges. Taking a length of strong thread and starting at the center of one side, make long stitches across the back of the board, lacing one edge of the fabric to the other. Repeat this process with the other two edges. Finally, reassemble the frame.

KEY

DMC 961	Anchor 76	+ Dark pink
DMC 3716	Anchor 75	▲ Mid-pink
DMC 818	Anchor 48	O Light pink
DMC 550	Anchor 102	− Purple

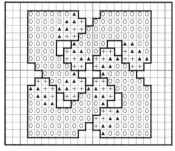

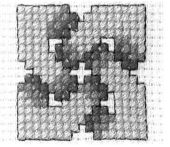

KNOTS AND PATTERNS

The 10 projects in this section all feature patterns based on Celtic designs. Knotwork designs are what many people think of first when they picture Celtic art: lines of jewel-bright colors or softer pastels continuously intertwining. Knots in Celtic art vary from simple twists through more complex braids and borders to elaborate carpet pages – whole pages in illuminated manuscripts dedicated to labyrinthine interweavings.

The Celts believed that the lines of knotwork showed the twist, flow, and complexity of life, and that the knot created from a single line echoed eternity. Celtic artists made the knotwork designs fit into any available space; the benefit of the undulating lines is that they can be made to meander in any direction! From only one or two separate lines, elaborate borders can be built up and made to go around corners or to fit into cross shapes or T-shapes.

The knotwork patterns in the following projects follow that tradition and feature circles, rectangles, squares, diamonds, triangles, borders, and quarter circles in both simple and complex patterns.

Spirals, too, were very popular with the Celts – they liked the movement and flow in their patterns. They also favored key and fret patterns, and ornamental designs similar to Greek patterns, or upright zigzags that generally fit into squares; the squares can be joined in repeat patterns or borders or fitted into stepped pyramids. Spirals and fret patterns are featured in the jewelry designs on page 26 and also appear on pages 120–121 in the Pattern Library.

CROSS BOOKMARK

eltic cross designs range from the simple to the elaborate – sometimes built up from knots or spirals, sometimes incorporating animals or birds. This design was based on a cross cut in marble in the old cathedral at Chur, Switzerland; although the knot looks complex, it is actually a fairly simple repeat.

Stitch count: 131 x 71
Design size: 6 x 3 in (15 x 7.5 cm)

MATERIALS
- One piece of white Aida or other even-weave fabric, 22 hpi, 10 x 6 in (25 x 15 cm)
- Stranded embroidery floss: green
- Fine tapestry needle

WORKING THE DESIGN
1 Press the fabric and fold it in half down the length to find the center line; mark this with a water-soluble pen.
2 Measure $1^{1}/_{2}$ in (4 cm) from the top of the fabric down the marked line. Mark this point with the water-soluble pen; this is where you will begin your stitching. The corresponding center line of the design is indicated with arrows on the chart.
3 Using only one strand of embroidery floss in the needle, work three cross stitches side by side, so that the middle one falls on the center line at your marked point. These three stitches are the ones at the center top of the charted design.
4 Continue working the stitches following the chart, using one strand of floss throughout. Keep checking that the lines of stitches match across the central line so that you will know if you have miscounted at any stage.
5 When the embroidery is complete, sponge away the water-soluble pen marks. Allow it to dry, then press on the back (see page 10).
6 Using sharp scissors, cut any excess fabric away from the top and sides of the embroidery to within six threads of the stitching. Cut the bottom $1^{1}/_{2}$ in (4 cm) down from the stitching. Fray three double threads away from each edge of the bookmark and press again on the reverse side.

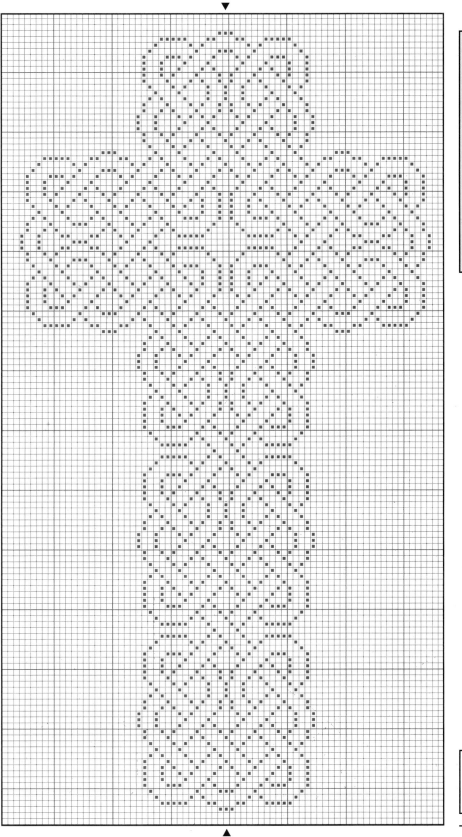

VARIATION
If you prefer a simpler cross design, you can try the more straightforward one on page 116 of the Pattern Library, filling in the central parts with a paler color.

KEY
DMC 699
Anchor 923 ■ Green

TRINKET BOX

This pretty circular design can be used on a square or circular trinket-box base; stitch it in the colorway shown here, or choose your own colors to fit in with your bedroom.

Stitch count: 57 x 57
Design size: 4¼ x 4¼ in (11 x 11 cm)

MATERIALS

For a box with a 4³/4–5¹/2 in (12–14 cm) square or circular opening, you will need:

- One piece of pale turquoise damask Aida, 14 hpi, 8 x 8 in (20 x 20 cm)
- Stranded embroidery floss in the colors given in the key
- Medium tapestry needle

WORKING THE DESIGN

1 Fold the square of fabric in half and then in quarters. Where the folds intersect is the center of the fabric square. Mark this point with a water-soluble pen (see page 10).

2 Using two strands of purple and beginning at the center of the design, which is indicated on the chart by arrows, follow the dark squares on the chart to work all of the purple outline stitches of the knot.

3 Use the purple to stitch the small patterns at the corners of the design.

4 Using two strands of turquoise floss, fill in the inside parts of the knot; because you have worked all the outlines, you should not need to count the squares.

5 Sponge away the water-soluble pen marks and allow the fabric to dry completely. Lay the completed embroidery face down on a soft surface and press it (see page 10).

6 Depending on the box that you are using, the exact way of inserting the embroidery into it will differ; follow the instructions that come with the box you buy.

KEY

| DMC 552 | Anchor 101 | ■ Purple |
| DMC 3761 | Anchor 9159 | O Turquoise |

VARIATION

You can stitch this design at different sizes to suit the different sizes of trinket boxes on the market. Choose your box first, then see what gauge of fabric you need in order to fit the design into the aperture (see page 11).

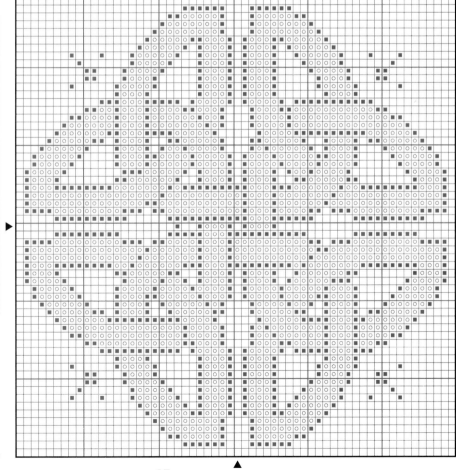

KNOTWORK GREETING CARDS

Two very different knotwork designs appear on these cards. The bright heraldic design would suit any occasion; the fan shape incorporates a heart and would be particularly suitable for a wedding, anniversary, or Valentine card.

Stitch count: Pink fan card, 47 x 31
Multicolored card, 57 x 57
Design size: Pink fan card: 4 x 3 in (10 x 7.5 cm)
Multicolored card: 4 x 4in (10 x 10cm)

MATERIALS

For the multicolored card, you will need:
- One piece of cream Aida, 14 hpi, 10 x 10 in (25 x 25 cm)
- Stranded embroidery floss in the colors given in the key
- One spool of fine turquoise metallic thread, such as Gütermann or Kreinik
- Fine tapestry needle
- Large pale jade card mount with an opening at least 7 x 7 in (18 x 18 cm)

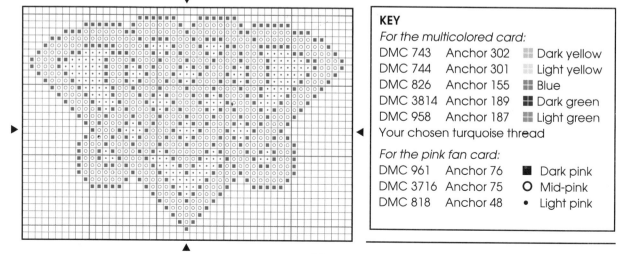

KEY
For the multicolored card:

DMC 743	Anchor 302	▦ Dark yellow
DMC 744	Anchor 301	▦ Light yellow
DMC 826	Anchor 155	▦ Blue
DMC 3814	Anchor 189	▦ Dark green
DMC 958	Anchor 187	▦ Light green

Your chosen turquoise thread

For the pink fan card:

DMC 961	Anchor 76	■ Dark pink
DMC 3716	Anchor 75	O Mid-pink
DMC 818	Anchor 48	• Light pink

For the pink fan card, you will need:
- One piece of cream Aida, 11 hpi, 7 x 6 in (18 x 15 cm)
- Stranded embroidery floss in the colors given in the key
- Medium tapestry needle
- One small piece of thin batting
- Large pale pink card mount with a quarter-circle aperture

WORKING THE DESIGNS
To make the multicolored card:

1 Fold the square of Aida in half and then into quarters, pressing gently. Unfold it and mark the point where the folds intersect (see page 10). This is the center of the fabric and corresponds with the central square of the chart, which is indicated with arrows.

2 Using two strands of floss for all the cross stitches, stitch the design in the appropriate colors, working outwards from the center.

3 Using one strand of turquoise metallic thread, outline the edges of the design with backstitch (see page 9) as marked on the chart.

To make the pink fan card:

1 Fold the fabric in half and press gently. Measure 1¹/2 in (4 cm) up from the bottom, along the fold, and mark this point. (see page 10). Begin your stitching here; this point corresponds to the tip of the fan on the chart.

2 Using three strands of floss, stitch the design in the appropriate colors, following the chart.

Press the embroidery, having removed the pen marks (see page 10). Follow the instructions on page 71 to make it into a card. Place batting behind the Aida when assembling the pink fan card.

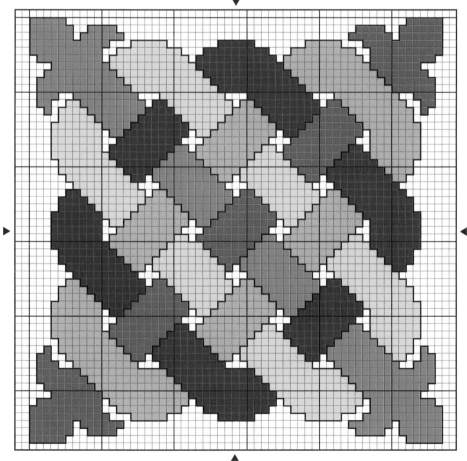

VARIATIONS
The fan design can be stitched in colors other than pink; try it in royal colors with a fine gold backstitch (see page 9) around the edges. The design is created from one line; for an unusual effect, try shading subtly from one color to another as you work around the knot.

DECORATED HAND TOWEL

T he distinctive knotwork border designs are some of the most attractive features of Celtic art; this hand towel makes use of a complex knot in two colors.

Stitch count: 35 deep
Design size: 2$1/2$ in (6.5 cm) deep

MATERIALS
- One maroon hand towel with a band specially made for working cross stitch: The stitching band on the towel should be at least 35 squares deep in order for this design to fit onto it.
- Stranded embroidery floss in the colors given in the key
- Medium tapestry needle

WORKING THE DESIGN
1 Fold the towel in half vertically to find the center, press and then mark the line with water-soluble pen. This indicates the center of your border.

2 Count to find the center of your stitching band from top to bottom and mark this point on your vertical fold. This indicates the exact center of your first motif.

3 Using three strands of embroidery floss for all the cross stitches, follow the chart to stitch the pink and blue portions of one whole motif. The horizontal center line is shown by arrows on the chart.

4 Stitch as many whole repeats of the motif as you can fit in each side of the central one; each repeat takes 24 stitches widthwise.

5 Finish off the pink and blue lines of stitching with the decorative finials shown on the chart; each finial requires nine stitches widthwise, so make sure you have space after your final motifs.

6 Using two strands of maroon floss, work backstitches (see page 9) over each of the lines marked on the chart – the places where the knotwork lines cross themselves or each other.

7 When all the stitching is complete, press the embroidery from the back (see page 10).

VARIATIONS

Try using one of the other border patterns from the Pattern Library on pages 118–119 to decorate your towels; work a narrow one on the smaller towels and a more complex one on wide Aida bands for large bath towels.

If you do not want to use a towel with a section woven in for cross stitch, you can buy one of the specially made Aida bands and work your design onto that. The bands come in several different colors, widths, and styles.

If you prefer a subtler look, work both of the knotwork lines in the same color and show where they overlap with the backstitches.

KEY

DMC 813	Anchor 977	● Light blue
DMC 604	Anchor 60	+ Pink
DMC 3803	Anchor 43	– Maroon

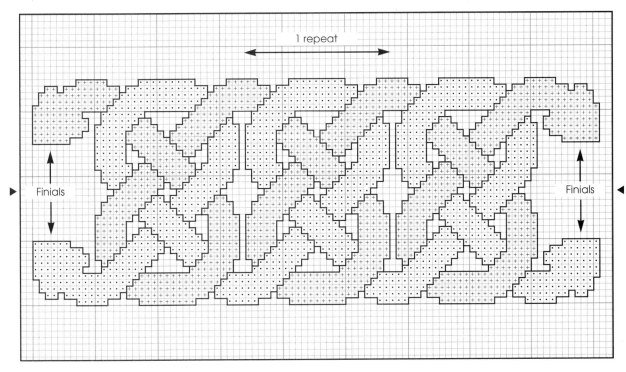

1 repeat

Finials

Finials

DOLL'S HOUSE RUG

C eltic designs can be used to decorate not only your own house, but also a doll's house; this miniature rug will be just the right size. The tiny cross stitches, similar to petit point, produce a firm, hardwearing texture, and the ends of the fabric are frayed to make the fringes of the rug.

Stitch count: 61 x 45
Design size: 3¹/₄ x 2¹/₄ in (8.5 x 6 cm)

MATERIALS

- One piece of cream Aida, 22 hpi, 6 x 4³/₄ in (15 x 12 cm)
- One piece of iron-on interfacing, 3¹/₂ x 2¹/₂ in (8.5 x 6 cm)
- Stranded embroidery floss in the colors given in the key
- Fine tapestry needle

WORKING THE DESIGN

1 Fold the Aida in half lengthwise and press lightly to mark the fold. Then fold it in half widthwise and press. Mark these lines with a water-soluble pen; they will be the center lines of your design.

2 Using one strand of dark blue, work the stitches outlining the knot, beginning at the center of the chart (indicated by arrows) and fabric and working outward.

3 Using one strand of light blue, fill in all the areas inside the knot outlines.

4 Using one strand of cream, fill in all the

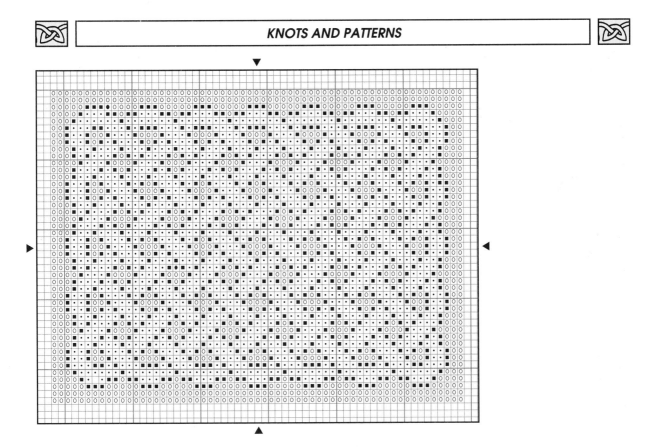

background areas within the pattern and outside it as marked on the chart.

5 When the embroidery is complete, spray or sponge the fabric to remove the pen marks. Leave it to dry completely. Trim the fabric to ¹/₂ in (1 cm) beyond the stitching all around the edges of the design. Fray the top and bottom edges of the rectangle, up to the stitching, by removing the horizontal threads.

6 Lay the embroidery face down and fold the excess fabric on the sides to the back of the embroidery. Position the rectangle of fusible stiffening fabric, adhesive side down, over the back of the embroidery and fuse it in place with a hot iron.

PRACTICAL TIP
When you are ironing the stiffening fabric onto the back of the rug, simply lay the hot iron on top of the fabric and press down; if you use the usual forward-and-backward ironing motion, the fabric may pucker.

KEY

DMC 809	Anchor 175	•	Light blue
DMC 797	Anchor 177	■	Dark blue
DMC Ecru	Anchor 885	0	Cream

VARIATIONS
If blue and cream do not match the decor of your doll's house, pick out colors from your carpet or curtains and work the chart in those. Use a darker and lighter version of the same color for the knot itself or combine two different ones, such as blue and peach, green and beige, orange and pale green.

To change the feel of the rug radically, work the knot in pale and medium shades of one color, and the background in a darker color, such as charcoal, navy, or burgundy; this will look particularly effective if you have a period doll's house.

PLACEMATS AND NAPKINS

$\boxed{A}$ cornerpiece from a richly illuminated letter "B" was the inspiration for this right-angled knot. The design is worked on an even-weave fabric with 28 threads to the inch (2.5 cm), but it can just as easily be worked on a piece of Hardanger or Aida at different sizes.

Stitch count: 49 x 49
Design size: $5^1/2$ x $5^1/2$ in (14 x 14 cm)

MATERIALS

For a set comprising one placemat and one napkin, you will need:

- Two pieces of pale green even-weave fabric, 28 hpi; one rectangle measuring 20 x 15 in (50 x 38 cm) and one square measuring 15 x 15 in (38 x 38 cm)
- Matching sewing thread
- Flower thread in the colors given in the key
- Medium tapestry needle

WORKING THE DESIGN

1 Turn under and press a small double hem around each piece of fabric, then sew by hand or machine. It is best to do this before you start the embroidery, partly to stop the fabric from fraying and partly so that you can make sure the design is positioned evenly on each piece. Press the hemmed pieces before stitching.

2 Measure $2^3/4$ in (7 cm) diagonally in from the top right and bottom left corners of the

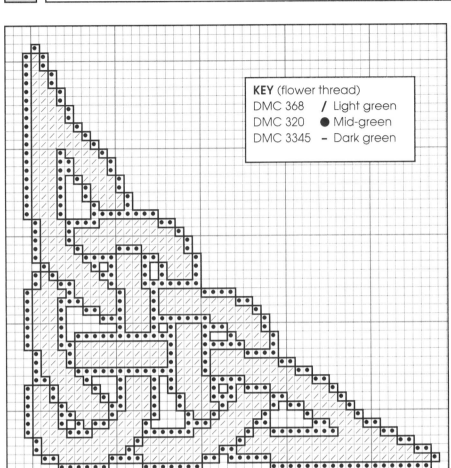

KEY (flower thread)
DMC 368   / Light green
DMC 320   ● Mid-green
DMC 3345   − Dark green

placemat and from one corner of the napkin. Mark the place with a dot of water-soluble pen and use these marks as guides for the corners of your designs.

3 Using one strand of flower thread across three threads of the background fabric, stitch the outline crosses of the design in mid-green. Fill in the areas marked inside the knot design with crosses in pale green.

4 Using one strand of dark green, work around the outside edges of the outline stitches in backstitch (see page 9). Make each backstitch across the width of one cross stitch − that is, across three threads of background fabric each time.

5 When the designs are complete, remove the dots from the water-soluble pen with a dab of

water. Let the fabric dry completely. Then lay the mat and napkin face down on a soft cloth and press the designs on the back with a steam iron (see page 10).

PRACTICAL TIP
If the fabric of your table linen is not even-weave, use waste canvas (see page 10) as a stitching guide for your cornerpieces.

VARIATIONS
Because the knot fits so well into a right angle, use the design for the corner of a bag, curtain, pillow, or any kind of table linen.

CELTIC JEWELRY

Rich colors and the addition of gold thread give these simple jewelry designs the opulence of gilded illuminations. The pendant is stitched directly onto a prepunched metal blank manufactured especially for cross stitch; the brooch is stitched on a fine even-weave fabric.

Stitch count: For the brooch, 21 x 29
Design size: For the brooch, 1³/₄ x 1¹/₄ in (4.5 x 3 cm)

MATERIALS

For the pendant, you will need:
- One gold-plated jewelry pendant for cross-stitching
- Stranded embroidery floss in the colors given in the key
- One spool of gold embroidery thread, such as Gütermann metallic 24
- Medium tapestry needle

For the brooch, you will need:
- One gilt oval brooch for cross stitching, approximately 2 x 1¹/₂ in (5 x 4 cm)
- One piece of white Aida, 18 hpi, approximately 4 in (10 cm) square

- Stranded embroidery floss in the color given in the key
- One spool of gold embroidery thread such as Gütermann metallic 24
- Fine tapestry needle

WORKING THE DESIGNS

To make the pendant:
1 Using three strands of embroidery floss, follow the chart to stitch the design on the metal pendant in blue and jade.
2 Using two strands of gold thread, work backstitch (see page 9) around the edges of the knot as shown on the chart.

To make the brooch:
1 Fold the square of Aida in half diagonally and press gently; fold diagonally in the other direction and press. Mark where the folds meet; this is the center of the fabric.
2 Beginning at the center of the fabric and the center of the chart, stitch the spiral design in one strand of red.
3 Using one strand of gold thread, work backstitch (see page 9) around the edges of the design as shown on the chart.
4 Trim the fabric and assemble the brooch according to the manufacturer's instructions.

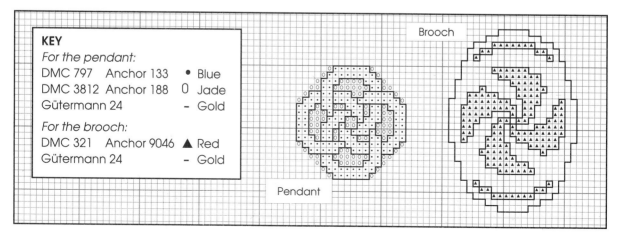

KEY

For the pendant:

DMC 797	Anchor 133	• Blue
DMC 3812	Anchor 188	0 Jade
Gütermann 24		− Gold

For the brooch:

DMC 321	Anchor 9046	▲ Red
Gütermann 24		− Gold

Brooch

Pendant

VARIATIONS

Many other simple Celtic designs can be substituted for the two shown in the photograph; here are some alternative designs in different shapes.

KNOTWORK PICTURE

M any Celtic knotwork designs can be made into simple pictures; this circular design, based on four heart shapes and edged in gold, is surrounded by a creamy yellow mount in a plain gold frame.

Stitch count: 49 x 49
Design size: 3¹/2 x 3¹/2 in (9 x 9 cm)

MATERIALS
- One piece of cream Aida, 14 hpi, 6¹/4 in (16 cm) square
- Stranded embroidery floss in the colors given in the key
- One spool of gold embroidery thread, such as Gütermann metallic 24 or a similar thread of your choice
- Medium tapestry needle
- One 5¹/2 in (14 cm) square picture frame, with or without mount

WORKING THE DESIGN
1 Fold the fabric in half lengthwise and press lightly. Then fold it in half widthwise and press. Mark where the two folds cross (see page 10); this is the center of your design.
2 Using two strands of embroidery floss and beginning at the center of the chart (indicated by arrows) and the fabric, stitch the design, working outward and following the colors as they are marked on the chart.
3 Using two strands of gold embroidery thread, work backstitches (see page 9) all around the outside edges of the knotwork line as marked on the chart.

4 Press the embroidery from the back (see page 10). Trim the fabric to the required size, then follow the instructions on the frame for mounting and assembling the picture.

PRACTICAL TIP
If you want to hang the finished picture diagonally, as shown here, you will need to position the hanging ring of the frame at one corner.

KEY

DMC 742	Anchor 303	●	Dark yellow
DMC 743	Anchor 302	•	Mid-yellow
DMC 744	Anchor 301	0	Light yellow
Your chosen gold thread		–	

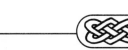

VARIATIONS

This versatile knot shape can be used in many different ways. Work it on smaller-gauge fabric as a greeting card, or use the waste canvas method (see page 10) to work it on a sweatshirt or blouse pocket.

Because the design is made up of heart shapes, it would be lovely stitched in shades of pink as a wedding or Valentine's Day card. Try using DMC 3716, 962, and 961, or Anchor 74, 75, and 76, outlined with red or silver metallic thread.

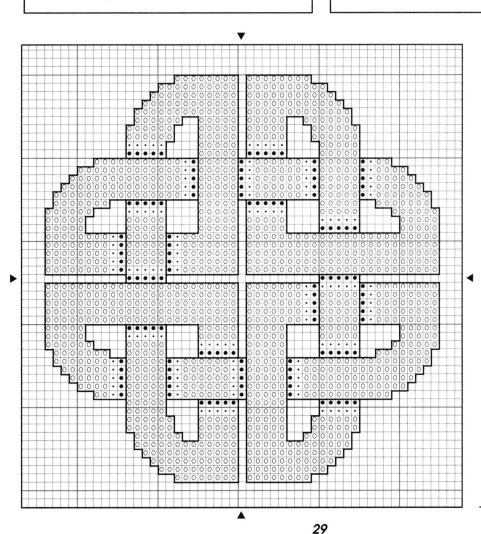

EMBROIDERED CHRISTENING GOWN

A special occasion calls for a special garment. This christening gown is decorated with a Celtic knotwork border design on the bodice and single motifs on the sleeves, yoke, and skirt.

Stitch count: Border, 19 x 73; Motif, 19 x 37
Design size: Border, 7 x 2 in (18 x 5 cm); Motif, 4 x 2 in (10 x 5 cm)

MATERIALS
- One pattern for a christening gown
- White, ivory, or cream silk fabric, in yardage required by the pattern
- Waste canvas, 11 hpi, 9 in (20 cm)
- White lining fabric, buttons, thread, etc., as required by the pattern
- Three skeins of stranded embroidery floss: DMC white or Anchor 1
- One spool of silver embroidery thread, such as Gütermann metallic 24
- Medium crewel needle
- Basting thread

WORKING THE DESIGN
1 Lay out the pattern pieces on the silk fabric to check their layout. Cut out the skirt pieces and set to one side; for the yoke pieces and

30

sleeves, baste the outlines onto single layers of silk and then remove the pattern pieces.

2 Cut a piece of waste canvas (see page 10) to fit the width of the front yoke inside the seam allowances; it needs to be 21 squares deep. Find and mark its center line by following the instructions on page 10, then baste the strip of waste canvas in position on the right side of the front yoke area marked on your fabric.

3 Using three strands of white floss and beginning at the center of the design (see the arrows on the chart) and working outward, stitch the border design onto the front yoke.

4 Cut five rectangles of waste canvas, 40 squares long and 21 squares wide. Baste one on each of the back yoke shapes marked on your fabric, making sure they are level and within the seam allowances. Baste one on the center line of each sleeve, about halfway down, and one on the center front of the skirt, 6–8 in (15–20 cm) up from the bottom.

5 Using three strands of white floss, stitch the smaller motif onto each of the five rectangles of waste canvas.

6 Follow the instructions on page 55 to remove the waste canvas. Dry the silk by securing the pieces to a large embroidery frame, pinning outside the pattern areas. This will prevent the silk from puckering.

7 Keeping the fabric on the embroidery frame and using two strands of silver thread, outline the knot designs with backstitch (see page 9) as shown on the charts.

8 Cut the pattern pieces out of the silk along the basted lines. Then sew the gown together, following the instructions given with the pattern.

PRACTICAL TIP

Remove the waste canvas before you work the backstitches (see page 10); otherwise the silver thread may catch some of the canvas threads and make them difficult to remove.

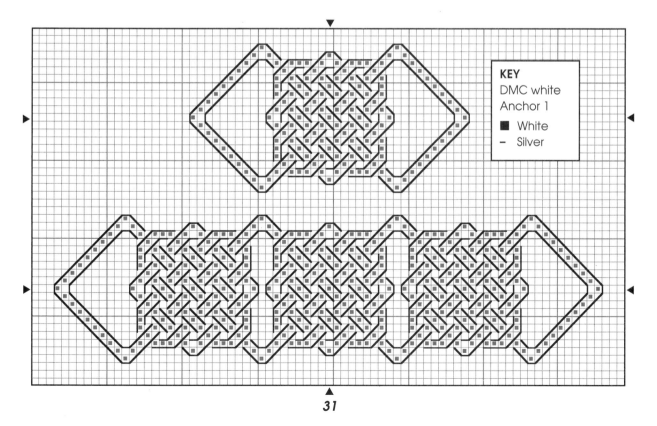

KEY
DMC white
Anchor 1
■ White
– Silver

SQUARE PILLOW

The Celts produced knotwork patterns that could fill any shape, whether regular or irregular. The design for this pillow began as a right-angled triangular knot; I have combined four identical knots and made the lines of the different sections flow into each other to form a square.

Stitch count: 111 x 111
Design size: 20 x 20 in (51 x 51 cm)

MATERIALS
- One piece of cream or gray binca, or Aida, 6 hpi, 25$^{1}/_{2}$ in (65 cm) square
- Anchor tapestry yarn in the colors given in the key
- Large tapestry needle
- Two rectangles of heavy, stiff gray fabric, such as sailcloth or twill, 16 x 22 in (40 x 55 cm)
- One spool of gray sewing thread
- Pillow form

WORKING THE DESIGN
1 Fold the binca in half lengthwise and press lightly. Then fold it in half widthwise and press. Where the two folds meet is the center of your fabric and the center of your design; mark it with water-soluble pen (see page 10).
2 Beginning at the center of the chart (indicated by arrows) on the next page and working from the center of the fabric, backstitch all the very dark aqua outline stitches.
3 When the outlines are complete, stitch the dark aqua and mid-aqua stitches as marked on the chart.
4 Fill in all the other squares within the outlines with the pale aqua; because the outlines are already in position, there is no need to count the squares.

5 Using dark gray, stitch a few isolated squares at random across the background, inside and outside the knot design (the background extends three squares beyond the outermost parts of the knot).
6 Using mid-gray, stitch a few more isolated stitches at random in the same way across the same parts.
7 Using light gray, fill in all the remaining parts of the background.
8 When all the embroidery is complete, press the design from the back (see page 10). Trim the edges of the binca to within $^{3}/_{4}$ in (2 cm) all around.
9 Turn under, press, and stitch a small double hem on one long side of each rectangle of gray fabric. Lay the embroidery face up on a flat surface, then lay the two rectangles of gray fabric, right sides down, on top, overlapping them so that their edges line up with the raw edges of the binca.
10 Pin and baste along the line made by the very edge of the embroidery. Then stitch around this line by machine twice, going over the corners several times to reinforce them. Clip the corners and trim the seams back to 3 in (7.5 cm). Turn the cover to the right side, pushing the corners out with the head of a knitting needle, and press from the back (see page 10).

PRACTICAL TIP
You don't need to follow the exact squares marked on the chart for the different grays; just scatter the dark gray and mid-gray stitches at random as described in the instructions, then fill in the rest with light gray. If you choose alternative colors for your pillow, follow the same instructions using your choice of three background shades.

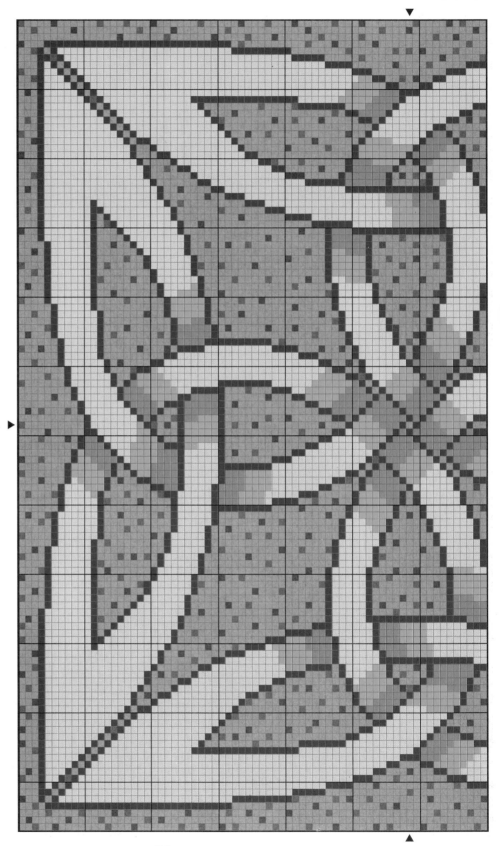

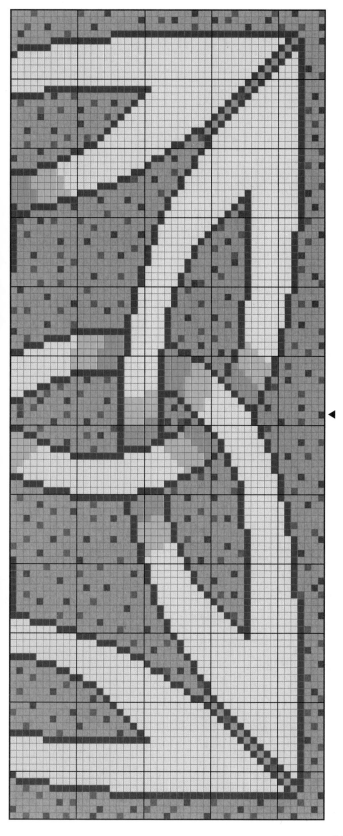

VARIATIONS

This design would look equally effective in different colorways; try picking out colors from your own decor. Make sure you buy the right number of skeins of each shade; the greatest number of skeins is needed for the palest background color and the palest color inside the knot, and seven skeins are needed for the color you choose for the outlines.

Because this design is stitched in yarn, it will withstand heavy use; you could use it for chair seats and upholstered chair backs, as well as for pillows.

KEY	SKEINS		
Anchor 9786	14		Light gray
Anchor 9790	2		Mid-gray
Anchor 9794	2		Dark gray
Anchor 8914	12		Light aqua
Anchor 8918	2		Mid-aqua
Anchor 8920	2		Dark aqua
Anchor 8922	7		Very dark aqua

ANIMALS AND PEOPLE

Living creatures of all kinds are frequently featured in Celtic art. Perhaps best known are the quaint birds, whose down-turned beaks often give them a baleful look. The birds come in all shapes and sizes, and although they are sometimes recognizable as a particular species — perhaps a duck or a peacock — they are usually adorned with elaborate stylized plumage. Fish are rarely depicted in Celtic art, and when they do appear, they get much the same stylized treatment as the birds, with their scales illustrated in the same patterns.

Even more extraordinary are the unrecognizable reptilian creatures that are often incorporated into elaborate knots; the serpents on page 48 are a legacy of this fashion. Celtic artists also had a fondness for depicting animals that were part horse and part seahorse, with equine heads and vaguely horse-like legs but with very long bodies that occasionally had fins. The design on page 122 shows some of these creatures. Animals such as lions, of which, presumably, the artists had never seen reliable pictures, gave rise to some very strange and fantastic creatures similar to the lion-dogs of Imperial Chinese art; the picture on page 46 features a Celtic lion.

Other creatures, however, were illustrated with more realism by Celtic artists, whose depictions of horses, boars, deer, and dogs were often surprisingly fresh. Humans and angels had mixed fortunes: some were realistic, some beautiful, while others were ugly enough to pass for gargoyles. The projects on the following pages reflect the different Celtic styles in portraying living creatures, from the simple and realistic to the fantastic.

HORSE CARD AND PICTURE

T he card and the picture (shown on page 6) use the same basic design. The card is worked small, in petit point on gray even-weave fabric, using just the horse's outline; the picture is a mirror image, with the outline stitched in the same dark turquoise on a white background but filled with paler turquoise.

Stitch count: 84 x 69
Design size: Picture, 6 x 5 in (15.5 x 13 cm)
Card, 3¹/2 x 3 in (9 x 7.5 cm)

MATERIALS

For the picture, you will need:
- One piece of white Aida, 14 hpi, 10 in (25 cm) square
- Stranded embroidery floss in the colors given in the key

- Fine tapestry needle
- Frame to fit the finished picture, with an opening at least 7 in (18 cm) square

For the card, you will need:
- One piece of gray even-weave fabric, approximately 25 hpi, 6 in (15 cm) square
- Stranded embroidery floss in the color given in the key
- Very fine tapestry needle
- White card mount with an opening at least 3¹/2 in (8.5 cm) square

WORKING THE DESIGNS
To make the picture:
1 Measure in 2 in (5 cm) from the right-hand side of the fabric and 2¹/2 in (6 cm) down from the top, and mark with water-soluble pen; this point is where you will begin stitching and corresponds to the tip of the horse's ear.
2 Using two strands of dark turquoise, stitch the outline of the horse, following the chart. Using two strands of light turquoise, fill in all the areas inside the horse.
3 Press the embroidery from the back on a clean surface (see page 10), then mount in the frame following the instructions on page 11.

To make the card:
1 Measure in 1¹/2 in (4 cm) from the left-hand edge of the fabric and 1³/4 in (4.5 cm) down from the top and mark with water-soluble pen. You will begin stitching at this point, which corresponds to the tip of the horse's ear.
2 Using one strand of dark turquoise, follow the chart to stitch the outline of the horse.
3 Press the embroidery from the back (see page 10), then follow the instructions on page 71 for mounting it in the card.

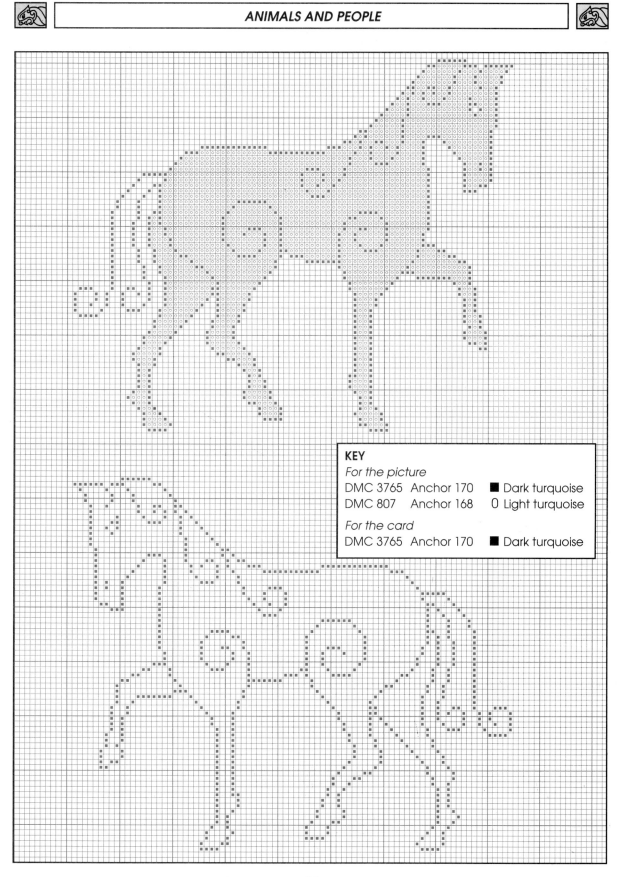

KEY

For the picture

DMC 3765	Anchor 170	■	Dark turquoise
DMC 807	Anchor 168	0	Light turquoise

For the card

DMC 3765	Anchor 170	■	Dark turquoise

BABY'S BIB

Ducks are always favorite animals to decorate baby items, and here a little detail from a Celtic manuscript has been turned into a design to adorn a baby's bib. The original had a head and neck outline made from white dots on a brown background; I have achieved the same effect with alternate squares of dark and light colors. If you wish, add some of the ducklings from page 41.

Stitch count: 50 x 39
Design size: 4 x 3 in (10 x 7.5 cm)

MATERIALS

- One baby's bib suitable for cross-stitching
- Stranded embroidery floss in the colors given in the key
- Medium tapestry needle
- Water-soluble pen for marking

WORKING THE DESIGN

1 Measure $1^1/2$ in (4 cm) up from the bottom of the bib. Draw a line across the fabric of the bib in water-soluble pen. This line will mark the bottom of your stitching and corresponds to the line marked on the chart.

2 Using two strands of brown floss, stitch the squares marked as the dark outlines on the chart. Begin with the front foot, starting it on the marked line $2^1/2$ in (6 cm) in from the left-hand edge.

3 Using two strands of embroidery floss throughout, stitch the colored portions of the chart as marked. Count the squares carefully from the duck's feet to the reeds, and stitch those following the chart.

4 Using one strand of brown floss, work backstitch (see page 9) around all the edges of the squares marked for backstitch.

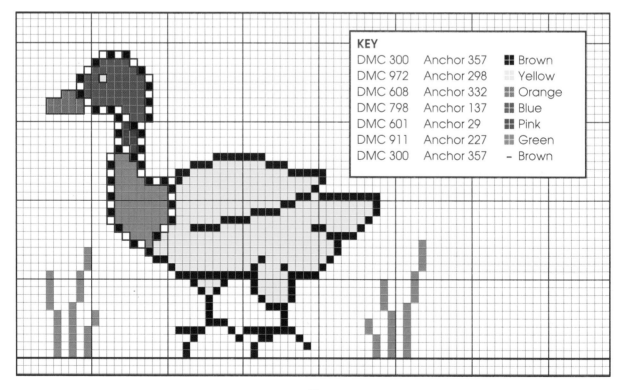

KEY			
DMC 300	Anchor 357	▓	Brown
DMC 972	Anchor 298	░	Yellow
DMC 608	Anchor 332	▓	Orange
DMC 798	Anchor 137	▓	Blue
DMC 601	Anchor 29	▓	Pink
DMC 911	Anchor 227	▓	Green
DMC 300	Anchor 357	–	Brown

VARIATION

This duck is so much fun that you might want to stitch a parade of them on a cross-stitch band to march across a baby's quilt or a crib bumper; use the chart below as a guide and add as many ducklings as you wish.

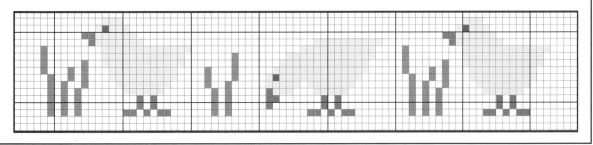

PEACOCK VEST

Bright peacocks decorate this flamboyant vest; the same design is worked on each front panel but as a mirror image. Although the area covered is large, soft matte embroidery cotton and large-gauge canvas make the work grow quickly.

Stitch count: 60 x 88
Design size: 15 x 10 in (38 x 26 cm)

MATERIALS

For an adult-sized vest, you will need:

- A vest pattern with simple front pieces
- Two pieces of cream binca or Aida, 6 hpi, the size of your vest front pattern piece
- Matte embroidery cotton as given in the key
- Large tapestry needle
- Unbleached muslin (in the amount indicated for the vest and lining on your pattern)
- Matching sewing thread
- Iron-on fusible web, two pieces to fit your pieces of even-weave fabric
- Basting thread

WORKING THE DESIGN

1 Press the binca. Cut out the paper pattern piece for your vest front and trace one side in each direction onto the fabric, using a water-soluble pen. Baste around these lines to mark the pattern shapes.

2 Count the squares of binca covered by the pattern piece and check that the peacock design will fit onto the pieces and still allow for the seams. If it does not, adjust your pattern piece slightly to accomodate the design. Using a water-soluble pen, mark the places on the binca where the designs need to go, so that they fit into the shapes and are level with each other; the best way to do this is to mark the level and position of the peacock's feet on each design.

3 Using black cotton, follow the charts to stitch the design outlines onto the binca, beginning from the areas you have marked. If you have marked the fabric correctly, the peacock designs will fall within your basted pattern areas on each piece of binca.

4 Fill in the solid areas in the appropriate colors as marked on the charts.

5 Using black, work backstitch (see page 9) around the edges of the pink squares on each peacock's tail.

6 Sponge away any marks left by the water-soluble pen. When the embroidered pieces are completely dry, iron them from the back (see page 10), pulling the binca square if it has become slightly distorted. Lay the pieces of fusible web, web sides down, on the backs of the embroidered pieces, and iron them to fuse them to the fabric. Cut around the basted lines marking the edges of the pattern pieces.

7 From the muslin, use your pattern to cut the vest back and fronts and the lining back and fronts. Peel the backing paper away from the web on the embroidered pieces. Lay the embroidered pieces face down, and position the muslin vest fronts on top. Iron to fuse the muslin to the web. You now have two embroidered vest fronts; construct the vest as instructed in the pattern.

PRACTICAL TIP

When you are checking that the peacock design fits your vest pattern, try the peacocks positioned back-to-back as well as face-to-face; the design may fit your vest more easily that way.

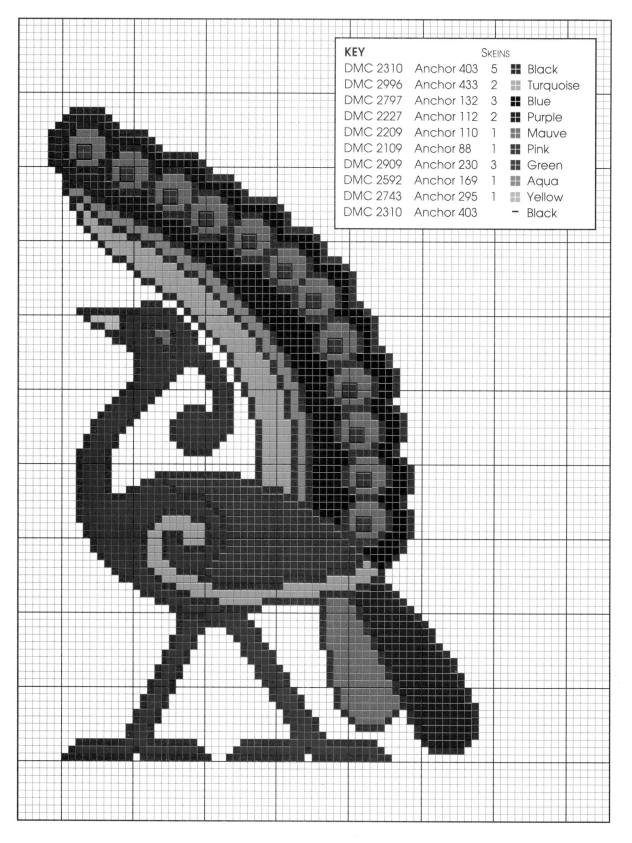

KEY		SKEINS		
DMC 2310	Anchor 403	5	▓	Black
DMC 2996	Anchor 433	2	▓	Turquoise
DMC 2797	Anchor 132	3	▓	Blue
DMC 2227	Anchor 112	2	▓	Purple
DMC 2209	Anchor 110	1	▓	Mauve
DMC 2109	Anchor 88	1	▓	Pink
DMC 2909	Anchor 230	3	▓	Green
DMC 2592	Anchor 169	1	▓	Aqua
DMC 2743	Anchor 295	1	▓	Yellow
DMC 2310	Anchor 403	−	−	Black

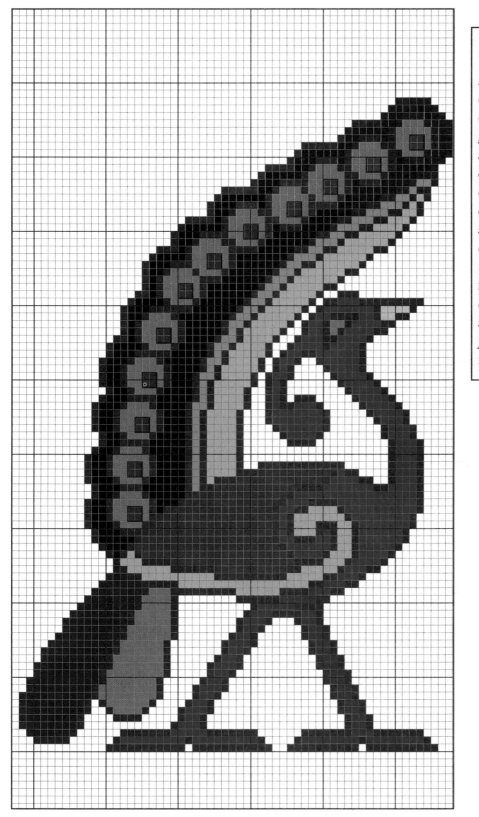

VARIATION

If you want to adapt the peacock design for a child's pattern, use a smaller gauge of canvas (such as 8- or 11-hpi Aida), and a finer thread, such as pearl cotton or flower thread. As with the adult vest, trace the pattern and count the squares of the fabric to make sure it will fit it.

LION PICTURE

Ferocious mythical beasts, such as the bizarre creatures that were half lion, half dog, were often depicted by Celtic artists. This roundel features a brightly colored version of just such a creature.

Stitch count: 62 x 52
Design size: 4¹/₂ x 4 in (11.5 x 10 cm)

MATERIALS
- One piece of white Aida, 14 hpi, at least 8 in (20 cm) square
- Stranded embroidery floss in the colors given in the key
- Medium tapestry needle

- One circular wooden picture frame with a 4³/₄–5 in (12–13 cm) opening

WORKING THE DESIGN
1 Measure 1¹/₂ in (4 cm) from the left-hand side of your square of fabric and 3 in (7.5 cm) down from the top; mark this point with a dot of water-soluble pen. This will be your starting point for stitching.
2 The marked dot corresponds to the tip of the lion's nose. Using two strands of black floss, begin working at the marked point and stitch all the black outlines marked on the chart.
3 Using two strands of embroidery floss throughout, fill in the different parts of the lion with the colors marked on the chart.

4 When the embroidery is complete, remove the dot of pen with a damp cloth. When the fabric is completely dry, press it from the back (see page 10).

5 Trim the fabric into a circle to fit the frame, then assemble the embroidery and frame according to the instructions on page 11.

VARIATIONS

The lion design looks outstanding in these bold, stained-glass colors. If you want to soften its appearance a little, try choosing mid-blue for the outline and gentler shades for the filled areas.

In contrast, if you want to make the design more visually striking, work the outlines in black or gold, and the colors in one strand of stranded embroidery floss and one strand of a bright metallic thread.

Embroider the lion as a crest on a blazer pocket, using the waste canvas method (see page 10), or work a matching pair as bookmarks or coaster designs.

KEY

DMC 608	Anchor 332	▦	Orange
DMC 702	Anchor 226	▦	Green
DMC 796	Anchor 133	▦	Blue
DMC 602	Anchor 63	▦	Pink
DMC 552	Anchor 112	▦	Purple
DMC 3765	Anchor 170	▦	Aqua
DMC 972	Anchor 298	▦	Yellow
DMC 310	Anchor 403	▦	Black

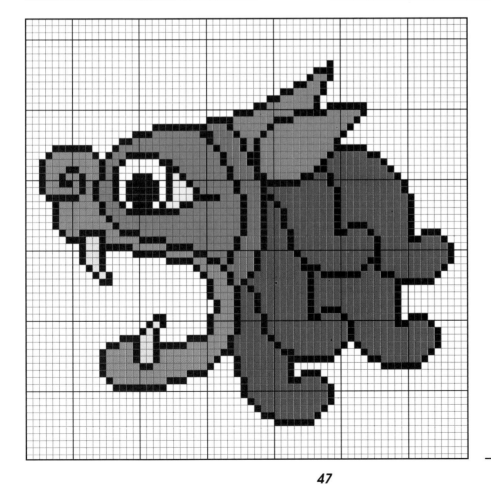

SERPENT PINCUSHION

Many Celtic designs combine knotwork with strange, elongated, snouted reptiles that are not immediately recognizable as any specific animal! The design for this pincushion echoes that favorite combination.

Stitch count: 57 x 41
Design size: 4 x 3 in (10 x 8 cm)

MATERIALS
- Two pieces of dark blue Aida, 14 hpi, 6 x 8 in (15 x 20 cm)
- Two pieces of iron-on interfacing, 6 x 8 in (15 x 20 cm)
- Stranded embroidery floss in the colors given in the key
- Matching blue sewing thread
- One spool of fine gold thread, such as Gütermann metallic 24
- Fine tapestry needle
- Water-soluble pen for marking
- Stuffing

WORKING THE DESIGN
1 Fold one piece of blue fabric lengthwise and press gently. Then fold it widthwise and press. Mark the point with water-soluble pen where the folds meet; this is the center of your work and will correspond to the center of the chart, as indicated by the arrows.
2 With two strands of dark yellow and one strand of gold in your needle, follow the chart and work all the outline stitches of the design.
3 Using two strands of the appropriate color for all the other cross stitches, follow the chart

to stitch the rest of the serpent design.

4 Using one strand of dark blue, work backstitch (see page 9) where marked on the chart – where the serpents cross over themselves or each other and around the orange stitches that form the pupils of the eyes.

5 Press the embroidery from the back (see page 10). Position the pieces of interfacing, adhesive sides down, on the backs of the embroidered pieces, and fuse them in place with a hot iron.

6 Place the two embroidered pieces right sides together. Pin, baste, and machine-stitch around three sides of the rectangle, making a 1/2-in (12 mm) seam. Clip the corners and trim the seam allowances, then turn the shape to the right side.

7 Turn under and press the seam allowance on the raw edge. Fill the pincushion firmly with the stuffing, then stitch the turned edges together with ladder stitch or overcasting.

8 From the remaining embroidery threads, cut several strands about 2 yd (2 m) long of each color. Gather them all together and tie one end of the hank to a firm object, such as a door handle. Twist the threads together firmly, then double them back on themselves and twist again to make a stable length of cord.

9 Remove the cord from the door knob and, leaving 3/4–11/4 in (2–3 cm) free at one end, begin stitching the cord to one edge of the pincushion. Cut the cord leaving 3/4–11/4 in (2–3 cm) free at the other end, then repeat for the other three sides of the pincushion. Work a few tight stitches around the tops of the free ends of cord to create a tassel, then trim the ends off evenly.

KEY			
DMC 743	Anchor 302	■	Dark yellow + Gold
DMC 745	Anchor 301	\	Pale yellow
DMC 797	Anchor 147	▲	Dark blue
DMC 334	Anchor 145	0	Mid-blue
DMC 3325	Anchor 144	+	Light blue
DMC 970	Anchor 324	•	Orange
DMC 797	Anchor 147	-	Dark blue

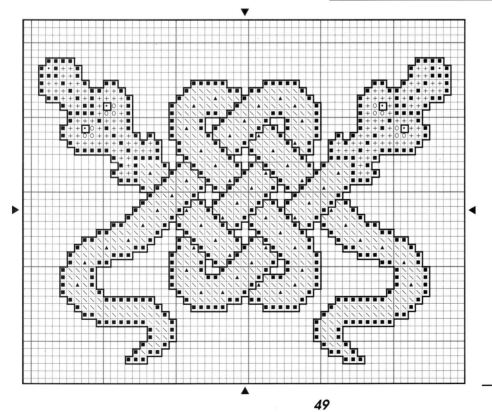

STAINED-GLASS ANGEL

E xotic saints and angels fill Celtic illuminations. **This Christmas design was inspired by several different figures. The black outlines and jewel-like colors make the design glow like a piece of stained glass.**

Stitch count: 112 x 183
Design size: 17 x 11 in (43 x 28 cm)

MATERIALS
- One piece of white Aida, 11 hpi, 26 x 16 in (65 x 40 cm)
- Stranded embroidery floss in the colors given in the key
- One spool of gold thread, such as Gütermann metallic 24
- Medium tapestry needle
- Frame with an opening approximately 18 x 12 in (45 x 30 cm) to fit the finished picture

WORKING THE DESIGN
1 Fold the fabric in half and press gently to form a crease from top to bottom. Measure 4³/4 in (12 cm) down this line from the top of the fabric, and mark with a water-soluble pen. The midline is shown with arrows on the chart.
2 Using three strands of black, begin stitching at the dot; the dot corresponds to the middle of the top line of the halo. Stitch all the black outlines as marked on the chart, and the "PAX" within the rectangular panel.
3 Using two strands of yellow and one strand of gold thread, stitch the areas marked as yellow on the chart: the staff, the halo, and the outside border of the rectagular panel.
4 Using three strands of the appropriate colors, stitch all the remaining areas of the design as marked on the chart. Using one strand of brown, work the nose, eyebrows,

chin, and eye outlines in backstitch (see page 9) as marked on the chart.
5 When the embroidery is complete, sponge away the mark from the water-soluble pen. Let the fabric dry completely, then iron it from the back (see page 10).
6 Assemble the frame according to the instructions given on page 11.

PRACTICAL TIP
When you are choosing your floss for this project, stick to either DMC or Anchor throughout; occasionally the colors do not correspond exactly across the brands, so if you mix them, the shades may not blend.

The halo and staff have a strand of gold worked with the yellow thread

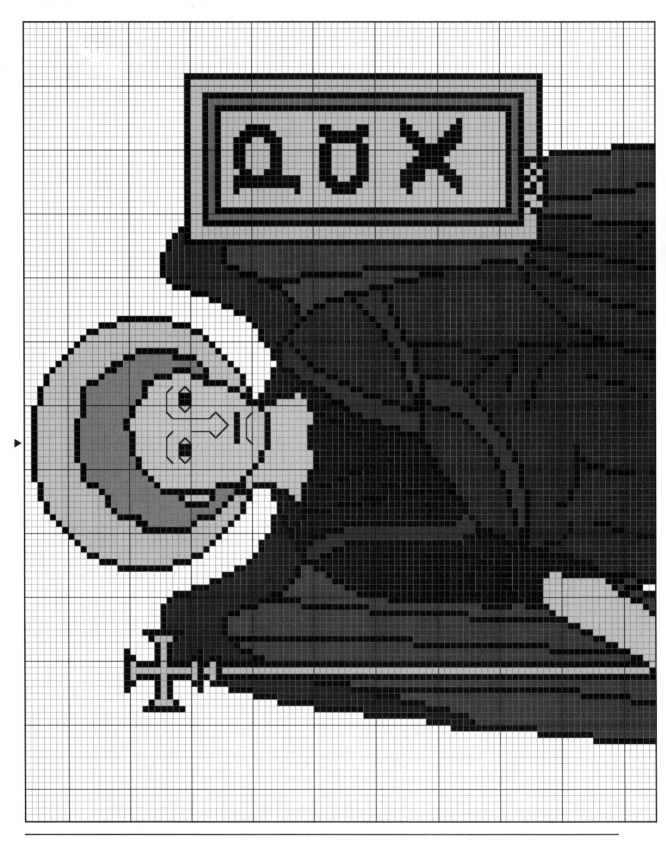

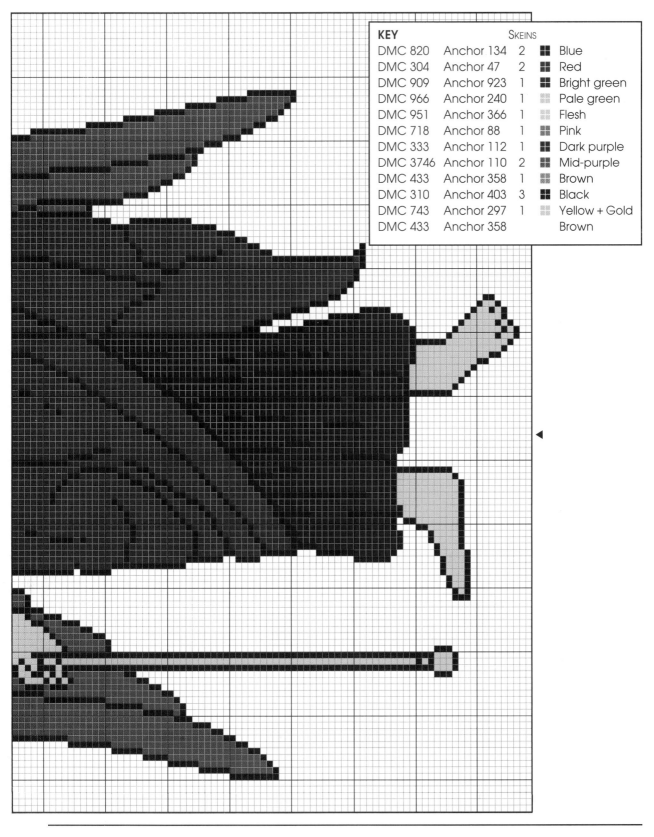

KEY		SKEINS		
DMC 820	Anchor 134	2	▪▪	Blue
DMC 304	Anchor 47	2	▪▪	Red
DMC 909	Anchor 923	1	▪▪	Bright green
DMC 966	Anchor 240	1	▫▫	Pale green
DMC 951	Anchor 366	1	▫▫	Flesh
DMC 718	Anchor 88	1	▪▪	Pink
DMC 333	Anchor 112	1	▪▪	Dark purple
DMC 3746	Anchor 110	2	▪▪	Mid-purple
DMC 433	Anchor 358	1	▪▪	Brown
DMC 310	Anchor 403	3	▪▪	Black
DMC 743	Anchor 297	1	▫▫	Yellow + Gold
DMC 433	Anchor 358			Brown

ROOSTER SWEATSHIRT

Brighten up a plain sweatshirt with a quirky Celtic bird; the design is stitched using waste canvas as a guide, so you can stitch it onto any sweatshirt or sweater – or even a T-shirt!

Stitch count: 54 x 48
Design size: 5¹/4 x 5¹/4 in (13.5 x 13.5 cm)

MATERIALS
- Dark blue sweatshirt
- Piece of waste canvas, 11 hpi, at least 6¹/4 in (16 cm) square
- Stranded embroidery floss in the colors given in the key
- Medium crewel needle
- Basting thread

WORKING THE DESIGN
1 Decide on the position of your motif; its finished size is 5¹/4 in (13.5 cm) square, so use this to help you see the space the design will take up on the background. When you have decided on the position, baste the piece of waste canvas onto the sweatshirt to cover the area.
2 Using three strands of embroidery floss, stitch the design, following the colors marked on the chart. Take each stitch across one double thread of the waste canvas (see page 10), down the hole in the canvas and into the fabric behind. Make sure that each stitch goes into the background fabric. Stitch the blue outlines of the bird first so that you do not have to count the stitches inside the outlines.

3 When the stitching is complete, dampen the whole design with a sponge and a little warm water; this dissolves the glue holding the canvas threads together.

4 When the glue has dissolved, pull the threads of the canvas out from under the stitches. You may find it useful to use tweezers for this task. When all the threads have been removed, you will be left with the embroidered design on a plain background. Let it dry, then press the design from the back with a steam iron (see page 10).

PRACTICAL TIP
Try not to pull the stitches too tight when you are working over the waste canvas; if you leave them a little loose, it will be easier to pull the canvas threads out later.

VARIATIONS
The waste canvas method (see page 10) allows you to work counted thread designs onto virtually any background; you could try this design on a pocket or a blouse front, or work it onto a plain fabric for an egg cozy.

Pairs of birds would look good on the corners of curtains or the ends of a table runner; just flip the chart from left to right for a mirror image.

Of course, you don't have to use waste canvas for this design; it can be stitched on Aida for a simple card or worked large for a bright pillow.

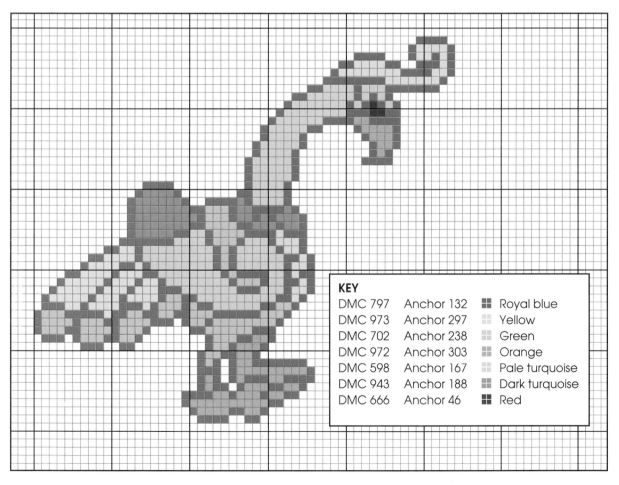

KEY			
DMC 797	Anchor 132	▓▓	Royal blue
DMC 973	Anchor 297	░░	Yellow
DMC 702	Anchor 238	▒▒	Green
DMC 972	Anchor 303	▓▓	Orange
DMC 598	Anchor 167	░░	Pale turquoise
DMC 943	Anchor 188	▒▒	Dark turquoise
DMC 666	Anchor 46	██	Red

CURTAIN TIEBACKS

F ish appear occasionally in Celtic art, usually as highly stylized and decorative features. The curving fish motif on this design fits the curve of the curtain tieback perfectly.

Stitch count: 123 x 75
Design size: 9 x 5¹/₂ in (23 x 14 cm)

MATERIALS
For each pair of tiebacks, you will need:
- Paper and pencil to enlarge the design
- One piece of moss-green Aida, 14 hpi, 28 x 20 in (70 x 50 cm)
- One piece of heavy iron-on interfacing, the same size as the Aida
- One piece of matching green cotton backing fabric, the same size as the Aida
- Two skeins of stranded embroidery floss in DMC white or Anchor 1
- Fine tapestry needle
- 3 yd (3 m) matching green bias tape, ¹/₂ in (12 mm) wide
- Four large curtain rings
- Basting thread
- Matching sewing thread

WORKING THE DESIGN
1 Enlarge the tieback outline to the correct size and cut out the shape. Using this as a guide, cut two shapes from the stiffening fabric and two from the backing fabric.
2 Trace the shape twice onto the green Aida using a water-soluble pen. On one shape, measure ¹/₂ in (12 mm) to the right of the central line and 2 in (5 cm) up from the bottom; mark the position with a dot of water-soluble pen. On the other shape, measure ¹/₂ in (12 mm) to the left of the central line and 2 in (5 cm) up and mark this

position in the same way. On each of the fish charts, you will see that there is a vertical line of four cross stitches at the tip of the head. The bottom stitch of the four will correspond with the dot marked on the fabric.
3 Using two strands of white embroidery floss throughout and beginning at the marked dots, stitch the designs onto the fabric.
4 When the stitching is complete, the fish shapes should sit comfortably within the marked outlines. (If by any chance they do not, redraw the outlines slightly to accommodate them.) Cut out the fabric shapes around the marked outlines. Sponge away the marked dots, then leave the fabric to dry completely. Press the embroidered pieces from the back (see page 10).
5 Lay each piece of embroidery face down, and position a piece of iron-on interfacing, adhesive side down, on top; fuse the layers together with a hot iron.
6 Lay the two pieces of backing fabric right sides down on a flat surface. Cover each piece with one of the embroidered pieces right side up. Pin and baste the bias tape face down around the edges of each piece, aligning the raw edges. Then stitch along the line by machine. Fold the free edge of the bias tape over the raw fabric edges, tuck it under, and slipstitch the bias tape to the back of each tieback.
7 Stitch a curtain ring to the back of each end of both tiebacks with a few strong overcasting stitches.

PRACTICAL TIP
Don't cut the fabric shapes out of the Aida before you embroider them; if you leave cutting until the stitching is done, the edges will not fray and lose their definition.

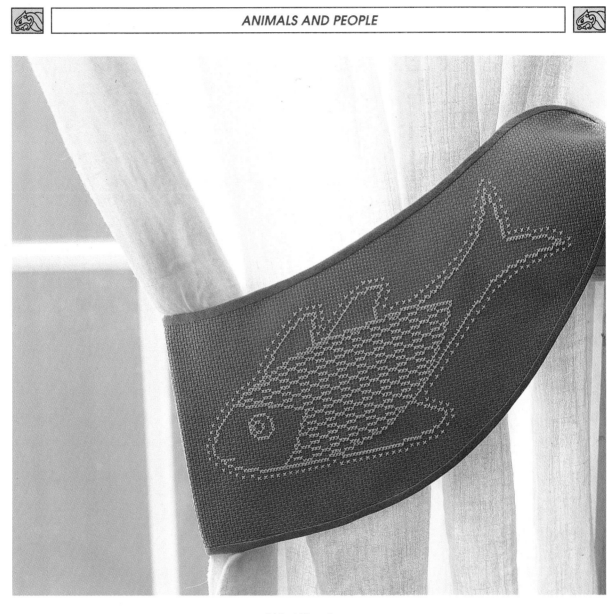

24 in (60 cm)

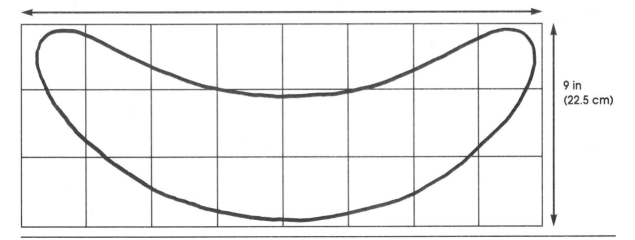

9 in
(22.5 cm)

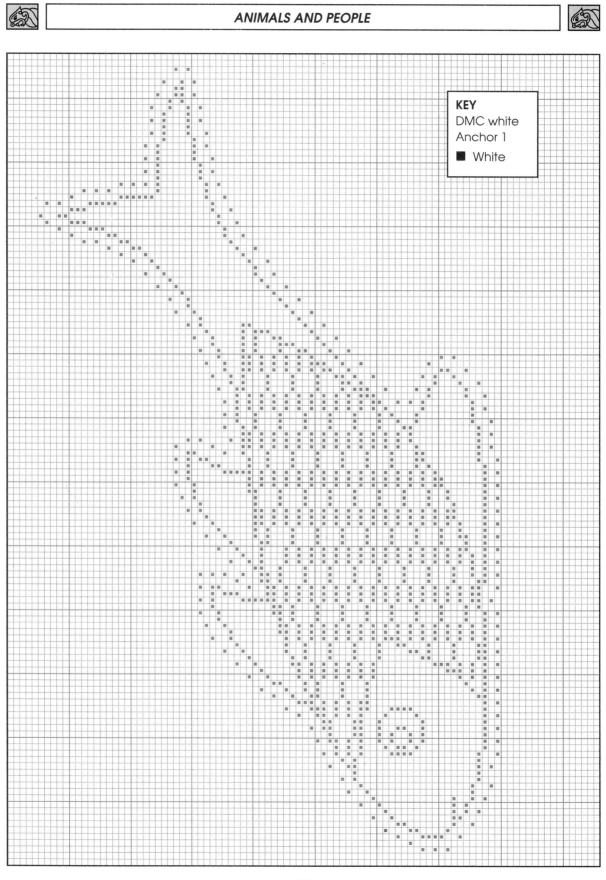

KEY
DMC white
Anchor 1
■ White

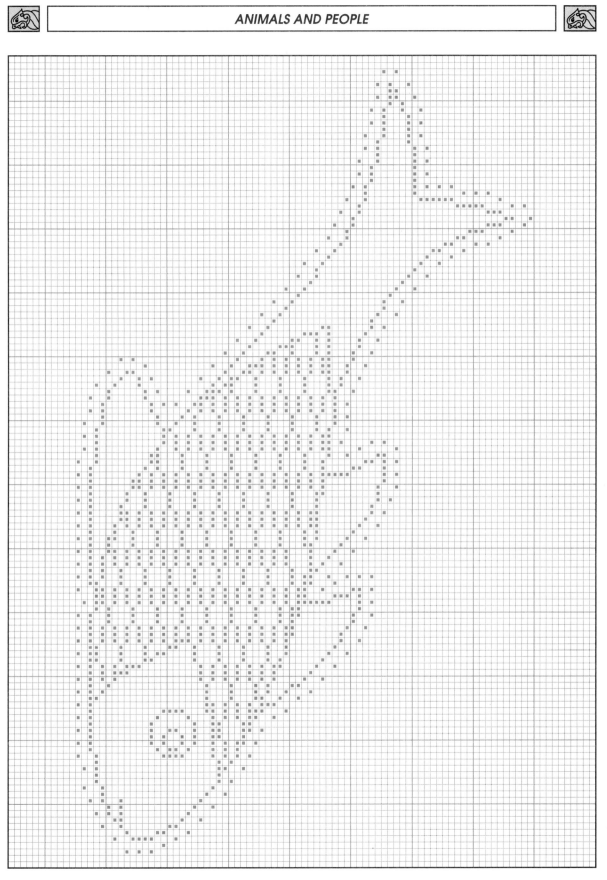

HORSEMAN PICTURE

W hen horsemen appear in Celtic designs, they are usually depicted realistically, dressed in simple clothing and armed with a basic sword and shield. This panel combines a realistic horse and rider with cross-topped columns taken from the borders of a carpet page; the colors are from the more subtle range of the Celtic palette.

Stitch count: 196 x 112
Design size: 14 x 8 in (36 x 20 cm)

MATERIALS

- One piece of cream Aida, 14 hpi, 18 x 12 in (45 x 30 cm)
- Stranded embroidery floss in the colors given in the key
- One spool of fairly heavy silver embroidery thread, such as Gütermann metallic 41
- Fine tapestry needle
- Frame to fit the finished picture, with an opening at least 16 x 10 in (40 x 25 cm)

WORKING THE DESIGN

1 Press the Aida. Measure up 2 in (5 cm) from the bottom of the fabric, and draw a horizontal line in water-soluble pen at that level. This will be the baseline, that you will use as a guide for positioning the design.
2 Measure in 2 in (5 cm) along this line from the edge of the fabric (measure in from whichever edge you prefer to start) and make a dot with the water-soluble pen. This dot is where you will start stitching and marks the outside edge of the dark pink base of the cross.
3 Using two strands of embroidery floss in the appropriate colors, follow the chart to stitch the cross at the side you have marked. When

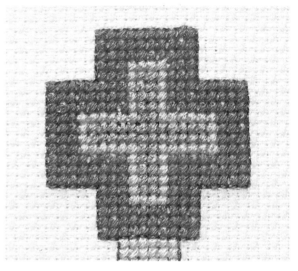

A detail of one cross, showing the backstitch outlines around the colored areas

the cross is complete, outline the different parts of it with backstitch (see page 9) in one strand of dark brown floss, as marked on the chart.
4 Count the squares of fabric carefully to see where to position the horse in relation to your stitched cross. Work all the dark brown outlines of the horse and rider next, and then work the horseman's beard, which is in the same color.
5 Using the appropriate colors, fill in all the solid areas of the horse and rider. Use one strand of dark brown to outline the horseman's eye and the circles on the shield.
6 Stitch the second cross in position, then finish it off with backstitch in the same way as the first.
7 When the embroidery is complete, sponge away the marks made by the water-soluble pen. When it is completely dry, press the embroidery from the back (see page 10), and then mount in your chosen frame, following the instructions on page 11.

PRACTICAL TIP

Many colors are needed for this horseman, and for most of them, only a small amount of floss is used. If you have a good selection of stranded embroidery floss from previous projects, you may be able to use some of them as substitutes for the colors listed — try them out together to check that they harmonize before you stitch with them.

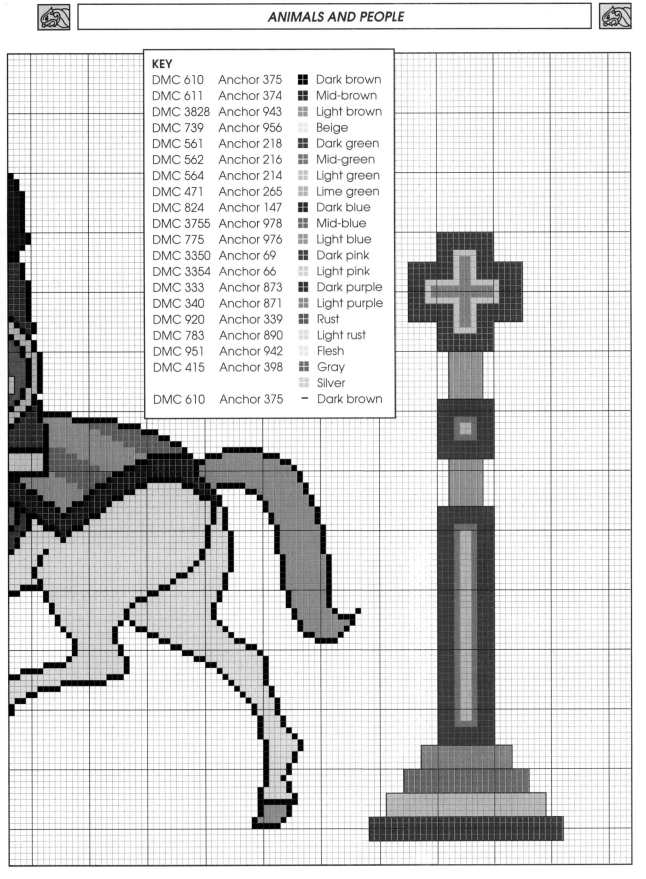

KEY

DMC 610	Anchor 375	■■ Dark brown
DMC 611	Anchor 374	■■ Mid-brown
DMC 3828	Anchor 943	■■ Light brown
DMC 739	Anchor 956	▦ Beige
DMC 561	Anchor 218	■■ Dark green
DMC 562	Anchor 216	■■ Mid-green
DMC 564	Anchor 214	▦ Light green
DMC 471	Anchor 265	▦ Lime green
DMC 824	Anchor 147	■■ Dark blue
DMC 3755	Anchor 978	■■ Mid-blue
DMC 775	Anchor 976	■■ Light blue
DMC 3350	Anchor 69	■■ Dark pink
DMC 3354	Anchor 66	▦ Light pink
DMC 333	Anchor 873	■■ Dark purple
DMC 340	Anchor 871	▦ Light purple
DMC 920	Anchor 339	■■ Rust
DMC 783	Anchor 890	▦ Light rust
DMC 951	Anchor 942	▦ Flesh
DMC 415	Anchor 398	■■ Gray
		▦ Silver
DMC 610	Anchor 375	− Dark brown

CELTIC RUG

Birds and knotwork are combined in this striking design. Although this is the largest project in the book, it is not as time-consuming as it looks because the stitching is in sport-weight knitting yarn on large-gauge canvas.

Stitch count: 259 x 187
Design size: 45 x 31 in (115 x 79 cm)

MATERIALS

- One piece of cream Aida or binca, 6 hpi, $3^1/_4$ x $4^1/_2$ ft (1 m x 1 m 40 cm)
- $3^1/_2$-oz balls of wool sport yarn in the colors given in the key
- Large tapestry needle
- One piece of heavy backing fabric, such as linen or heavy muslin, the same size as the Aida or binca
- Matching sewing thread

WORKING THE DESIGN

1 Fold the Aida or binca in half along its length and mark the line with a water-soluble pen. This will serve as a stitching guide for the different parts of the design. The center line is also indicated on the chart to help you.

2 Measure in 6 in (15 cm) from one end of the fabric and mark a line with the water-soluble pen. The edges of the first two knotwork borders will lie along this line. Using one strand of dark blue, begin stitching the two knotwork border outlines at this end of the fabric, making sure you leave one empty square between them. When the outlines of the first two knotwork borders are complete, stitch the outlines of the other two, again leaving one square between them.

3 Fill in the knotwork outlines with light blue as marked on the chart.

4 Using dark blue, stitch in the outlines of the inner and outer borders as marked on the chart. Counting the stitches and squares carefully, stitch in the outlines of the birds, making sure that their beaks and stomachs are five squares apart.

5 Using red, yellow, green, and purple, fill in the colored areas of the birds and the straight borders as marked on the chart.

6 Using cream, fill in all the background areas behind the birds and the knots.

7 Sponge away any marks left from the water-soluble pen. When the embroidery is completely dry, press it gently from the back (see page 10). Pull the fabric to make it square if it has distorted.

8 Trim the raw edges of the rug to within $1^1/_2$–2 in (4–5 cm) of the stitching. Cut the backing fabric to the same size. Lay the backing fabric face up and cover it with the embroidery, face down. Pin and baste a seam just at the edge of the embroidery; stitch around this twice by machine, reinforcing the corners and leaving about 20 in (50 cm) open for turning.

9 Clip the corners and trim the seams to about $^3/_4$ in (2 cm), then turn the rug to the right side. Press under the seam allowances of the open edge and close it with slipstitch or ladder stitch. Press the rug gently from the back (see page 10).

PRACTICAL TIPS

Stitch the outlines of all the knotwork borders before you fill any of them in and before you stitch the plain borders; it is much easier to see if you have miscounted before the light blue is added.
Keep checking your stitching to make sure that the birds align exactly.

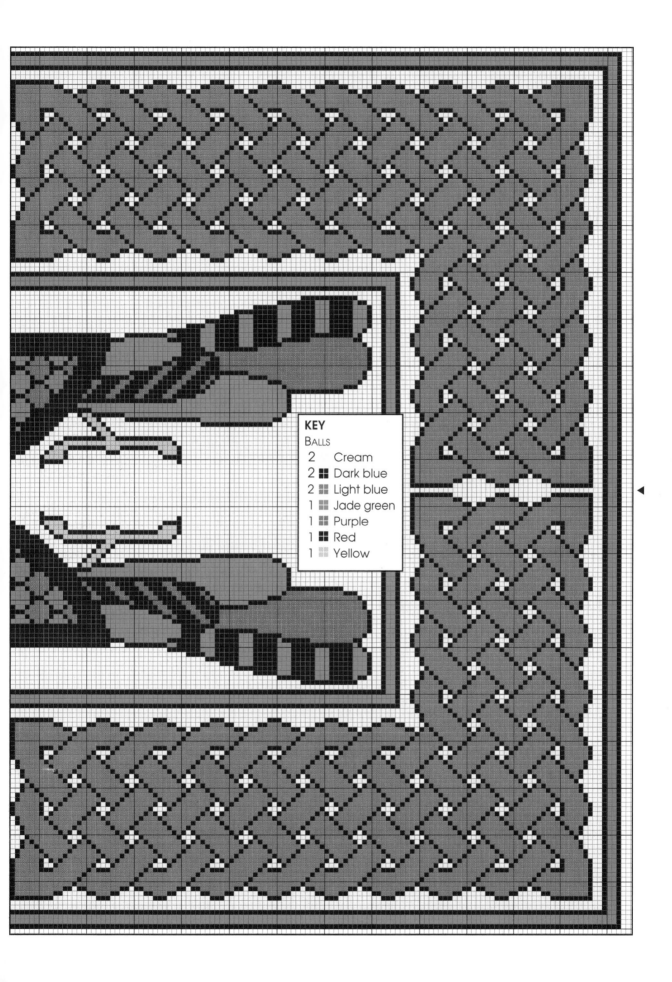

KEY

Balls

2   Cream

2 ▦ Dark blue

2 ▦ Light blue

1 ▦ Jade green

1 ▦ Purple

1 ▦ Red

1 ▦ Yellow

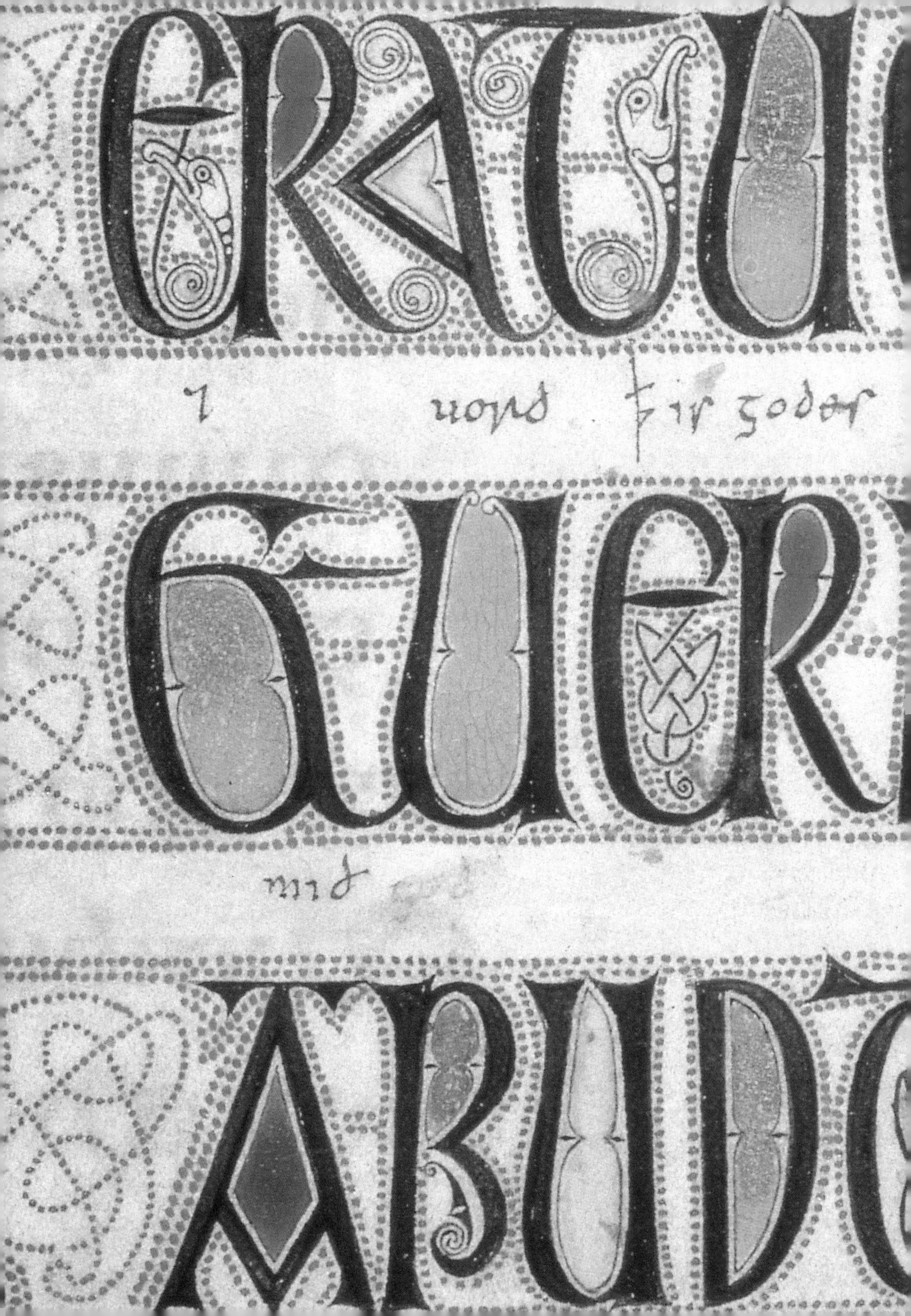
ERATU
ETUER
ABUD

LETTERING

Celtic lettering is some of the most beautiful in history. In decorating their letterforms, Celtic scribes combined an exuberant use of color with an aesthetic sensitivity that laid the foundation for the wonderful illuminated manuscripts of the Middle Ages.

There is no one style of Celtic lettering; even the great sourcebooks, such as the *Book of Kells* and the *Book of Durrow* (written in Ireland in the eighth or early ninth century), contain several different styles within their pages. A typical illuminated page began with an elaborately decorated initial letter, sometimes made in the shape of a fantastic animal. Such letters were loosely based on forms known as versals, but often they are so tortuous and interwoven that they are virtually unrecognizable as a letter; the "S" on page 112 is based closely on one of these letters.

The illuminated letter might be followed by several lines of strange, angular lettering, with or without extra angular knots within the shape, again often stylized beyond immediate recognition, and with the spaces between them filled with flat, bright colors. The letters on pages 80–85 and 86 reflect these particular styles.

Then the "ordinary" text would begin, which was often some variation of the styles known as uncial and half-uncial. The letters on page 108 echo some uncial forms, and those on pages 72–77 are based on half-uncials from the *Book of Kells*. Occasionally throughout the text, at a break such as a new chapter, there might be a smaller, less elaborately decorated initial; the letters of the Christmas decoration on page 90, and the animal letters on pages 100–107 reflect this simpler kind of illumination.

INITIAL CARDS

T hese wonderfully bright initials were taken from the *Book of Kells*; the monks working on that manuscript often filled in the counters (the spaces within letters) with areas of flat color in mid-green, chalk blue, mauve, or pink and then surrounded them with an outline of red brush dots or squares.

MATERIALS
For each large card, you will need:
- One piece of cream Aida, 11 hpi, 8 in (20 cm) square
- One card mount with an opening large enough to show your finished design
- Stranded embroidery floss in the colors given in the key, plus one skein of your chosen filling color
- Medium tapestry needle

For each small card, you will need:
- One piece of cream Aida, 14 hpi, 8 in (20 cm) square
- One card mount with an opening large enough to show your finished design
- Stranded embroidery floss in the colors given in the key, plus one skein of your chosen filling color

- One spool of fine red metallic embroidery thread, plus one spool of fine metallic thread to tone in with your chosen filling color
- Fine tapestry needle

WORKING THE DESIGN

1 If you are working on 11-hpi fabric, use three strands of embroidery floss for your stitching. If you are working on 14-hpi fabric, use two strands of embroidery floss. Find the center of your fabric by folding it twice (see page 10) and mark it with water-soluble pen. Count the squares on the chart to find the central point; this will correspond with mark on your fabric. Begin with black, and stitch all of the main letter first.

2 If you are using 11-hpi fabric, stitch the filling block (or blocks) in three strands of your chosen filling color, and stitch the outline dots in three strands of red. If you are using 14 hpi, use two strands of embroidery floss and one strand of the matching metallic thread for the filling block and the outline dots.

3 Press the design on the back using a steam iron (see page 10).

4 Follow the instructions on this page for assembling the cards.

PRACTICAL TIP
Metal threads tend to shred quite easily, so only use short lengths.

KEY
For both cards:

DMC 310	Anchor 403	■ Black
DMC 326	Anchor 19	+ Red
Your chosen filling color		/

ASSEMBLING CARDS

1 *Check that your design fits behind the opening in the card front, then trim the fabric so that it fits inside the card with the design showing correctly at the front.*

2 *Lay the card mount face down on a flat surface, and spread some paper glue around the edges of the opening, making sure the glue does not go onto the front of the card. Use a medium amount of glue; if you use too much, the card will buckle.*

3 *Carefully position the embroidered design so that it shows through the opening. Smooth the edges of the fabric so that there are no wrinkles and the edges are caught by the glue.*

4 *With the card face down again, put a little glue around the edges of the left-hand flap. Don't put glue over the middle of this flap; otherwise it might come through the embroidery and spoil it. Fold the flap over the back of the embroidery and press into place.*

5 *Leave the card to dry completely, pressed between two heavy books.*

VARIATIONS

These initials would look pretty worked in paler colors as birth congratulation cards. Stitch the main letter in a mid-pastel color, then pick up toning pastels for the filling blocks and the dots around the outside.

Try stitching two initials on the same piece of background fabric for an unusual wedding or anniversary card. You could stitch the initials very small, perhaps using one strand of floss on 18- or 22-hpi fabric.

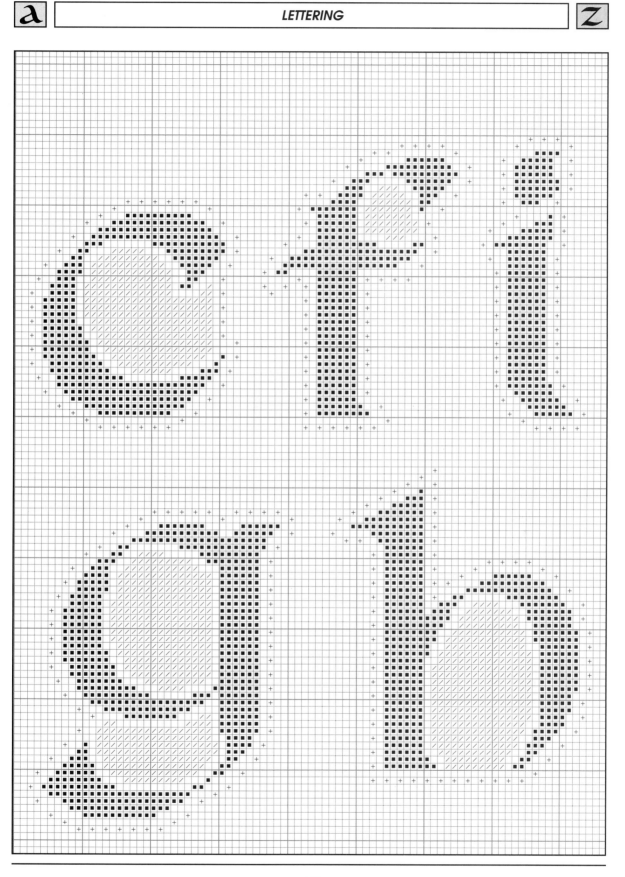

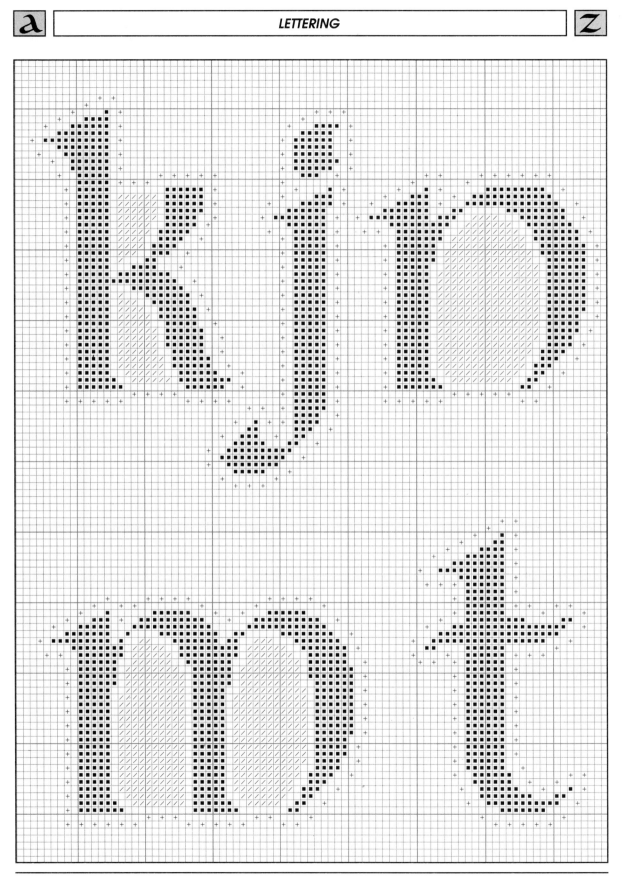

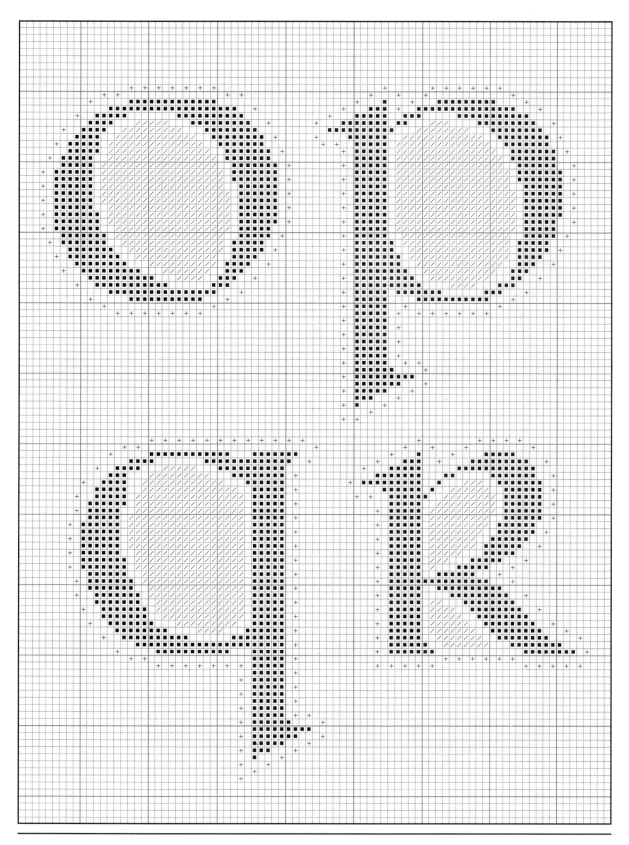

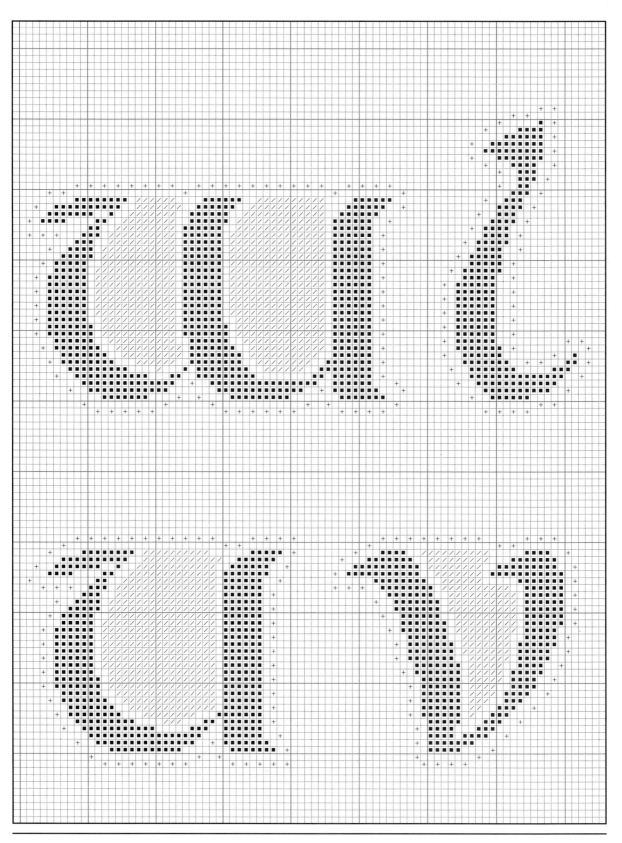

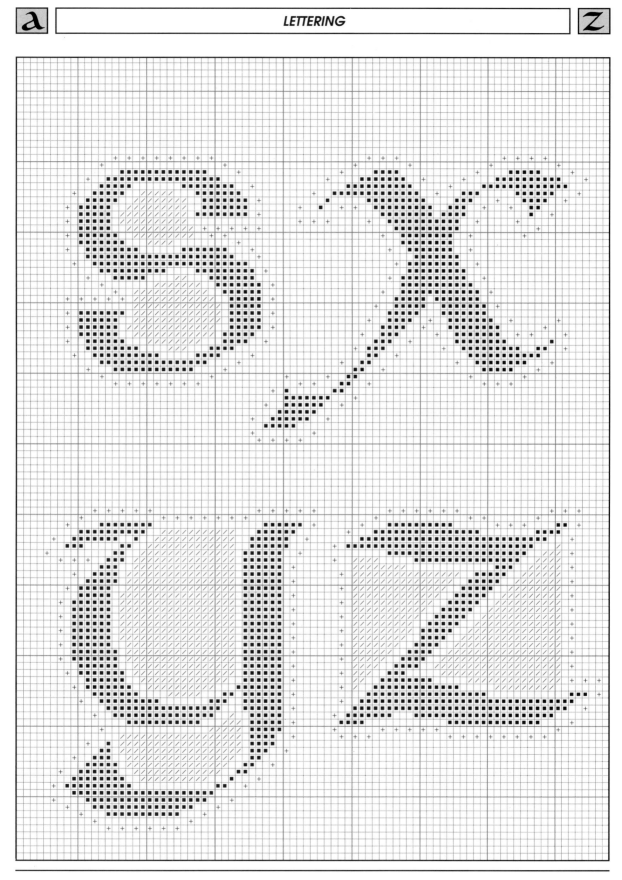

STITCHED NAMEPLATE

Personalized presents are always well received. In this project, one of the Celtic alphabets has been used to make a nameplate; you could adapt the same idea for a card or sampler.

MATERIALS
- Graph paper
- One strip of white Aida, 11 hpi, 6 in (15 cm) wide; for length, see step 3 in the instructions
- Stranded embroidery floss in the colors given in the key
- Medium tapestry needle
- Mat board in a matching color, or frame to fit the finished embroidery

WORKING THE DESIGN

1 On the graph paper, chart the name that you want to use on the nameplate, using the letters from the sampler design on page 108. Space the letters so that they look correct visually; note that some go slightly above or below the standard level of the others.

2 Around your lettering, draw in the border design. There should be three empty squares between the edges of the lettering and the border at the sides and between the standard letters (those that do not go above or below the level of the others) and the border at the top and bottom. Count or fold

your chart to find the center line of the design.

3 Count the number of squares horizontally that your design now occupies; your strip of fabric will need to be that number of squares long plus $1^1/4$–$1^1/2$ in (3–4 cm) at each end.

4 Fold the fabric strip in half to find the center line, and mark the line with a water-soluble pen. Measure down $3^1/2$ in (8.5 cm) from the top of the strip and mark a horizontal line at this level, again with the water-soluble pen; this line is the baseline guide for all the standard letters in your design.

5 Use three strands of embroidery floss for all the cross stitches. Beginning at the center of your chart and fabric, stitch the letters in light green, aligning the bottoms of the standard letters with your baseline guide. Stitch the border, following the chart for the colors.

6 Using one strand of dark green, outline the letters in backstitch (see page 9). Using one strand of dark peach, outline the light peach border in backstitch as shown on the chart.

7 Sponge the embroidery to remove the water-soluble pen marks, then let dry completely. Press the embroidery from the back (see page 10).

8 Cut a mat from a matching piece of mat board or fit the the nameplate into a frame to complete it.

PRACTICAL TIP

It is important to space the letters by eye rather than by calculation when you are drawing the chart. The different shapes of letters make some combinations look closer together than others when they are positioned with the same gap between them.

KEY			
DMC 561	Anchor 210	+	Dark green
DMC 350	Anchor 11	■	Dark peach
DMC 352	Anchor 8	0	Light peach
DMC 350	Anchor 11	–	Dark peach
DMC 562	Anchor 208		Light green *(for letters)*

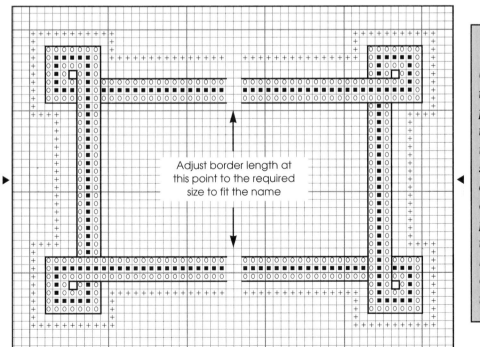

Adjust border length at this point to the required size to fit the name

VARIATIONS
Use this letterform to create a personalized card, taking just one initial and surrounding it with a shortened version of the border. Or put two names together and lengthen the sides of the border to take them both in.

PINCUSHION AND NEEDLE CASE

Knotted letterforms adorn this pincushion and needle case set in toning colors. On the needle case, the initial is worked in peach on a white background; on the pincushion, the pale peach letter on a darker background gives a more subtle effect.

MATERIALS
- One needle case made for cross-stitching in white Aida, 14 hpi
- One piece of peach Aida, 14 hpi, 6 in (15 cm) square
- Stranded embroidery floss in the colors given in the key
- Fine tapestry needle
- Circular pincushion base with 4 in (10 cm) diameter cushion

WORKING THE DESIGN
1 Press the peach fabric and the needle case. Fold the fabric in half lengthwise and press gently. Then fold in half across the width and press. Make a dot in water-soluble pen where the folds cross to mark the center of the fabric. Do the same with the needle case front (ignore the fact that two of the corners are rounded).

2 Choose the initials that you want to use from the charts on the following pages. On each initial you choose, find the center square and mark it with a pen dot; this will correspond to the dot you have marked on the fabric.

3 Using two strands of pale peach floss, follow the chart for your chosen letter to stitch the design onto the peach fabric for the pincushion. Using two strands of peach, stitch your chosen initial onto the front of the needle case.

4 Using one strand of dark orange, work

backstitch (see page 9) around the edges of each letter and across the knotted part of each letter as marked on the charts.

5 Sponge away the marks made by the water-soluble pen. When the embroidered pieces are completely dry, press them from the back (see page 10).

6 Assemble the pincushion according to the manufacturer's instructions. This generally requires unscrewing the padded area from the base, stretching the embroidery over the pad (making sure that it is positioned in the center), gluing or taping the fabric in place underneath the pad, and reassembling the pincushion.

PRACTICAL TIP
The center point of each letter is not always in the center of the knot, so make sure you measure and mark it correctly for each different initial that you work.

VARIATIONS
The whole alphabet is included in the charts, so you can personalize anything appropriate or put several letters together to make a monogram.

Because these letters are so ornate, they tend not to work very well together for spelling out names, but they look effective worked into a sampler design.

KEY		
DMC 3341	Anchor 8	+ Peach *or*
DMC 3824	Anchor 6	+ Pale peach
DMC 606	Anchor 334	− Dark orange

BRIGHT SAMPLER

T he unusual design of this sampler is based on a style Celtic scribes often used in illuminated manuscripts. The first row of words following an ornate capital letter would be written in straight-sided, sometimes bizarre letterforms, with the gaps inside and between them (the counters) filled with bright colors.

Stitch count: 148 x 128
Design size: 11$^{1/2}$ x 9$^{1/2}$ in (29 x 24 cm)

MATERIALS

- One piece of white Aida, 14 hpi, 16 x 13$^{1/2}$ in (40 x 34 cm)
- Stranded embroidery floss in the colors given in the key
- Fine tapestry needle
- Frame to fit the finished embroidery, with an opening at least 13 x 11 in (33 x 28 cm)

The brightly colored counters within and between the letters are outlined with black backstitch.

WORKING THE DESIGN

1 Press the fabric. Measure down 2$^{3/4}$ in (7 cm) from the top of the fabric and 3 in (7.5 cm) in from the right-hand side; make a dot at this point in water-soluble pen. This is where you will begin stitching; it corresponds with the top right corner of the "J" on the chart.

2 Using two strands of black floss, stitch the top row of letters, working from the "J" across to the "A."

3 Count the squares and stitches carefully to see exactly where to begin the middle row of letters, then stitch them in the same way. Do the third row in the same way.

4 Using two strands of embroidery floss in the appropriate colors for all the cross stitches, fill in the colored areas of the design as marked on the chart.

5 Counting the squares and stitches carefully to check that the positioning is correct, stitch the black borders in cross stitch.

6 Using one strand of black, work backstitch (see page 9) around the edges of all the colored panels.

7 Sponge away any marks left by the water-soluble pen. When the embroidery is completely dry, press it from the back (see page 10).

8 Assemble the embroidery in the frame, following the instructionson page 11.

PRACTICAL TIPS

If you are left-handed or prefer to work from left to right, begin at the top left corner. In this case, measure 2$^{3/4}$ in (7 cm) down and 3$^{1/2}$ in (8.5cm) in from the left; this spot corresponds to the top left of the bar at the top of the "A." Work the lettering before you stitch the border so that it will be easier to count the stitches of the border correctly.

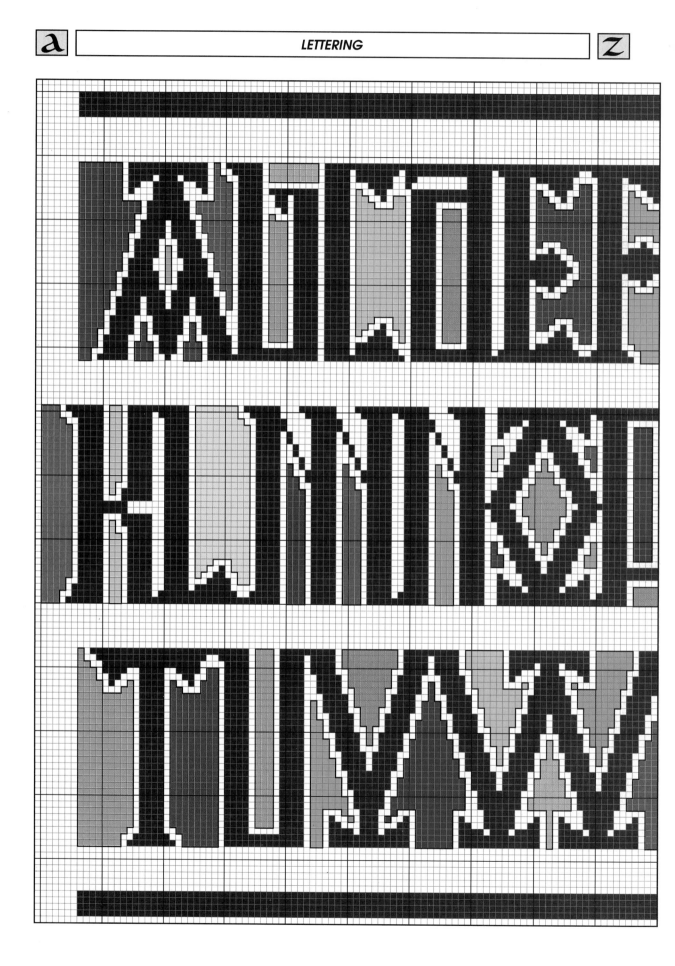

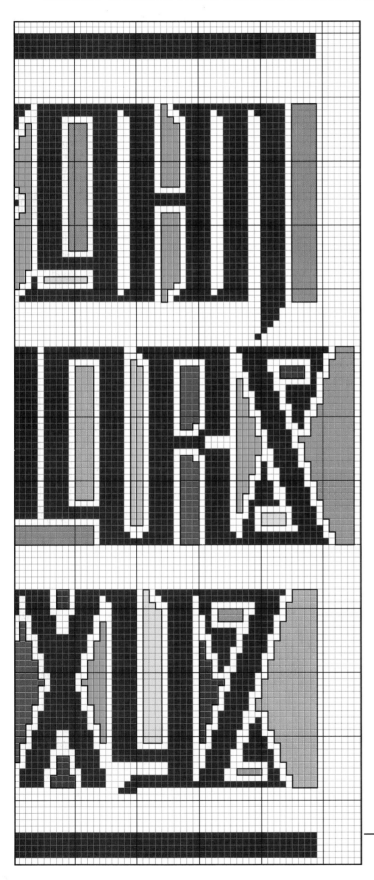

KEY

DMC 310	Anchor 403	▦ Black (*4 skeins*)
DMC 550	Anchor 102	▦ Dark purple
DMC 333	Anchor 111	▦ Light purple
DMC 820	Anchor 134	▦ Royal blue
DMC 3812	Anchor 189	▦ Jade green
DMC 742	Anchor 303	▦ Yellow
DMC 740	Anchor 316	▦ Orange
DMC 600	Anchor 63	▦ Pink
DMC 995	Anchor 410	▦ Turquoise
DMC 910	Anchor 228	▦ Bright green
DMC 666	Anchor 9046	▦ Red
DMC 310	Anchor 403	- Black

VARIATION

This alphabet is composed of such strangely designed letters that they do not work very well for making words; however, some of them look effective singly or in pairs as monograms.

NOEL CHRISTMAS DECORATION

Bright Christmassy colors are used in this richly illuminated Noel decoration; the glittering goldfingering and the sheen on the pearl cotton give extra opulence and will catch the light from candles or Christmas tree lights.

Stitch count: 100 x 31
Design size: 10¹/₂ x 3¹/₂ in (27 x 9 cm)

MATERIALS

- One piece of plastic canvas, 12 x 4³/₄ in (30 x 12 cm)
- Gauge-5 and gauge-3 pearl cotton in the colors given in the key
- One spool of dark or light gold goldfingering, or other fine gold metallic thread
- Large tapestry needle

WORKING THE DESIGN

1 Measure ³/₄ in (2 cm) in from the right-hand side of the plastic canvas (see page 9), and 2 in (5 cm) up. Mark with a water-soluble pen. This is where to begin stitching, and corresponds to the top gold stitch on the right-hand edge of the tail of the "L" on the chart.

2 Using one strand of goldfingering, stitch all the gold squares as marked on the chart.

3 Using one strand of red or green, as appropriate, follow the chart to fill in all the complete and partial cross shapes formed by the gold lattice.

4 Using one strand of gauge-5 blue, follow the chart to stitch the outlines of the letters.

5 Using small sharp-pointed scissors, cut the shape out of the plastic canvas; make sure you leave the edges intact of any holes that have stitching in them.

6 Using one strand of the gauge-3 thread, neaten the cut edges of the plastic shape by working a variation of cross stitch over the edges themselves; work a series of diagonal overcasting stitches in one direction, then cross them with stitches in the other direction. When you come to the top left of the "N" and the top right of the "L," make a buttonhole loop for hanging.

PRACTICAL TIP
When cutting the intricate areas inside the letters, cut one hole at a time, with the points of the scissors held away from the embroidery.

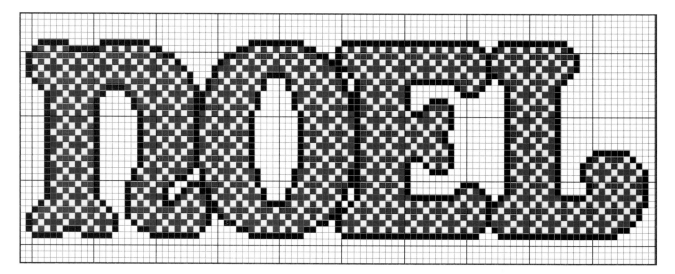

VARIATION

This design looks attractive worked on any scale; stitch it small on a long rectangle of even-weave fabric for a very special Christmas card.

KEY

Gauge 5:

DMC 498	Anchor 47	▦	Red
DMC 820	Anchor 134	▦	Blue
DMC 909	Anchor 923	▦	Green
Goldfingering			Gold

Gauge 3:

DMC 796	Blue *(for edging)*

WEDDING INITIALS

Stitch a pair of square initial pictures as a perfect wedding present. These chunky versal letterforms are each worked inside a square border and embellished with pearl beads; the charts for each letter can be worked in blue or in pink.

Stitch count: 71 x 71
Design size: 6$\frac{1}{4}$ x 6$\frac{1}{4}$ in (16 x 16 cm)

MATERIALS

For each blue letter, you will need:
- One piece of white Aida, 11 hpi, 10 in (25 cm) square
- Stranded embroidery floss in the colors given in the key
- Pack of small white pearl beads
- Medium tapestry needle
- White sewing thread
- Frame to fit the finished initial, with an opening at least 7 in (18 cm) square

For each pink letter, you will need:
- One piece of white Aida, 11 hpi, 10 in (25 cm) square
- Stranded embroidery floss in the colors given in the key
- Pack of small white pearl beads
- Medium tapestry needle
- White sewing thread
- Frame to fit the finished initial, with an opening at least 7 in (18 cm) square

PRODUCING THE DESIGN

1 Press the fabric. Mark your starting point 2 in (5 cm) from the top and 2 in (5 cm) in from the right-hand side; make a dot with a water-soluble pen. The dot corresponds to the top right-hand stitch inside the border.

2 Using three strands of either dark blue or dark pink, depending upon your chosen color scheme, follow the chart to work the alternating cross stitches that form the inner pattern of the border. Using three strands of light blue or light pink, work the light cross stitches as marked on the chart. Surround the pattern with the solid outlines of the border in one of the darker colors.

3 Fold the fabric (see page 11) to find the center of the white square left inside the border; mark this with a dot of water-soluble pen. Choose the initial you want to use from the charts, and mark the center of it. Using three strands of the appropriate colors as marked on the chart, and matching the center of the chart with the central dot on your fabric, stitch the initial. Where a square is marked for a bead, leave it clear of stitching.

4 Sponge the fabric to remove any marks left by the water-soluble pen. When the fabric is completely dry, press it from the back (see page 10).

5 Using the white sewing thread, sew a pearl bead into each of the squares indicated on the charts for the letter and border.

6 Mount and frame the pictures together or separately.

KEY				SKEINS
For each blue letter:				
DMC 798	Anchor 146	2	■	Dark blue
DMC 809	Anchor 140	2	+	Light blue
Bead			●	
For each pink letter:				
DMC 603	Anchor 68	2	■	Dark pink
DMC605	Anchor 60	2	+	Light pink
Bead			●	

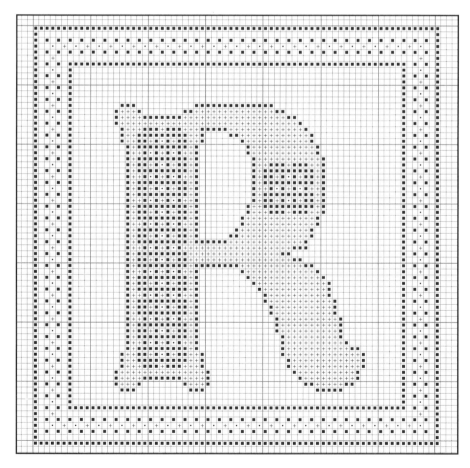

VARIATION
You don't have to use blue and pink for the initials; you can choose colors that match a particular room or stitch the pictures in shades of yellow with gold, or gray with silver, for gold or silver wedding anniversaries.

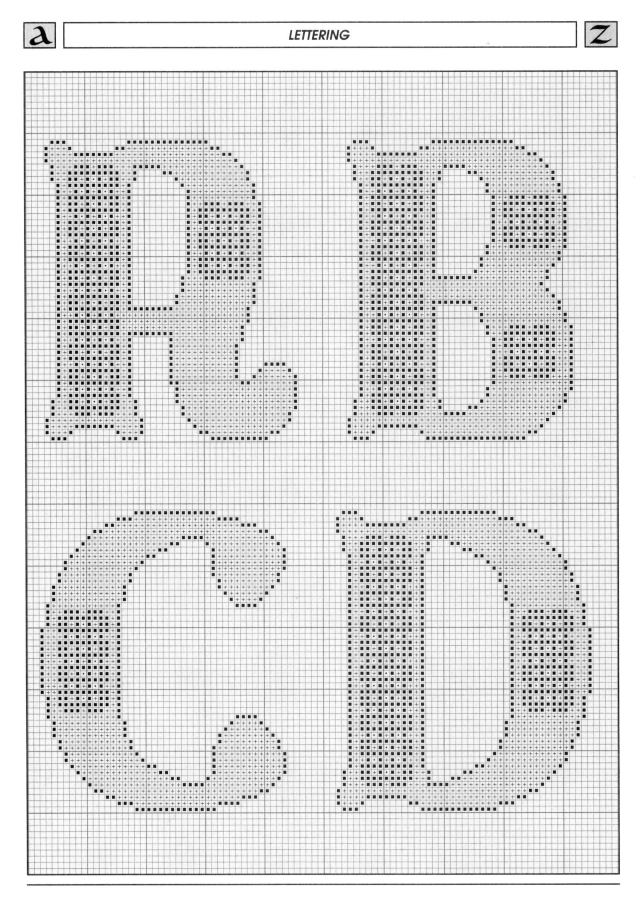

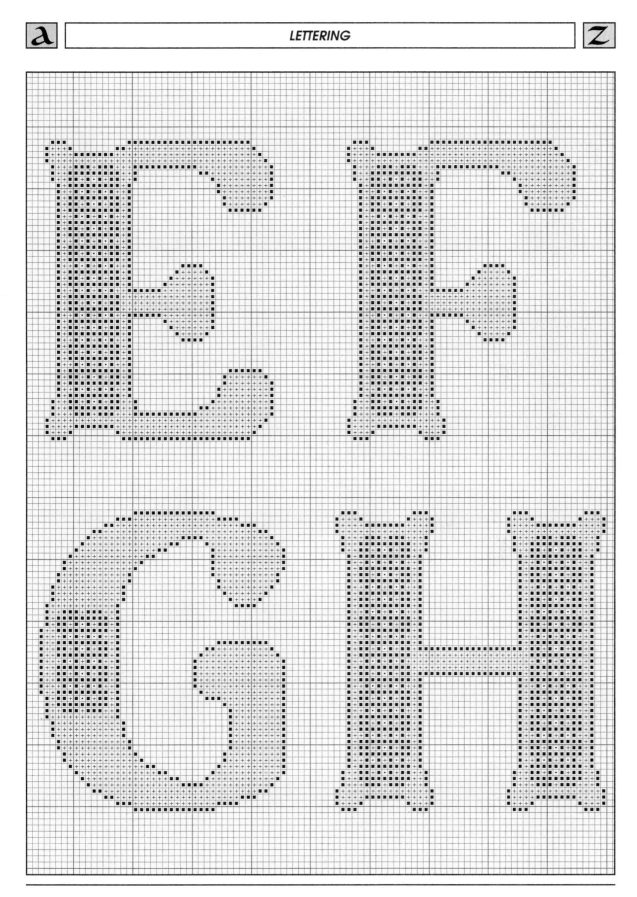

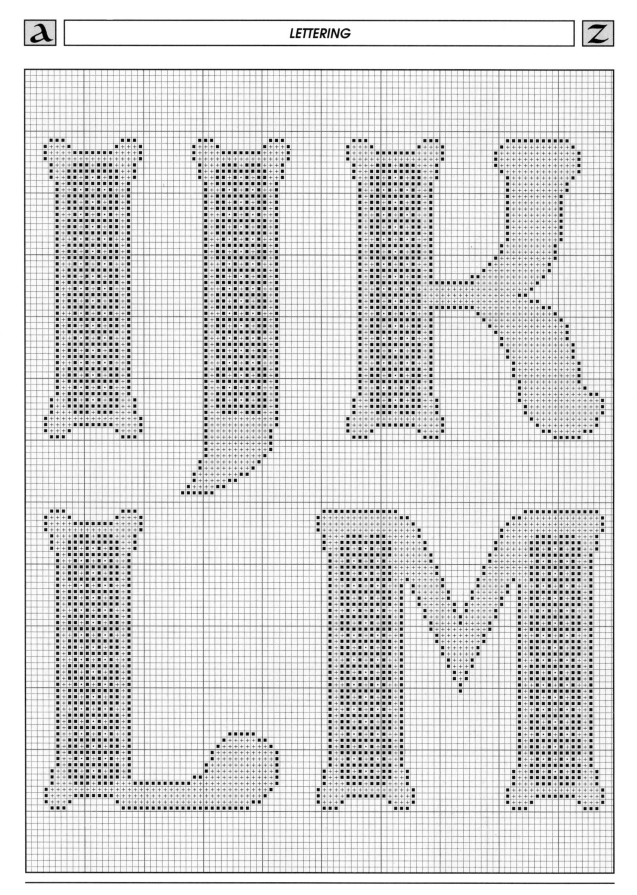

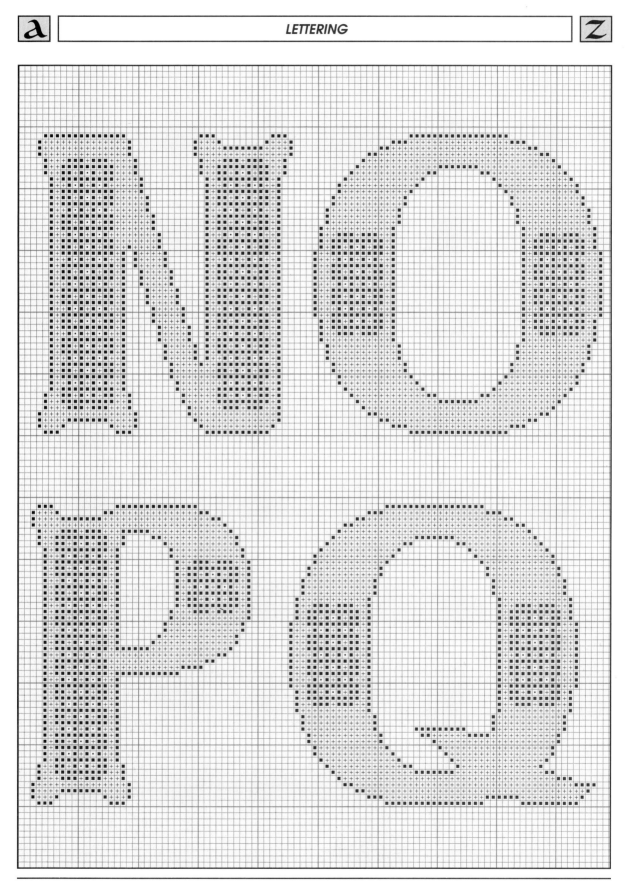

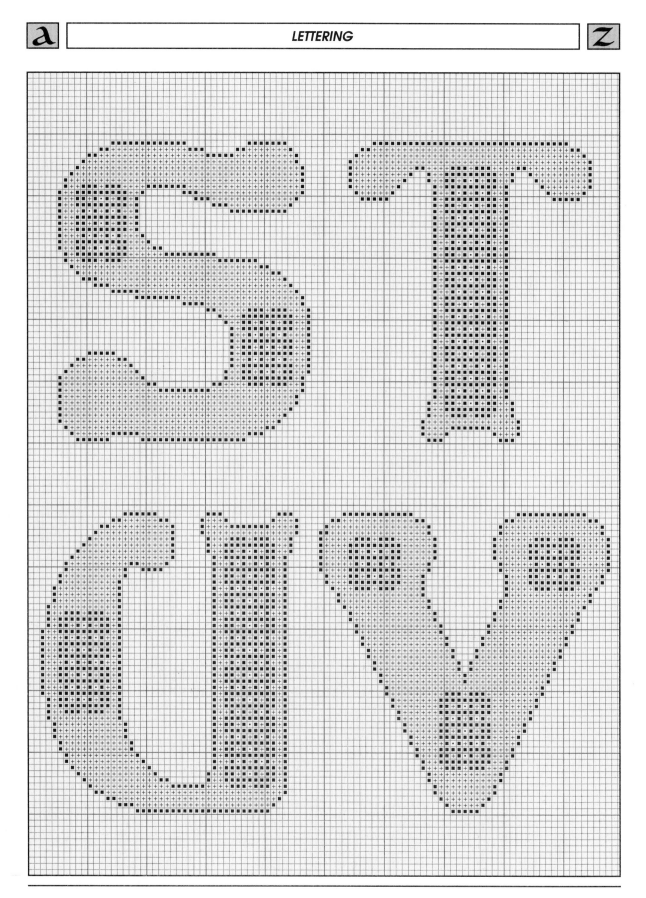

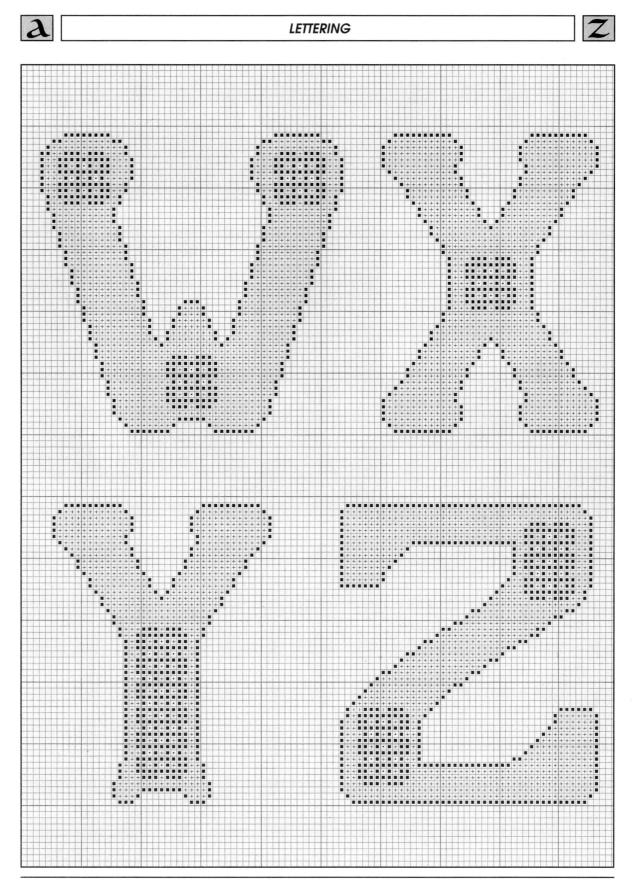

INITIAL PICTURES

A lphabets combining letterforms with strange animals appear frequently in Celtic art. The top finials of these letters are made from two birds' heads linked by a knot, with a simpler finial at the bottom.

MATERIALS

For each picture, you will need:
- One damask embroidery square with a central panel at least 49 squares wide and 49 squares high
- Stranded embroidery floss in the colors given in the key
- Fine tapestry needle
- Frame to fit the finished picture

WORKING THE DESIGN

1 Fold the fabric square in half and then in quarters, and mark the center point with a

dot of water-soluble pen (see page 10).
Count and mark the corresponding center
point of your chosen initial on the chart.

2 Starting at the center and using two strands
of embroidery floss in the appropriate colors,
follow the chart to stitch the initial on the
damask square.

3 Using one strand of dark blue floss, work
backstitch (see page 9) around the edge of
the initial and on the finials as indicated
on the chart.

4 Sponge the fabric to remove any marks from
the water-soluble pen. When it is completely
dry, iron it from the back (see page 10).

5 Assemble the picture in the frame, following
the instructions on page 11.

PRACTICAL TIP

*These initials use only a small amount of
thread; even if you are stitching several letters,
you will still only need one skein of each color
of stranded embroidery floss.*

VARIATIONS

*These initials have been worked as small
pictures on damask squares, but they can be
worked just as easily on any counted thread
fabric.*

*If you want to use them as monograms on
non-even-weave fabric, such as a bag or a
bathrobe, use the waste canvas method
(see page 10).*

KEY

DMC 986	Anchor 211	•	Dark green
DMC 989	Anchor 243	0	Light green
DMC 891	Anchor 29	+	Dark pink
DMC 893	Anchor 27	\	Light pink
DMC 796	Anchor 178	■	Dark blue
DMC 796	Anchor 178	−	Dark blue

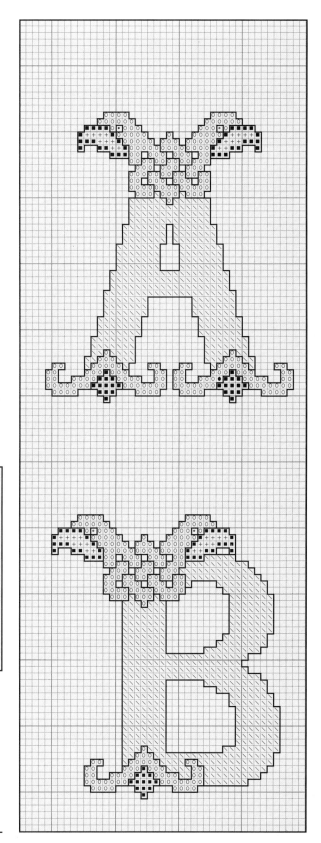

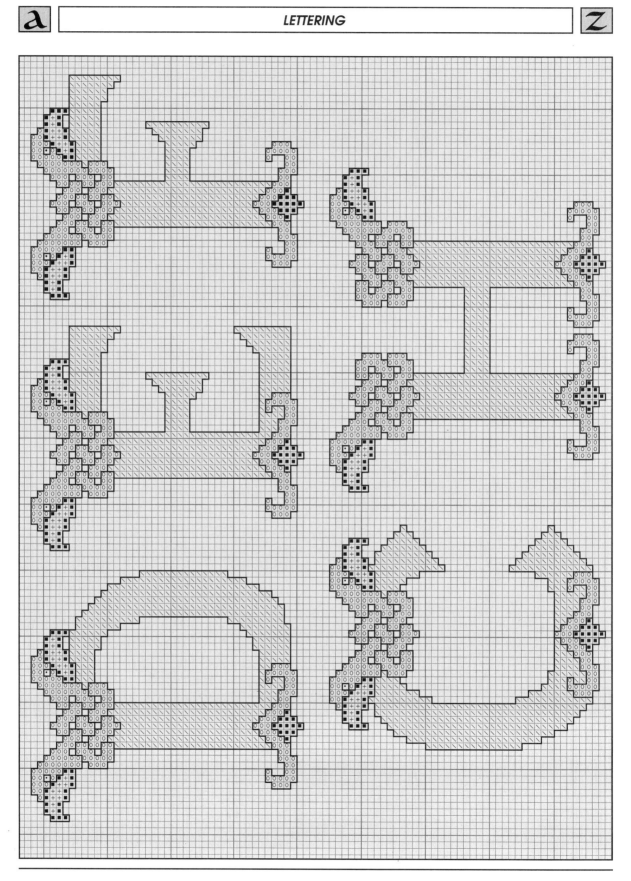

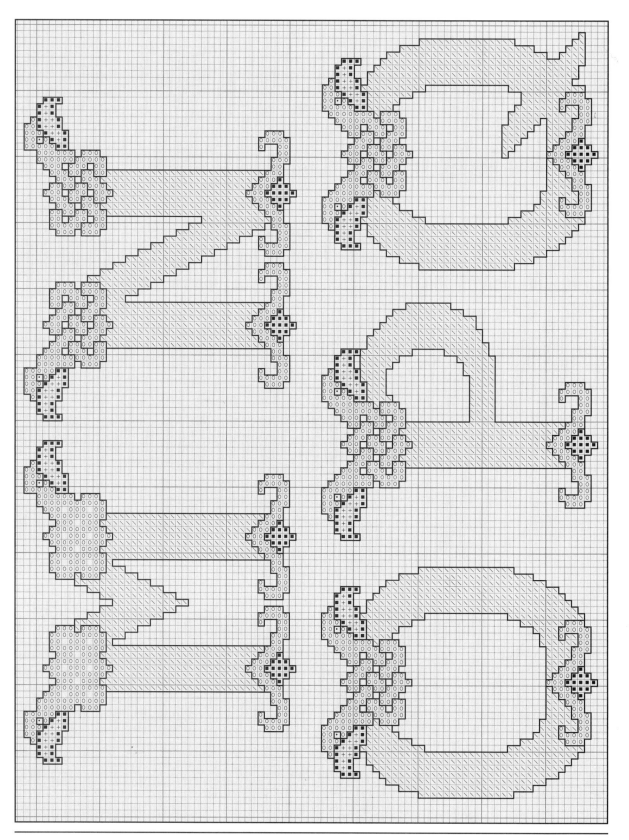

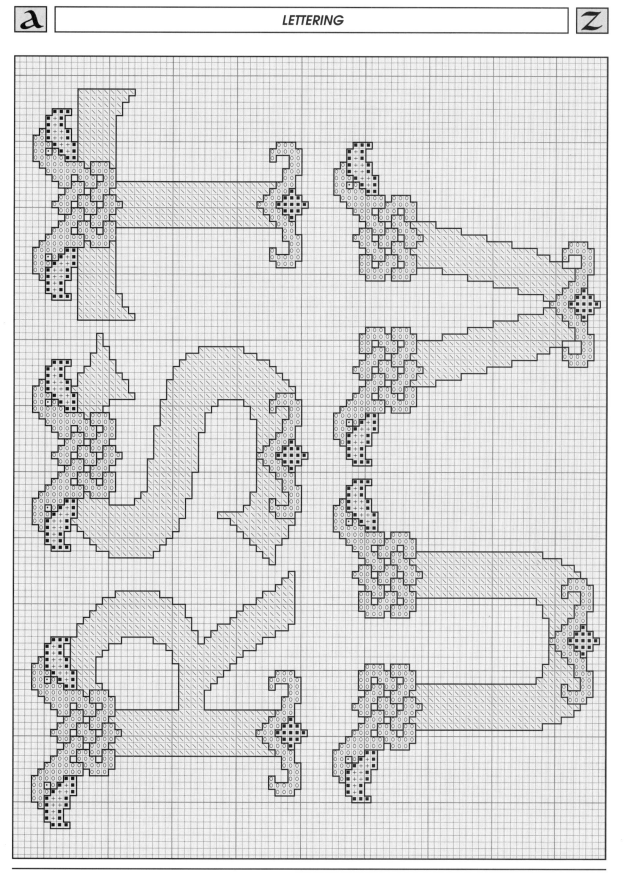

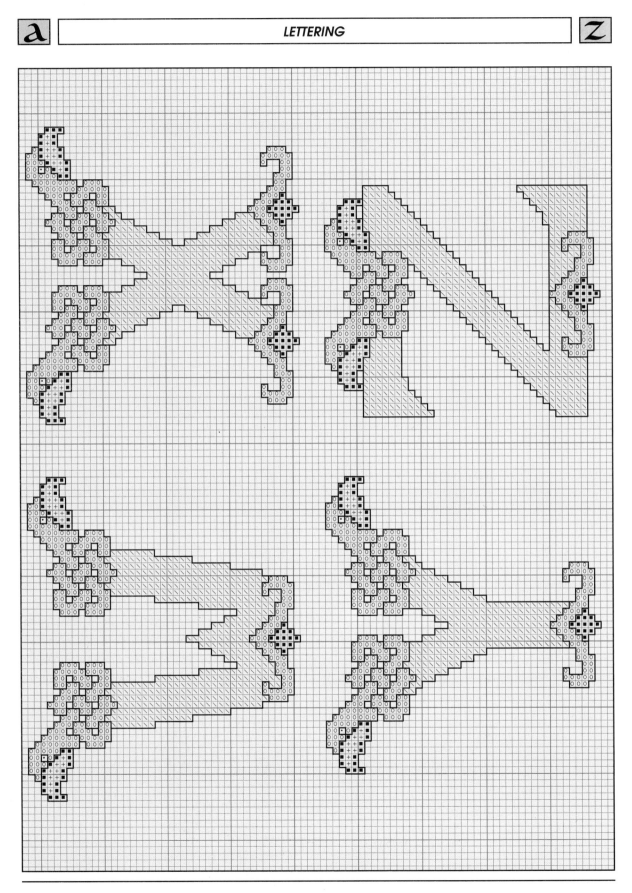

TIE AND HANDKERCHIEF

Personalize a plain tie and a white handkerchief using Celtic letters and motifs. The tie is embroidered with a monogram, while the handkerchief sports the birds' head finial from the decorated initials which can be found on pages 101–106.

MATERIALS
- One plain blue tie
- One plain white handkerchief
- Anchor Marlitt thread in colors given in the key
- Waste canvas, 11 hpi, approximately 4 x 4 in for each initial
- Medium crewel needle

WORKING THE DESIGN
1 Select the initial you want to use, then cut a piece of waste canvas covering the required number of squares. If you are decorating a tie, find the center by folding it in half lengthwise. Baste the waste canvas (see page 10) in position onto the front of the fabric. Using two strands of silver-gray Marlitt, stitch the initial over the waste canvas.

2 Cut a piece of waste canvas 3¹/₂ x 1¹/₂ in (8.5 x 4 cm); baste it to one corner of the handkerchief so its central line is at 45° to each side of the fabric, and the bottom is about 3¹/₂ in (8.5 cm) in from the corner.

3 Follow any of the charts with the double birds' head, using two strands of silver-gray for the main part, blue for the beak outline, purple for the beak, and red for the eye. Use one strand of dark gray for the backstitch (see page 9).

4 Follow the instructions on page 10 for removing the waste canvas.

KEY (Marlitt)		
Anchor 845	O	Silver-gray
Anchor 836	■	Blue
Anchor 817	+	Purple
Anchor 815	•	Red
Anchor 846	–	Dark gray

VERSAL SAMPLER

T he letterforms in this sampler are based on the forms known as missal versals; these shapes were used for the decorative initials in many illuminated manuscripts. The color scheme of yellow, green, and purple picks up one of the more unusual colorways used by Celtic artists.

Stitch count: 141 x 165
Design size: 12 x 10 in (30 x 26 cm)

MATERIALS
- One piece of pale yellow Aida, 14 hpi, 14 x 16 in (35 x 40 cm)
- Stranded embroidery floss in the colors given in the key
- Fine tapestry needle
- Frame to fit the finished embroidery, with an opening at least 12 x 10½ in (30 x 27 cm)

This detail shows the attractive shapes of some of the letterforms.

WORKING THE DESIGN
1 Press the fabric, then fold it in half to give a line down the center. Mark the line with a water-soluble pen. Measure 2¾ in (7 cm) down this line from the top of the fabric, and make a dot with a water-soluble pen. This corresponds with the central stitch of the upper line of the cross at the top of the chart. The arrows on the chart mark the center line.
2 Using two strands of dark purple stitch the outline cross shape; then stitch the inner sections in light purple and dark purple, as shown on the chart.
3 Using two strands of dark green, stitch the outline squares to the right and left of the cross; using light green, stitch the patterns inside them.
4 Continue working around the frame of the sampler in the same way, following the colors and patterns marked on the chart.

5 Counting the stitches and squares carefully, stitch the letters inside the border using two strands of light green floss.
6 Sponge away the marks made by the water-soluble pen. When the embroidery is completely dry, press it from the back (see page 10).
7 Assemble the embroidery in the frame, following the instructions on page 11.

PRACTICAL TIPS

It might be tempting to stitch all the outlines of the border blocks first, but if you fill them in with the appropriate patterns as you go, you will be able to see more quickly if you have miscounted anywhere.

When you come to stitch the letters, you may find it easier to begin at the center line of each row of letters and work outward to the sides.

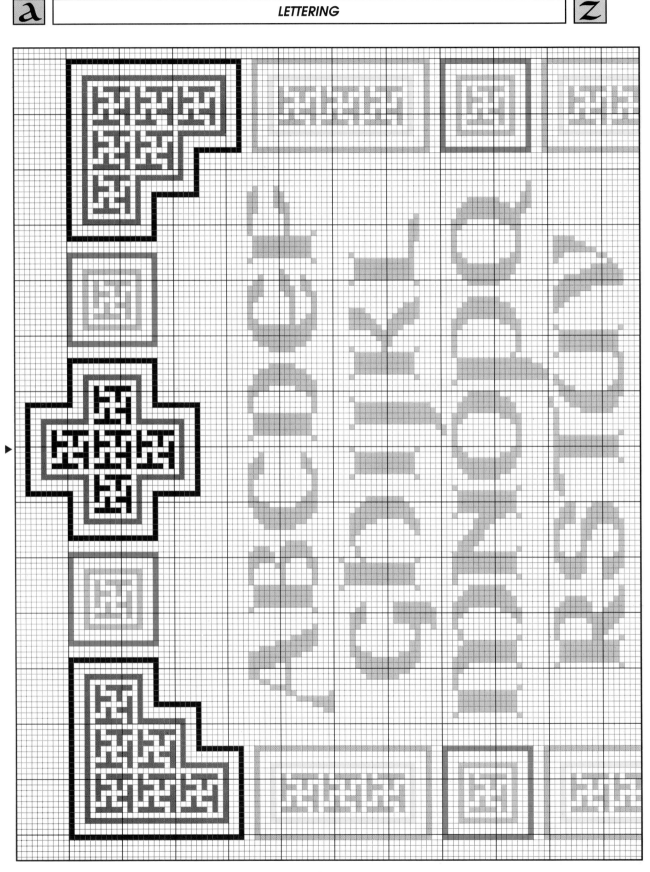

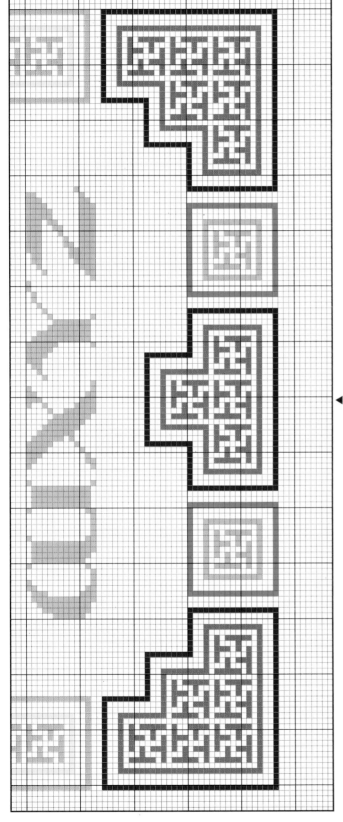

KEY

DMC 333	Anchor 101	■■	Dark purple
DMC 340	Anchor 98	■■	Light purple
DMC 912	Anchor 243	■■	Dark green
DMC 954	Anchor 240	■■	Light green (*2 skeins*)
DMC 743	Anchor 302	■■	Dark yellow
DMC 744	Anchor 301	■■	Light yellow

ILLUMINATED INITIAL

This opulently illuminated letter "S" makes a wonderful picture; the gold outlines show off the bright colors of the solid sections, and the cream backing fabric imitates the color of vellum or parchment. The design is based on an initial taken from a French psalter.

Stitch count: 114 x 139
Design size: 10 x 12 in (26 x 30 cm)

MATERIALS
- One piece of cream Aida, 11 hpi, 16 x 18 in (40 x 45 cm)
- Three spools of gold thread, such as Gütermann metallic 24
- Stranded embroidery floss in the colors given in the key
- Medium tapestry needle
- Frame to fit the finished embroidery, with an opening at least 11 x 14 in (28 x 35 cm)

The colored areas of the design are set off by gold outlines.

WORKING THE DESIGN
1 Press the fabric. Measure in 2³/₄ in (7 cm) from the right-hand side of the fabric and 2³/₄ in (7 cm) down from the top. Mark the point with a dot of water-soluble pen. This dot marks the point at which you will begin stitching and corresponds to the top right corner of the frame on the chart. Using three strands of gold thread and beginning at the marked dot, stitch all the gold outlines and diagonal lines of the frame.
2 Using three strands of embroidery floss, fill in the red and blue stripes of the frame.
3 Using three strands of gold thread, stitch all the gold outlines and dots of the "S" design. Using three strands of embroidery floss in the appropriate colors, fill in all the solid areas as marked on the chart.
4 Sponge away the dot made by the water-soluble pen. When the embroidery is completely dry, iron it from the reverse side (see page 10).
5 Assemble the embroidery in the frame, following the instructions given on page 11.

PRACTICAL TIPS
Because there are strong diagonal lines in this design, you may find that the fabric is no longer square when you have finished. You may wish to use an embroidery frame to avoid this problem (see page 10). Alternatively, to reshape the finished embroidery, dampen the fabric with a water mister, then pin it out square, using rust-resistant T-pins on a blocking board protected by clean paper. When it is dry, iron it with a little spray-on starch to keep it square. If you are left-handed, begin your stitching at the topleft corner of the frame; in this case, measure in from the top and the left-hand side of the fabric.

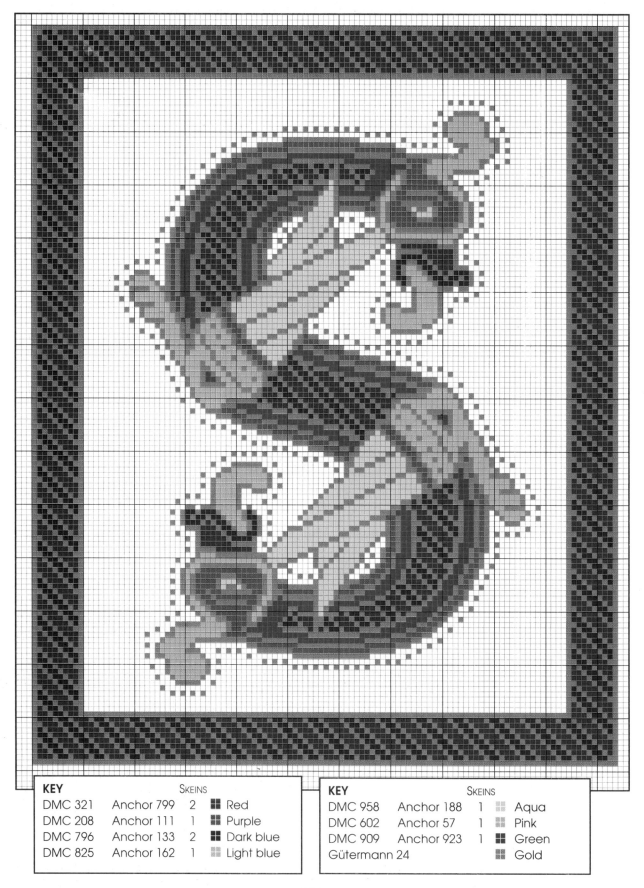

KEY				
DMC 321	Anchor 799	2		Red
DMC 208	Anchor 111	1		Purple
DMC 796	Anchor 133	2		Dark blue
DMC 825	Anchor 162	1		Light blue

KEY				
DMC 958	Anchor 188	1		Aqua
DMC 602	Anchor 57	1		Pink
DMC 909	Anchor 923	1		Green
Gütermann 24				Gold

PATTERN LIBRARY

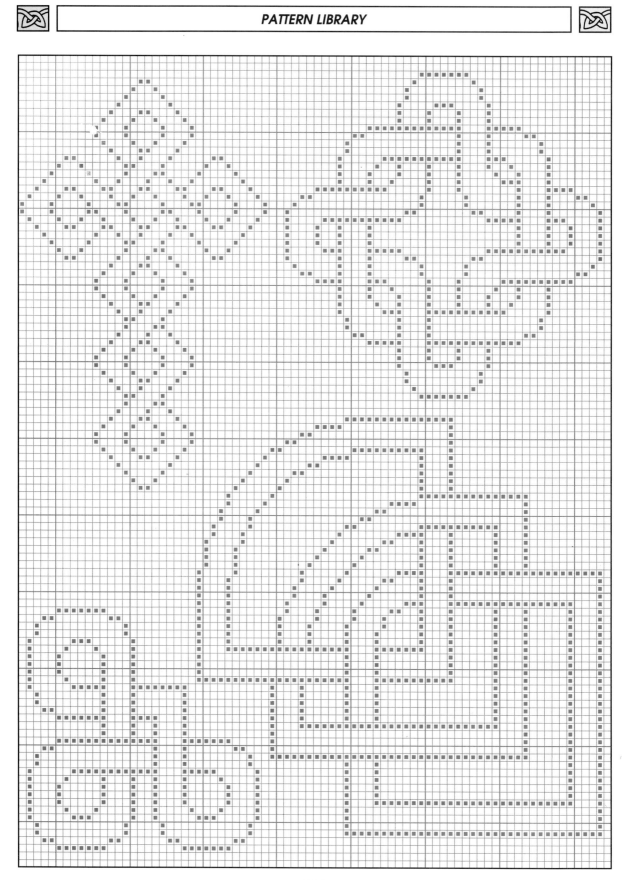

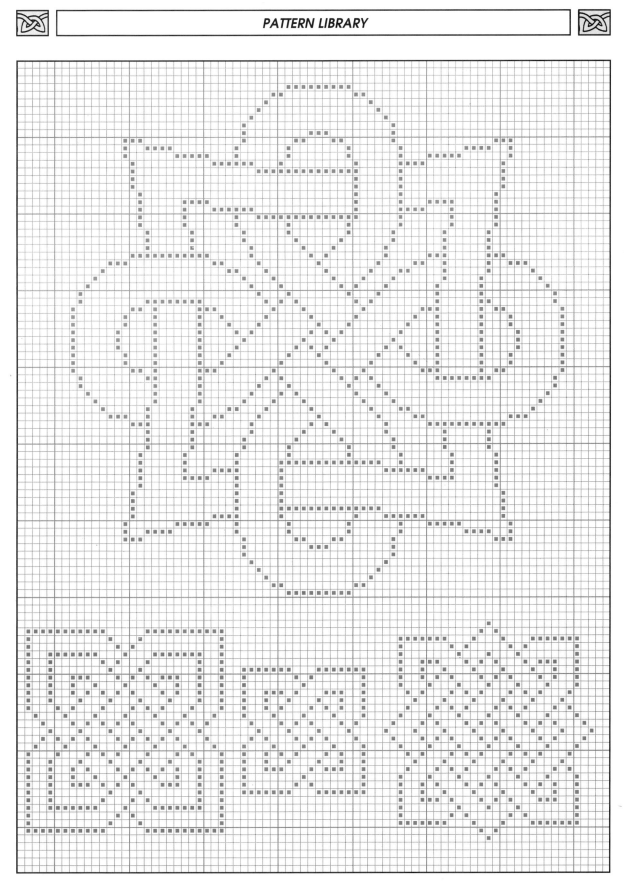

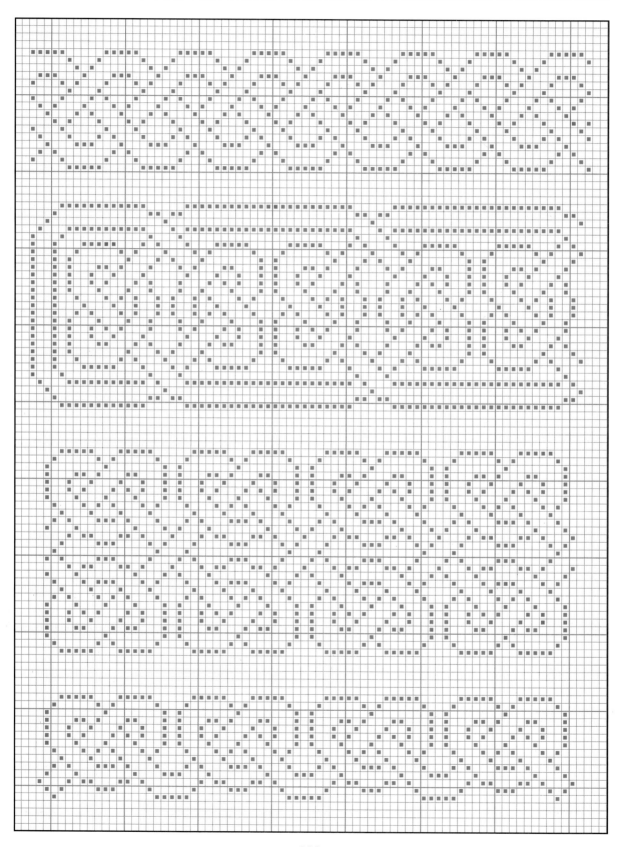

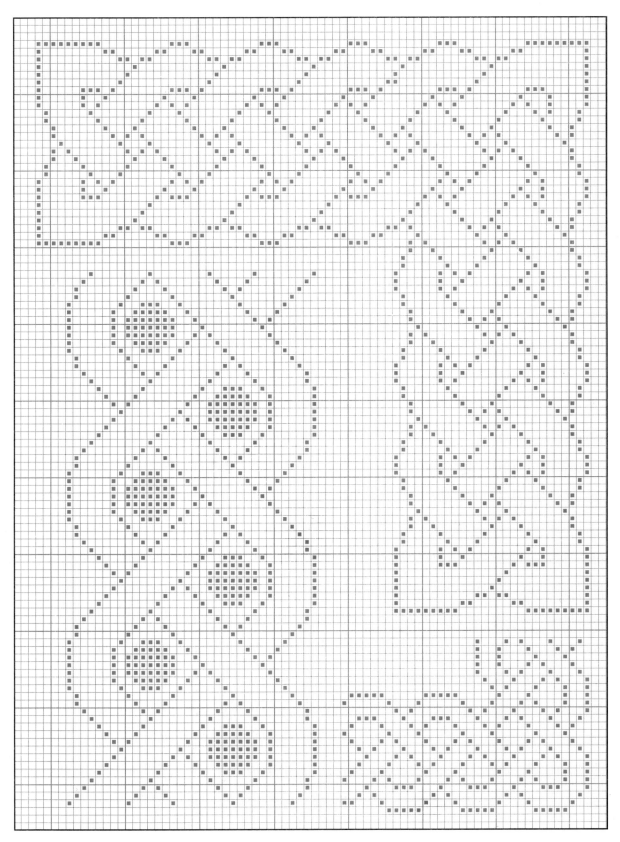

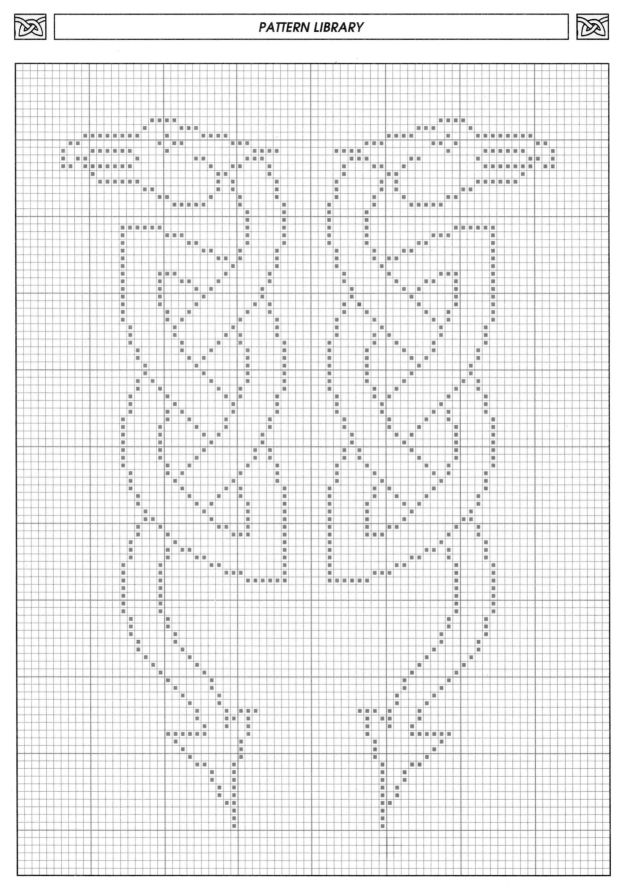

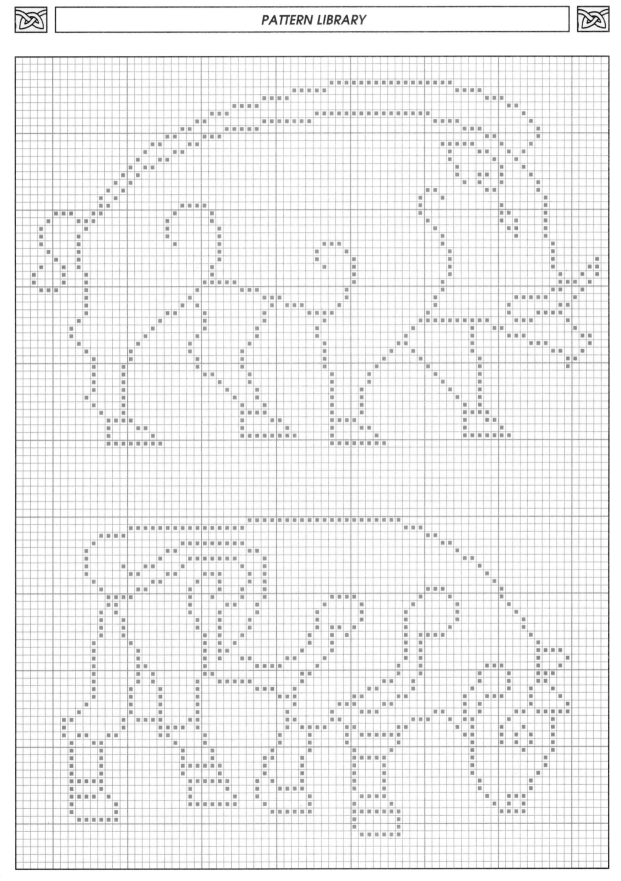

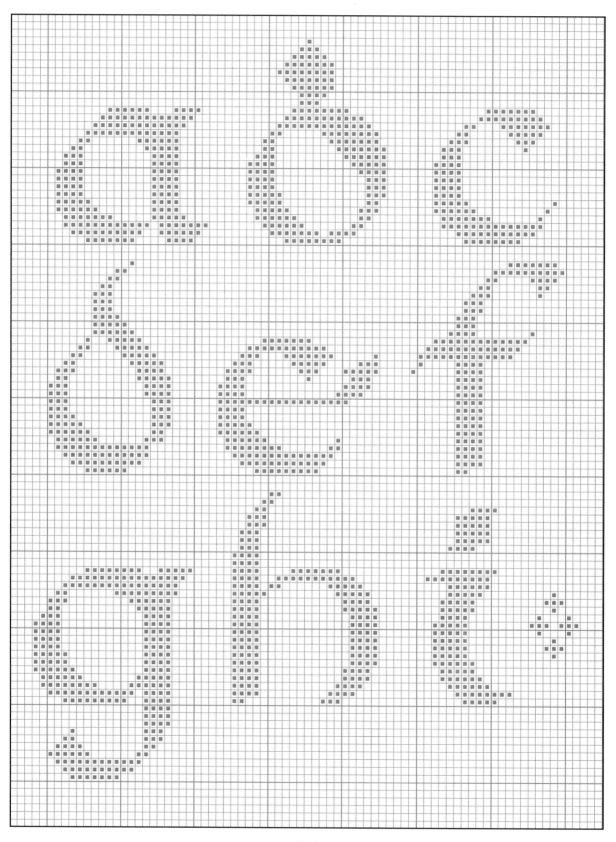

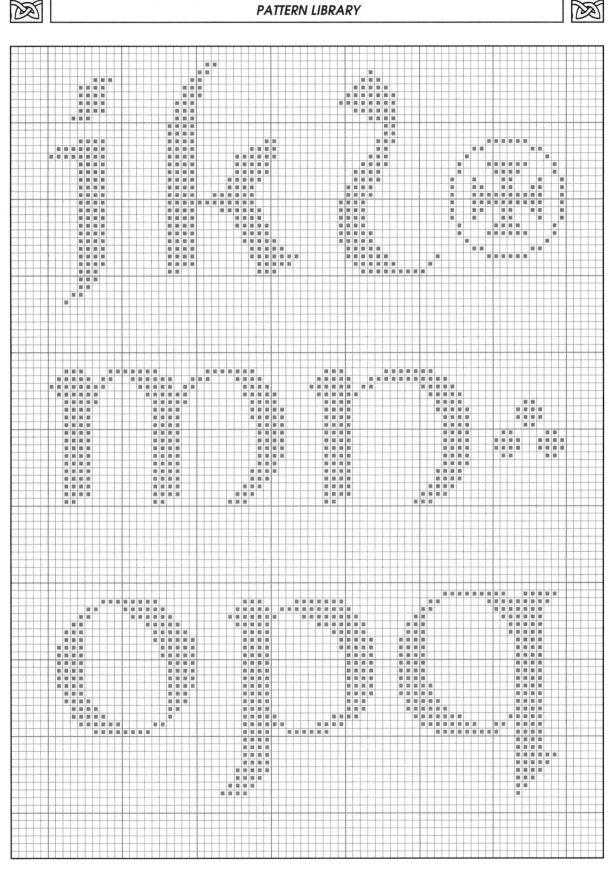

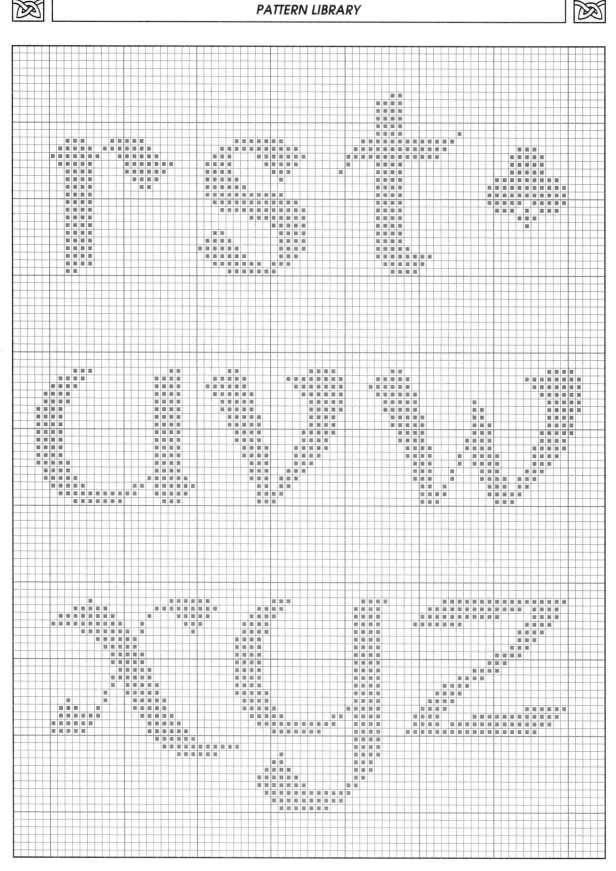

ACKNOWLEDGMENTS

All designs are by Gail Lawther. Many thanks to the following embroiderers for stitching some of the designs:
Beryl Hoad: *knotwork pillow, serpent pincushion.* Sarah Hoad: *horse picture, lion picture, stitched nameplate.* Liz Lance: *placemats and napkins, initial pictures.* Christopher Lawther: *Celtic rug.* Doreen Newnham: *trinket box, wedding initials.* Pauline Oakes: *stained-glass angel, pincushion and needle case.* Jennie Ring: *curtain tieback.* Sue Slide: *initial cards, knotwork cards, knotwork picture, illuminated initial.*

Photograph credits:
The illustrations on the section opening pages are all taken from the late-seventh-century manuscript book *The Lindisfarne Gospels* and used by permission of The British Library.
pages 12–13 Cotton Ms Nero D. iv G 138b
pages 36–37 Cotton Ms Nero D. iv G 210b
pages 2, 68–69 Cotton Ms Nero D. iv G 211

SUPPLIERS

Items for cross-stitching can be bought in numerous craft stores and from many mail-order craft companies. The following is a list of just a few of the many suppliers.

General needlecraft suppliers
Appleton Bros. of London, West Main Road, Little Compton, RI 02837

The Golden Eye, Box 205, Chestnut Hill, MA 02167

Paternayan Yarn, Johnson Creative Arts Inc., West Townsend, MA 01474

Kreinik, Mfg. Co., Inc. 3106 Timanus Lane, Baltimore, MD 21244

Susan Bates, PO Box E, Route 9A, 212 Middlesex Avenue, Chester, CT 06412

DMC Corporation, 107 Trumbell Corporation, Elizabeth, NJ 07206

Kits and materials for cross-stitching
Dimensions, 641 McKnight Street, Reading, PA 19601

Brucilla Corporation, 1 Oak Ridge Road, Hazeltown, PA 18202

Stitch & Frame Shop, Dept. CM-9508, 1627 Celanese, Rock Hill, SC 29732

Canadian addresses of suppliers of cross-stitching kits and materials
Dick & Jane, 2352 West 41st Avenue, Vancouver, BC V6M 2A4

Jean McIntosh Ltd, 1115 Empress Street, Winnipeg, MB R3H 3H1

The Nimble Thimble, 3201A Yonge Street, Toronto, ON M4N 2K9

S.R. Kertzer Ltd, 105A Winges Road, Woodbridge, ON L4L 6C2

INDEX

Aida, 9; tape, 21
Angels, 7, 37, 51
Animals, 7, 14, 37, 38, 46, 48, 69, 100, 122–23
Assembling cards, 71

Baby's bib, 40
Backstitch, how to work, 9; on charts, 11
Binca, 9
Birds, 7, 14, 37, 40, 42, 54, 64, 100
Book of Durrow, 69
Book of Kells, 7, 69, 70
Bookmark, 14

Canvas, 9
Carpet pages, 13, 60
Celtic, art, 7, 13, 37, 69; patterns, 7, 8, 13; peoples, 7
Christening gown, 30
Christmas decoration, 90
Color schemes, 7, 13, 60, 109
Cross patterns, 14, 60, 116
Cross stitch, charts, 10, 11; paper, 9; tips, 8–9; ways of working, 8–9
Curtain tiebacks, 56

Design size, 11
Doll's house rug, 22
Durrow, Book of, 69

Even-weave fabric, 9

Fabric gauge, 11
Fading pen, 10
Fish, 37, 56
Floss, 10
Flower thread, 10
Frames, embroidery, 10
Framing, 11

Greeting cards, 18, 38, 70
Half-uncial letterforms, 69
Handkerchief, 107
Hand towel, 20
Hoops, embroisery, 10
Horse card and picture, 38
Horseman picture, 60

Illuminated initial, 112
Illumination, 7, 13, 26, 51, 69, 86, 109, 112
Initial, cards, 70; illuminated, 112; pictures, 100; wedding, 92
Ireland, Celtic tradition in, 7, 69

Jewelry, 26

Kells, Book of, 7, 69, 70
Key and fret patterns, 7, 13, 120–21
Knitting yarns, 10, 64
Knotwork patterns, 7, 8, 13–35, 64, 100, 115–19

Letterforms, 7, 69, 70–114, 124–26
Linen, 9
Lion picture, 46

Marking pens, 10
Marlitt, 10
Matte embroidery cotton, 10
Metallic threads, 10

Nameplate, 78
Needle case, 80
Needles, 9, 10
Noel Christmas decoration, 90

Peacock vest, 42
Pearl cotton, 10
People, 7, 37, 51, 60

Petit point 22, 38
Picture, angel, 51; horse, 38; horseman, 60; initial, 100; knotwork, 28; lion, 46; wedding initials, 92
Pillow, 32
Pincushion, knotted, 80; serpent, 48
Placemats and napkins, 24
Plastic canvas, 9
Pressing embroidery, 11

Rooster sweatshirt, 54
Rug, Celtic, 64; doll's house, 22

Samplers, bright, 86; versal, 109
Serpent pincushion, 48
Sewing equipment, 10
Silk gauze, 9
Spiral patterns, 13, 14, 26, 120
Stained-glass angel, 51
Stitch count, 11
Stranded embroidery floss, 10
Sutton Hoo jewelry, 7
Sweatshirt, rooster, 54

Tapestry, needles, 9,10; yarn, 10
Tie and handkerchief, 107
Trinket box, 16

Uncial letterforms, 69

Versal letterforms, 69, 109
Vest, peacock, 42

Waste canvas, 10, 25, 29, 30, 54
Water-soluble pen, 10, 11
Wedding initials, 92
Yarns and threads, adjusting for different designs, 11; types of, 10; untwisting, 9